Economic Breakdown & Recovery

Economic Breakdown & Recovery

Theory and Policy

John Cornwall

With a Foreword by David Colander

M.E. Sharpe
80 Business Park Drive
Armonk, New York 10504

Copyright © 1994 by M. E. Sharpe, Inc.

All rights reserved. No part of this book may be reproduced in any form
without written permission from the publisher, M. E. Sharpe, Inc.,
80 Business Park Drive, Armonk, New York 10504.

Library of Congress Cataloging-in-Publication Data

Cornwall, John.
Economic breakdown and recovery: theory and policy
/ John Cornwall.
p. cm.
Rev. ed. of Theory of economic breakdown, 1990
Includes bibliographical references and index.
ISBN 1-56324-304-0.—ISBN 1-56324-305-9 (pbk.)
1. Business cycles—History—20th century.
2. Capitalism—History—20th century. 3. Economic history—1971–
I. Cornwall, John. Theory of economic breakdown.
II. Title.
HB3711.C644 1994
338.5′42—dc20
93–22648
CIP

Printed in the United States of America

The paper used in this publication meets the minimum requirements of
American National Standard for Information Sciences—
Permanence of Paper for Printed Library Materials,
ANSI Z 39.48-1984.

∞

BM (c) 10 9 8 7 6 5 4 3 2 1
BM (p) 10 9 8 7 6 5 4 3 2 1

TO JAMES S. DUESENBERRY

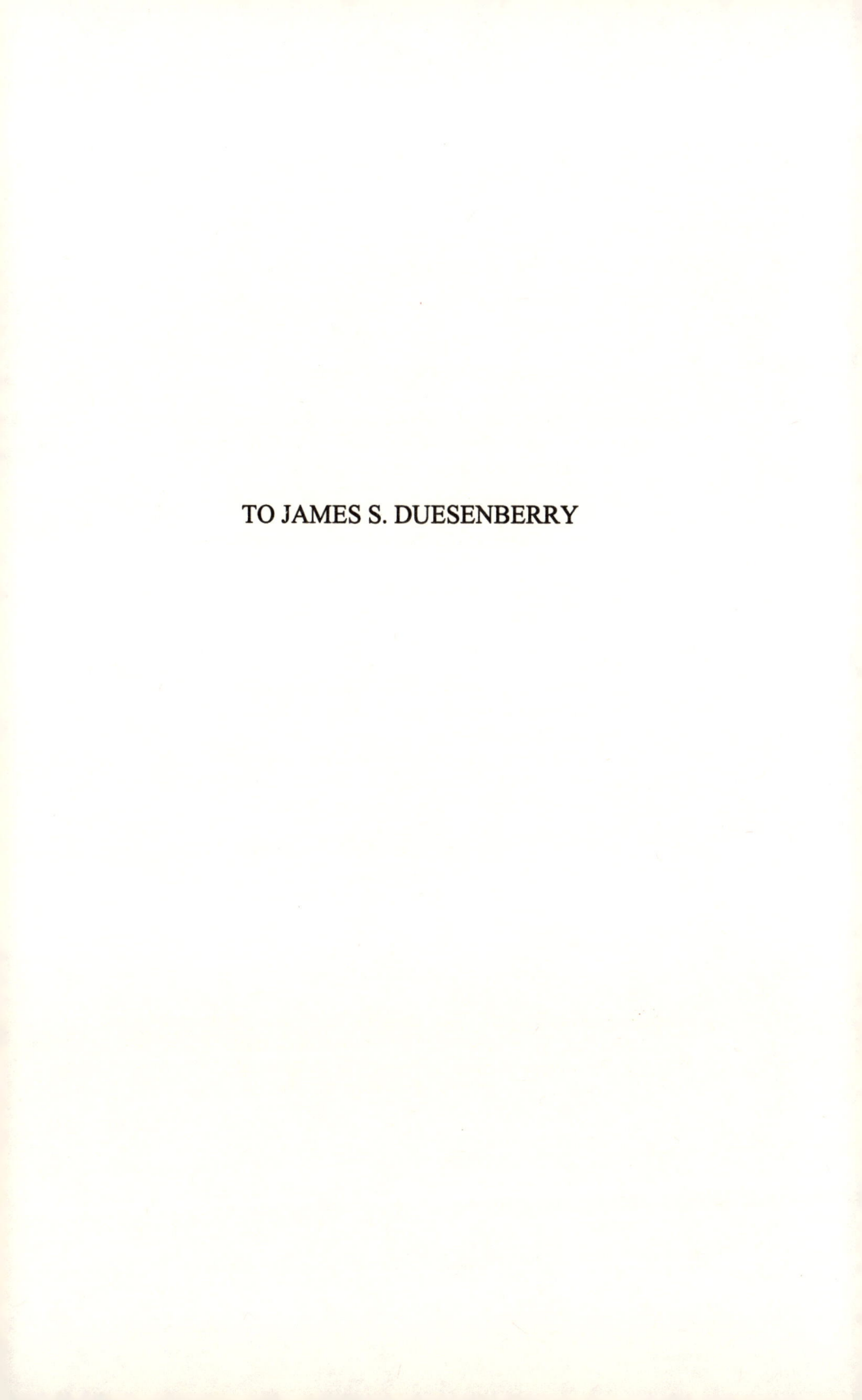

Contents

Foreword: Economic Breakdown and Recovery   xiii
Preface to the 1994 Edition   xix
Preface to the 1990 Edition   xxv

PART I FRAMEWORK

Introduction I: Framework   1

    I.1   Must Democratic Capitalism Fail?   1
    I.2   Can Democratic Capitalism Succeed?   3
    I.3   A Keynesian View   5
    I.4   Understanding Today's Difficulties   7
    I.5   An Extended Framework of Analysis   8
    I.6   Unemployment is the Issue   9
    I.7   The Tasks Ahead   13

1   How should we do Macroeconomics?   15

    1.1   Introduction   15
    1.2   Why Do Governments Choose Unemployment Policies?   16
    1.3   The Basic Causes   17
    1.4   A Framework for Studying Performance   20
    1.5   The Second Blade of the Scissors   20
    1.6   The Second Limitation   22
    1.7   An Institutional-Analytical Approach   23

2   The Evolutionary Nature of Twentieth-century Capitalism   26

    2.1   Introduction   26
    2.2   A Comparison of Unemployment and Growth Rates   27
    2.3   The Rise of the Welfare State   28
    2.4   The Rising Power of Labor   31
    2.5   Industrial Relations and the Rising Power of Labor   34
    2.6   Strike Activity and the Size of the Welfare State   35

	2.7	Inflation and the Rising Power of Labor	37
	2.8	The Breakdown in the Early 1970s	39
	2.9	Conclusions	42
3	**A Reappraisal of Vertical Phillips Curve Analysis**	44
	3.1	Is Keynes Irrelevant?	44
	3.2	The Natural Rate Hypothesis Once More	45
	3.3	New Strands in Vertical Phillips Curve Analysis	49
	3.4	The Alpha Strand	50
	3.5	Vertical Phillips Curves: The Beta Strand	55
	3.6	Some Counter-arguments	57
	3.7	Hysteresis Effects	60
	3.8	Conclusions	62
	Appendix A: The Reliability of Nonaccelerating Inflation Rate of Unemployment Estimates	65
	Appendix B: Pigou Reborn	67
4	**Some Basic Determinants of Unemployment**	69
	4.1	Introduction	69
	4.2	Public Choice Theory	70
	4.3	Policy Outcomes and Organizational Competition	72
	4.4	Party Control as an Explanation of Policy Choices	73
	4.5	Cross-country Analysis	75
	4.6	Party Control and Economic Policy	76
	4.7	A Political Economist's Analysis of Unemployment	79
	4.8	The Basic Causes of Unemployment	81
	4.9	A Question of Terminology	82
	4.10	A Multitude of Constraints	83
	4.11	The Relevant Institutional Constraints	84
5	**Macroeconomic Performance and Institutions**	87
	5.1	Introduction	87
	5.2	Party Control and Unemployment before the Breakdown	88
	5.3	The Impact of Unions on Inflation	90
	5.4	Inflation as a Prisoner's Dilemma	92
	5.5	Why Phillips Curves Differ	94
	5.6	Corporatism	97
	5.7	Social Democratic Corporatism	99

	5.8	Pluralist Economies	100
	5.9	Bourgeois Democratic Corporatism	101
	5.10	Alternative Forms of Corporatism—Switzerland	103
	5.11	Alternative Forms of Corporatism—Japan	104
	5.12	Why the Cross-country Phillips Curve is Horizontal	106
	5.13	Conclusion	108
6	**Econometric Tests of Institutional Influences**		109
	6.1	Introduction	109
	6.2	Measures of Social Bargains	109
	6.3	Simple Correlations	112
	6.4	Unemployment Rates, 1963–1973	113
	6.5	Unemployment Accounting	116
	6.6	Cross-country Differences in the Misery Index, Price Inflation, and Wage Inflation, 1963–1973	118
	6.7	Tarantelli's Study	119
	6.8	An Evaluation	120
	6.9	What Can We Learn from the Experience before the Breakdown?	122
	6.10	Why Were Unemployment Rates So Low in the OECD?	123
	6.11	Conclusions	125

PART II BREAKDOWN

Introduction II: Breakdown — 129

II.1	Introduction	129
II.2	Stability Downward—Instability Upward	132
II.3	Instability Downward—Stability Upward	133
II.4	A Misdirected Research Program	133

7	**Unemployment Performance since the Breakdown**		135
	7.1	A Look at the Record	135
	7.2	Regression Analysis: Unemployment in the Post-war Period	138
	7.3	Why Did Some Succeed?	142
	7.4	Conclusions	145
	Appendix A: A Formal Analysis of the Immediate and Basic Determinants of Unemployment and Inflation		146

8	High Inflation and Policy-induced High Unemployment	152
	8.1 Starting Over	152
	8.2 The Variable-coefficient Phillips Curve	153
	8.3 Fairness and the Dynamics of Inflation	155
	8.4 Variable-coefficient Models of Inflation	157
	8.5 The Eckstein-Brinner Model of Inflation	158
	8.6 The Workings of the Model	160
	8.7 Are Workers Fooled?	162
	8.8 The Shifting Long-run Variable-coefficient Phillips Curve	162
	8.9 Hysteresis and the Variable-coefficient Phillips Curve	167
	8.10 Conclusions	169
	Appendix A: Analytical Solutions	173
	Appendix B: Regression Analysis	178
9	Explaining the Breakdown	181
	9.1 Introduction	181
	9.2 The "Great Post-war Inflation"	182
	9.3 Stages of the "Great Inflation"	183
	9.4 Breakdown	186
	9.5 The Rising Inflation Costs	188
	9.6 The Ineffectiveness of Traditional Payments Policies	190
	9.7 Conclusions	194
10	A Model of Long-run Mass Unemployment	197
	10.1 Weak and Strong Corporatist and Pluralist Economies	197
	10.2 Exporting Unemployment	200
	10.3 A Coordinated Stimulative Policy is Not Sufficient for World Recovery	200
	10.4 Looking to the Future	202
	10.5 Why Restrictive Aggregate Demand Policies Are So Costly	204
	10.6 Why Restrictive Aggregate Demand Policies Are Ineffective in the Long Run	207
	10.7 Conclusions	208

PART III RECOVERY

Introduction III: Recovery	213
III.1 Introduction	213
III.2 Outline of Part III	214

11	The Boom of the 1980s and its Aftermath	216
	11.1 Introduction	216
	11.2 The Booms of the 1960s and 1980s	216
	11.3 A Non-linear Model of the Cycle	219
	11.4 The Relationship between Booms and Slumps	221
	11.5 Path Dependence in the 1959–73 and 1982–92 Periods	223
	11.6 The Aftermath	227
12	A Program for Economic Recovery in the United States	230
	12.1 Introduction	230
	12.2 Paradigms and Recovery Programs	231
	12.3 The Unemployment Record in the Twentieth Century	233
	12.4 An Outline of the Program	236
	12.5 Creating the Ideological Climate—Keynes Reborn, Part One	239
	12.6 Creating the Ideological Climate—Keynes Reborn, Part Two	240
	12.7 Budget Dynamics and the Interaction of the Budget and the Economy	242
	12.8 Creating the Ideological Climate—the Social Bargain	244
	12.9 The Hierarchy of Policy Goals	245
	12.10 A Diagrammatic Exposition	247
	12.11 The Clinton Program for Recovery	249
	12.12 What About the Demand Side?	250
	12.13 What About the Supply Side?	251
	12.14 Conclusions	253
13	Choosing the Future	256
	13.1 Policy Options	256
	13.2 Recreating the Nineteenth Century	257
	13.3 A Program for the Future	262
	13.4 Studying Economic Breakdown	263
	13.5 Path Dependence in Capitalist Development	264
	13.6 Choosing the Wrong Future	266
Bibliography		269
Index		277

Foreword: Economic Breakdown and Recovery

When George Aiken, a former United States Senator from Vermont, was asked what to do about the Vietnam War, he said the United States should declare that it had won the war and get out. While the United States did not follow his prescription, macroeconomists, and Western economies, did. Instead of addressing the main macroeconomic concern of the post-war era—how to achieve full employment (by which they meant, at most, 2–3 percent unemployment, or at a level at which there were more vacancies than unemployed people—they declared victory and achieved it by defining as natural whatever unemployment existed. They stopped asking how to achieve the old definition of 2–3 percent unemployment and focused on explaining why 6 percent, 7 percent, or even 8 percent unemployment should be accepted by society as natural. This left about 5 million more people in the United States out of work than would have been the case if the lower level of unemployment had been achieved. After all, we wouldn't want to go against nature.

Achieving Full Employment

Instead of exploring how we might restructure economic institutions to achieve 2 to 3 percent unemployment, economists were playing mind games and expanding the Walrasian model in multiple directions, most of which involved high levels of math, making the work look impressive. The result was good for the macroeconomists' egos; their impressive-looking set of models made them look like economic rocket scientists. The result wasn't so good for the unemployed.

Now, it is possible that the record of Western economies is the best that could have been achieved. It is unclear whether politically acceptable, administratively feasible, and cost-effective policies could have been designed to put those people to work. I think, had economists and politicians put their minds to it, 2.5 percent unemployment would have been achievable. But whether it would have will never be known, because most macroeconomists explored neither the question nor the institutional changes that might have led us there.

One major exception is John Cornwall. His work has continually focused on real problems and he has never lost sight of the ultimate goal of macroeconomics—to understand the macro economy so that we can find policies that can improve the general welfare of the population. In keeping this goal in mind he follows in the footsteps of early macroeconomists such as John Maynard Keynes and James Duesenberry.

Early in his career John Cornwall recognized that impressive macro models that don't correspond to the institutional reality of our economy serve little purpose. He recognized that much of the currently-in-vogue theoretical work in macroeconomics violates the law of significant digits, and that there is little sense in being more exact than the least exact dimension of the issue one is looking at. Given that many of the dimensions of the macroeconomic problems are ambiguous, most of the models in macroeconomics are needlessly exact and, worse, misleading because they pretend to be modeling relationships with functional forms that are unable to capture the complexity of those many dimensions. Put simply, there is no fit between most macro models and reality. By becoming increasingly lost in abstract models, macroeconomic theory has lost sight of the unemployment problem and has simply modeled it away—losing it in the micro foundations of macroeconomics.

Multiple Equilibria and the Macro Foundations of Microeconomics

After many years of work on these impressive-looking models, the modelers are now finding that the old way of looking at issues—building into one's analysis an understanding of institutions—is essential to attacking the problem. As they have formally specified the large number of assumptions necessary to arrive at a unique solution to a model of an aggregate economy, they have made it clearer and clearer that unique analytic solutions are not forthcoming. Many outcomes consistent with rationality are possible, and without assuming some institutional structure that limits individuals' choices, macro models arrive at no outcome.

But how does one choose the institutional structure that limits individual choice? The way macro modelers have chosen is backward induction. They ask: what structure will achieve a desirable aggregate equilibrium? When one designs models using that backward-induction approach, one comes up with the tautological conclusion that, given the assumptions, the macro economy arrives at a desirable equilibrium! (The limited usefulness of the above tautological results is generally hidden in the impressive mathematics.)

The likely existence of multiple equilibria in the economy has profound implications for macro economic theorizing and policy. These implications are only now beginning to become apparent to macro theorists; the most important of these implications is that multiple equilibria require theorists to include some way of determining at which of the multiple equilibria the economy will come to rest, how and why it will move from one equilibria to another. Since markets in choosing equilibria do not exist, it makes no sense to assume that the market will choose which equilibria the economy will arrive at; one needs an institutional theory that determines the structure within which people operate. This is important because one's theory of markets makes sense only if one takes account of the limitations that institutional theory places on that theory. It is those limitations that New Classical, and many New neo-Keynesian, theorists have forgotten in their search for a micro foundation for macroeconomics.

When one takes seriously the implications of multiple equilibria one quickly discovers that the weak link in macroeconomic theorizing is not micro foundations of macroeconomics; the weak link is *macro foundations of microeconomics*. Taking seriously the macro foundations of microeconomics requires one to account explicitly for the constraints which macro institutions place on individual decision makers.

Let me give two examples. Economists have devoted enormous amounts of thought to providing a microeconomic explanation of why prices and wages are sticky. They are trying to explain why people don't immediately adjust their prices to competitive equilibrium prices. In most of that sticky-price literature economists pose the question about sticky prices in a model of an economy with neither a numeraire nor money, implicitly assuming that it is meaningful to use such a model as a reference point for understanding sticky wages and prices in our real-world economy. But without money or a numeraire, a modern market economy could not exist, and without some fixity in relative and nominal prices and wages, a monetary economy could not exist. Put simply, the existence of a monetary economy requires the wage and price level not to fluctuate too much. If the above argument is true, and a strong argument can be made that it is, the explanation of wage and price stickiness lies in the macro foundations of a monetary economy. Stickiness is, and must be, built into the institutional structure of a monetary economy. The use of money imposes societal constraints, and hence individual constraints, on price-setters, that their prices not fluctuate too much. So the comparison of our real-world economy with a model of an economy without money is an irrelevant one. No necessity of sticky wages and prices is built into the appropriate macro foundations of microeconomics.

A second example concerns the level of unemployment at which an economy equilibriates in a steady state. Economists generally think of that aggregate equilibrium in reference to partial equilibrium supply-demand analysis, and, at least implicitly, picture in their minds some equivalency between excess supplies and excess demands at a "natural rate" equilibrium. Such a conception of aggregate equilibrium is not necessarily appropriate for a monetary economy. The use of money by an economy imposes a non-accelerating price level constraint for the economy as a whole. If the price level can be expected to explode, it will destroy the institution of money. Thus, again, the macro foundations of microeconomics impose constraints on the individual market equilibria that makes up the interdependent parts of the aggregate economy.

When seller monopolies and seller-set nominal pricing institutions predominate, as they do in our economy, this non-accelerating price level constraint means that in a competitive supply–demand equilibrium the representative seller will be pushing for a nominal price which exceeds the competitive price. Without some macro institution to anchor the nominal price and offset this tendency, so that the expectation of an accelerating inflation does not get built into price-setting expectations, the price level would explode. So, in a seller-set monetary economy, for a monetary macro equilibrium to exist, the representative market must make its contribution to the non-accelerating price level constraint by maintaining excess supply. It follows that the equilibrium level of unemployment at which a monetary economy will equilibrate depends on constraints imposed on individuals by the aggregate institutional structure and it cannot be analyzed independent of the constraint that monetary aggregate institutional structures impose on price setters in individual markets. Monopolistic competition is not the cause of the macro problem; it is the result of a necessary macroeconomic constraint.

This constraint of a non-accelerating price level as an integral element of macroeconomic foundations gives one a quite different conception of a steady state equilibrium in a monetary economy. Moreover, it illuminates more accurate insights into the effectiveness of alternative macro policies. Steady state unemployment is not a reflection of individual choice. It is a reflection of an institutional macroeconomic constraint imposed by the economy's use of nominal prices and money. Because the cause of unemployment is integrated with the economy's use of nominal money, the level of steady state unemployment can be reduced by policies that affect nominal wages and prices—by an incomes policy.

The above ideas are still novel to most economists. However, as macroeconomists further develop these insights, the macroeconomic issues of the 1990s will increasingly concern the macro foundations of microeconomics and the macro foundations of macroeconomics, rather than the micro foundations of macroeconomics.

Cornwall's Approach to Macroeconomics

The above discussion of recent developments in macroeconomic theory is important to this book, because John Cornwall is one of those few macroeconomists who has never forgotten the need of the economy to choose among alternative equilibria. Moreover, he offers a reasonable way of choosing among multiple equilibria—assume the existing institutional structure is descriptive of the equilibrium structure the appropriate model of the economy would have. As a result, the limitations that the real-world institutional structure imposes on real-world decision makers are the appropriate limitations to consider when developing a micro foundation for macroeconomics. Because he recognizes this fact John Cornwall is significantly beyond most macro theorists in his thinking about the macro economy.

This book, however, is not primarily about theory. For Cornwall, abstract theory is only a stepping stone to policy discussions. Consistent with his earlier work, Cornwall develops only the theory necessary to discuss the policy issues meaningfully.

The book is divided into three parts. The first part sets the framework, the second part develops the theory of breakdown, and a third part deals with a program for economic recovery.

His introduction to part I and his first chapter set the stage for his approach to macroeconomics. He convincingly pulls the various streams of macro analysis together and focuses his approach right where it belongs—on the contextual nature of our real-world economy. Chapter 2 considers the history of Western institutions, setting the institutional stage for the analysis. This institutional-analytic approach, which as Cornwall explains, is an approach that examines how institutions shape policy and performance and simultaneously how policy and performance change institutions, is a minimal requirement for meaningful macroeconomics. Yet, as Cornwall explains in chapter 3, such an approach is not the way most macro analysis has been done recently.

Chapters 4 and 5 develop his thesis in a logical manner. They distinguish his approach to political economy from the public choice approach, and provide a convincing argument for explaining why his approach is preferable. In chapter 6 he provides empirical support for his argument and explains how the political responses of institutions led to the high unemployment Western economies experienced before the breakdown in the early 1970s.

Part II develops his theory of economic breakdown in more detail, nicely outlining his approach and relating it to other approaches. Chapter 7 employs econometric techniques to explain the rise in unemployment since 1973; chapter 8 explains the rising inflation costs of any unemployment policy over time. Chapters 9 and 10 develop his model of breakdown and explain its relevance.

This 1993 edition has been updated and revised from the earlier edition. The biggest change in the book from the earlier edition is the addition of part III which provides a discussion of a Program for Recovery. In it Cornwall explains how he believes the United States can get out of its current economic malaise. He develops the case for increased government spending which, combined with institutional changes on the wage- and price-setting fronts, could help get the economy out of the breakdown it has fallen into.

Throughout his analysis John Cornwall's value judgments are clear. We, as economists, and as a society, need to be reminded that there is a normative aspect to the questions we ask and the framework in which we ask them. Most would agree that the unemployment created by Western economic systems is unfair to the unemployed. But then we, as economists and as members of society, drop the issue. By raising it, and putting it in an analytic framework of economic breakdown, John Cornwall has taken an important step toward relevance for macroeconomics.

Not everyone will agree with, or be convinced by, Cornwall's analysis. But because he develops his arguments so logically and smoothly, his analysis will provide insight for all.

—David Colander

Preface to the 1994 Edition

When Dick Bartel suggested I revise and expand my 1990 book, *The Theory of Economic Breakdown*, I was more than happy to comply.[1] Much of the analysis and certainly the key predictions of the 1990 book were controversial. The mere passage of time provided me with opportunities to gather new information and to reevaluate some of my earlier ideas. These results are incorporated in this edition.

I wrote in the first edition:

> it is the universal nature of the high involuntary unemployment which has persisted for so long, together with an inability to foresee its end, that most clearly defines the present era of capitalist development. (p. 9)

Some reviewers challenged my prediction that "everything was in place for continued mass unemployment into the 1990s." Others were of the opinion that I had got my facts wrong, writing about the 1980s as if it were a period of mediocre performance rather than one signaling the rebirth of the golden age of the 1950s–1960s. For some critics in the English-speaking countries, macroeconomic developments in the second half of the 1980s were even seen as a cause for celebrating the victory of capitalism, the Thatcher and Reagan records revealing conclusively the miracles in store for any government willing to unleash the forces of the free market.

My own view by the late 1980s was that despite substantial growth in GDP, the Thatcher and Reagan "miracles" were nothing more than weak recoveries, given the failure of unemployment rates to decline to levels achieved in the earlier postwar booms. The Reagan boom was often incorrectly referred to as the longest peacetime boom. I would describe it as the longest nonsustainable recessionary boom in history. This reflects the failure of the Reagan Administration to do anything about the structural changes that were poised to generate strong inflation.

---

[1] *The Theory of Economic Breakdown: An Institutional-Analytical Approach*, Basil Blackwell, Oxford, 1990.

This new edition has given me the chance, not only to reach a wider audience, but to bring the historical record up to date and to fill some important gaps in the earlier edition. Thus I have been able to provide more recent historical data to support my original prediction of continued malfunction into the 1990s. In addition this edition has allowed me to expand the study to take account of macroeconomic development in the 1980s in much more detail. As a result, I concluded that not only was the boom of the 1980s weak and nonsustainable, but in the English-speaking countries the 1980s boom increased the difficulties of improving performance in the 1990s. This new finding has become an important supportive element in my evaluation of future world prospects.

Most important, the timing of the publication of this edition called for a treatment of the prospects for policy-induced recovery. Since the first edition there has occurred a rather belated change in attitudes in influential circles that unemployment and not inflation is the number one macroeconomic problem. Quite simply the unemployment problem has become too large and has gone on far too long to be ignored by policymakers, with the possible exception of central bankers. The most noticeable example of this shift is in the attitude and pronouncements of the Clinton Administration with respect to macro policy intervention. This is all to the good. World recovery requires the implementation of an entirely new set of macro policies, especially in the English-speaking economies. In response to these developments, this edition has been expanded to three parts. While the focus of Part III is on the United States, the program advocated for recovery is relevant to a number of other economies now experiencing high unemployment, e.g., Canada and the United Kingdom.

This program is at complete odds with the failed policies employed since the early 1970s in the English-speaking economies; these are designed to depress the economy until inflation is under control (the short-term pain) and then allow the alleged self-healing and self-correcting properties of the system to generate a return to non-inflationary, full employment growth (the long-term gain). However, the recommended program is similar to programs adopted in other OECD economies that have succeeded in keeping the unemployment level low.

The vast differences between the recovery program offered in Part III and what would be considered the more "mainstream" view in, say, the United States is often attributed simply to differences in underlying economic theories. For example, a believer in demand-pull inflation would advocate one type of policy while a cost-push theorist would recommend another type. An investigation of the institutional structures of the different capitalist economies, that is, the rules, laws, and customs of behavior, led me to the conclusion that differences in recovery programs were related to something more basic.

The notion of a paradigm is insightful and useful in this regard.[2] The concept has come to represent the set of metaphysical beliefs, assumptions, and values accepted by a particular school of thought (in economics in this case), together with the choice of problems considered important and the techniques deemed appropriate for analyzing these problems. The reigning paradigm in economics is clearly the neoclassical one. Viewed as a paradigm, a basic tenet of neoclassical analysis is that the private sector of a modern capitalist economy is self-regulating. For example, while deviations from some long-run rate of growing full employment output may arise because of shocks, the system automatically and quickly moves back to its growth path in the absence of ill-advised government intervention.

This study challenges the belief that capitalism is a self-regulating system and offers in its place a basic tenet of an alternative paradigm. For want of a better expression, it will be referred to as the institutional-analytical paradigm. It rejects the neoclassical view that capitalism is self-regulating, maintaining that it is instead a system capable of generating economic and political conflict as well as other basic structural changes in the normal course of its evolution. This evolutionary process, moreover, can generate long periods of poor as well as exemplary macroeconomic performance, as the historical record cited in Part III shows.

Adherence to the institutional-analytical paradigm is a necessary condition for understanding the workings of a modern capitalist system. Without such understanding the cause and possible cure for breakdowns, such as that from which we are currently suffering, will continue to elude us. The prevailing ideology contains elements that form a barrier to a true understanding of modern affluent capitalism. As a result, policymakers of the neoclassical persuasion derive their intellectual authority from a world view that leads to self-defeating policies. Recovery requires what the philosophers of science refer to as a paradigm shift.

Having said this, it follows that the acceptance of a recovery program that can succeed involves discarding deeply-rooted and strongly-felt beliefs, assumptions, and values. In my efforts to contribute to this

[2]Kuhn, T. *The Structure of Scientific Revolution*, University of Chicago Press, Chicago, 1962.

change, the strategy I have adopted in Part III is to summarize the historical evidence that clearly refutes the self-regulating tenet of neo-classical analysis and to outline the elements of a new approach to the workings of capitalism that must be accepted before recovery is possible.

In defense of the recovery program offered here, two points are worth making. First, it bears a strong resemblance to programs adopted throughout the post-war period in those OECD economies that have consistently performed well, e.g., Austria, Japan, and Switzerland. In contrast, economies that adopted policies of short-term pain for long-term gain, e.g., Canada, the United Kingdom, and the United States, have performed relatively poorly, measured in terms of unemployment and productivity growth. Obviously other factors are involved, but the association between performance and policies (and ultimately basic beliefs) has a rationale and a persistence that can no longer be written off as coincidental.

Second, supporters of the mainstream view have consistently been wrong in their appraisal of the seriousness of the current breakdown. The McCracken report of the mid-1970s marked the beginning of a long series of reports and pronouncements, each envisaging recovery as imminent, provided the authorities would just implement the available policies correctly. A "credible" attack on inflation (through restrictive aggregate demand policies) was all that was required to recreate the golden age of capitalism. This persistent and false optimism can also be traced to a set of widely-held but erroneous beliefs about the functioning of a capitalist economy.[3]

In summary, the tasks of the book remain as before, to explain the causes of the worldwide breakdown, the reasons why economic performances differed across economies, and to offer a program for recovery. As mentioned, this edition expands greatly on the third task by devoting a substantial part of the study to a recovery program. In response to comments by a reviewer of the first edition, chapter 7 has been completely rewritten. Rather than focus on cross-country differences in performance between countries after the early 1970s, the econometric analysis focuses on the causes of the rise in unemploy-

[3]The extremely restrictive aggregate demand policies of the early 1980s reduced average inflation rates to approximately 2 percent in the seven large OECD economies by 1986, following six consecutive years of unemployment rates averaging over 7 percent. If ever there was an example of the resolve of the authorities to "whip the inflationary psychology once and for all," this should have been it. Yet by 1989 when unemployment rates fell from 7.1 to 5.7 percent, rates of inflation rose from 2.2 to 4.5 percent.

For an earlier statement of a less optimistic prognosis see the author's *The Conditions for Economic Recovery*, M. E. Sharpe, Armonk, NY, 1983, Part II.

ment over time. No conclusions from the earlier study are affected.

In bringing the analysis up to date, my explanations of the economic breakdown in the early 1970s, the predictions for the 1990s, and the policies I find essential for recovery remain unchanged. The introduction of more recent data serves to support the main conclusions of both editions.

As before, my main indebtedness is to my wife, Wendy Cornwall. Additional assistance was received from Mark Setterfield, Michael Bradfield, Peter Burton, and Alasdair Sinclair. I would also like to express my thanks to my research assistants, Jennifer McDonald and Sean Rogers. Financial support from the Social Sciences and Humanities Research Council of Canada and the Dalhousie University Research Development Fund is acknowledged and greatly appreciated. Permission to use the remark of John Maynard Keynes cited in Volume 21, page 45 of *The Collected Writings of John Maynard Keynes* was given by the Royal Economics Society.

Preface to the 1990 Edition

To some readers the title of this study may seem both pretentious and misguided. *A Theory* rather than *The Theory of Economic Breakdown* would seem to be the appropriate level of modesty, and the performance over the past several years in the largest capitalist economy hardly suggests a breakdown. With respect to the appropriate article, I have deferred to the wishes of the publisher. Regarding the appropriate designation of the current state of developed capitalism, I offer no excuse.

It is true that the new classical macrotheorists do not see the rise in unemployment since the early 1970s as a form of malfunction, and there are those who choose to evaluate macroperformance in terms of the behavior of output. They find the recent growth of gross domestic product in a limited number of economies to be a more significant measure of capitalist performance than the mass unemployment of the 1980s.

However, along with a sizable number of government officials and economists, I see the current situation as a serious market failure. The belief that the rise in unemployment in the countries of the Organization for Economic Cooperation and Development from approximately 10 million in 1973 to a predicted level of over 29 million in 1990 is primarily, if not totally, a massive intertemporal substitution of leisure for work appears to me to be quite absurd. Nor do I think that the welfare dimensions of macroeconomic performance can be correctly evaluated without focusing first and foremost on the unemployment record. Furthermore, as I will argue, the current breakdown represents not only a tremendous loss in human welfare with no immediate end in sight, it is also inducing structural and institutional changes that reduce dynamic efficiency. For example, there is no better way to destroy the work ethic than to create a labor force in which an increasing proportion is accustomed to unemployment; those prone to unemployment will invent lifestyles that downplay the importance of regular work, while the rest, seeing this, will lose their fear of unemployment.

Therefore the focus of this study is on unemployment, especially its pervasive and prolonged character, why it has taken on these characteristics, and what, if anything, can be done. The question of why unemployment rates differ across countries is also studied, partly because the answers throw light on the causes of the intertemporal rise in unemployment.

The framework of the analysis is a blend of conventional and somewhat unconventional approaches. The mainstream analytical techniques of macroeconomic theory play a prominent role and standard econometric tests prove to be useful in supporting various hypotheses. A multicountry approach has found increasing favor among economists and is given prominence here as well. Even the emphasis on institutions suggested in the subtitle of the book would not find too much disapproval. With the recognition that economic performance, even during the period of general collapse, has varied widely has come a recognition that institutions matter and may be subject to economic analysis.

A concern in the following pages with economic and political power is probably more suspect among economists. Despite structural changes in the real world that have given rise to unions, multinationals, takeovers, and conglomerates, economists have increasingly chosen to model economic events within the competitive framework. There is no room for economic, let alone political, power in such an orientation. Furthermore, this study incorporates historical developments in the capitalist world, and economic history has been subjected to the same level of abuse as sociology among large numbers of economists.

Nonetheless, I have felt it necessary to incorporate power and historical developments in the analysis. I find it impossible to explain why macropolicies and unemployment records differ between countries and over time without taking account of differences in the distribution of economic and political power. I also find it impossible to explain the current performance of economies, including the policies now in effect, without taking account of their past histories. Whether designated hysteresis or path dependence or history dependence, the present has to varying degrees been created in the past and, in the same way, the future is now being determined.

The framework is decidedly dynamic, to a large extent because of a recognition of path dependence. There has always been disquiet among some economists over the use of the static neoclassical framework with its assumptions of fixed tastes and technology. Changes in these and in other institutional features have become so rapid in modern times, relative to the rate at which an economy can adjust, that the convergence tendencies become less important and less interesting than the structural changes themselves. However, a recognition of path dependence emphasizes the necessity of a dynamic historical approach in which structural change itself is explained. Thus, in neoclassical analysis a given institutional structure, including given tastes and technologies, is assumed and the values of the economic variables, for example outputs, incomes, and unemployment, are determined. Similarly the impact of once-over changes in this structure on the economic variables is studied. Throughout this study what is stressed is the dynamics of causation running from the performance variables, for example total output, aggregate demand, and unemployment, to the institutional structure. These induced changes in institutions, in turn, lead to constraints on future performance and future policy options. Together the process describes a form of path dependence whereby performance at one point in time, through its effects on institutions, influences performance at a future point in time. This can only be captured within a dynamic historical context.

To those who find my approach no better than "sociology," I answer in the following manner. Beginning in the second half of the 1960s an increasing number of economists, including many who refer to themselves as "Keynesians," have resurrected the distinctly pre-Keynesian notion of unique equilibrium unemployment tendencies when modeling macroperformance. Moreover, they see no need to take account of the stance of aggregate demand policy in deriving this equilibrium since it is determined by "supply" factors. Changes in aggregate demand cannot affect the real sector in the long run; they affect only nominal values.

Modeling performance in this manner might be understandable if the past two decades had been a continuation of the booming low unemployment era of the 1950s and 1960s. Advocates of the unique equilibrium approach could maintain that their models were merely reflecting the ability of capitalist economies to operate close to full employment. However, in the face of the rising and persistent unemployment since the early 1970s, many proponents of the unique equilibrium framework no longer maintain that this equilibrium rate has the optimal property of low or zero involuntary unemployment. Furthermore, they recognize that this equilibrium, while unique, is also constantly changing. But surely the rising popularity of unique equilibrium unemployment models during a period of prolonged and rising unemployment throughout the OECD countries suggests the inappropriateness of much of our macroresearch. It is time to explore different ways of modeling a capitalist economy.

As emphasized in this book, the macroequilibrium of a capitalist system cannot be determined without specifying the stance of aggregate demand policy. This was the central message of Keynes's *General Theory* and remains as true today as it did a half century ago. More than this, I will argue that it is impossible to understand events of the recent past and of the present and to implement a recovery program without adopting the eclectic approach of this study.

Modeling capitalist economies in terms of an institutional-analytical framework has dictated to a large extent the style of the book. Because the approach is somewhat novel, I have tried to outline my views in as nontechnical a manner as possible so that the ideas are easily grasped. This is particularly true of some chapters, where appendices are included to handle the more technical ideas. In many instances the finer points have been relegated to footnotes, enabling the reader to comprehend the central issues immediately. Even so, the chapters vary in character primarily because institutions play a key role in the study, and as a result some of the chapters are quite descriptive.

In addition, I have tried to set out my arguments so that the reader will have no difficulty in determining the relative merits of my position and of more popular, but what I consider incorrect, views. For example, I have found it useful to go over once more the basic natural rate hypothesis step by step in chapter 3. In this way the unrealistic but essential assumptions of this form of modeling inflation and unemployment are clearly in mind when proceeding to evaluate the embellishments and extensions of the natural rate concept.

The dominant view among economists (and governments) today is that inflation is the main macroproblem and must be contained. When asked at what cost, the public is not told that high unemployment for 5, 10, or 15 more years may be required. It is told that there are no alternatives. This reluctance of the economics profession to inform governments and the public of the likely course of events and the costs of current policies over, say, the next decade is, of course, an easy option. Instead of intensifying our efforts to explain a very complex issue and to correct a serious malfunctioning beginning its third decade, economists are free to contemplate yet another optimization problem. I have taken a more speculative approach. I have tried to indicate what I think are the costs and consequences of present policies. I contend that current policies are merely aggravating already undesirable conditions and that unless new policies are adopted the future looks decidedly bleak. It is the difficulty in implementing policies to induce further institutional changes that gives rise to this pessimism.

Before proceeding to explain the marked deterioration in macroperformance, I use the first four chapters and an introduction to provide an elaboration of my approach in order to gain the reader's confidence. Two more chapters follow before I undertake an explanation of economic breakdown of the last two decades. These two chapters illustrate how the institutional-analytical approach can be used to explain events during a period of superior performance—the decade preceding the general rise in unemployment. However, they also provide aid in understanding why macroperformance has worsened since then with no immediate sign of improvement.

In one sense, I hope that my prognosis is incorrect and that an early return to something like full employment conditions is likely. Yet even if my pessimism proves to be unjustified, I believe that much of the analysis will prove useful in other applications.

I am indebted to many colleagues for assistance. Specifically, I wish to thank Swapan Dasgupta, David Braybrooke, William S. Brown, James W. Dean, James Duesenberry, Daniel V. Gordon, Tony Myatt, Tomson Ogwang, Shelley Phipps, Gouranga Rao, Kurt Rothschild, Mark Setterfield, Alasdair Sinclair, Peter Skott, and Brendan Walsh. Special thanks go to Wendy Cornwall and R. M. Sundrum, both of whom carefully read the entire manuscript and offered numerous suggestions and helpful criticisms. Sundrum's visit to Dalhousie in the fall of 1988 was like manna from heaven. I hope that the exchange of ideas this made possible was as helpful to him (and to my wife) as it was to me. I also wish to thank the Social Sciences and Humanities Research Council of Canada for financial support and Monique Comeau who typed most of the manuscript.

Parts of chapters 1 and 10 are reprinted from the *Journal of Economic Issues,* June 1987, by special permission of the copyright holder, the Association for Evolutionary Economics, and *Inflation and Income Distribution in Capitalist Crisis: Essays in Memory of Sidney Weintraub* (ed. J. A. Kregel), Macmillan, London, and New York University Press, 1989.

PART I

Framework

Introduction I: Framework

I.1 Must Democratic Capitalism Fail?

The overloaded capitalist democracies

The acceleration of rates of inflation during the late 1960s and early 1970s and the failure to substantially reduce these rates without the creation of the mass unemployment of the 1980s and 1990s have been responsible for a mood of extreme pessimism within the capitalist world. For over two decades, writers of what would be considered the political right as well as the left have (for different reasons) announced the end of an era of capitalism. The golden age of the 1950s and 1960s is allegedly over and will be replaced by something not yet clearly seen, but possibly something ominous. For one reason or another capitalism has been sowing the seeds of its own destruction, and without drastic changes in basic institutions and attitudes it will continue to do so.

Consider the type of pessimistic view popular in the 1970s, expressed in the notions of an "overloaded" economy and the "ungovernability" of the capitalist systems.[1] This expressed the view that the growing affluence and sustained high employment enjoyed for over two decades following the Second World War led to rising aspirations and expectations. These were eventually expressed in excessive economic demands, particularly on governments. Since these demands could not all be satisfied, the capitalist democracies became overloaded and inflation prone (such as in the early 1970s) as weak governments bought time by promising pressure groups programs and rewards that could not be realized. Widespread dissatisfaction resulted, leading to disillusionment within democratic capitalism.

---
[1] See A. King, "Overload: problems of governing in the 1970s," *Political Studies,* 23, June–September 1975, 284–96; and S. Brittan, "The Economic contradictions of democracy," *British Journal of Political Science,* 5, April 1975, 130–59.

2   *Framework*

Variations on a theme

The idea that democracy leads to inflation also found support in the revival of monetarist economics. This influential body of doctrine would have it that, despite the 1930s and the more recent breakdown, there is an inherent tendency for capitalist systems to gravitate toward a long-run position in which involuntary unemployment is minimal in the absence of irresponsible behavior on the part of the authorities. Any attempt to push the unemployment rate below this "natural" rate would prove to be fruitless in the long run, leading only to accelerating rates of inflation. Unfortunately, since the fiscal and monetary authorities are assumed to be weak and have an incentive to push the unemployment rate below the natural rate, an inflationary bias develops under capitalism—the same result seen by those who envisaged a tendency toward an overloaded economy. The theory of the inflationary "political business cycle" is a variation on this theme.

A reserve army of the unemployed

At the very least these views saw capitalist governments, through weakness and shortsightedness, reinforcing an underlying inflationary bias. Some saw government intervention as the cause of the bias. Governments were said to respond to pressures in such a way as to sacrifice price stability for high employment or full employment (FE), as they stand ready to "supply" full or high rates of employment upon demand, whatever the consequences.

If nothing else, recent events show that an economic theory of democracy that assumes accelerating inflation to be inevitable is only one special and highly simplified theory of the way in which political institutions interact with economic forces in determining policy. In fact, since the early 1980s governments have been willing to push unemployment rates to double-digit levels in order to reduce inflation. Based on more recent experience it could be concluded that, if anything, democracies are doomed to mass unemployment.

This entirely different but equally pessimistic forecast of the workings of democratic capitalism can be found in Kalecki's theory of the "political business cycle"—a theory with opposite implications from the more recent inflationary version.[2] In this formulation, the ruling

---

[2] See M. Kalecki, "Political aspects of full employment," *Selected Essays on the Dynamics of the Capitalist Economy 1933–1970,* Cambridge University Press, Cambridge, 1977, ch. 7.

capitalist classes would not tolerate prolonged periods of FE let alone serious inflation. Mass unemployment of the 1930s variety would not be permitted, but a situation in which labor could develop such strength as to lead to an overloaded economy was alleged to be intolerable to those in power. Neither inflation nor an overloaded economy was predicted by Kalecki. Whatever the strength of the demand for FE, it would not be supplied by means of real aggregate demand (AD) policies. In this scenario democratic capitalism leads to a reserve army of the unemployed.

Long-run views

Such divergent reasons for pessimism do not inspire confidence in the pronouncements of economists. However, even taking a somewhat longer view, events do not lend themselves to any clear interpretation of the future course of capitalism. A period of accelerating rates of inflation followed by a period in which inflation rates are reduced substantially (but remain high) at the cost of two decades of mass unemployment is neither a commendable record nor a good omen for the future. Such events describe quite well an economic breakdown. In contrast, the dismal performance of the recent period was preceded by a quarter of a century of unprecedented growth and prosperity. Even today, while productivity growth rates have fallen almost everywhere, some capitalist economies have managed to keep unemployment rates low without accelerating rates of inflation. While developments since the 1920s clearly suggest that capitalism is not a self-regulating economic system with little need for government macrointervention, a return to something like the "golden years" of market capitalism cannot be considered out of the question.

I.2 Can Democratic Capitalism Succeed?

If the historical record provides few clues to the future, longer run explanations of economic performance also lead to varying predictions. "Eurosclerosis" is an explanation of economic breakdown and a source of pessimism for the future because its policy implications are so radical. Low rates of growth of productivity and high rates of unemployment are traced to increased rigidities in capitalist economies induced by the prolonged period of full employment following the Second World War. New institutional barriers have reduced innovations, thereby reducing productivity growth, and have created labor markets in which real wages are rigid downward. Given such rigidity, shocks often result in a non-market-clearing real wage above the equilibrium level and, therefore, in unemployment. Recovery must await the removal of those institutional barriers that are responsible for the rigidities in the economic system, and this will likely require a comprehensive decartelization program with special emphasis on reducing the power of the trade unions.

A more optimistic view has been given new life with the recent change in administration in Washington. The Clinton campaign and election generated a flood of policy suggestions for revitalizing the American economy, including proposals for reducing unemployment and stimulating growth. A successful implementation of most of these (and additional) policies would have widespread benefits, as the American economy plays a determining role in the economic health of the world economy. Even if the program suffers from errors of commission and omission, as will be maintained in a later chapter, the general thrust of Clinton's message is commendable. Following a period in which government has been seen as part of the problem and not of the solution, the new administration rightly sees an expanded and necessary role for government if economic recovery is to be achieved.

This certainly is its strength. Relative economic success in the past and the present has been most apparent in economies that have rejected "Thatcherism" and "Reaganism" and have instead foreseen the need for some kind of economic partnership between government and the private sector. This includes an acceptance of discretionary AD policies as an instrument of stabilization. This in itself is an important change in government attitude, as the rise of Thatcherism and Reaganism has been accompanied both within government circles and the Economics profession by a rejection of AD policies as ineffective and harmful, and this mistaken belief has been a major impediment to recovery.

What is lacking in the Clinton recovery program is a recognition that the United States, as well as other economies, has inherited a set of institutions that interfere with the proper macroeconomic functioning of the economy. In particular, the institutions surrounding the labor market generate politically unacceptable inflation at rates of unemployment in excess of FE in these economies. A need to have the right kind of institutions in order to perform well will be stressed throughout the study. Because of the critical position played by the United States in the success or failure of any worldwide recovery program, a chapter will be devoted to outlining a program of policy-induced institutional change to supplement the Clinton program. A central message of this book is that democratic capitalism can succeed but its success involves an expansion and not a contraction of the role of government.

I.3 A Keynesian View

Three propositions

It will be argued in the pages to follow that the origins of the current difficulties are to a large extent institutional; it will also be maintained that they cannot be overcome without further radical institutional adjustments. However, arguments which deny the role of restrictive AD policies in today's breakdown and a place for stimulative AD policies in a program for recovery are factually incorrect and dangerous. Their acceptance guarantees continued mass unemployment. Rather, it will be argued that AD policies played a key role in the recent past and must have an important part in any recovery program. This will be a recurring theme throughout, and the argument is supported at some length.

However, since there is widespread misunderstanding of the place of AD policies, whether stimulative or restrictive, in a stabilization program, it is important at the outset to clarify the function of AD policies in any recovery program. This role can be summarized in the following three propositions to be supported in later chapters.

1. AD policies are appropriate instruments for regulating aggregate output and employment and their impact is symmetrical, that is, increases in AD reduce unemployment when there are involuntarily unemployed workers and reductions in AD increase unemployment. This symmetry lies at the heart of Keynes's message and is correct. It will be referred to as the Keynesian symmetry. Many believers in the nonaccelerating inflation rate of unemployment (NAIRU) and Eurosclerosis deny that stimulative AD policies can be effective. Their views are discussed and rejected.
2. AD policies are inappropriate instruments for regulating inflation and their impact on inflation is asymmetrical, that is, increases in AD are more likely to cause inflation rates to accelerate than are decreases in AD to cause inflation rates to decelerate. This will be referred to as the post-Keynesian or neo-Keynesian asymmetry.[3]
3. Keynesian AD policy recommendations are necessary but not sufficient for economic recovery.

[3] See J. Cornwall, *The Conditions for Economic Recovery*, Blackwell, Oxford, 1983, ch. 6.

6 *Framework*

Underlying these propositions is the assumption that capitalist economies are not self-regulating. Not only is there no inherent tendency for the private sector to gravitate unaided toward some unique "equilibrium" unemployment rate (whether designated as the NAIRU, the natural rate, or the FE rate of unemployment), there is no inherent tendency for capitalist economies to experience non-accelerating rates of inflation at low rates of involuntary unemployment.

The unwillingness in the past to accept proposition 2 has led the authorities to vastly underestimate the unemployment costs of their restrictive AD policies. Their current unwillingness to accept proposition 1 has led them to deny the importance of stimulative AD policies in reducing unemployment. Together, these mistaken views reflect a belief that AD policies have strong price and weak output effects. Such a belief is ultimately based on a view that capitalist economies are self-regulating with strong FE tendencies. Proposition 3 merely summarizes what has just been said: that our inability to implement policies for recovery stems from a failure to develop additional policy instruments to accompany a stimulative AD program. Thus Keynes's *General Theory* laid out a framework for understanding the causes of the Great Depression and for formulating a recovery program. With inflation not a serious problem and economic interdependence less likely to cause difficulties, greater public expenditures or reduced taxes were sufficient to offset the inadequate level of private demand without drastic adverse side effects. As it was, economic recovery had to wait for the increase in AD and output associated with rearmament and the war effort.

New obstacles to recovery

Recovery today is not simply analogous to dentistry, as Keynes once envisaged the future role of macroeconomic policy. Events since the mid-1970s suggest that the obstacles to economic recovery are large and numerous and cannot be overcome solely by stimulating AD. One of the more important obstacles is the belief held by fiscal and monetary authorities (as well as by economists and civic leaders) in most of the countries of the Organization for Economic Cooperation and Development (OECD) that any stimulation of AD, at least under existing institutional arrangements, will lead to a politically unacceptable acceleration of inflation rates or serious balance-of-payments difficulties or both. As a result, it can be expected that most governments will continue to restrain

AD, thereby allowing unemployment rates to remain substantially above their levels of the 1950s and 1960s. This will also result in reduced innovative investment and therefore productivity growth.[4]

It will be argued below that, under currently prevailing institutions, stimulative AD policies do have serious adverse side effects. Consequently the current breakdown will persist until the development of additional policy instruments that will ensure a noninflationary, externally balanced recovery. Only then can it be expected that stimulative AD policies will be put into effect in the United States and throughout the OECD. While the development of the required policy instruments requires substantial institutional change, the point here is not that AD policies have no important role to play in a recovery program, but only that Keynes's program for recovery is incomplete in today's world.

I.4 Understanding Today's Difficulties

A historical perspective

The overload thesis goes wrong in its failure to foresee the authorities' reaction to accelerating inflation. The response beginning in the 1970s to these inflationary pressures was to implement restrictive AD policies which led to stagnation. However, there is truth in the claim of the overload thesis that the extended period of growth and affluence following the Second World War caused new problems for modern capitalism, one of which was to strengthen an inflationary bias. Gradually the OECD economies became increasingly prone to upward movements in inflation rates, especially at FE. In later pages this will be viewed as an induced adverse side effect of the prolonged period of FE and its impact on the institutional framework. After a rather detailed explanation of the framework to be employed and an analysis of the post-war period before the breakdown, the book takes up this theme.

Moreover, large-scale unemployment can only be ended by eliminating or at least reducing the impact of those forces that generate the inflationary bias. It is the difficulty of finding means to reduce this impact that gives support to the views of those who see a future of mass unemployment. However, understanding these issues requires a careful study of the period leading up to the breakdown. This is especially true in view of the development of alternative explanations of high unemployment such as the Eurosclerosis theory with its markedly different policy implications.

[4]Iceland is the only capitalist economy that chose to pursue FE policies despite the extremely adverse inflationary consequences. However, it did so for only a short period during the 1980s.

The comparative approach

Considered as part of a long-term historical performance of each country, the 1950s and the 1960s were high points for almost every OECD economy. Unemployment rates were very low and inflation was of manageable proportions. However, economic performance varied widely across countries, with a few economies experiencing relatively high rates of unemployment. A rather wide dispersion in performances is evident in the current period as well. A further distinguishing feature of the more recent period has been the ability of only a few countries to keep unemployment low as reflected in the rise of the OECD average rate of unemployment. Explaining these cross-country differences in macroperformance is a useful undertaking in its own right. In addition, comparisons between economies at given periods of time provide support for the theory advanced to explain developments over time. For example, explaining why some economies have managed to maintain low unemployment rates both before and after the early 1970s and why most others have not provide valuable clues to the explanations of the more recent overall decline in OECD (and world) activity and of the means to recovery. The objective is to determine those features that permit a few economies to withstand the unfavorable effects of widespread economic decline. Hence it is necessary to study many economies as well as the period of success preceding the breakdown.

I.5 An Extended Framework of Analysis

The greater difficulty in achieving economic recovery today has dictated the framework adopted here for understanding economic breakdowns. In addition to being historical and multicountry, it is decidedly institutional as well as analytical. It will be argued in later chapters that the ability of some economies to realize FE without accelerating rates of inflation and payments problems and the inability of others to achieve these goals is closely related to the prevailing institutions of the country. These determine whether the policy instruments for superior performance can be developed and successfully implemented.

The importance of institutions in influencing macroperformance has been stressed by other writers recently and comparison will be made with their works. It will be maintained here that in all countries institutional developments during the 1950s and 1960s have made the traditional instruments of macropolicy, for example, monetary, fiscal, and exchange rate policy, either much less effective in achieving the usual macrogoals or unable by themselves to realize the intended goals without generating intolerable adverse side effects. As a result new instruments of policy that operate more directly on behavior are needed in most economies to supplement the traditional policy instruments.

It will also be argued that past institutional developments in some countries have made it virtually impossible to develop and successfully implement the required new instruments. Further drastic policy-induced institutional changes will be required before this can be achieved. For example, before a successful incomes policy can ever be implemented, the industrial relations system of some countries will need to be overhauled. Without such changes, the authorities will choose to maintain restrictive AD policies and high unemployment will continue indefinitely.

I.6 Unemployment is the Issue

One final point: the term "stagnation" is used widely to denote low rates of growth of productivity and per capita incomes as well as high rates of unemployment, and is so used here. The emphasis and concern throughout this book is explaining the large increase since the early 1970s in the number of involuntarily unemployed, that is, workers who try to obtain jobs for which they are qualified at prevailing real wages (or less) but fail because there are none.[5] There are at least two reasons for this. First, the forces that have led to high rates of unemployment have also been partly responsible for low growth of investment, productivity, and per capita income. To a large extent, explaining high unemployment will explain the poor performance record of the other dimensions of stagnation. Second, and more important, it is the universal nature of the high involuntary unemployment which has persisted for so long, together with an inability to foresee its end, that most clearly defines the present era of capitalist development. It also most profoundly indicates the welfare losses incurred.

Some of the dimensions of the seriousness and general nature of the breakdown are given in figure I.1 and table I.1. Figure I.1 shows the number of recorded unemployed workers in North America, OECD-Europe, and OECD-total from 1962 to 1992 along with the forecast for

---

[5] "Ask the following simple question of job losers and job leavers: would you willingly take your previous job back on the terms now available in the market? If the answer is yes, the person is involuntarily unemployed" A. Blinder, "The challenge of high unemployment," *American Economic Review, Papers and Proceedings*, 78, May 1988, 1–15. For reasons presented below, the FE rate of unemployment is assumed to be around 2–2.5 percent (see section 5.2).

10 *Framework*

Figure I.1 Unemployment in the OECD area 1962-94

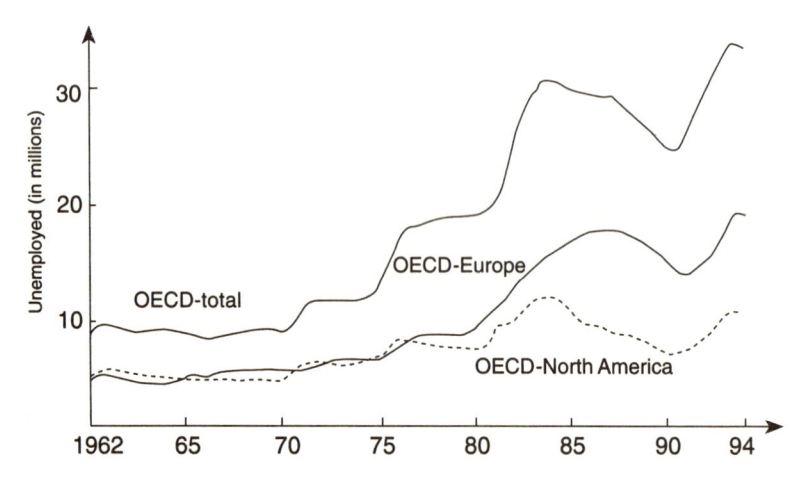

Sources: OECE, *Labour Force Statistics*, various issues, and *Economic Outlook*, December 1992, table 49, OECD, Paris

1993 and 1994. For the OECD as a whole, the number of unemployed rose from a low of 8.9 million in 1962 to a high of 31.1 million in 1983 followed by a decline to 24.4 million in 1990. It then rose to 32.3 million in 1992 and was forecasted to rise to 33.8 and 33.4 million in 1993 and 1994, respectively. Even if these forecasts are not overly optimistic, and more recent preliminary data indicate they are, a rise in the number of unemployed of such magnitudes can hardly be voluntary. Nor can it be ignored as something "natural."

Table I.1 records the unemployment rates and the proportion of unemployed in long-term (one year or more) unemployment in 15 OECD countries. Taking the period 1979–91 as a whole, the trends in both unemployment rates and long-term unemployment are clearly upward. By 1989, in almost half the economies treated in table I.1, the long-term unemployed comprise approximately a third or more of the unemployed. This also indicates a sharp rise in involuntary unemployment.

Increasingly, economists have ignored these important facts. Partly this lack of concern with unemployment can be traced to a rising fear of inflation and, related, to a general acceptance by the economics profession that higher unemployment has been and continues to be a necessary cost of containing inflation. When this fear is formalized within the context of the NAIRU and its alleged increase since the early 1970s, both the difficulty in reducing unemployment through

Table I.1 Unemployment rate and proportion of unemployed in long-term unemployment in selected OECD countries (percent)

	1979 Rate	1979 Pro-portion	1981 Rate	1981 Pro-portion	1983 Rate	1983 Pro-portion	1985 Rate	1985 Pro-portion	1987 Rate	1987 Pro-portion	1989 Rate	1989 Pro-portion	1991 Rate	1991 Pro-portion
Australia	6.2	18.1	5.7	21.0	9.9	27.5	8.1	30.9	8.0	28.6	6.1	23.0	9.6	24.9
Austria	1.7	8.6	2.1	6.5	3.7	9.0	3.6	13.3	3.8	10.8	3.2	13.1	3.7	15.2
Belgium	7.3	58.0	10.0	52.4	12.9	62.8	12.0	68.3	11.2	74.9	9.3	76.3	9.3	—
Canada	7.4	3.5	7.5	4.2	11.9	9.8	10.5	10.3	8.9	9.4	7.5	6.8	10.3	7.2
Finland	6.0	—	4.9	—	5.4	22.3	5.0	21.1	5.1	19.0	6.5	6.9	7.6	—
France	6.0	30.3	7.6	32.5	8.4	42.2	10.2	46.8	10.6	45.5	9.4	43.9	9.4	37.3
Germany	3.3	19.9	4.6	16.2	8.2	28.5	8.3	31.0	7.9	48.2	5.6	49.0	4.3	—
Ireland	7.1	31.8	9.9	30.5	14.0	31.0	17.3	41.2	18.7	66.4	15.6	67.3	15.8	—
Japan	2.1	16.5	2.2	13.5	2.6	15.5	2.6	11.8	2.8	20.2	2.3	18.7	2.1	17.9
Netherlands	5.6	27.1	9.2	22.0	15.0	43.7	14.2	55.3	12.6	46.2	7.4	49.9	5.9	—
Norway	2.0	3.8	2.0	3.0	3.3	6.7	2.5	8.3	2.1	5.0	4.9	11.6	5.5	20.2
Spain	9.5	27.5	14.3	43.4	17.7	53.5	21.9	56.8	20.5	62.0	17.3	58.5	16.3	51.1
Sweden	1.7	6.8	2.1	6.0	2.9	10.3	2.3	11.4	1.9	8.0	1.4	6.5	2.7	—
UK	4.5	24.8	9.1	22.0	11.3	36.5	11.7	41.0	10.4	45.9	6.2	40.8	8.3	—
USA	5.8	4.2	7.6	6.7	9.6	13.3	7.1	9.5	6.2	8.1	5.3	5.7	6.7	6.3

Source: OECD, *Employment Outlook*, OECD, Paris, September 1987, July 1992

policy as well as its high costs are highlighted. As a result the plight of the unemployed is pushed well into the background.

Much of this study is given to refuting a NAIRU interpretation of the current difficulties. While the practical determination of just what rate of unemployment can be considered the FE rate will always involve some arbitrariness, it is important to stress at the outset that the FE rate of unemployment is not to be confused with the NAIRU. Here, as in most studies until recent times, FE is defined in terms of the nature of unemployment and not the behavior of prices.

A second factor detracting from a concern with the poor unemployment record arises from the ability of a country to experience periods of growth in total output, and even in productivity and per capita income, while unemployment remains high. The Reagan and Thatcher "recoveries" are two cases in point. Starting from the bottom of the severe recession of the early 1980s, substantial (but nonsustainable) growth in gross domestic product (GDP) occurred in both countries until 1990. However, if measured on a consistent basis, unemployment exceeded double-digit rates in the United Kingdom and at rates that during the 1950s and 1960s would have been considered recession highs in the United States.[6] This remains true despite the recent rapid growth of employment in both countries. Seen in another way, from 1974 to 1990 official unemployment rates in the United Kingdom and the United States have averaged 8.1 percent and 6.9 percent respectively compared with an average of 3.2 percent and 4.5 percent respectively from 1963 to 1973.

Consider the following related fact. In 1988 unemployment rates in the United States fell below 6 percent, to 5.4 percent, for the first time since 1979. However, even when the unemployment rate fell to 5.6 percent in 1974 in the United States, almost half the weeks of unemployment experienced in that year were experienced by persons unemployed for 27 or more weeks.[7] Moreover, data on the reasons for being unemployed in the United States (mostly losing one's job) strongly describe a situation in which most of the rise in unemployment since the early 1970s is a rise in involuntary unemployment.

Throughout this study, growth of output and employment even if

---

[6]When unemployment is measured on a basis that was used up until November 1982, the seasonally adjusted UK unemployment rate for January 1993 was 14.2 percent with 4.2 million unemployed workers. See Paul Convery, *Working Brief 42*, Unemployment Unit, London, 1993, table 1.

[7]See L. Summers, "Why is the unemployment rate so very high near full employment?" *Brookings Papers on Economic Activity*, No. 2, 1986, table 5.

sustained in a few economies with mass unemployment throughout the capitalist world is not treated as a cause for celebration. The success or failure of any system's macroperformance will be evaluated primarily through its unemployment record. So that these points can be kept clearly in mind, the difficulties everywhere beginning in the late 1960s are more often referred to as an economic breakdown, as in the title of this study, rather than stagnation.

I.7 The Tasks Ahead

An outline of the adopted framework of analysis is contained in chapter 1, and is fully developed in the following three chapters. It is shown that this approach is more appropriate than any other to the tasks of (a) explaining the causes of the current worldwide breakdown, (b) explaining the differences in economic performance between countries today, and (c) pointing the way to a program for economic recovery. Some of the more important macrodevelopments since the First World War, including trends in macropolicies in the developed capitalist world, are summarized in chapter 2. This historical chapter is designed to illustrate how macroproblems and policy responses have arisen out of past developments within the capitalist system. Chapter 3 is a critique of what is essentially a pre-Keynesian view of the role of policy. It is maintained that the Keynesian symmetry is as true today as it was a half century ago. An examination of the determinants of unemployment policies and performances in the OECD countries is initiated in chapter 4. By utilizing both cross-country and intertemporal approaches, the forces that have led to a rise in the average rate of unemployment throughout the OECD can be isolated from those responsible for differences in unemployment rates across countries at any point in time.

In chapters 5 and 6 the period of success of post-war capitalism (i.e. the period up until 1974) is analyzed in terms of the framework developed in chapters 1–4. In chapter 6 simple econometric tests are undertaken to support the qualitative institutional explanations of differences in unemployment performances between countries put forward in chapter 5. Many of the ideas developed in earlier chapters are also pulled together in chapter 6. If chapters 5 and 6 document the success of modern capitalism, the remainder of the study explains its failure. Following a brief introduction, econometric tests to refute alternative explanations of the current breakdown are employed in chapter 7. This chapter also indicates how conventional Phillips curve analysis is related to the econometric models. Chapter 8 considers mathematical models of inflation and unemployment giving a better understanding of the difficulties that have arisen since the early 1970s. These difficulties are detailed in chapter 9. Chapter 10 outlines a model of long-run mass unemployment. The special role of the English-speaking economies in holding back world recovery is stressed. Chapter 11 discusses the Reagan boom of the 1980s. Its special nature (including its non-sustainability) has had much to do with the slowness and weakness of the long-awaited recovery in the 1990s. Chapter 12 presents a program for recovery in the United States. It has the additional benefit of describing a recovery program for Canada and the United Kingdom as well. Chapter 13 contains the conclusions.

1 How should we do Macroeconomics?

1.1 Introduction

In introduction I it was stated that, in order to understand the causes and cure of the current mass unemployment, an extended framework of analysis is required. The analytical techniques of traditional macroeconomics are essential for this purpose but in addition it is necessary to introduce institutional influences and to consider the problem in a historical and comparative framework. In this chapter the nature of this proposed approach is discussed at greater length, indicating the outline, at least, of the method of analysis followed throughout the study to explain the current difficulties. Detail and substance will be added in later chapters. The nature of the extended framework is made clearer by a comparison first with what can be considered the mainstream or traditional view of political economy.

Consider the rather obvious point that one of the main tasks of macroeconomics is to develop models to explain the macroperformances of real economies. For example, why rates of inflation or unemployment have risen, while productivity growth has slowed down, and the payments positions worsened; or why one country has succeeded in its macroperformance much more than another. Given the propensity of governments to intervene in order to influence macro-outcomes in the real world, these models must therefore incorporate the impact of policies, for example, how changes in monetary, fiscal, or exchange rate policy affect employment, as well as the interaction between the traditional economic variables. In this sense alone, explaining the performance of any economy requires a political economy perspective.

A good example of this rather traditional approach is contained in the *General Theory*—an acknowledgement that capitalism is not a self-regulating system with strong FE tendencies. According to Keynes, political intervention in the form of discretionary AD policies is required from time to time in order to guarantee a decent overall output and employment performance. As a result, understanding the actual performance of any economy requires a model that incorporates such macropolicy variables and their interactions with economic variables.

However, the first point to be stressed is that modeling the macroperformance of an economy today requires an extended political economy perspective that can explain why the authorities choose the AD policies that they do. Why, for example, were stimulative AD policies implemented in the 1950s and 1960s and restrictive policies more recently? As will be clear, the "why policy" question must be posed because it leads to the more basic issues of the costs of AD policies and why they might vary over time (and across countries).

The second point to stress is that the impact of political intervention often reaches beyond its economic targets. It is capable of inducing changes in economic and social institutions—changes that can result in new constraints on future policy decisions and therefore future economic performance. Because of this, the framework must also encompass policy-induced institutional changes and their impact on future performance. Without these two added dimensions, this study seeks to make clear that no analysis can adequately explain the rise in unemployment almost everywhere and therefore find a way to bring about recovery.

1.2 Why Do Governments Choose Unemployment Policies?

Consider first the need to explain why different policies, in particular restrictive unemployment policies, have been chosen in different countries recently. Beginning in the early 1970s the macroperformance of most developed capitalist economies deteriorated markedly. Unemployment rates rose and productivity growth fell sharply almost everywhere. Until the recent monetarist revival, few doubted that FE policies would succeed should governments choose to use them, but they chose not to do so.[1]

An explanation of macropolicy choices popular with political scientists before the breakdown maintained that (cross-country) differences in unemployment rates can be explained by differences in the strength of organized labor and of the political parties that represent it.[2] Accord-

---

[1] Taking the OECD as a whole, it was found that 70 percent of the rise in unemployment rates from 1979 to 1983 could be attributed to fiscal and monetary restraint. See J. McCallum, "Unemployment in the OECD countries in the 1980s," *Economic Journal*, 96, December 1986, 942–60.

[2] This view can be found in D. Cameron, "Social democracy, corporatism, labour quiescence and the representation of economic interest in advanced capitalist society," in J. Goldthorpe (ed.), *Order and Conflict in Contemporary Capitalism,* Clarendon Press, Oxford, 1984; and D. Hibbs, "Political parties and macroeconomic policy," *American Political Science Review,* 71, December 1977, 1467–87.

ing to this view, labor is willing to trade off price stability for lower unemployment and registers this preference at the ballot box through its choice of political party. If these cross-country findings are applied uncritically to intertemporal events, a political explanation of the reversal of AD policies in the early 1970s emerges; there has been a shift in political power away from pro-labor governments.

Whatever the merits of the argument, however, if policy choices and macro-outcomes could be explained solely in terms of political power (or other noneconomic forces), the question of why governments choose particular macroeconomic policies might best be left to non-economists. However, political influences underlying differences in AD policies and unemployment records are only one possibility. Explanations based on economic causes are readily available. For example, a common argument made since the early 1970s is that restrictive AD policies have been utilized throughout the OECD because governments considered the costs too high, in terms of inflation and payments problems, and this was understood by many economists as reason enough for their refusal to pursue the FE goal. According to this line of argument there have been adverse shifts in the Phillips curves facing the different economies and governments have responded to this. Mass unemployment is very much an economic as well as a political phenomenon.

1.3 The Basic Causes

However, even if such a political economy explanation of differences in unemployment policies is correct, it is rather superficial. What must concern policy-makers in this case is why the Phillips curve is so unfavorably placed and what can be done to shift it in a favorable direction. It is at this point that cross-country analysis becomes useful in reaching the more basic causes. What must be noted is that, since 1973, some governments have successfully pursued stimulative AD policies and have been able to maintain low rates of unemployment. They have thereby avoided the most important dimension of the stagnation problem and have done so while experiencing inflation records often as good as, if not better than, the countries with high unemployment. The question arises as to why they have succeeded where others have not.

To see how this question must be answered, first allow that in all modern capitalist economies wage negotiations and price setting are carried out in such a way that wage–wage and wage–price inflationary mechanisms are always in danger of being activated. Furthermore, the potential inflationary pressures emanating from these mechanisms intensify as the unemployment rates fall, other things being equal. The point to be emphasized is that across countries other things are not equal; institutions will differ and "institutions matter" in the sense that they will determine whether these potential inflationary forces become activated, resulting in high rates of inflation under low unemployment conditions. In this case explaining differences in Phillips curves and therefore in unemployment rates between countries (and over time) involves determining what the critical institutions are that influences wage–wage and wage–price responses as the unemployment rate varies. These findings must then be incorporated in any explanation of policy choice and ultimately of macroperformance.

To anticipate some of the findings of this study, stimulative AD policies lead to high and even accelerating rates of inflation while unemployment rates are still high in some countries but not in others because of a relatively unfavorable configuration of institutions in the former group which is absent in the latter. Chief among these are an adversarial industrial relations system, a fragmented union movement with decentralized collective bargaining, and a lack of any tradition of government leadership in reconciling distributional conflict.[3] In these countries determining the ultimate causes of a poor unemployment record involves explaining how a reduction in unemployment rates interacts with, say, the adversarial industrial relations system so as to cause accelerating wage and price increases at relatively high rates of unemployment. This amounts to tracing the origins of the unwillingness of the authorities to stimulate AD.

The question arises as to who in these circumstances is best able to analyze these problems—to trace out in systematic detail the manner in which institutions work to prevent or allow the use of policies for reducing unemployment. Clearly economists are in the best position to determine the relationship between AD conditions and the inflationary forces, but their expertise is also needed to understand how inflationary

[3]For examples of a rapidly expanding literature on the importance of institutions for macroeconomic performance, see M. Bruno and J. Sachs, *The Economics of Worldwide Stagflation*, Harvard University Press, Cambridge, MA, 1984; Cornwall, *Conditions for Economic Recovery;* C. Crouch, "The conditions for trade union wage restraint," in L. Lindberg and C. Maier (eds.), *The Politics of Inflation and Economic Stagnation,* Brookings Institution, Washington, DC, 1985; J. McCallum, "Inflation and social consensus in the seventies," *Economic Journal*, 93, December 1983, 784–805; and "Unemployment in the seventies," *Economic Journal*, 93, December 1983, 784–805; and "Unemployment in the OECD countries."

Figure 1.1 A causal chain

Poor institutional-policy fit ⟹ High costs of FE ⟹ Restrictive AD policies ⟹ High unemployment

forces are shaped by institutions and what institutional changes are needed to relieve some economies of their strong inflationary bias under low unemployment conditions. To put this last point differently, economists are needed to see what kind of incomes policy, if any, is workable.

What has just been outlined is a strategy for determining the more basic causes of AD policy differences. It serves to underline a key point of this study: that the assignment of questions of *why* macroeconomic policies are adopted to political scientists and limiting economists to the questions of *what* are the effects of alternative macropolicies is not a useful division of labor but a prescription for continued misunderstanding of how economies really function. When this is acknowledged, the explanation of economic breakdown proceeds along a causal chain. High unemployment is seen primarily as the result of inadequate AD. AD does not passively and automatically adjust to aggregate supply guaranteeing full employment of labor and capital as in a neoclassical world. The failure of AD to generate FE and renewed growth is then traced to an unwillingness of governments to provide the fiscal and monetary stimulus required. The reasons for this unwillingness are then sought; among them may be the high costs of FE policies, such as accelerating inflation and external disequilibria. These are finally related to the institutional framework of the economy. In this way economic breakdown is seen as a failure to achieve an "institutional-policy fit."[4] Some AD policies cannot be implemented and some employment goals cannot be thereby realized because such policies are so costly and therefore unacceptable, and these high costs can be attributed to prevailing institutions. This causal chain is shown schematically in figure 1.1. Obviously a similar causal chain can also be used to explain relative success. However, when the failure to achieve an institutional–policy fit is widespread across countries, mass unemployment results.

[4]F. Scharpf, "The political economy of inflation and unemployment in Western Europe: an outline" and "Economic and institutional constraints of full-employment strategies: Sweden, Austria and West Germany," IIM/IMP Discussion Papers 81–2 and 83–20, Wissenschaftszentrum, Berlin, 1981, 1983.

1.4 A Framework for Studying Performance

Section 1.7 indicates how this causal chain can be extended to explain macrodevelopments over time for any economy as well as cross-country differences. First, however, some additional points must be made. The concepts of a causal chain and an institutional–policy fit are hardly a blueprint for studying the political economy of economic breakdown. A framework for analyzing how policies influence performance and institutions and how institutional influence policy needs structure and some detail. The possibility that economic performance and choice of policy may be dictated by relative political power or party control rather than economic constraints was mentioned earlier. These alternative explanations suggest a method of extending and improving the causal chain concept.

Thus Kalecki's theory of the political business cycle and more recent work outside economics point up the importance of the strength of the demand for high employment or FE as a determinant of the actual policies chosen and, therefore, of economic performance.[5] Kalecki among others has argued that capitalists have the upper hand in the governance of capitalist economies and (for reasons which are not well explained) are able to dictate the kind of AD policy adopted. Periodic high unemployment is perceived as necessary to maintain labor discipline. According to this theory the relative demand for FE is all-important and it is found to be weak.

Studies that have been more careful recognized that the strength of demand for FE can vary widely across countries. The point is that in understanding why certain AD policies are chosen and why unemployment rates are what they are, the preferences, demands, and relative power of organized interest groups must be taken into consideration. For example, some of these groups may prefer to substitute reduced unemployment for more inflation.

1.5 The Second Blade of the Scissors

But this is only "one blade of the scissors." The basic framework of market demand and supply analysis suggests that policy choices and outcomes will depend upon both the demand for some policy, FE in this case, and the willingness of the authorities to supply it. From what has just been said, it should be apparent that institutional factors may

---

[5]Kalecki, "Political aspects of full employment."

constrain policy-makers and thereby limit the supply of policy forthcoming, and these should be considered. Two such supply constraints limiting stimulative AD policies have already been mentioned—an inflationary bias and balance-of-payments difficulties at FE—but others come to mind, for example, legal constraints on deficit spending and a politically divided fiscal authority.

The manner in which demand and supply forces interact in determining why some AD or unemployment policy is chosen can be seen in the following example. AD policies can influence unemployment rates whenever there is involuntary unemployment. It is also correct to argue that powerful unions and other social forces may intensify the demand for FE. This may induce governments to introduce various labor market policies, for example, policies to facilitate job search or to retrain workers, in order to reduce the costs of stimulative AD policies. However, as long as governments have the option of stimulating or restricting AD, the AD policy is still indeterminate. Governments may be simply unwilling to "supply" FE or even to stimulate AD marginally because it is felt that (despite their best efforts) the political and economic side effects of FE policies are too costly.[6] As a result the supply of AD policies for pursuing high or FE goals is constrained.[7] Furthermore, recent AD policies throughout the OECD attest to the unwillingness of governments to pursue FE whenever the inflation or payments problems at FE are considered to be serious. As already suggested in sections 1.2 and 1.3, the continued existence of serious adverse side effects despite the authorities' efforts can be traced to the inability to develop additional policy instruments to counter them, for example, the inability to develop a workable incomes policy. Ultimately, the limitation on the number of available instruments can be traced to basic institutional influences.

It is intended that in analyzing historical performances in terms of the demand for and supply of FE, a clearer picture will emerge of the determinants of policy choice, macro-outcomes, and the basic causes of today's difficulties. It is also intended that by isolating and weighing the demand and supply factors determining policies and outcomes, a critical step in formulating a policy for ending mass unemployment will be achieved. It must be noted also that since ending mass unemployment involves eliminating the inflation and pay-

---

[6]The idea of explaining macroeconomic policies in terms of demand and supply factors is found in R. J. Gordon, "The demand for and supply of inflation," *Journal of Law and Economics*, December 1975, Vol. 18 (3), pp. 807–836.

[7]For example, throughout the post-war period even governments favorable to labor have been forced to restrict AD because of payments difficulties, and this despite the fact that in countries like Britain labor is highly unionized.

ments problems that can arise under FE conditions, a successful policy must achieve all these goals.

1.6 The Second Limitation

So far the first shortcoming of the traditional political economy perspective—its failure to consider the role of institutions in determining why policies are adopted—has been considered. Consider next a second limitation. It was noted that mainstream political economy of the Keynesian type was limited in the way that it studied the impact of a policy on the economy; it was concerned only with the effect of policy on economic variables. However, if the evolution of capitalist economies in the post-war period tells us anything, it is that policy can affect the performance of an economy in such a way as to cause radical changes in its institutional structure.

Two cases should be mentioned. First, active pursuit of FE by governments in the 1950s and 1960s strengthened the power of labor relative to capital, as did the extension of the welfare state. These policies greatly altered the workings of labor markets in a way that gave rise to potentially strong inflationary problems. Labor was simply put in a stronger position for enforcing its wage demands under FE conditions. In some countries, FE would have led to politically unacceptable rates of inflation as labor exercised its power, and in those countries unemployment rates were allowed to remain high.

Other countries were more fortunate. Inflation was not eliminated, but even in countries with extremely powerful trade union movements, unemployment rates were reduced to the bare minimum, yet the inflation record compared well with the high unemployment economies. As will be argued, this was no accident but arose out of the determination of governments and other key actors to reduce inflationary pressures at FE. In this important sense, a long-run workable incomes policy was implemented. An understanding of how FE policies altered labor markets and price mechanisms, giving rise to potentially strong inflationary problems everywhere and forcing some authorities to accept relatively high rates of unemployment even before the current period of mass unemployment, is fundamental for comprehending the current situation.

Second, the current breakdown reveals just as clearly how important it is to study the impact of policies on institutions if we are to find a solution. Policy-induced periods of slack, particularly when they are prolonged, lead not just to long-term unemployment, low profits, the destruction of human capital through the deterioration of skills, and the destruction of infrastructure and other forms of physical capital. They also lead to a marked decline in labor force participation rates, the acceptance of short-term spells of employment and long-term spells of unemployment as a way of life, and the substitution of paper entrepreneurship for the Schumpeterian type. Such marked changes in attitudes toward work and unemployment are bound to alter the impact of AD policies on unemployment and inflation. A fuller understanding of these and other impacts of restrictive AD policies on the basic structure of the economy is needed if we are to bring mass unemployment to an end.[8]

1.7 An Institutional-Analytical Approach

If the current breakdown is to be ended, it must first be understood. This requires a model that can explain how institutions shape policy, and how policy induces changes in institutions as well as in purely economic variables. The more traditional approaches that work within a framework of fixed tastes and technologies can never get to the heart of the current problem. Tastes and technologies are only part of an institutional framework that is evolving constantly and rapidly enough that our theories must be constantly modified to take account of these changes.[9] Institutions do influence policy options and some institutional structures severely restrict the authorities in their ability to fight mass unemployment.

Seen in this way the political economy view of economic breakdown is nothing more than an example of a more comprehensive political economy perspective that seeks to explain economic outcomes as the result of a joint interaction: one in which the policies chosen affect the economy and its institutional environment and another in which the institutional structure of the economy in its turn affects the policies chosen. However, all of this must be seen in dynamic terms as part of the process of growth in which economic growth takes place in a most

---

[8] A widely adopted way to emphasize the impact of policy on performance and ultimately institutions is discussed at length in chapters 3, 8, and 9. There the focus is on the impact of policy and performance on the position of the Phillips curve.

[9] Explaining economic events, such as the behavior of GDP, in terms of fixed tastes and technologies when the latter are in fact determined by the events that are supposed to be explained, that is, the behavior of GDP, is considered ad hoc theory by Popper. See K. Popper, *Objective Knowledge: An Evolutionary Approach,* Oxford University Press, Oxford, 1972, pp. 15–16.

Figure 1.2 Path dependence

Distribution of power and institutional framework ⇒ AD policies adopted ⇒ Unemployment performance ⇒ Institutional framework

unbalanced way. Industries rise and fall, new goods and processes are introduced, and resources are constantly reallocated. In short, economic growth must be seen as a transformation of the economy. As the economy grows and transforms itself, institutional changes also occur—some induced by macroeconomic events (including policies) and others largely exogenous to the economic transformation process. It is thus a recursive process as suggested by the earlier expression—the causal chain. But whatever the relative importance of economic or noneconomic causes, at any point in time the institutional framework will act as a constraint on current and future policy options open to the authorities. Macroperformance is always "path or history dependent" in this important sense.

Figure 1.2 illustrates this dynamic interaction by expanding on figure 1.1. Starting at some point in time, the existing institutional framework acts as a constraint limiting and shaping economic performance whatever the AD policies adopted. But it also constrains the set of policy options available to the authorities. However, the distribution of political and economic power must also be taken into account as it influences the strength of demand for AD policies. The policies adopted then influence the actual unemployment performance of the economy and eventually have significant effects on the institutional framework itself as seen by moving from left to right across the diagram. Projecting further into the future, the process can be repeated, emphasizing path dependence as it applies to historical changes in institutional structures.

This dynamic process, however, will be continuously subject to external shocks and trends independent of the workings of the economy. For example, in chapter 9 the impact of the formation of the Organization of Petroleum Exporting Countries (OPEC) cartel is discussed as an example of a severe outside disturbance influencing the growth and transformation process, while in chapter 2 the rising economic and political power of labor, a development to a large extent independent of the performance of the economy, is considered as a prime determinant of the nature of this chain of events. Influences such as these have been operative in all economies.

It is true that because different countries experience different disturbances and are influenced by their own unique histories, the actual chain of macroevents will differ between countries. Fortunately, the multicountry approach reveals that there has been sufficient similarity in economic developments to establish the usefulness of the framework in analyzing many economies. In addition, because of this similarity, the impact of differences in institutional arrangements, especially those institutions that allow the authorities to manage their economies more adequately, can be better isolated. The multicountry approach is essential for establishing this point as well.

This proposed framework has many affinities with traditional "institutional economics." These include an emphasis on the diversity of institutional arrangements, their constant state of flux, the many important ways in which institutions influence outcomes, and a rejection of "universal laws" in the social sciences holding for all time and in all places. However, traditional institutional economics has suffered from an over-reaction to what it sees as the sterility of mainstream economic theory. It is true that much of neoclassical theory can be rejected as of little use for analyzing and understanding contemporary problems. For example, the fixed tastes and technology framework and the competitive model, including the assumption of flexprice markets that always clear, will have no role to play here. But the position taken in this study is that an understanding of current developments and difficulties requires a careful blending of institutional analysis with a more realistic and relevant form of analytical economics. Some of the key trends in the distribution of power and the evolving institutional framework that figure so importantly in capitalist development this century are discussed in greater detail in chapter 2.

2 The Evolutionary Nature of Twentieth-century Capitalism

2.1 Introduction

Some of the major macrodevelopments common to all the developed capitalist economies since the First World War are outlined in this chapter. This is done in such a manner as to provide further understanding of the dynamic process described at the end of chapter 1. Extending the period of analysis to consider events prior to the Second World War provides the reader with a deeper grasp of the causal chain underlying developments. Furthermore, in order to comprehend what has gone wrong and what, if anything, can be done to end the current difficulties, a comparison with earlier periods of capitalist development is essential. This allows a better understanding of how the policy options available today depend upon institutional developments left over from the past. In particular, a good deal of attention must be paid to the period of approximately a quarter of a century leading up to the early 1970s. Special emphasis is given to the shift in economic and political power to labor and its impact on policy and the labor market, as well as the subsequent effects of these developments on the policy choices available to the authorities in the more recent period.

The focus is initially on unemployment, growth trends, and the rise of the welfare state. These are then related to important shifts in political and economic power, suggesting the forces behind the changing demand for FE and welfare policies. The impact of the growing strength of labor on industrial relations and inflation is next taken up. Following that, the strong policy responses to the accelerating inflation of the late 1960s–early 1970s and their consequences are outlined. These policies are then causally linked to the early boom period. The tone is somewhat assertive, but supportive arguments are contained in later chapters. The period is divided into three subperiods: the interwar period, roughly the quarter of a century following the Second

Table 2.1 Unemployment rates U, growth rates of output per person employed, $\dot{q}$, and growth rates of gross domestic product, $\dot{Q}$, in selected OECD countries during 1929–1937 and 1960–1973

	1929–37			1960–73		
	U	$\dot{q}$	$\dot{Q}$	U	$\dot{q}$	$\dot{Q}$
Canada	12.3	−0.9	−0.3	5.2	2.7	5.6
Denmark	6.3	1.5	2.2	1.6	3.1	4.4
France	3.3[a]	−1.3	−2.1	1.8	4.9	5.6
Germany	9.3	2.1	3.2	0.8	4.2	4.4
Italy	4.4[b]	1.6	1.9	4.8	5.8	5.3
Japan	–	4.6	5.4	1.3	8.5	9.9
Netherlands	7.7	0.3	0.2	1.2	4.1	5.0
Sweden	5.3	2.1	2.4	1.6	3.5	4.1
UK	9.6	1.6	2.3	2.7	2.9	3.1
USA	16.5	0.4	0.1	4.8	2.0	4.0

[a] Average of 1931, 1936, and 1938.
[b] Average excluding 1935 and 1936.

Sources: *National Institute Economic Review*, July 1961, table 13; A. Maddison, *Economic Growth in the West*, Twentieth Century Fund, New York, 1964, p. 220; OECD, *Labour Force Statistics, 1960–1971*, OECD, Paris, 1973; OECD, *Labour Force Statistics, 1970–1981*, OECD, Paris, 1983; OECD, *Economic Outlook, 1980, 1981, 1983*, OECD, Paris; OECD, *Historical Statistics, 1960–1983*, OECD, Paris, 1985

World War, and the period of economic decline beginning in most countries in 1973 and continuing up to the present.

2.2 A Comparison of Unemployment and Growth Rates

Table 2.1 brings out certain key features of the macroeconomic performances of several OECD countries during the Great Depression and the period of steady growth before the general collapse of the early 1970s. The marked improvement in the employment records in the more recent of the two periods is apparent. Only Italy experienced a rise in unemployment rate U in the more recent period. A noticeable improvement is also evident for the growth rate of total output $\dot{Q}$ and for the more critical measure of the growth rate of output per employed worker, $\dot{q}$. In every country rates of growth of GDP increased substantially in the period following the Second World War, while rates of growth of productivity were typically at least double those of the interwar period.

The superior unemployment and growth performances in the more recent period are related. Tight labor markets have their counterpart for capital in the form of high capacity utilization rates. The latter reduce

28 *Framework*

macrorisks and induce business to undertake investment projects, especially the innovational kind. Conversely, the low capacity utilization rates that often accompany high rates of unemployment inhibit investment, thereby slowing down rates of growth of productivity and output. As will be shown below, the deterioration in economic conditions since 1973 has generated an economic climate similar to that of the 1930s.[1]

Which elements of final demand were responsible for the favorable employment performance is a matter of debate. Certainly, the resulting unemployment records during this post-war period can at least be interpreted as an unwillingness of governments to allow unemployment rates to rise further.[2] Behind this lay a desire by governments to respond to the problems arising out of the Great Depression and the Second World War, reinforced by the rising economic and political power of labor and underlain by the extension of suffrage and expanded access to free education throughout the century. However, for the majority of the OECD economies, the pre-1974 rapid expansion of private investment and exports contributed importantly to the booming demand conditions. Equally important, the growth in investment contributed to the rapid growth of productivity outside the North American economies, lessening payments problems in these other economies. The period after 1973 was to see a major change in government attitudes in these matters—a change related to new difficulties arising from severe shocks to the OECD economies and from the conditions of affluence prior to 1974.

These trends are well known. Table 2.1 also reveals that there were substantial differences in unemployment and growth rates between countries in the more recent period. Canada, Italy, and the United States stand out as the economies with the highest unemployment, while the three English-speaking economies were at the bottom of the per capita growth league. Performances since 1973 are discussed in section 2.8.

2.3 The Rise of the Welfare State

The rapid and sustained rates of growth of productivity and per capita incomes in the first quarter of a century following the Second World

---
[1] Extending the post-war period back to, say, 1950 or to other OECD economies would not affect any of the conclusions of this section.

[2] It has been argued that merely a belief that government can and will do something to stabilize output and employment will lead to greater stability. See M. Baily, "Stabilization policy and private economic behavior," *Brookings Papers on Economic Activity*, No. 2, 1978.

Table 2.2 Social security expenditure as a percentage of gross domestic product in Scandinavia, Austria, and Germany, 1933–1977

Year	Denmark	Norway	Sweden	Austria	Germany
1933	6.2	4.1	3.5	7.0	11.4
1950	7.5	4.6	8.8	10.1	11.7
1977	23.3	19.1	29.7	20.1	22.4

Source: E. Esping-Andersen and W. Korpi, "Social policy as class politics in post-war capitalism: Scandinavia, Austria and Germany," in J. Goldthorpe (ed.), *Order and Conflict in Contemporary Capitalism*, Clarendon Press, Oxford, 1984, table 8.1

War facilitated an institutional change in the post-war period that was to have a lasting impact. This was the rapid expansion of the welfare state. The dramatic nature of the change from the pre- to the post-war era cannot be adequately illustrated by statistics as unfortunately few comparable data are available for the pre-war period. Table 2.2 illustrates some of this development with data for social security expenditures as a percentage of GDP for five European economies.[3] In every economy, this percentage has risen dramatically since the 1930s. The broad picture, however, is not difficult to describe: a pronounced substitution of nonmarket for market allocative mechanisms took place everywhere in the post-war period.

Much more data are available beginning early in the post-war period. For example, social security transfers, that is, social security benefits for sickness and old age, family allowances, unemployment and social assistance grants, and unfunded employee welfare benefits paid by general government, increased as a share of the GDP in the seven largest OECD economies from 7.3 percent in 1960–67 to 17.6 percent in 1980–83.[4] However, the welfare state has been usefully treated as something more than a series of income maintenance programs under the title of social security. In addition, public education and health programs have also been considered since they are deliberate attempts "*to improve future earnings possibilities and to protect the position of the most vulnerable groups in society.*"[5] Table 2.3 gives details of this social expenditure measure of the welfare state where direct public expenditures on education, health services, pensions, unemployment compensation, and other income maintenance programs and welfare services are given as a share of GDP for selective post-war years. The

---
[3]See also P. Flora, *State, Economy and Society in Western Europe, 1915–1975*, Vol. 1, Campus Verlag, Frankfurt, 1987, ch. 9.
[4]OECD, *Historical Statistics, 1960–1983*, OECD, Paris, 1985, table 6.3.
[5]OECD, *Public Expenditure Trends*, OECD, Paris, 1985.

30 *Framework*

Table 2.3 Social expenditures as a share of gross domestic product (at current prices) for seven large OECD countries

	1960	1973	1981
Canada	12.1	19.5	21.5
France	13.4[a]	17.2[a]	29.5
Germany	20.5	26.3	31.5
Italy	16.8	24.2	29.1
Japan	8.0	10.7	17.5
UK	13.9	19.3	23.7
USA	10.9	17.3	20.8
Average	13.7	19.2	24.8

[a] Excluding education.

Source: OECD, *Social Expenditure Statistics 1960–1990*, OECD, Paris, 1985, table 1 and annex C

Table 2.4 Real social expenditure in OECD countries, 1960–1981[a]

	Real expenditure share		Annual growth rate of real social expenditure		Real income elasticity of social expenditure	
	1960	1981	1960–75	1975–81	1960–75	1975–81
Canada	12.3	22.1	9.5	2.7	1.9	0.8
France	13.4[b]	29.1	7.5[b]	5.9	1.5	2.1
Germany	20.4	29.2	6.7	1.9	1.8	0.6
Italy	18.1	26.2	7.0	3.8	1.5	1.2
Japan	10.2	13.7	9.7	7.3	1.1	1.6
UK	14.8	23.1	5.0	2.5	1.9	2.5
USA	11.3	20.2	7.7	2.8	2.3	0.9
Average[c]	14.4	23.4	7.6	3.8	1.7	1.4

[a] Or latest year.
[b] Excluding education.
[c] Unweighted average.

Source: OECD, *Social Expenditures, 1960–1990*, OECD, Paris, 1985, table 4

increasing scope and size of the welfare state measured in this manner stand out clearly.

Even though the growth of these programs relative to the growth of the economy has slowed since the 1970s, social expenditure still remained a "luxury good" almost everywhere, at least until 1981. This is brought out clearly in table 2.4 in which levels and rates of growth of real social expenditure (nominal expenditure deflated by a social expenditure index) and real GDP (nominal GDP deflated by the GDP implicit price index) are compared for each country. The first two columns show the rising ratio of social expenditure to GDP even after eight years of reduced economic growth. The third and fourth columns depict a slowing in the rate of growth of real social expenditure after 1975, and the fifth and sixth columns reveal a decline in real growth elasticities after 1975 (i.e. ratio of rate of growth of real social expenditure to rate of growth of real GDP), although on average the growth elasticity remains greater than unity until 1981.

Of equal interest, when the growth rate of real social expenditure is "decomposed" into the parts due to changes in the demographic composition of the population, changes in the coverage of each program and changes in the average real benefit of each person covered, the rapid growth of average real benefits of the various programs accounts for more than half the expansion of the four major programs. This is shown in table 2.5 for the seven major OECD countries. Taking the four major programs as a group reveals that the growth of real expenditure attributable to the growth of average real benefits was approximately 58 percent in the period 1960-75 and 62 percent from 1975 to 1981. It should also be noted that in both periods much of the growth in unemployment compensation can be attributed to higher "average real benefits." However, more recent data indicate a decline in average real benefits.[6]

Finally, it should be noted that even tables 2.3 and 2.4 fail to measure the full extent of the rising importance of the nonmarket allocative mechanisms in the post-war period. For example "tax expenditure" and occupational welfare measures financed by the private sector are neglected and, in general, the entire role of government in stimulating private spending for programs designed for income maintenance and improved future earnings is left out of consideration.

2.4 The Rising Power of Labor

The historical decline in unemployment rates and the expansion of the welfare state from the interwar period to the quarter of a century following the Second World War has been attributed by social scientists largely to the rising power of organized labor.[7] Workers as well as their union leaders perceive, for example, a tradeoff between lower unemployment and higher inflation (if necessary) as in their material

---

[6] See A. Atkinson, in R. Dornbusch and R. Layard (eds.), *The Performance of the British Economy*, Clarendon Press, Oxford, 1987.

[7] See, for example, K. Schott, *Policy, Power and Order: The Persistence of Economic Problems in Capitalist States*, Yale University Press, New Haven, CT, 1984.

Table 2.5 The decomposition of the growth rate of average social expenditure of the seven major OECD countries, 1960–1975 and 1975–1981

	Annual growth rate (%)[a]			
	Real expenditure	Demography	Coverage	Average real benefit
1960–75				
Education[b]	6.2	0.6	1.4	4.1
Health	9.0	1.0	1.3	6.5
Pensions	8.2	2.4	1.8	3.8
Unemployment compensation	12.7	4.4	1.5	6.4
Total of above programs	8.0	1.6	1.6	4.6
Total social expenditure	7.5	–	–	–
1975–81				
Education	1.4	–0.4	0.4	1.4
Health	3.4	0.5	0.1	2.8
Pensions	6.8	2.1	1.1	3.5
Unemployment compensation	5.7	6.5	–2.9	2.2
Total of above programs	4.2	1.2	0.4	2.6
Total social expenditure	3.9	–	–	–

[a] Average compound growth rates, calculated as the geometric mean of the individual country growth rates.
[b] Six-country average, excluding France.

Source: OECD, *Social Expenditures, 1960–1990*, OECD, Paris, 1985, table 5

interest, as it reduces labor's dependence on any specific employer for employment. Table 2.6 brings out clearly the rising economic strength of labor when measured by "union density," that is, the percentage of the labor force that is unionized. Compared with previous periods, the period 1946–60 saw an increase in union density everywhere but in Germany.[8] The period after 1960 is more mixed but, again with the exception of Germany, union density in the period 1961–76 was greater than in the pre-war period.

The growth of the union movement was a source of rising political as well as economic power, as it strengthened the political power of leftist (i.e. socialist, labor, and communist) parties. Table 2.7 attempts to capture this trend by recording votes for leftist parties in 18 OECD economies during the twentieth century. Again, comparing the period before the Second World War with 1946–60, the increased percentage vote for leftist parties is very marked with declines only in Germany. The trend from 1946–60 to 1961–80 is also mixed, but the political

[8] In Germany wage settlements and other terms of employment in the unionized sector are very often automatically granted to the non-unionized labor force.

Table 2.6 Union membership as a percentage of the nonagricultural workforce: 1900–1976

	Before the First World War	Interwar	1946–60	1961–76
Austria	6	43	54	56
Belgium	5	28	42	52
France	7	12	28	19
Ireland	–	15	33	40
Italy	11	19	27	18
Germany	16	46	36	34
Netherlands	16	27	31	33
Switzerland	6	15	25	22
Australia	30	37	52	48
Canada	8	12	25	27
New Zealand	17	25	44	39
Denmark	16	34	48	50
Finland	5	8	30	47
Norway	6	19	47	44
Sweden	11	30	65	76
UK	15	29	43	44
Japan	–	20	26	28
USA	8	10	27	26

Source: W. Korpi, *The Democratic Class Struggle*, Routledge and Kegan Paul, London, 1983, p. 31

power of the left, measured in this way, remained substantially above the pre-war percentages. A similar long-term trend emerges when the representation of members of left-of-center parties in cabinet posts is calculated. Using the political affiliation of government in 12 Western European countries in the period 1960–84 as a measure of relative political power, Rothschild found an increase in left and left coalition governments from the 1960s to the 1970s followed by a smaller decline in the 1980s.[9]

The upward trend in the political and economic power of labor has had much to do with the nature of the growth and transformation process of modern capitalist economies. In particular, the rise of unionized labor has altered the way in which labor markets work and has led to a change in behavior of wages and prices, as will be shown presently. The accompanying increase in labor's political power has led to radical changes in macropolicies, comparing the post-war period with the period before the Second World War as noted. However, causation works in the other direction as well. Not only has the increased economic and political power of labor had much to do with the adoption of high employment

[9] See K. Rothschild, " 'Left' and 'right' in Federal Europe," *Kyklos*, 39 (3), 1986, appendix, 359–76.

34 *Framework*

Table 2.7 Left percentage of valid votes in 18 OECD countries, 1900–1980

Country	Before the First World War	Interwar	1946–60	1961–80
Austria	23	41	48	40
Belgium	23	38	42	40
France	13	32	43	41
Ireland	–	10	12	15
Italy	18	26	35	41
Germany	31	40	34	41
Netherlands	13	25	36	33
Switzerland	16	28	30	28
Australia	37	45	50	47
New Zealand	5	35	48	44
Canada	0	3	13	17
USA	4	5	1	0
Denmark	26	39	45	46
Finland	40	39	48	46
Norway	15	36	52	50
Sweden	13	46	52	51
UK	5	33	48	45
Japan	–	–	32	41

Source: W. Korpi, *The Democratic Class Struggle*, Routledge and Kegan Paul, London, 1983, p. 38

policies and the expansion of the welfare state, these policies have in turn strengthened labor's economic and political power.

2.5 Industrial Relations and the Rising Power of Labor

The increased unionization of labor and the increased share of votes cast for left-of-center pro-union parties together with the extension of the welfare state were important common features in all of what we now refer to as advanced capitalist economies. This would suggest that the level and nature of industrial conflict would be evolving in a similar way throughout the capitalist world. However, from early in the twentieth century through to the 1980s, levels of strike activity reveal no universal pattern for the developed capitalist economies regardless of whether the volume of strike activity or the relative involvement of strikes is the measure.[10] In the period before the First World War strike

---

[10]See D. Hibbs, "On the political economy of long-run trends in strike activity," *British Journal of Political Economy*, 8, 1978, 153–76; and W. Korpi and M. Shalev, "Strikes, power and politics in the Western nations, 1900–1976," in M. Zeitlin (ed.), *Political Power and Social Theory*, Vol. 1, JAI Press, Greenwich, CT, 1980.

Strike involvement I is the product of the frequency F for strikes and their average size S or $I = SF$ where F is the ratio of the number of strikes to the number of workers in the labor force and S is the ratio of the number of workers involved in strikes to the number of strikes.

activity measured by involvement rose almost everywhere to be followed by a general decline in the 1920s. The pattern varies considerably from country to country in the 1930s, often reflecting radical political changes occurring in some of the countries at the time. The post-war developments resulted in even greater variation between countries by the 1970s. Compared with the earlier periods, some economies experienced sharp declines in strike activity, in others strike activity increased sharply, and in still others it continued more or less at its earlier levels. This wide post-war dispersion in strike activity measured by involvement is altered somewhat when volume measures are used.[11] Hibbs's study reveals a sharp reduction in strike volume in about half his sample countries, comparing the interwar and post-war periods, and a noticeable rise in the rest. The result was a bimodal distribution of the volume of strike activity across countries in the post-war period.[12]

2.6 Strike Activity and the Size of the Welfare State

Party control, the welfare state, and strike activity

The fact that this general secular rise in the economic and political power of labor was not accompanied by a uniform trend in strike activity requires an explanation. It is useful to begin with Hibbs's distinction between the distributional conflicts between capital and labor that occur in the marketplace and those that take place in the political arena, for example, parliament.[13] Following this division, conflicts produce strikes in the marketplace, and legislative debate and legislation in the political forum to determine the amount of resources to be devoted to collective consumption.

Consider next what is termed the "party control" hypothesis—a theory of policy determination or public decision-making widely advocated by social scientists outside economics. According to this view, the distribution of conflict is determined by party control. As this struggle is shifted from the market to the political arena in an age of rising economic and political power for labor, strike activity declines. The main determinant of the size of the shift is seen in the first in-

---

[11] Volume of strikes $V = ID$ where I has the meaning given in note 10 and D is the ratio of man-days lost in strikes to the number of workers involved in strikes.

[12] Hibbs, "Political economy of long-run trends in strike activity"; see also M. Paldam and L. Rasmusen, "Data for industrial conflicts in 17 OECD-countries, 1948–77," Memo 80–4/5, Institute of Economics, Aarhus University, 1980 and chapter 6, table 6.1 below.

[13] Ibid.

stance as the extent to which left-of-center parties succeed in obtaining control or at least influence in government, for example trends in cabinet posts held by members of left-of-center parties. Thus, comparing the interwar with the post-war period up to the early 1970s, in those countries in which the share of cabinet posts held by left-of-center parties rose dramatically, for example, the Scandinavian countries, strike volume fell perceptively. In contrast, when left-of-center parties were virtually excluded from cabinet posts in both periods, strike activity actually rose along with unionization.[14]

However, party control *per se* is not seen as the determinant of strike activity. Rather, it is the extent to which governing parties actively intervene in the economy in such a way as to modify the distributional outcomes that would be dictated by the market alone, that is, roughly the size of the welfare state. In the final analysis, the party control explanation of industrial conflict explains the variation of strike activity over time (and across countries) in a period of rising and high unionization as primarily a matter of the degree to which the welfare state has been implemented. In the period up until the First World War, for example, strike activity increased along with unionization because distributional conflicts had to be resolved primarily in the marketplace. Only later, when governments intervened actively to modify market-determined distributional outcomes, did industrial conflict decline. Moreover, it is alleged that the extent of the decline from country to country depended on the extent to which the welfare state was expanded.

An evaluation

There is much to be said for this explanation of changes in industrial conflict, and it does provide a useful antidote to the view that affluent capitalism signals the "end of ideology" and therefore automatically leads to reduced industrial conflict. However, there are at least two important caveats. There are countries in which strike activity has fallen or remains low or both that have not introduced large-scale governmental redistributional measures, for example Japan and Switzerland.[15] In addition, there was a strong upward trend in strike activity from the 1960s to the 1980s in the United Kingdom, a country in which social expenditures are large, left-of-center parties have held office, and unionization of workers is widespread. Explaining the

[14] Ibid.
[15] Neither of these countries is considered by Hibbs in his sample.

strike performance of these three economies requires important modifications to any party control theory of policy choice and outcomes. A large welfare state is neither a necessary nor a sufficient condition for industrial harmony. The conditions required for industrial harmony as well as other desirable responses by business and labor, for example wage and price restraint, are taken up presently.

2.7 Inflation and the Rising Power of Labor

There is an additional impact of the shift in power to labor that must be treated—its influence on inflationary pressures. Consider first the long-term trends in money wages. Although the data are limited and subject to error, the behavior of money wages and developments in the labor movement can be divided into three distinct phases.[16] Beginning in the second half of the nineteenth century before unionization was evident, money wage rates had a procyclical movement but in general grew less rapidly than productivity, allowing for declines in the price level until about 1890. From 1890 to the First World War, the formative years of the trade union movement in several European countries, wage inflation accelerated slightly but was moderate compared with the current period as unions concentrated on improving the nonpecuniary aspects of work. Rising union strength was accompanied, however, by a growth in money wages in excess of productivity growth. This explains the reversal of price trends that began around the turn of the century. The period after the Second World War saw a further rise in the power of labor augmented by what can be considered pro-labor policies. An important result of this was the ability of labor to introduce "fairness considerations" in wage settlements, that is, money wage increases would be related to the cost of living and wage settlements in other labor markets. This led to an increase in rates of wage (and price) inflation at every rate of unemployment, but especially whenever the economy approached FE.

The shift in economic and political power to labor over the past century or so has had much to do with the upward trend in wages and prices throughout the developed capitalist world. This has often led to a rather uncritical acceptance that the greater the unionization of the labor force, the more extensive the welfare state, and the more leftist the government, the more inflation prone will be the economy. But

[16]See E. Phelps Brown, *A Century of Pay*, Macmillan, London, 1968; and W. Lewis, *Growth and Fluctuations: 1870–1913*, George Allen & Unwin, London, 1978.

38 *Framework*

Table 2.8 Annual average rates of inflation of consumer prices in 18 OECD countries for selected years

	Average rate of inflation (%)			
	1955–65	1966–70	1971–73	1974–79
Australia	2.4	3.1	7.1	12.2
Austria	2.8	3.3	6.2	6.3
Belgium	1.9	3.5	5.6	8.5
Canada	1.6	3.9	5.1	9.2
Denmark	3.9	6.7	7.2	10.8
Finland	5.2	4.7	8.1	12.9
France	4.4	4.4	6.3	10.7
Germany	2.3	2.4	5.9	4.7
Ireland	3.4	5.3	9.7	15.1
Italy	3.3	3.0	7.1	16.1
Japan	3.3	5.4	7.4	10.2
Netherlands	2.9	4.8	7.8	7.2
New Zealand	2.8	4.9	8.5	13.8
Norway	3.4	5.0	7.0	8.7
Sweden	3.6	4.5	6.7	9.8
Switzerland	2.1	3.5	7.3	4.0
UK	2.9	4.6	8.6	15.7
USA	1.5	4.2	4.6	8.6

Sources: OECD, *Economic Outlook,* December 1988, OECD, Paris, table R11; and D. Grubb, *The OECD Data Set,* Working Paper No. 615, Centre for Labour Economics, London School of Economics, March 1984.

cross-country comparisons give different insights. For example, if average rates of inflation between countries are compared from 1955 through 1970, the period before the rapid acceleration of rates of price and wage inflation of the early 1970s, then rather similar behavior in inflation rates is revealed (table 2.8). The same is true across countries in the explosive period from 1971 to 1973.

The point is not that inflation rates did not differ but that they often differed so little across countries compared with the vast differences between countries in the frequently alleged determinants of inflation, for example, differences in union strength (table 2.6), left-wing votes (table 2.7), and size of the welfare state (tables 2.2 and 2.3). Countries in which the labor force was most extensively unionized, for example, while reducing unemployment to a minimum did not experience above-average rates of price inflation. Thus the common view that unions raise inflationary problems that were absent in the earlier period before widespread unionization is essentially correct as far as it goes. The point to be made here is that, while the rise of unions has been a major contributor to the upward historical trend in inflation rates in almost every country, the trends have differed substantially between countries (as have trends in strike activity). As a result, in any period such as the quarter of a century following the Second World War there is no simple relationship between, say, the degree of unionization of the labor force and the severity of inflation. Unions do make a difference but the nature of that difference varies across countries—a matter to be discussed more fully.

2.8 The Breakdown in the Early 1970s

The post-war era of low unemployment, rapid productivity growth, and rapid expansion of foreign trade came to an end in most economies in 1973. Various theories have been advanced to explain the end of the post-war boom and the continuing mass unemployment. Adopting the terminology of chapter 1, the explanation offered in this study proceeds through a chain of causation, ascribing the severity of the downturn in the early 1970s and the rising unemployment in the first instance to declines in AD. These were largely brought about by restrictive AD policies throughout the OECD. These in turn are attributed to an increase in unwillingness of the authorities to supply FE because of an inability of the various governments to curtail inflation or to correct balance-of-payments difficulties in any other way than by increasing the slack in the economy. The institutional changes that took place during the previous prolonged boom gave the authorities no other choice.

The marked deterioration in the inflation record before the stagnation is seen in table 2.8 in which the rapid acceleration of inflation rates is recorded for most of the OECD countries. Beginning with the second half of the 1960s, there was a general acceleration in rates of inflation with double-digit inflation rates commonplace by 1973–74. Comparing the periods 1955–65 and 1966–70, rates of inflation accelerated everywhere except Finland and Italy. By 1971–73 the acceleration was universal with rates of inflation doubling in many countries between 1966–70 and 1971–73 and accelerating almost everywhere again in 1974–79.

The strong restrictive measures introduced almost everywhere by 1974 are reflected in the unemployment records. In part these measures were a response to domestic inflation, and in part they could be traced to widespread efforts to correct payments difficulties by "beggar-your-neighbor" policies. During the period of expansion of the OECD economies most economists heralded the beneficial effects

40 Framework

Table 2.9 Average unemployment rates U, rates of real gross domestic product $\dot{Q}$, and the rates of growth of productivity $\dot{q}$ in 18 OECD countries 1974–1979 and 1980–1990 (%)

Country	U 1974–79	U 1980–90	$\dot{Q}$ 1974–79	$\dot{Q}$ 1980–90	$\dot{q}^a$ 1974–79	$\dot{q}^a$ 1980–90
Australia	5.0	7.5	2.7	3.1	1.8	0.6[b]
Austria	1.5	3.2	2.9	2.3	2.5	1.2
Belgium	6.3	10.5	2.2	2.2	2.2	2.0
Canada	7.2	9.2	4.2	2.8	1.3	1.1
Denmark	5.5	9.0	1.9	1.9	n.a.	1.2
Finland	4.4	4.7	2.3	3.4	1.6	2.6
France	4.5	9.0	3.0	2.1	2.4	2.0
Germany	3.2	5.9	2.3	2.0	2.7	1.4
Ireland	7.6	14.2	4.6	3.4	3.7	3.6
Italy	4.6	7.0	2.6	2.4	2.8	1.9
Japan	1.9	2.5	3.6	4.1	2.9	2.9
Netherlands	5.1	9.5	2.7	1.7	2.2	0.7[c]
New Zealand	0.8	4.7	0.2	1.5	–0.9	1.4[b]
Norway	1.8	3.0	4.9	2.6	2.7	2.0
Sweden	1.5	2.1	1.8	1.9	0.5	1.2
Switzerland	1.0	1.8	–0.4	2.3	0.6	0.9[d]
UK	5.1	9.7	1.5	2.1	1.3	1.6
USA	6.7	7.0	2.4	2.6	0.0	1.0

[a] Rate of growth of real GDP per person employed.
[b] Data for 1986 not available.
[c] Data for 1981 and 1987 not available.
[d] Data for 1980 not available.

Sources: OECD *Historical Statistics, 1960–1990*, OECD, Paris, 1982, tables 3.1 and 3.7; OECD, *Economic Outlook*, OECD, Paris, June 1987, tables R10 and R12; and R. Layard et al., *Unemployment: Macroeconomic Performance and the Labour Market*, Oxford University Press, Oxford, 1991, table A3.

of increased economic interdependence, for example, the ability to take advantage of scale economies through specialization. However, in periods of worldwide restriction of AD, such a high degree of interdependence had harmful implications for economies, beginning in the 1970s. Worse still, a comparison of unemployment rates in the period 1974–79 (given in table 2.9) with figures given for 1960–73 in table 2.1 reveals that, despite a pronounced increase in unemployment rates, rates of inflation remained high into the second half of the 1970s in most countries. Only by the mid-1980s, when double-digit unemployment rates were becoming common, did rates of inflation come down as seen in table II.1 below. But even with continued high rates of

Table 2.10 Surplus on current transactions with the rest of the world as a percentage of gross national product/gross domestic product in seven major OECD economies and the total OECD economy for selected years and periods between 1963 and 1980

	1963–73[a]	1974	1975–78[a]	1979	1980
USA[b]	–0.3	0.1	–0.3	0.0	0.0
Japan[b]	0.8	–1.0	0.7	–0.9	–1.0
Germany[b]	0.7	2.8	1.0	–0.7	–1.7
France	0.0	–1.4	0.2	0.9	–0.6
UK	–0.1	–4.0	–0.4	–0.3	1.2
Italy	1.6	–4.1	0.4	1.5	–2.2
Canada	–0.7	–0.9	–2.3	–1.7	–0.4
Total major countries	0.4	–0.4	0.2	–0.2	–0.5
Total OECD	0.3	–0.7	–0.1	–0.4	–0.9

[a] Annual average.
[b] Percentage of GNP.

Sources: OECD, *Economic Outlook*, OECD, Paris, December 1983, table R20; and June 1992, table R21

unemployment in the 1980s, inflation rates remained substantial compared with rates in the 1950s and 1960s. This worsening in the unemployment-inflation "mix" has been subject to much study, which has resulted in widely divergent explanations and policy proposals. It is discussed at length in the second half of the book.

Table 2.10 reveals the severe deterioration in the balance of payments of the industrial economies following 1973, despite depressed economic conditions. Particularly significant is the impact of the increase in oil prices in 1973–74 and 1979–80 on the payments position of the industrial countries, a factor also leading to restrictive AD policies in many countries. The impact of the breakdown on unemployment rates U, GDP growth rates $\dot{Q}$, and productivity growth rates $\dot{q}$ for 18 OECD economies are given in table 2.9. The data cover the period following the first oil shock up to the second large increase in oil prices and the period since. In every country unemployment rates rose and rates of growth of GDP and productivity fell, comparing the two more recent periods with the post-war period until 1974. For example, relating the unemployment rates of the ten economies considered in table 2.1 for 1960–73 with their record in 1974–79 reveals a sharp rise over time everywhere. A doubling and even a tripling of rates was not uncommon. Comparing the two period detailed in table 2.9 shows that unemployment rates increased further everywhere from the second half of the 1970s to the 1980s.

2.9 Conclusions

This chapter has discussed several important economic developments of this century, distinguishing and contrasting the quarter of a century following the Second World War from both the interwar period and the period of collapse beginning in the early 1970s. As indicated, the overriding policy response to the collapse of the interwar period and the hardships of the Second World War was to ensure that the benefits of capitalism became more widely and equally distributed than in the past. The growing power of organized labor spearheaded the changes, with AD policies supplementing private demand when necessary and an expanded welfare state being the main instruments employed. The historically unprecedented (and unexpected) rapid rate of growth of per capita incomes that occurred during the period was the key enabling factor and proved to be a major source of social and economic harmony. Together, FE, rising living standards, and the expansion of the welfare state interacted in such a way as to further shift the distribution of economic and political power toward labor. Events in the late 1960s and early 1970s brought an end to this remarkable period of capitalism, and high rates of inflation and high rates of unemployment have characterized the performance of most of the economies ever since.

The developments just outlined are meant to suggest the following points. All capitalist economies undergo far-reaching structural and institutional changes during their evolution. This transformation is to a large extent an induced response to growth and can be traced chiefly to rising per capita incomes interacting with policy variables and exogenous trends. Together these strongly influence the institutional changes that give the growth process its changing direction and form. Unfortunately, these induced structural changes create problems that require government intervention if the economy is to give a decent macroeconomic performance. Not only that, resolving one problem can create new requirements for macromanagement. For example, while the rising affluence of the 1920s in many countries introduced the possibility of periods of insufficient AD such as the 1930s, the affluence of the 1950s and 1960s, together with the rising power of labor, was the source of a new problem—a potentially strong inflationary bias. Ironically, the affluence of the 1950s and 1960s and the resulting bias can be partly traced to policies to relieve economies of the problems arising in the 1930s.

The potential inflationary pressures became accelerating rates of inflation in the late 1960s and early 1970s and high rates of inflation accompanying high rates of unemployment up to the present. This sequence was described in introduction I as an economic breakdown. Determining the causes of this breakdown, and especially the deterioration in the employment records throughout the OECD, is the major aim of this study. A framework of analysis separating influences affecting the demand for FE from those affecting the willingness of the authorities to supply FE was outlined in chapter 1. The present chapter singled out the rising political and economic power of labor in this century as reflected in growing unionization and leftist political control as a strong demand factor determining employment policies and records.

However, the rise in unemployment since the early 1970s is not likely to be due to any noticeable decline in the strength of the demand for FE. In Europe, political power during the 1970s shifted in favor of leftist governments. Even the subsequent shift to the right in many countries in the 1980s has not been sufficient to recreate pre-1974 political conditions.[17] A theory of economic breakdown must, therefore, seek out the changes in the post-war period that have caused governments to be less willing to supply FE since the early 1970s. The immediate task is to develop detailed arguments that link together these events according to the framework developed in chapter 1. Chapter 3 begins this task.

---

[17] See Rothschild, " 'Left' and 'right' in Federal Europe." Rothschild's study deals with all the European countries considered in this study except Ireland.

3 A Reappraisal of Vertical Phillips Curve Analysis

3.1 Is Keynes Irrelevant?

One link in the causal chain outlined in figure 1.2 is that which connects policies with economic performance. In particular, it was assumed that stimulative AD policies can reduce unemployment when it is involuntary, that is, when there are unemployed workers for whom leisure is less valuable than the prevailing real wage in jobs for which they are qualified.[1] Furthermore, a creditable unemployment record depends upon a willingness of the authorities to intervene in such cases.

Paradoxically, the period of rising rates of inflation beginning in the late 1960s and followed by rising rates of unemployment has been accompanied within the economics profession and government circles by a marked shift in views of how the capitalist system operates and, more specifically, of the role of AD policies. Increasingly, the Keynesian view that a modern capitalist system is not self-regulating and requires government intervention has given way to a rebirth of the classical notions. These perceive capitalist economies as self-regulating, so that government intervention in the form of discretionary AD policy is at best ineffective and at worst destabilizing. Many of the difficulties of the past quarter of a century are then attributed to too much rather than too little intervention by government. According to this view, differences in unemployment rates reflect supply side forces that are not affected by AD. In some versions of the argument, AD adjusts to these supply forces automatically. These views have been developed in great detail and sophistication by macroeconomists with substantial influence on policy-makers. They have been particularly influential during the period since the early 1970s, arguing that stimulative AD policies

---

[1]Defined in this way, unemployed economics professors who refuse to set up a business of selling apples are not considered to be voluntarily unemployed.

are inflationary and cannot have a permanent effect on unemployment rates.

Clearly this position is completely at odds with the arguments of chapter 1. If it is true that the immediate cause of differences in unemployment cannot be attributed largely to differences in AD, then the framework of analysis sketched earlier collapses, for differences in AD (and AD policies) are but the first stage of explanation offered here which seeks to determine the more basic institutional–political causes of differences in unemployment records both over time and between countries.

Resolving this issue requires determining the impact of AD policies on unemployment and inflation. Phillips curve analysis is therefore taken up before proceeding to an analysis of the basic determinants of inflation and unemployment. For the most part this chapter deals with theories of policy ineffectiveness that find their origin in the natural rate hypothesis (NRH). Collectively, they will be referred to as theories of the vertical Phillips curve (VPC) or simply VPC analysis. Some of the theories assume that capitalism has automatic FE tendencies and most assume simply that capitalism displays unique equilibrium tendencies, but all assume that AD policies have a limited role in reducing unemployment. As serious a challenge as these policy-ineffectiveness theories may be, it is contended that they are inherently flawed and present misleading views of the way economies operate, and therefore must be rejected. In addition, the thrust of this body of literature has unfortunately misdirected the attention of economists. The crucial issue is why high inflation persists despite post-war high rates of unemployment. Unfortunately, the acceptance of the VPC has led economists to seek explanations other than insufficient AD for the persistence of high unemployment.[2]

3.2 The Natural Rate Hypothesis Once More

The "expectations-augmented" Phillips curve

Consider the familiar "expectations-augmented" Phillips curve for wage inflation:

$$\dot{w}_t = b_0 + b_1 U_t^{-1} + b_2 \dot{p}_t^e \qquad (3.1)$$

---

[2]See chapter 8. See also B. Bernheim, "Ricardian equivalence: an evaluation of theory and evidence," *NBER Working Paper Series, No. 2330*, July 1987, for a negative evaluation of another form of the policy-ineffectiveness argument dealing with the "crowding-out" issue.

where $\dot{p}_t^e$ is the expected rate of inflation in period t. Given certain simplifying assumptions, a second relationship between wage and price inflation can be derived:

$$\dot{p}_t = \dot{w}_t - \dot{q} \tag{3.2}$$

where $\dot{q}$ is the rate of growth of labor productivity.

A key assumption is the manner in which inflation expectations are generated. Assume as in the early formulations that in the labor market employers' expectations of the current rate of price (and wage) inflation are always correct, that is, $\dot{p}_t^e = \dot{p}_t$ (and $\dot{w}_t^e = \dot{w}_t$), while workers base their price expectations completely on the last period's actual rate of price inflation, that is, $\dot{p}_t^e = \dot{p}_{t-1}$ (and correctly predict the actual current rate of wage inflation). Some rather elementary substitution yields two short-run Phillips curves:

$$\dot{w}_t = b_0 + b_1 U_t^{-1} + \dot{p}_{t-1} \tag{3.1'}$$
$$\dot{p}_t = b_0 + b_1 U_t^{-1} + \dot{p}_{t-1} \tag{3.2'}$$

where, as in Friedman's formulation, $\dot{q} = 0$ and $b_2 = 1$ are assumed.[3]

Allow further that the law of diminishing marginal product of labor holds and that the demand for labor is a decreasing function of the real wage w/p, while the supply of labor is an increasing function of the expected real wage w/p^e. Finally, assume that the rate of price inflation in the current period is equal to the last period's rate of price inflation so that all expectations on the part of employers and labor are realized initially.

The workings of the model

This equilibrium situation is represented in figure 3.1 by point A which lies on the short-run Phillips curve SPC₁ with a rate of current price inflation $\dot{p}_0$ and an unemployment rate U_0. Suppose that in the next period AD is increased by an increase in the rate of growth of the money supply, resulting in a reduction in unemployment to U_1 U_0 and an increase in the rate of inflation to $\dot{p}_1$ as given by point A'. By assumption the rise in employment implied by a fall in unemployment

[3] See M. Friedman, "The role of monetary policy," *American Economic Review*, 58, March 1968, 1–17. For a related development see E. Phelps (ed.), *Microfoundations of Employment and Inflation Theory*, Norton, New York, 1970.

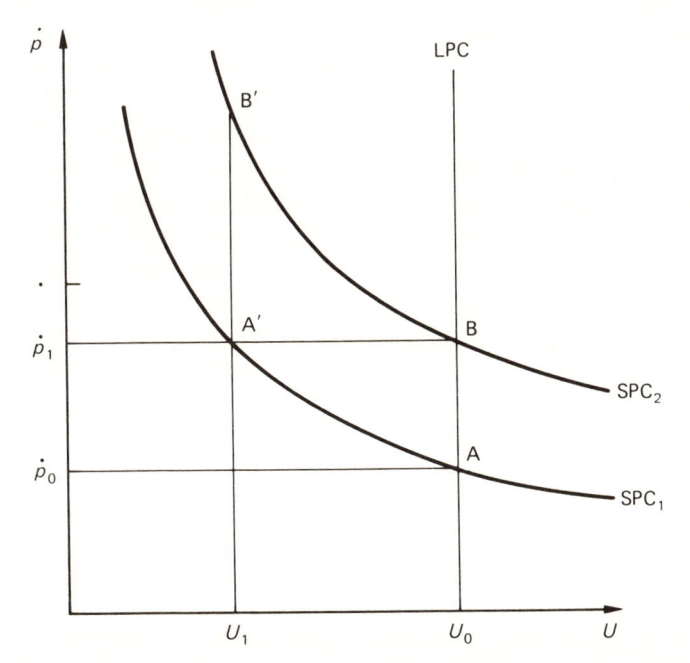

Figure 3.1 The long-run and short-run Phillips curves

from U_0 to U_1 must be accompanied by a fall in the real wage; otherwise the omniscient employers would not have taken on more workers (since $\dot{q} = 0$). However, workers, while correctly anticipating the higher rate of wage inflation generated by the increase in the money supply, do not correctly anticipate the rise in the rate of price inflation since by assumption their expectations are that $\dot{p}_t^e = \dot{p}_{t-1}$, that is, they are subject to "price surprises." Thus, even though the real wage has fallen, workers' expected real wage has risen as the economy moves to point A'.

In the next period the short-run Phillips curve must shift up to SPC_2 to take account of the workers' revised expected price inflation which is assumed to occur with a one-period lag. The authorities now have a choice: they can continue to stimulate AD further and move to point B' by fooling labor once more, or they can maintain the rate of growth of the money supply and therefore the rate of price inflation $\dot{p}_1$. Assume that the latter choice is made and that no further acceleration of inflation occurs. As workers realize that the real wage has actually declined, those who were induced into employment in the previous period are assumed to withdraw from employment, and the unemployment rate returns to U_0, but at a higher rate of inflation as indicated by point B. In the long run the policy-maker has really no discretion in his choice of AD policies. Any rate of unemployment other than the so-called "natural rate" U_0 can only be maintained if inflation rates are allowed to accelerate or decelerate without limit. Therefore the long-run Phillips curve LPC denotes the lack of tradeoff between inflation and unemployment over time. The policy, if not the welfare, implications are clear.

Some critical assumptions

All this is well known and would seem to belabor the obvious. However, a host of critical assumptions underlying the NRH, which have been carried over to subsequent developments, have been forgotten and need to be made explicit in any appraisal of VPC analysis. For example, underlying the NRH is the competitive model with strong FE tendencies. The voluntary nature of unemployment is reflected in the work–leisure choice presented to labor and is suggested by the assumption that wage bargaining is always in real terms. Given a downward-sloping demand curve and an upward-sloping supply curve for labor, a real wage which, based on the information available, always clears the market is somehow determined in the labor market through a "haggling" process between individual workers and their employers.

What is novel about this version of self-regulating capitalism is its use of the expectations-augmented Phillips curve to explain deviations of the unemployment rate around the natural rate and its use in determining the condition for long-run equilibrium. Thus the following statements provide a useful summary of the NRH.

1. Changes in the rate of inflation lead to changes in the rate of unemployment, and not the other way around, because of incomplete information on the part of workers or "price surprises." The only way in which unemployment can permanently deviate from the natural rate is by permanently surprising or fooling labor through acceleration or deceleration in the rate of growth of the money supply. To put the matter otherwise, capitalist economies are always teetering on a "knife-edge" in which deviations from the natural rate lead either to accelerating or decelerating rates of inflation.
2. Only at the natural rate, where the rate of inflation is constant, is long-run equilibrium realized in the sense that the expected and actual rates of inflation are equal.

Following upon the NRH, it is helpful to think of VPC analysis developing in two quite divergent directions. On the one hand, the new classical macroeconomics retains the competitive assumptions of NRH analysis with continuous and instantaneous market clearing. In addition, expectations are generated in such a way (i.e. "rationally") that, assuming that the model correctly describes reality and is adopted by all, the short-run Phillips curve disappears. Unemployment might deviate from the natural rate U_0, but only if shocks are introduced. Given the unreality of the competitive model with continuous market clearing, this popular development need not be considered further. However, the other line of development of VPC analysis includes an effort to incorporate some of the rigidities and market imperfections of the real world and so deserves to be analyzed.

3.3 New Strands in Vertical Phillips Curve Analysis

The prolonged period of historically high and often rising rates of unemployment right up to the present, better explanations of why markets do not clear, and the accumulation of additional data on the causes and nature of unemployment, for example the large component of layoffs among the unemployed and the long duration of much of the unemployment, have led to a questioning of the assumption of zero involuntary unemployment and the realism of the NRH. This is shown, for example, in an increased tendency to substitute a distinction between "classical" and "Keynesian" unemployment for that between voluntary and involuntary unemployment. By definition, Keynesian unemployment can always be reduced through stimulative AD policies, while classical unemployment cannot, at least in some long-run sense. But classical unemployment may contain an involuntary element along with the usual "frictional" part.[4]

In addition, there have been efforts to model wage setting as part of an institutionalized bargaining process and not as something resulting from haggling between individual buyers and sellers of labor. In so doing, various explanations of real and money wage rigidity have been developed in which the labor market may not clear. Many of these explanations, when combined with other elements, are then used to illustrate the ineffectiveness of stimulative AD policies. Thirdly, an instability of the VPC has been acknowledged, even by its advocates.

[4]See, for example, P. Layard and S. Nickell, "The causes of British unemployment," *National Institute Economic Review*, 111, February 1985, 62–85.

However, prolonged mass unemployment has not led to a rejection of other critical assumptions surrounding the NRH. The aggregate demand curve for labor always slopes downward to the right. Wage bargaining is always in real terms even though large-scale involuntary unemployment may exist and the real wage is somehow set in the labor market. In effect, a long-run VPC is still widely accepted by economists, certainly in the sense that stimulative AD policies are ineffective in reducing unemployment until FE has been achieved. However, the unemployment rate corresponding to some long-run VPC is less likely to be referred to as something natural; rather it has been increasingly termed the NAIRU or "equilibrium" rate of unemployment. Furthermore, whatever it is that determines this equilibrium rate, it does not respond to AD policy. Thus policy remains largely ineffective.

In order to correctly evaluate these developments, a somewhat restrictive but nevertheless useful analytical device will be adopted in order to cull the salient features from the many writings in VPC analysis. Specifically, it is useful to distinguish between two strands in the further development of VPC analysis: one a simple logical extension of the NRH, and the other more institutional and radical in its departure. The major differences between what will be termed the alpha and beta strand are as follows: (a) their different reliance on the expectations-augmented Phillips curve, in particular the role of price surprises in explaining fluctuations in unemployment and therefore their reliance on the knife-edge implications of this Phillips curve; (b) related to this, the mechanism utilized to explain why unemployment in the long run is unresponsive to stimulative AD policy; (c) the mechanism, if any, by which the economy is assumed to converge to some kind of unemployment equilibrium. While much that has been written in VPC analysis contains elements that can be assigned to both strands, the point to be stressed is that these writings demonstrate serious contradictions and inconsistencies.

3.4 The Alpha Strand

The new–old vertical Phillips curve

In this section the focus is on those VPC models that continue to assume, in addition to the assumptions listed in section 3.3, that "price surprises" generate short-run fluctuations in unemployment rates around the NAIRU and that the fulfillment of price expectations is a condition of long-run equilibrium.[5] From this flows the standard explanation of the knife-edge properties of the NAIRU and the convergence properties of some of the models. In the long run, stimulative AD policies are ineffective in the sense that there is only one level of AD consistent with a position in which all wage and price expectations are realized. This is the "natural" level of demand that generates the NAIRU.[6] Any attempt to reduce unemployment to a lower rate leads to results identical with those sketched in the discussion of the NRH. If Keynesian AD policy plays any role at all in a stabilization policy, it is an extremely limited one—to regulate the level of AD so that it will be at the natural level. To do otherwise would result in continuous acceleration or deceleration of inflation rates. But even that role may be superfluous. Some second-generation model builders, including many who would consider themselves "Keynesians," have retained the automatic equilibrium unemployment tendencies of the NRH. Consider the following:

> ... there is no such trade-off [between unemployment and inflation] in the long-run. The economy's self-correcting mechanism ensures that unemployment eventually will return to the "natural rate," no matter what happens to aggregate demand.[7]

To ensure this "self-correction," real balance effects are often resurrected as the long-run equilibrating forces, recalling Pigou's rebuttal of a key feature of Keynes's *General Theory*.

Forces behind the shift of the nonaccelerating inflation rate of unemployment

The assumptions and implications of the alpha strand of analysis suggest in effect a world little different from that envisaged in the NRH

[5]Consider the following quotations: "In order to reach a new equilibrium [following a disturbance] in which expectations are fulfilled real demand must fall. This can happen both automatically as a result of the real balance effect and a decline in competition, and autonomously as a result of changes in fiscal and monetary policy" and "Attempts to raise [AD] above (below) [the level corresponding to the NAIRU] will raise (lower) employment only as long as the wage and price expectations of firms and workers differ from levels actually realized." C. Bean, P. Layard, and S. Nickell, "The rise in unemployment: a multi-country study," *Economica* (Supplement), 53, 1986, pp. S17 and S18.

[6]Ibid., p. S15.

[7]See W. Baumol and A. Blinder, *Economics: Principles and Policy* (2nd ed.), Harcourt Brace Jovanovich, New York, 1982, p. 303. See also R. Dornbusch and S. Fischer, *Macroeconomics*, McGraw-Hill, New York, 1981, ch. 13. In appendix B the use of "Pigou effects" to guarantee convergence to some unique equilibrium is strongly challenged.

52 Framework

analysis of section 3.2. Indeed, since unemployment can only be reduced below the NAIRU by fooling the previously unemployed into thinking that the real wage has risen, the observer can be excused for thinking that much of the recent work in NAIRU analysis implicitly assumes a world in which all unemployment is still voluntary while often explicitly denying it.

However, the decision to no longer assume that all unemployment is voluntary at the rate corresponding to the vertical long-run Phillips curve has opened up a whole new area of investigation in VPC analysis, and that is finding those various forces that determine the unemployment rate at which the VPC cuts the horizontal axis. For example, consider the following equations for explaining rates of wage and price inflation:

$$\dot{w}_t = c_0 + c_1 U_t^{-1} + \dot{p}_{t-1} + \dot{q}^T \qquad (3.3)$$

and

$$\dot{p}_t = \dot{w}_t - \dot{q} + \dot{p}^I \qquad (3.4)$$

where, for convenience, it is assumed that variables are so measured in equation (3.4) (and in similar equations throughout the text) as to take account of the relative weights assigned to labor and nonlabor costs. Equations (3.3) and (3.4) incorporate two additional influences on the inflationary process that have loomed large in the recent literature: the rate of productivity growth expected by wage earners and incorporated in their demands as a target rate of growth of real wages, $\dot{q}^T$, and the rate of growth of prices of imports, $\dot{p}^I$. As before $\dot{p}_t^e = \dot{p}_{t-1}$ is assumed and $\dot{q}$ is some given rate of growth of productivity. The sense of equation (3.3) is that in wage settlements workers are not merely mindful of the need to protect their real wages, hence the coefficient of unity before the variable $\dot{p}_{t-1}$, but desire a "bonus" over and above this in the form of higher rates of growth of money wages that will enable real wages to grow. Inclusion of the variable $\dot{p}^I$ in the price equation points out one aspect of the current high degree of economic interdependence and the importance of inflationary movements in international commodity markets.

Substitution of equation (3.3) into (3.4) gives

$$\dot{p}_t = c_0 + \dot{q}^T - \dot{q} + \dot{p}^I + c_1 U_t^{-1} + \dot{p}_{t-1} \qquad (3.4')$$

Long-run equilibrium in these models is defined by $\dot{p}_t = \dot{p}_{t-1}$ $(= \dot{p}\,?)$ or

$$\dot{p}_t - \dot{p}_{t-1} = c_0 + \dot{q}^T - \dot{q} + \dot{p}^I + c_1 U_t^{-1} = 0 \tag{3.5}$$

This expression is then solved for U giving

$$U = U_0 = \frac{c_1}{\dot{q} - \dot{q}^T - c_0 - \dot{p}^I} \tag{3.6}$$

where U_0 is the NAIRU.[8]

It is clear from equation (3.6) that either a rise in the target growth rate of real wages or in the rate of inflation of import prices will increase the NAIRU. To prevent accelerating rates of inflation in either case, the authorities must allow the actual unemployment rate to rise. A decline in the rate of growth of labor productivity $\dot{q}$ has a similar impact. Obviously many other variables thought to affect wage and price inflation, for example unemployment benefits which alter the NAIRU if they themselves change, can (and have been) included in equations such as (3.3) and (3.4).

An evaluation

What this strand of NAIRU analysis has added to the NRH analysis is a catalog of determinants of the position of the VPC and empirical estimates of their impact on the NAIRU.[9] At the same time much of NAIRU analysis tends to avoid the issue of whether unemployment at the NAIRU is all voluntary or not as already pointed out. It is all classical, that is, unresponsive in the long run to an increase in AD, but may be voluntary, involuntary, or a mixture of the two. However, while some of these forces which position the NAIRU qualify as influences on the work–leisure decisions, others are clearly unrelated to the "work ethic," for example a change in the rate of growth of import prices $\dot{p}^I$ or in the rate of growth of productivity $\dot{q}$, and this raises some difficulties.

[8]Similar results follow if the wage equation is used. See G. Johnson and P. Layard, "The natural rate of unemployment: explanation and policy," *Discussion Paper, No. 206*, Centre for Labour Economics, London School of Economics, October 1984. Econometric studies used to estimate the NAIRU in this manner constrain the estimate of the lagged price inflation variable by using $\dot{p}_t - \dot{p}_{t-1}$ or some variant as the dependent variable. See, for example, D. Grubb, R. Jackman, and R. Layard, "Causes of the current stagflation," *Review of Economic Studies*, 49, 1982, 707–30.

[9]For estimates see, for example, Layard and Nickell, "Causes of British unemployment," tables 6 and 8; and Bean et al., "Rise in unemployment," table 4. See also M. Bruno, "Aggregate supply and demand factors in OECD unemployment: an update," *Economica* (Supplement), 53, 1986, S35-S52.

Consider a decrease in $\dot{q}$. According to the NAIRU model, even if this results in a rise of the NAIRU from, say, 5 to 20 percent, wage bargaining continues to be in real terms, leading to an inability of the authorities to permanently reduce unemployment rates below the new higher NAIRU without rates of inflation accelerating without limit. But clearly this conclusion is unwarranted unless it can be assumed either that at the new NAIRU all unemployment is voluntary or that some other mechanism prevents the involuntary unemployed from obtaining jobs if AD is increased.

It would be difficult to argue that voluntary unemployment has increased because productivity growth has slowed, and if the higher unemployment is involuntary it would be expected that an increase in AD would reduce unemployment permanently (although inflation rates may rise substantially) as previously unemployed workers willingly take jobs at less than the going real wage and not because they were fooled. They are likely to be quite indifferent to, say, a moderate acceleration of inflation rates that reduces the real wage. Even the long-run Phillips curve would have some curvature and the lower rate of unemployment would not lead to continuous acceleration of inflation rates.

Some important implications are clear. If involuntary unemployment is allowed to exist at the NAIRU, some other explanation must be found to support the assumption that wage bargaining is always in real terms and that stimulative AD policies cannot permanently reduce unemployment rates below the NAIRU without a permanent acceleration of inflation rates. Unemployment changes should not be explained in terms of price surprises since these are only appropriate explanations of changes in unemployment (if at all) in a world of no involuntary unemployment. Their continued use in models allowing involuntary unemployment involves a contradiction even though they are incorporated in much of current VPC writings.

Furthermore, once involuntary unemployment is possible and price surprises rightly eliminated as a cause of fluctuations in unemployment, the knife-edge and any convergence properties of the model must be dropped. The impact of unemployment movements on inflation is now indeterminate. Other explanations of real wage bargaining and mechanisms of policy ineffectiveness free from contradiction are offered by the beta strand in VPC analysis. They are also unacceptable.

3.5 Vertical Phillips Curves: The Beta Strand

Involuntary unemployment

Another rather different strand in VPC analysis can be isolated that provides a more obvious break with the earlier NRH models. This development arises out of a recognition that it is not enough to merely assume that wage bargaining is in real terms, no matter what the level of unemployment. Some explanation is required as to why, in the face of mass unemployment, bargaining is in real terms, why the real wage can rise above its market-clearing level, and why the resulting increase in (classical) unemployment cannot be eliminated through stimulative AD policies.

The beta strand of VPC analysis does not rely on price surprises to explain fluctuations in unemployment about the equilibrium or the realization of price expectations as a condition for equilibrium, nor does it show an interest in any possible convergence properties of the model. Indeed, the analysis often dispenses with the use of the expectations-augmented Phillips curve entirely and shows little interest in the knife-edge symmetry properties accepted by advocates of the alpha strand of VPC analysis.

It does retain the assumptions that the real wage is determined in the labor market, and that rates of inflation accelerate without limit if AD policies are used to achieve FE. However, it must be stressed that the inability of stimulative AD policies to reduce the real wage and eliminate classical unemployment has little to do with the absence of involuntary unemployment. Various institutional features of the economy serve to thwart the Keynesian policy-makers from getting at this form of involuntary unemployment according to this strand.

Involuntary unemployment and the vertical Phillips curve

There are several institutional explanations of why the labor market fails to clear, thus causing involuntary unemployment, and why such unemployment might rise over time.[10] The framework of analysis can be described as that of modeling optimizing behavior subject to constraints in a static neoclassical tradition.[11] Whatever the explanation,

---

[10] One such explanation, the monopoly-union model, often refers to "household-involuntary but union-voluntary" unemployment.

[11] Three useful surveys are A. Lindbeck and D. Snower, "Explanations of unemployment," *Oxford Review of Economic Policy*, No. 2, 1985; L. Katz, "Efficiency wages theories: a partial evaluation," *NBER Working Paper Series*, No. 1906, April 1986; and Johnson and Layard, "Natural rate of unemployment." In the latter survey the authors impose, in effect, an expectations-augmented Phillips curve onto models that were often originally developed with little or no consideration of expectations.

the analysis leads to a kind of NAIRU conclusion: at an employment and therefore an unemployment rate corresponding to some prevailing excessive real wage, there is no tradeoff between unemployment and inflation in at least one direction. The key issues can be seen more clearly with the use of figure 3.2.

The real wage is measured on the vertical axis and both real aggregate demand and real aggregate supply (AS) are measured on the horizontal axis. The downward sloping line DD indicates those combinations of real wages and AD at which firms will supply an amount equal to the amount demanded. Assuming that technology and the capital stock are given, it is downward sloping given the usual profit-maximizing and diminishing marginal productivity assumptions. The vertical line at Y^* represents full employment output or supply and is drawn to indicate that labor is supplied inelastically. Therefore, points A, B, C, and G all represent situations of involuntary unemployment.[12]

Assume that the economy is at point B with the real wage at $(w/p)_1$ and that the level of aggregate demand is equal to Y_1. Then, even if the real wage is unchanged, a stimulation of AD can move the economy to point A and output Y_2, as AS responds to increased AD by assumption. The reduction in unemployment in the movement from Y_1 to Y_2 is, by definition, a reduction in Keynesian unemployment. However, supply (and the corresponding employment) cannot be increased beyond Y_2 without a fall in the real wage since the latter is required to induce firms to employ more workers and supply more output. If the real wage is stuck at $(w/p)_1$ for any reason and AD rises to an amount greater than Y_2, the only effect is an acceleration of inflation rates since the difference between the unemployment corresponding to Y^* and Y_2 only measures the remaining involuntary but classical unemployment.

However, if for some reason the real wage should fall to $(w/p)_2$, a stimulative AD policy could be employed to move the economy from point C to the full employment point E. The expression "real wage gap" is used to measure the difference between the current real wage, say $(w/p)_1$, and that required to clear the labor market, that is, $(w/p)_2$. Whenever such a gap occurs, stimulative AD policies are supposedly unable to move the economy to the FE level of output Y^*.

[12]The vertical line at Y^* is the supply of output forthcoming when the total labor force less frictional unemployment is employed. The figure is that used by R. Dornbusch, "Macroeconomic prospects and policies for the European Community," in O. Blanchard, R. Dornbusch, and R. Layard (eds.), *Restoring Europe's Prosperity*, MIT Press, Cambridge, MA, 1986.

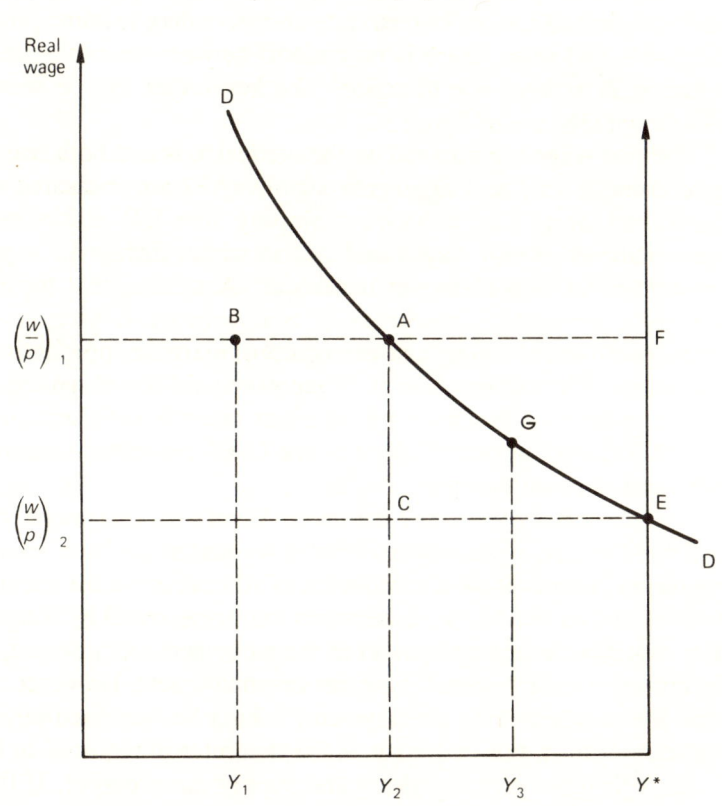

Figure 3.2 Classical and Keynesian unemployment

3.6 Some Counter-arguments

There are two separate assertions in this policy-ineffectiveness argument: (a) the labor market does not automatically clear and at prevailing wages an excess supply of labor exists, and (b) it is not possible to reduce unemployment by means of stimulative AD measures. Since there are a number of plausible theories explaining why the labor market does not clear, it is possible to accept the first proportion without agreeing to the second.[13] The important issue is whether the involuntary but supposedly classical unemployment that arises would respond

[13] See the references cited in note 11 and Blinder, "Challenge of high unemployment," for explanations of wage "stickiness."

to AD stimulus.[14] An affirmative argument, one that parallels the discussions in the years following the publication of Keynes's *General Theory* and has been updated, is appropriate.[15]

Stated briefly, this argument has two parts:

1. Keynes's view, voiced in the *General Theory*, that the real wage can be reduced through AD stimulation if producers so choose is correct.
2. A decline in the real wage is not a necessary condition for an expansion of output and an increase in employment.[16]

Consider the first part. Implicit in most of the policy-ineffectiveness arguments of this chapter is the assumption that the real wage is in some unspecified way determined in the labor market. This assumption can and has been strongly disputed, the counter-argument being that, with one important exception, the real wage is set in the product market once the money wage is determined, when firms set price.[17] Given a world of low price elasticities of demand in an age of affluence (and flexible exchange rates), firms have a good deal of flexibility in their pricing policies. If they so desire they can raise prices by enough to cover any additional wage costs that might be involved in hiring additional workers. As a result, if AD is stimulated when involuntary unemployment exists, the real wage falls. Reverting to figure 3.2, the economy then moves down the DD line from point A and, ignoring

[14]There is an empirical side to this debate centering on the evidence offered that the real wage is "too high." See McCallum, "Unemployment in the OECD"; and J. Helliwell, "Comparative macroeconomics of stagflation," *Journal of Economic Literature*, 26, March 1988, 1–28.

[15]The text conclusions need not hold for "equipment-deficient unemployment," a form of classical unemployment stressed by E. Malinvaud, *Mass Unemployment*, Blackwell, Oxford, 1984, and "Wages and unemployment," *Economic Journal*, 92, March 1982, 1–12. For rebuttals of this policy-ineffectiveness argument see F. Modigliani, M. Monti, J. Dreze, H. Giersch, and R. Layard, "Reducing unemployment in Europe: the role of capital formation," in R. Layard and L. Calmfors (eds.), *The Fight Against Unemployment*, MIT Press, Cambridge, MA, 1987; and O. Blanchard and L. Summers, "Hysteresis and the European unemployment problem," *NBER Working Paper Series*, No. 1950, June 1986.

[16]There is a related argument to the effect that if wage and prices were in fact very flexible it would make the economy less stable downward. This is neglected.

[17]See, for example, T. Scitovsky, "Market power and inflation," *Economica*, 45, August 1978, 221–34; and R. Solow, "Unemployment: getting the questions right," *Economica* (Supplement), 53, 1986, S23-S34. See note 24 for the important exception.

Bruno and Sachs construct an inflation model in which labor's share of value added rises with an increase in the rate of inflation and when labor's real wage target $\dot{q}^T$ exceeds productivity growth $\dot{q}$. This suggests that labor is in a position to increase the real wage above its market-clearing rate. However, their results depend upon a lag in the adjustment of prices to rising labor costs. Without this unrealistic lag, the text conclusion holds; the real wage is determined in the product market. See Bruno and Sachs, *Economics of Worldwide Stagflation*, pp. 174–76.

inflation costs, the authorities could choose to move to the FE output Y^*. The fact that in the process productivity increases which affect labor costs will probably be induced merely emphasizes the point that firms have a wide latitude in their determination of the real wage. However rigid the money wage is, the real wage can show a good deal of flexibility. This leads to the second part of the rebuttal.

Even if it were true that stimulative AD policy could not lead to a reduction in the real wage (for example, because of universal and complete indexation of money wages), there is an additional difficulty in accepting the excessive real wages explanations of high unemployment. This arises because of the likelihood that a reduction in the real wage is not even a necessary condition for the expansion of employment.[18] Put simply, the issue centers on the relationship between employment (or unemployment) and the real wage. In figure 3.2 it is assumed that, given the capital stock and technology, the relationship is negative since declining marginal productivity requires a rise in price relative to the money wages as employment and therefore output rise to induce firms to take on more workers. Consider the following alternative possibilities. Once the importance of monopoly elements in markets is recognized together with the objective to protect or expand market shares, then a willingness of firms to reduce their mark-up may offset rising labor costs leading to an expansion of employment with little or no change in the real wage. Alternatively, allow that technology is such that there are constant or increasing returns to labor. Then with a constant mark-up, a rise in employment will be accompanied by a constant real wage or a rising real wage respectively.[19] In each case, the behavior of real wages depends upon how firms react to ongoing events, illustrating how real wages are determined in the product market.

Alternatively, higher demand may induce short-run and long-run changes in production processes and the amount of capital services extracted from the physical capital already in place. In the latter case, any stimulative AD measure will then lead to a joint expansion of labor and capital services.[20] In the longer run all sorts of additional

[18]Figure 6.2 indicates that a fall in real wages is not a sufficient condition for an increase in employment.
[19]These points and supporting evidence are given by L. Summers, "Comments," *European Economic Review*, 31 (3), April 1987, 606–14; and O. Blanchard and L. Summers, "Beyond the natural rate hypothesis," *American Economic Review, Papers and Proceedings*, 78, May 1988, 182–7. Section III of the latter contains a useful bibliography of explanations of constant or increasing returns.
[20]See T. Dernburg, *Macroeconomics* (7th ed.), McGraw-Hill, New York, 1985, ch. 11.

possibilities open up. For example, the increase in AD may well induce an increase in productivity according to Okun's law or Verdoorn's law or both. In terms of figure 3.2 this can be interpreted as a very flat or even rising DD curve or a shift in the DD curve to the right as an increase in AD moves the economy from, say, point A to point F. All these considerations indicate that it is thoroughly misleading to assume that technology or capital are given when drawing an AD curve for labor.

3.7 Hysteresis Effects

An inadequate framework

These points have some rather far-reaching implications. In addition to the recognition that AD policies will be an important determinant of performance, two are worthy of mention. First, the whole notion of employing a fixed-technology (and fixed-taste) framework in analyzing important macroproblems becomes suspect. As outlined in chapter 1, the actual performance of an economy, including the stance of macropolicies, has an impact on the institutional framework including its technology. The above examples illustrate the response on the supply side to booming AD conditions. The argument is symmetrical. With respect to restrictive AD policies, there is increasing evidence that high levels of unemployment and persistent stagnation destroy human and physical capital, lead to a general loss of the "work ethic" within the labor force and management, and reduce productivity growth.

Second, given that the demand side of the economy induces changes on the supply side, when this is combined with a model incorporating an equilibrium rate of unemployment, the latter is said to have the property of hysteresis or path dependence. The equilibrium rate of unemployment depends upon the actual rate of unemployment. As a result, there is no unique equilibrium rate of unemployment.[21] This special form of hysteresis has an important role to play in this study.

---

[21] See S. Hargreaves Heap, "Choosing the wrong natural rate: accelerating or decelerating employment and growth," *Economic Journal,* 90, 1980, 611–20; and R. Cross (ed.), *Unemployment, Hysteresis and the Natural Rate Hypothesis,* Blackwell, Oxford, 1988.

Other examples of important hysteresis effects concentrate on the impact of AD on long-term unemployment, considering both the effect of the duration of unemployment on the morale of unemployed workers and firms' attitudes toward hiring such workers, and the lack of impact of the long-term unemployed on wage determination. These effects are considered in chapter 8.

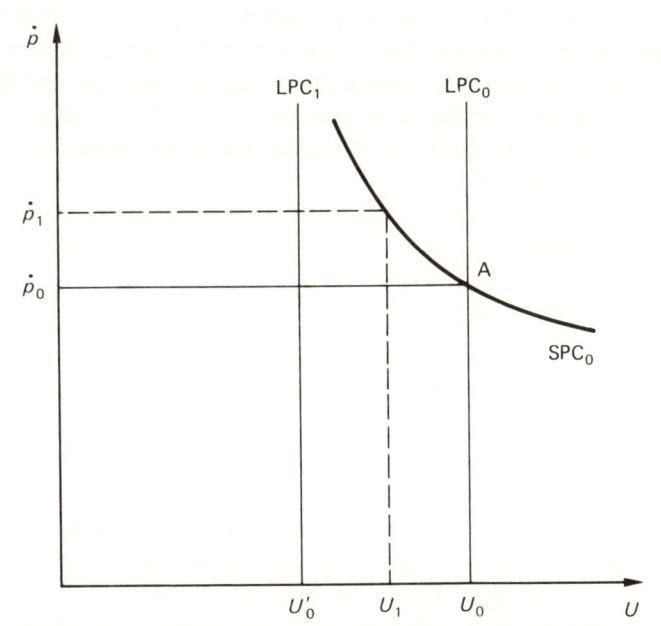

Figure 3.3 Hysteresis and the nonaccelerating inflation rate of unemployment

A nonaccelerating inflation rate of unemployment interpretation

These results can be given a more exact NAIRU interpretation. Recall from section 3.4 that the NAIRU can be written as (equation (3.6))

$$U_0 = \frac{c_1}{\dot{q} - \dot{q}^T - c_0 - \dot{p}^I}$$

where $\dot{q}$, $\dot{q}^T$, and $\dot{p}^I$ are, as before, the rate of growth of productivity, the expected rate of growth of productivity, and the rate of increase of prices of imported goods respectively. A long-run Phillips curve, LPC$_0$, is drawn in figure 3.3 to intercept the horizontal axis at this unemployment rate U_0, together with a short-run Phillips curve cutting the long-run curve at A.

Assume that the economy is initially at point A experiencing a rate of price inflation $\dot{p}_0$. According to conventional NAIRU analysis, following an increase in AD the rate of price inflation must rise as indicated by a movement along SPC$_0$ from $\dot{p}$ to $\dot{p}_1$ as unemployment falls to U_1. This gives rise to price surprises that lead to a continuous upward shift of the short-run Phillips curves (not shown) and accelerating inflation as long as unemployment remains below U_0.

However, if the rate of growth of productivity $\dot{q}$ is negatively related to the actual unemployment rate, this short-run–long-run NAIRU sequence must be discarded, for what equation (3.6) reveals is that a rise in $\dot{q}$ reduces the NAIRU to, say, U'_0 in figure 3.3. As a result, rates of inflation will eventually decelerate if unemployment is maintained at $U_1 > U'_0$ as the policy-induced change in the NAIRU has, in this example, made the economy less rather than more inflationary. If AD is increased again, the process may repeat itself with another leftward shift of the LPC and the NAIRU (not shown). At the very least, this effect will improve the unemployment–inflation tradeoff as unemployment falls.

Whatever the assumed determinants of the NAIRU, when one or more of them are functions of the performance of the economy, multiple equilibria result. There is no unique NAIRU.[22]

3.8 Conclusions

A great deal of space has been allocated for discussing developments in the study of VPCs. For good reasons the discussion was carried out using only the simplest techniques. A vast literature has developed which modifies and embellishes the original NRH, and almost all of it is highly technical. As a result, many of the strong assumptions underlying VPC analysis have been lost sight of. When these are made explicit, much of the argument becomes highly questionable.[23] Hence there is a need to conduct the discussion and criticism in as simple a manner as possible while retaining the main elements of the argument.

The importance of VPC analysis in policy debates and inflation–unemployment studies warrants the lengthy discussion. It is fair to say that VPC analysis has been one of the most important challenges to the Keynesian position on the effectiveness of discretionary AD policy and the nature of the current unemployment. This has remained true despite some extremely implausible assumptions and implications. In these models, if the economy is not always teetering on a knife-edge, in the sense that any maintained deviation of the actual rate of unem-

---

[22]Figure 3.3 is drawn in such a way that the change in the actual rate of unemployment induces an even larger change in the NAIRU. This is only done for emphasis. It is shown in chapter 8 that the policy implications are little changed whether "full" or "less than full" hysteresis effects are assumed.

[23]In addition, much of the econometric work in support of the theory has been little more than "curve fitting," with lagged dependent variables, time trends, and time-shift variables, to name a few, introduced as explanatory variables.

ployment from the NAIRU leads to ever-accelerating or decelerating rates of inflation, at the very least it is faced with the prospect of accelerating rates of inflation if AD should be increased in an effort to reduce what is assumed to be classical unemployment. Stimulative AD policy has no long-run role to play in either case.

All the various models of VPC analysis considered are unacceptable. The NRH must be rejected for a number of reasons, but its built-in automatic FE tendencies, largely because of a competitive-haggling wage-setting process, is more than sufficient cause. Indeed, as the discussion of the alpha and beta strands of development makes clear, much of subsequent VPC analysis has dispensed with this assumption. Also unacceptable is VPC analysis that admits the possibility of involuntary unemployment while still explaining fluctuations in unemployment in terms of price surprises and real wage bargaining (i.e. the alpha strand). It makes little economic sense to allow for both possibilities.

The positive features of the beta strand analysis are that it allows for involuntary unemployment and dispenses with price surprises. Nevertheless, its argument against the effectiveness of stimulative AD policies must also be rejected. When it is recognized that the real wage is determined in the goods market, it becomes difficult to maintain that the real wage is too high and thereby prevents FE.[24] However, even if it is allowed that bargaining is always in real terms, there is a basic difficulty with this form of the policy-ineffectiveness argument. Whether the argument is phrased in terms of a fixed technology generating constant returns to labor, induced changes in technology in the form of dynamic scale economies, or hysteresis effects in which AD policies affect the rate of growth of productivity, a decline in the real wage is not a necessary condition for an expansion of employment.

What is implied by the "Keynesian symmetry," that is, increases in AD reduce unemployment when there are involuntarily unemployed workers and reductions in AD increase unemployment, is a rejection of the position that an economy is always tending toward some unique equilibrium unemployment rate with desirable properties. Even in the absence of hysteresis effects, advocates of the NAIRU admit to its instability, and when path dependence exists any "equilibrium" is very much dependent upon what policy-makers choose to make it.

[24]The real wage can be too high in one sense. If money wages are set so that, given some markup, domestic prices of tradable goods are high relative to foreign prices, a depreciation of the currency and a decline in the real wage could improve the payments position and reduce unemployment.

However, beyond the recognition that policy affects the equilibrium lies the more general challenge that any shock, should it affect the performance of the economy, influences the NAIRU. For example, equation (3.6) indicates that the NAIRU is determined by the actual growth rate of productivity, the growth rate of productivity expected by wage earners and reflected in their wage demands, and the growth rate of import prices. Other factors stressed by NAIRU proponents, for example the willingness to take jobs, the level of unemployment compensation, and union power, should be added to this. In every case reasonable arguments can be advanced that each is strongly dependent upon the state of the economy, whatever the stance of policy, and would be affected by, say, demand disturbances.

The argument here is that even when wage bargaining is in real terms, the uniqueness of an equilibrium unemployment rate is most unlikely. If it is admitted that wage bargaining is not always in real terms, the case against modeling the economy within the context of a unique equilibrium which is independent of AD policy becomes even stronger.[25] Thus, while this chapter began as a rebuttal of policy-ineffectiveness arguments, it ends as a challenge to the concept of modeling macroperformance within a unique equilibrium framework, particularly one centered on the long-run VPC, which ignores the kinds of induced supply and institutional effects just stressed.

In this book, an alternative framework is offered that stresses both the role of AD policy in performance and the forces influencing the choice of AD policy and therefore the future path of the economy. Chapter 4 proceeds to the next link in the causal chain of figure 1.2—the manner in which the distribution of economic and political power and the institutional framework jointly determine AD policy decisions.

---

[25] In chapter 8 this additional argument strengthens the case for multiple equilibria.

Appendix A: The Reliability of Nonaccelerating Inflation Rate of Unemployment Estimates

Consider table 3.1 in which NAIRU calculations for nine OECD countries are recorded along with average rates of unemployment and price inflation for the various time periods listed. According to NAIRU analysis, if the actual unemployment rate is greater (less) than the NAIRU, the rate of inflation will fall (rise). For example, using the estimates in the fourth and fifth columns, in the German case the actual unemployment is greater than the NAIRU in 1976–80, that is, 3.6 percent compared with the two NAIRU estimates of 3.1 and 2.4 percent. This should have led to a deceleration of inflation rates in 1976–80 compared with 1971–5, which it did, that is, the rate of inflation fell from 6.1 to 4.1 percent as seen in the seventh column. Whether or not inflation rates rise or fall during periods in which the estimated NAIRU is below or above actual unemployment rates provides a simple "test" of this kind of analysis.

Table 3.1 shows 65 such "tests" of the NAIRU hypothesis of the period 1961–83, if the period 1981–83 in Italy is excluded on the grounds that the change in the inflation rate over the previous period is too small to be of significance. The NAIRU hypothesis passes the above test in 36 out of 65 cases or 55 percent of the time.

NAIRU estimates do far better in correctly "predicting" acceleration than deceleration of inflation rates. Thus there are 25 observations when the NAIRU estimates were greater than the actual unemployment rates and 40 when the NAIRU estimates were less than the actual rate. In 22 of the 25 cases when NAIRU estimates were greater than actual unemployment rates, inflation rates actually rose. However, in only 14 of the 40 cases in which NAIRU estimates were lower than actual unemployment rates was there a deceleration of inflation rates.

At best, all this suggests an attitude of caution, if not skepticism, in the use of the NAIRU as a guide to policy. It is almost as likely as not to give the wrong AD policy signal. This is especially true during those periods in which NAIRU estimates are found to be lower than actual unemployment rates. According to NAIRU analysis, stimulative AD policies are called for, and yet the calculations in table 3.1 reveal that inflation rates usually accelerated in any case.

However, all this assumes that there is such a thing as a unique NAIRU. What the failure of inflation rates to fall when NAIRU estimates are less than the actual unemployment rate does suggest is that, whatever the NAIRU is supposed to measure, it has no knife-edge property.

66 Framework

Table 3.1 Nonaccelerating inflation rate of unemployment estimates

	Time period	Average unemployment rate	NAIRU estimates This study	NAIRU estimates Other studies	Average inflation rate
USA	1961–9	4.7		4.8 5.9	1.1
	1967–9	3.6	4.1 5.7	5.9	4.1
	1970–3	5.4	6.0 5.4	6.0 5.8	7.9
	1974–81	6.9	7.3 6.5	6.8 7.1	9.4
	1982–3	9.7	4.2 6.1	6.8	4.7
Japan	1972–5	1.5	1.2 1.2		13.1
	1976–80	2.1	1.9 1.9		6.6
	1981–3	2.2	2.3 2.3		3.2
Germany	1967–70	1.0	0.9 0.7	1.3	2.4
	1971–5	1.8	1.6 3.3	1.2	6.1
	1976–80	3.6	3.1 2.4	3.5	4.1
	1981–3	6.3	8.0 3.6	6.2	5.0
France	1966–70	2.1		2.2	4.4
	1971–5	2.7	4.6 4.5	3.3	8.9
	1976–80	5.2	3.3 4.8	5.2	10.5
	1981–3	8.3	9.0 7.7	6.9	11.6
UK	1967–70	2.2	2.6 7.1	2.4	4.8
	1971–5	3.0	7.2 4.2	4.0	13.2
	1976–80	5.4	7.3 7.6	4.7	14.4
	1981–3	10.6	5.9 9.4	9.2	8.4
Italy	1966–70	5.5	4.8 7.5	7.8	3.0
	1971–5	5.8	7.2 5.4	6.6	11.5
	1976–80	7.1	6.0 5.2	6.5	16.8
	1981–3	9.1	6.1 5.4	7.5	16.7
Canada	1967–9	4.2	3.8 6.4		4.0
	1970–3	5.9	4.1 4.7		4.7
	1974–9	7.2	7.2 5.8		9.2
	1980–3	8.5	6.9 7.4		9.9
Austria	1969–73	1.4	1.0 1.1		5.2
	1974–9	1.8	1.4 1.4		6.3
	1980–3	3.0	2.4 2.4		5.5
Netherlands	1969–73	2.5	2.2 3.0		6.9
	1974–9	5.2	5.4 4.5		7.2
	1980–3	9.3	10.6 8.7		5.5

Sources: D. Coe and F. Gagliardi, "Nominal wage determination in ten OECD economies," *Working Papers*, OECD, Paris, March 1985, table II

Appendix B: Pigou Reborn

Proponents of the unique equilibrium unemployment concept, whether it has the property of FE or not, emphasize certain automatic tendencies within capitalist systems that generate rapid convergence of the economy to that equilibrium. The belief in such automatic tendencies is as old as the invisible hand. In modern macroeconomics this invisible hand usually comes in one of two forms. As in the original NRH formulation, it is merely assumed that the economy is at FE or else employment deviates around this rate owing to temporary disturbances. Other interpretations of the invisible hand rely on real-balance effects but are rather vague about the nature of unemployment at the equilibrium rate. Thus any tendency for unemployment to deviate from the NAIRU generates accelerating or decelerating rates of inflation. With a given rate of growth of the nominal supply of money, the money supply in real terms then falls or rises. Since real balances are assumed to be positively related to levels of real consumption, AD falls or rises until the economy moves back to the NAIRU.[26]

Advocates of this type of unique equilibrium tendency have merely resurrected arguments brought against Keynes's *General Theory* almost half a century ago. There is no more evidence of this kind of convergence mechanism today than there was then. As a result, this justification of an automatic tendency toward some equilibrium unemployment rate is little better than the assertion of the NRH proponents.

What is new is the framework within which the argument is made—one based on a misleading partial equilibrium methodology and an incorrect modeling of the impact of price and wage formation. This form of mixed static–dynamic methodology can be characterized in the following manner. An essentially static model is assumed with a dynamic subsector: in this case prices and wages are allowed to change over time and affect the stock of real balances. While this is taking place, activity in the remainder of the economy is unchanged. Without this question-begging framework, a convergence is rather unlikely.

For example, if the unemployment rate is pushed above the NAIRU because of a decline in investment, this is not assumed to reduce capacity utilization rates and profits and therefore does not lead to further declines in investment, a likely sequence of events in the real world. If it did have these effects, given even the most extreme estimates of the impact of real balances on AD, unemployment rates would be pushed up further because of the more than offsetting additional declines in investment. The result would be a recession and not the assumed movement of the economy back towards some NAIRU.

This argument is strengthened by an acknowledgment that the actual per-

[26] See the references cited in notes 5–7.

formance of the economy strongly affects such "supply" factors as labor attitudes, labor supply, and productivity. For even if it could be assumed that the initial increase in the rate of unemployment does not have, say, adverse effects on investment and income through the multiplier, the very idea of a kind of convergence to some predetermined equilibrium must now be rejected. This was brought out clearly in section 3.7 where the NAIRU was seen to have the property of hysteresis. With induced effects on the supply side leading to path dependence, if it can be said that the economy is converging toward anything at all, it is very likely converging towards something determined by whatever policy the authorities adopt, including a passive AD policy.[27] All things considered, analyzing problems of inflation and unemployment within a framework that assumes automatic convergence to some unique equilibrium gives little help in understanding how the real world operates.

---

[27] See the model developed by Blanchard and Summers, "Hysteresis and the European unemployment problem."

4 Some Basic Determinants of Unemployment

4.1 Introduction

Little more than casual empiricism was offered in chapter 2 in support of the importance to policy formation of the historical shift in power towards labor and its supportive political parties. Yet the rising power of labor was cited in chapters 1 and 2 as one of the more important factors influencing policy developments and therefore the nature of the growth and transformation process in this century.

This chapter considers more closely the connection between political and economic power and AD and welfare policies, that is, the party control theory of policy formation. This theory and several alternative theories of policy formation are discussed and criticized. The second half of the chapter then discusses some of the institutional forces influencing the willingness of the authorities to supply these policies.

The approach recommended to explain unemployment rates and the size of the welfare state will seem completely inappropriate to most economists and actually wrong-headed to many other social scientists. After all, the theory of political or collective decision-making most familiar to economists—public choice theory—has a long and respectable tradition in economics and is based on a mode of analysis quite different from what is being suggested here. The point emphasized in the next two sections is that, useful as it may be for some problems, traditional public choice theory does not lead to an understanding of the kinds of political decisions that led to, say, FE and the expansion of the welfare state before the mid-1970s. A radically different approach is required.

Similarly, a large body of social scientists see "politics" playing a subsidiary role in economic policy, with the latter being dominated by certain imperatives or requisites that are determined by socioeconomic institutional forces, including technology. Thus various Marxist writers see policy outcomes as dictated by technological imperatives and the interests of capitalists and their need to accumulate. Non-Marxists dismissive of the party control theory start from a different persuasion. Politics or party control is not an important consideration because there is an inherent logic in industrialization and technological development that reduces party and class conflicts everywhere. This convergence of interests, both within a country and between countries, signals an "end of ideology" and a lessening of class and party differences, and therefore a reduced role for politics in economic policy-making.

This study provides an answer to these critics. It rejects a dogmatic Marxian view that capital prevails whatever the economic strength of the trade union movement or of left-of-center political parties. The non-Marxian critique of the party control position is also rejected. Although socioeconomic, institutional, and technological forces have a part to play, party control does influence policy.

4.2 Public Choice Theory

Economic theories of democracy

At a very general level, public choice theory can be viewed as the economic study of nonmarket collective decision-making. Schumpeter was one of the first economists to formalize an "economic theory of democracy," explaining collective decision-making as the outcome of politicians competing with one another for votes by promising to supply programs and public goods according to the electorate's preferences or demands.[1] Voters are simply consumers who spend their votes in a political marketplace indirectly purchasing programs by buying (electing) officials who will implement their preferences.

Schumpeter's economic theory of democracy finds its modern counterpart in abstract formal models of public choice in which individual voters, each seeking only to maximize his own self-interest, interact with politicians and bureaucrats who are similarly motivated. These models, based on the individual as the unit of analysis, assume voters to be influence seekers maximizing their own economic well-being, politicians to be adopting and implementing policies solely with a view to maximizing the number of votes that they will receive, and bureaucrats to be maximizing the budgets of their bureaus. Given some additional assumptions, determinate but very general policy implications are then derived; for example, the median voter's preferences or demands are the key in determining policy outcomes.

[1] J. Schumpeter, *Capitalism, Socialism and Democracy*, Harper, New York, 1942.

As should be clear, such models of decision-making, based on individual choice and fixed preferences, are a counterpart of the modern form of the competitive general equilibrium model: the assumption of a large number of price-takers is replaced by an assumption of a large number of voters, none of whom is assumed to have any special influence on policy choices; the assumption of fixed preferences of consumers gives way to one of fixed preferences of voters for public policies; the absence of cartels and oligopolies is replaced by a virtual absence of institutions, special interests, and power. If the same static framework as general equilibrium theory is utilized, under certain very strong assumptions a Pareto optimum emerges through competition of the political parties, that is, no policy changes are possible that would improve the welfare of any voter without harming some other.

Some criticisms

As might be expected, modern public choice theory has been subject to a number of criticisms similar to the standard criticisms of the competitive equilibrium model. By assuming that voter preferences are fixed and exogenous (and clearly articulated), public choice theory ignores efforts by governments to alter preferences, that is, to alter the political agenda. Governments do not lead because they are assumed not to be mission oriented. Nor do governments deny voter demands because their own actions might be constrained by institutions, laws, or the costs of their policies.[2] Constraints are allowed for, but they are rather few in number and of a special kind; for example, the need for politicians to be re-elected. Policy is essentially demand determined.

The impact on voter behavior or policy outcomes of a lack of voter information on issues or on the views actually held by politicians has not been well researched. Needless to say misinformation and outright lying have not found a prominent place in the more formal theories of public choice. The assumption that politicians and bureaucrats each have only one goal—vote maximization and enlargement of their budgets respectively—has brought criticism. Unfortunately, it has not been made clear what modes of political conduct will be forthcoming when politicians and bureaucrats are realistically treated as actors with multiple goals.[3] Furthermore, politicians seeking office are alleged to give

---

[2]The notion that democratic capitalism inevitably becomes overloaded is seen by many as a corollary of this economic theory of democracy.

[3]R. Goodin, "Rational politicians and rational bureaucrats in Washington and Whitehall," *Public Administration*, 60, Spring 1982, 23–41.

equal importance to the support of each and every voter—hence the importance of the median voter.[4]

For these and other reasons public choice theory does not serve the purposes of this study and a major departure from this theory of collective decision-making is required. To be useful in this study the proper unit of analysis must be the organized interest group. In addition, policy decisions and outcomes cannot be understood solely or even primarily as responses by governments to political demands. Public choice theory (as well as party control theories of policy) consistently overlooks institutional constraints operating both inside and outside the political process that limit the willingness of governments to supply policies on demand.

4.3 Policy Outcomes and Organizational Competition

There are several reasons for viewing collective decision-making as the result of competition and interaction between organizations rather than individuals, and this is especially true with respect to FE and welfare policies. One obvious point will suffice: attempts to influence governments and their agencies are in fact overwhelmingly carried out through the efforts of organized interest groups. There are good reasons why this is the case. For example, groups' interests become more effective by developing links with bureaucratic agencies. Consequently, such agencies tend to neglect, relatively, private citizens and loosely formed coalitions. Furthermore, it is widely accepted that special interest groups are able to exercise great power through their ability to provide information to voters and politicians, thereby often altering the latter's preferences, and to provide financial aid to politicians, thereby affecting policy choices. Aside from the rather formal treatment of the impact of political parties and bureaucrats on decision-making, the impact of organized interests on policy choices and outcomes is largely neglected in public choice theory. For these and other reasons, social scientists outside economics have developed formal models of collective decision-making in which attention is focused on the behavior of organized groups and their interactions rather than on

[4]This is related to the lack of consideration of institutions and organized interest groups in public choice theory and it can lead to some misleading results. For example, the important role played by the median voter suggests that if somehow those whose political preferences are close to the median would organize, something approximating the "general interest" might result. Yet the logic of collective choice tells us that the general interest, as reflected in some kind of majority interest, is unlikely to organize because of the free-rider problem. This leads to a situation in which special interests which do organize become over-represented in real life.

the behavior of individuals in the determination of policy. The party control theory of collective decision-making is one such model.

4.4 Party Control as an Explanation of Policy Choices

The party control theory of policy determination offers an explanation of differences in macropolicies, particularly policies that determine the scope of the welfare state and unemployment goals, in terms of the relative power of political movements. Underlying this view is the belief that the social and economic divisions within any society are reproduced in the political system, usually in the form of political parties and their programs. For example, the extent to which left-of-center parties actually dominate government is often explained in terms of the strength of the trade union movement. More elaborate versions consider both the extent to which workers are unionized and the organizational structure of the union movement.[5] It is argued that the more highly centralized the trade union structure and the more powerful the confederation in collective bargaining, the more likely are left-of-center parties to achieve control of the government. More complex theories seek to take account of differences within the political system as these affect the ability to translate voter and party preferences into policies.[6]

Given, then the relative strength of organized labor (variously measured), leftist, centrist, or rightist government control can be expected, allegedly giving rise to a predictable economic program. As one leading to advocate has put it:

> The single most important determinant of variations in macroeconomic performance from one industrialized democracy to another is the location of the left-right spectrum of the governing political party. Party platforms and political ideology set priorities and help decide policies. The consequence is that the governing party is very much responsible for major macroeconomic outcomes—unemployment rates, inflation rates, income equalization, and the size and rate of expansion of the government budget.[7]

This same concept is taken further in figure 4.1 where the political spectrum is defined from left to right in terms of three party positions,

---
[5] See Cameron, "Social democracy, corporatism."
[6] See Esping-Andersen and Korpi, "Social policy as class politics in post-war capitalism."
[7] E. Tufte, *Political Control of the Economy,* Princeton University Press, Princeton, NJ, 1978, p. 104.

74 Framework

Figure 4.1 Preferences of political parties in advanced industrial societies regarding various economic goals. *Source*: D. Hibbs, "Political parties and macroeconomic policy," *American Political Science Review*, December 1977

	Socialist-Labor	Center	Conservatives
Decreasing importance of goals	Full employment		Price stability
	Equalization of income distribution		
		Price stability	
	Economic expansion		
		Economic expansion	Balance-of-payments equilibrium
		Full employment	
		Equalization of income distribution	
	Price stability		Economic expansion
		Balance-of-payments equilibrium	
	Balance-of-payments equilibrium		Equalization of income distribution

while the relative preferences of each party regarding macrogoals are ranked from top to bottom in descending order. A clear reversal of relative preferences is apparent on moving from left to right. Thus the "equalization of income distribution" along with FE ranks at the top of the agenda for "socialist-labor" parties and at the bottom for "conservatives." Following this line of reasoning, differences in AD policies and welfare programs are interpreted to a large extent as the result of the relative strength of the competing demands of labor and business interests that provide the political support for the different parties, together with the relative ability of each party to win office and hold it.

Naturally, such a starkly simple explanation of policy choices and outcomes refers to tendencies, since members of different social and economic groups are bound to have overlapping preferences and interests in many policy areas. Nonetheless, advocates of the party control theory of policy have argued that these tendencies are particularly strong in the areas of employment and welfare policies, so that a strong causal relationship holds on average between the strength of economic and social divisions in society, political parties, and national economic policies.

4.5 Cross-country Analysis

A standard method of supporting the party control explanation of historical changes in AD and welfare policies would be to set up a model specifying the relationship between power (somehow measured) and policy outcomes, collect data, and then test the model statistically. This has been done by others. Unfortunately, the kinds of econometric time series analyses that have been undertaken to support this position have been inconclusive.[8] This in itself need not seriously undermine the party control theory of policy formation as an explanation of historical policy developments since the available data may not be sufficient to provide a fair test. Thus over time, as the distribution of economic power has shifted in response to the unionization of labor and the franchise has been extended (as has been free public education), the political power of labor would have increased also. This would have acted to shift the whole political spectrum to the left, forcing even nonleft parties to adopt a more favorable attitude toward policies advocated by labor as the political "climate" slowly changed.

In the absence of wars and natural catastrophes, such changes tend to be slow and drawn out over long periods of time. As a result, this gradual but persistent displacement of the political agenda, together with other important slow-changing institutional and structural influences also at work, would have imparted a great deal of continuity over time in policy outcomes.[9] Hence, unless data are available over a wide span of time and are of high quality, the impact of political control on policy and the importance of the strength of demand would not be readily determined. Furthermore, even when comparable historical data are available, this approach may fail to provide a fair test of the party control theory of decision-making. Over time, external developments such as worldwide stagnation can place severe constraints on the policy options open to governments, including those that might otherwise wish to pursue FE.

There is an alternative strategy that offers a means of determining the impact of political and economic power on policy and of supporting the framework outlined in chapter 1. As the data in chapter 2

---

[8]See, for example, D. Cameron, "The growth of government spending: the Canadian experience in comparative perspective," in K. Banting (ed.), *State and Society: Canada in Comparative Perspective*, University of Toronto Press, Toronto, 1986; and Korpi and Shalev, "Strikes, power and politics."

[9]See P. Hall, *Governing the Economy: The Politics of State Intervention in Britain and France*, Oxford University Press, New York, 1986.

76 *Framework*

reveal, the degree of expansion of the welfare state and unemployment records differs widely between countries. These differences have not gone unnoticed by social scientists, and efforts in using cross-country analysis to explain the connection between political and economic power, on the one hand, and policy choices, on the other, have been commonplace. Moreover, in these studies the relative power of economic and political groups is interpreted as a measure of the demand for the kinds of policies being discussed. Cross-country analysis, because it allows a comparison of diverse institutional arrangements while holding external developments constant across countries, can be of critical importance in isolating the influence of political power on policies and performance. By averaging party control variables and economic policy outcomes within a country over some period of time and comparing the relationships across countries during this period, some additional insight into the question of whether "party control matters" can be provided. The same conclusion can be drawn when utilizing cross-section analysis for isolating influences on the supply-of-policy side.

There are important benefits from proceeding along these lines. Among other things, it sets the stage for a more extended treatment of the forces behind the demand for policies. Following that, supply influences can be introduced which, together with insights gained from these cross-section demand studies, allow a more explicit formulation of the framework suggested in chapter 1. The focus will initially be on unemployment and welfare policies, but by the end of the chapter attention will be centered on unemployment. Welfare programs are reconsidered from a different perspective in later chapters.

4.6 Party Control and Economic Policy

Party control and labor power

Consider the relationship between the socioeconomic divisions in society and party control. Various measures of both variables have been used in cross-country studies to test for a possible correlation. The percentage of the labor force unionized or union density is the most commonly used measure of the underlying strength of "leftist" movements. Unionization of workers is thought to increase "class consciousness" and to channel political energies into forming pro-labor parties. A cross-country correlation of this variable with the control of government by leftist parties, that is, an index measuring the percentage of cabinet portfolios and parliamentary seats held on average by social democratic and labor parties, for 18 countries over the period of 1965–82 yielded a positive correlation (r = 0.74). Some improvement in the correlation ($r = 0.79$) was found if account was taken of certain organizational features of the labor movements in each of the countries; for example, the likelihood of control by leftist parties is enhanced when labor is organized into a single confederation and when collective bargaining is carried out at the confederation level.[10]

Party control and unemployment

Cross-country correlation analysis has been less successful in establishing a relationship between party control variables and employment performances. Based on their own subjective views of what is good for themselves as well as the actual behavior of incomes over the cycle, low and middle income groups are expected to prefer low unemployment even if it causes increased inflation. Therefore party control theory advocates predict a negative correlation between leftist party control of government and unemployment rates. However, while correlation studies usually show significant negative correlations, more than half the variance is left unexplained.[11]

Party control and the welfare state

Slightly stronger support for the party control hypothesis is found when party control variables are correlated with social expenditures. For example, table 4.1 gives the correlation between the three components of social expenditure and of total social expenditure for 1960, 1974, and 1981 and the percentage of parliamentary seats held by right-wing parties in 1951–60, 1960–74, and 1975–81 respectively.[12] According to party control explanations of policy choice, social expenditure should be negatively correlated with right-wing party control. In 1960 this was the case only for educational expenditure and total expenditure with the correlation of the latter and party control weak. The

[10] See Cameron, "Social democracy, corporatism," p. 166.
[11] Cameron, ibid., obtained $r = 0.44$ when the average rate of unemployment and leftist party control on average were correlated for 18 OECD countries for the period 1965–82. Hibbs, "Political parties and macroeconomic policy," obtained $r = 0.68$, but the sample excluded Japan and Switzerland. These two low unemployment countries have consistently elected right-wing governments.
[12] See F. Castles, "Social expenditure and the political right: a methodological note," *European Journal of Political Research*, 14, 1986, 669–76. Similar results were found by Hibbs, "Political economy of long-run trends in strike activity," and Korpi and Shalev, "Strikes, power and politics."

Table 4.1 Correlations between social expenditure as share of gross domestic product in 18 OECD countries and percentage of parliamentary seats held by right-wing parties for selected years

	Pearson's r		
	1960	1974	1981
Educational expenditure	−0.53	−0.64	−0.68
Health expenditure	0.03	−0.43	−0.48
Pension expenditure	0.16	−0.18	−0.25
Total social expenditure	−0.20	−0.61	−0.69

Source: F. Castles, "Social expenditures and the political right: a methodological note," European Journal of Political Research, 14, 1986, table 2

hypothesized relations are better borne out for 1974 and 1981, although pension expenditure was only slightly related to party control.

Expanding the analysis

Whatever the truth of the party control theory of politics, the findings of the statistical studies just summarized are inconclusive at best. Something else is influencing the choice of policy goals besides party control. What is being suggested is that before the party control hypothesis can be accepted or rejected on statistical grounds, additional variables must be included in the analysis. There are two ways that the analysis could proceed. Some variant of the view that certain basic socioeconomic institutions and technological developments dominate policy decisions could be resurrected in one or more of its forms and evaluated, but as a complement to party control theory. This approach would seek to determine the relative importance of the basic institutional determinants which are operative irrespective of shifting power sources, on the one hand, and political influences, on the other.

Alternatively, an economist's strategy could be pursued with one important modification: a political economy approach would be adopted and consideration would be given to what were referred to in chapter 1 as the basic determinants of macropolicy decisions. Fortunately it is an easy matter to show that these two procedures come to the same thing. In the next two sections this modified economist's approach will be utilized to achieve a deeper understanding of why governments choose particular employment goals. The forces ultimately influencing welfare programs will not be considered further.

4.7 A Political Economist's Analysis of Unemployment

Inflation costs as constraints on policy

In drawing up a list of determinants of differences in unemployment rates between countries, economists would include in their lists one or more of the following: the level of aggregate demand, the rate of growth of the money supply, the "natural rate of unemployment," the level of real wages, structural features of the labor market and labor force, the NAIRU, or even work-leisure preferences. Those economists who see an inherent tendency for capitalist economies always to be in the neighborhood of FE would choose, say, differences in the natural rate of unemployment or the NAIRU as the explanation of unemployment differences, while those of a more Keynesian persuasion would select differences in AD pressures or the rage of growth of the money supply.

In today's world of mass unemployment there is a good deal of support from economists for a Keynesian interpretation of unemployment differences between countries. Accordingly, differences across countries in unemployment rates are attributed largely to differences in AD pressures and therefore differences in AD policies. Not only that, Keynesian economists would be quite willing to push the chain of causation one step further back and maintain that behind these differences in AD policies lie differences in the inflation or payments costs of FE. In countries in which the costs of FE are low, the authorities are able and willing to stimulate AD. When they are high, employment rates are allowed to rise.

Next, consider the case of strong political pressures on government to pursue a FE policy and assume that inflation is the only possible cost of FE. In the absence of any inflation cost constraint on the use of AD policy for realizing full employment, believers in demand-determined macroeconomic policies would argue strongly that, on average, unemployment rates will be very low in this case. However, it may well be that a stimulative AD policy in some countries leads to an acceleration of inflation rates because of the structural features of their labor markets. If the governing authorities consider these rates of inflation too high a cost to pay for FE, AD policy instruments will be constrained, even in a country with a strong union movement and leftist control of government, by certain structural features of the economy. As a result policies and employment outcomes will not reflect simply demand pressures from the governing party's constituencies but

80 *Framework*

Figure 4.2 Differences in Phillips curves, party control and policy choices

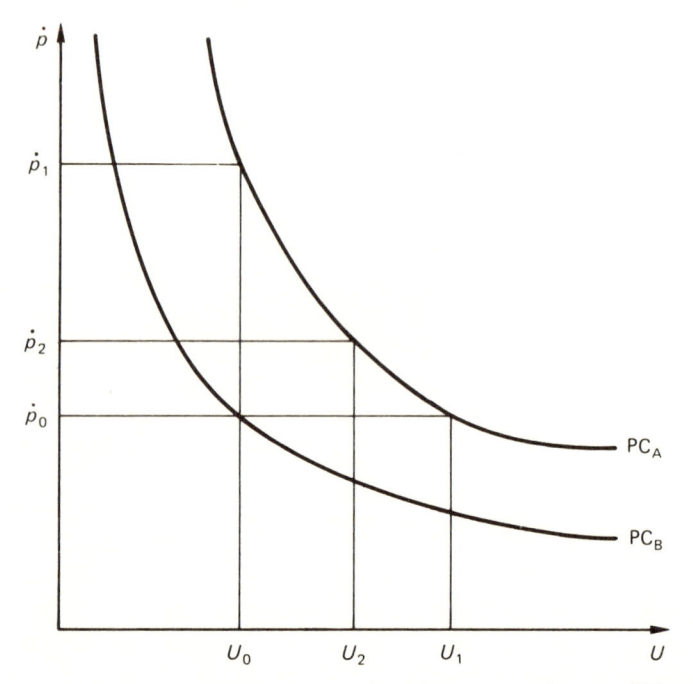

rather supply influences as well, due in this case to the unwillingness of governments to supply enough AD stimulus to achieve FE.

Differences in Phillips curves

The argument can be formulated as a modified Phillips curve theory of why unemployment rates differ across countries. Consider figure 4.2 in which two Phillips curves are drawn for two countries. The curves are drawn in such a way that country B can experience unemployment rates as low as U_0 with an inflation cost of $\dot{p}_0$ while country A would suffer a price inflation rate of $\dot{p}_1$ if it reduced unemployment to U_0. One possible impact of this difference is that the authorities in country A will constrain AD, leading to an unemployment rate of, say, U_1. Differences in unemployment rates can therefore be traced to differences in inflation costs or Phillips curves. However, this is only one possibility, as can be seen if the influence of party control on policy has force. Thus, assume that country A has a strong trade union movement and is dominated by a pro-labor government. Then, despite an unfavorably placed Phillips curve, the authorities may choose to accept a rate of unemployment somewhat higher than U_0, but less than U_1, say U_2, at the cost of a rate of inflation of $\dot{p}_2$.

Unfortunately, explaining differences in unemployment by differences in the position of the Phillips curve and political power takes the analysis only part of the way. It fails to consider why Phillips curves differ across countries. This requires a determination of what institutions lead to, say, an unfavorably positioned Phillips curve and why policies have not been or cannot be implemented to shift the Phillips curve in such a way that lower unemployment or even FE without serious inflation can be achieved. With respect to policy, the introduction of extensive government-run manpower programs and various kinds of incomes policies are examples of efforts to shift the Phillips curve. In some countries great effort has been made in this direction, often quite successfully. What is needed is an explanation of why some governments were willing or able to alter institutions and implement supplementary policies in order to reduce or eliminate an inflation constraint on expansionary AD policies and why others were not.

4.8 The Basic Causes of Unemployment

It is at this point that the political economist's approach, if pushed to its logical conclusion, meets the approach which extends the party control theory of policy-making to take account of institutional features of economies. Differences in Phillips curves between countries can be and often are attributed by economists to differences in structural or institutional factors, and those who stress the importance of political power and control, but see this as only one important factor, are also prone to look for institutional forces as important additional influences on unemployment policy. However, it must be emphasized that, while economists have often been concerned with finding institutional explanations of the position of Phillips curves, what they have traditionally treated as causes of why Phillips curves differ has until recently been rather restricted. For example, differences in geographic size, mismatch between job openings and job applicants, and differences in unemployment benefits are traditional economic explanations of differences in Phillips curves. Recent unemployment studies centering on the NAIRU concept have expanded this catalog of forces influencing the position of the long-run (vertical) Phillips curve. Additions to the list include the size of labor's "targeted" rate of growth of real wages, the strength of the union move-

82   *Framework*

ment, and institutional features of the labor market. While the assumption of a vertical long-run Phillips curve has already proved unacceptable in this study, a stress on such factors as these in determining the position of the (non-vertical) Phillips curve is quite in keeping with the views present here.

In order to highlight the issues, the early explanations by economists of why Phillips curves may differ between countries (or shift over time), for example differences in the demographic composition of the labor force or the system of unemployment benefits, will be played down. This is not meant to downgrade their importance. However, in explaining differences in Phillips curve relations between countries, it will be argued that certain other more lasting institutional forces dominate.[13] What is required is an expanded inventory of institutions that play a role in determining the position of the Phillips curve and the rate of inflation at FE. For, given the propensity of governments everywhere to restrict AD if inflationary pressures become serious when FE is approached, it can be expected that any government saddled with an unfavorable collection of institutions and a poorly positioned Phillips curve will be constrained in its use of stimulative AD policies. This will cause unemployment to be high. By combining this expanded inventory with an analysis of political demand pressures, it is possible to explain cross-country differences in macroperformance. It will also throw light on the causes of the rise of unemployment rates throughout the OECD since the early 1970s.

4.9 A Question of Terminology

The economics of institutions has become one of the most active areas of study in economics. On the one hand, the study of the influence of institutions on economic events has received attention. For example, in chapter 1 the impact of institutions on economic policy variables was stressed. In addition, however, economists have turned their attention to explaining the origin and evolution of institutions with the aid of economic theory.[14] An example of this kind of interest is again pro-

---

[13]For an attempt to combine traditional explanations of why Phillips curves differ with the kinds of institutional influences stressed here see R. Jackman, "Wage formation in the Nordic countries viewed from an international perspective," *Seminar Paper No. 4151*, Institute for International Economic Studies, University of Stockholm, August 1988. See also the references cited in note 3 of chapter 1.

[14]For a more formal summary see R. Langlois, "The new institutional economics: an introductory essay," in R. Langlois (ed.), *Economics as a Process*, Cambridge University Press, Cambridge, 1986.

vided in chapter 1—the impact of FE conditions and the extension of the welfare state on the structure of the labor market.

Some definitions are needed before proceeding further. For the purposes at hand, institutions or the institutional framework will be defined as the conventions or norms that describe acceptable ways of behavior, especially when they refer to relations between individuals and groups. This institutional framework of a society will describe the way in which authority can be used and delegated, rules for compliance, and the rights and obligations of individuals and groups. The legal system of a society can be thought of as part of its institutional framework.

Economic institutions are defined as the norms or conventions describing what is acceptable behavior in economic relations. For example, a labor contract (agreement) enforceable in law may contain a "last-hired-first-fired" written clause. The same contract may contain no explicit restrictions limiting the job classifications into which new workers may be hired. Yet it may have become customary to always hire outsiders into the low skill, low paying jobs, while filling better jobs through promotion from within. In the sense used here, the rule of laying off workers as well as the custom of promoting from within are both part of the institutional framework describing this labor market. They act to constrain the way in which economic activities can be carried out at the firm.

4.10 A Multitude of Constraints

The notion that certain institutional features of a society significantly constrain economic policy-making can be extended in several ways. In every case, constraints can be seen as a source of discrepancy between the demands and preferred policies associated with the party in control and their constituencies and the actual policy choices and performances. First, there may be economic costs associated with FE policies other than inflation that act to constrain AD policies and compromise the FE target. The most obvious is the existence of serious payments disequilibrium at FE. This cost will receive further consideration below. Second, other economic goals such as welfare programs may be seriously constrained by institutional factors. Third, noneconomic as well as economic constraints are liable to be operative limiting the pursuit of FE. More specifically, a distinction between constraints that arise from within the political system, its institutions, and processes and those arising out of the economic structure is often useful. A popular allegation made during the 1970s was that policy options open to governments were constrained by their need to be re-elected.

Going further, legal restrictions on the use of AD policies can vary from constitutional restrictions against deficit financing to a division of fiscal and monetary powers within a federalist system of governance. The existence of a central bank with powers to conduct an independent monetary policy provides an example of a constraint which is best viewed as both political and economic. Given the tendency of central bankers everywhere to stress the importance of price stability even if it implies an increase in unemployment rates, the more independent of legislative and executive direction is the central bank, the more constrained will be stimulative AD policies, other things being equal.[15] Finally, a distinction can be made between the kinds of policy instruments needed to relieve the policy-makers of any constraint, for example a simple legislative act or a need to change the behavior of market participants.

4.11 The Relevant Institutional Constraints

Clearly, to determine the causes of mass unemployment, it is necessary to identify those institutions that affect macroeconomic performance by placing constraints on the use of AD policies. It is only recently that economists have concerned themselves with the economic impact of institutions on performance, but there is now a sizable and growing literature in this area.[16] It is a literature that differs profoundly from conventional welfare economics. While the latter is ostensibly concerned with the conditions for improving welfare and therefore the well-being of the citizenry, it defines these conditions within the framework of the static competitive model. In contrast, much of the literature developed to explain the current breakdown and to explain why some countries have performed better than others has recognized that the real world is full of market imperfections and that some institutional imperfections are better than others.

This study concentrates on those institutional features of the economy that constrain the use of AD policies and therefore affect unemployment rates. In this study two constraints are emphasized. These are

---

[15] See J. Woolley "Monetary policy instrumentation and the relationship of central banks and governments," *Annuals of the American Academy*, 434, November 1977, 151–73.

[16] See chapter 1, note 3, for several references.

a political constraint and a (relative) balance-of-payments or simply a payments constraint. The first corresponds to a stance of AD policy beyond which a more stimulative policy, while reducing unemployment, generates or is expected to generate a rate of inflation or an increase in the size of the budget deficit or an increase in labor's power, any one of which is unacceptable to the authorities. For example, any higher rate of inflation than that at which the constraint takes hold is considered an evil in its own right. An important feature of this constraint is that a more stimulative AD policy would not be implemented even if the payments position could be sustained. As defined, this constraint arises from a mixture of political and economic forces underlying the willingness to supply FE.

The second constraint finds the chief harm of stimulative AD policies in their ability to undermine the country's external position. Thus, as AD is increased and unemployment falls, other things being equal, imports rise and exports tend to fall owing to diversion of output to the home market. These income effects are reinforced if any divergence of domestic rates of inflation from foreign rates is not compensated by movements in the exchange rate, and the payments position becomes unsustainable. Since in some long-run sense the payments position must balance, or at least the deficit may not exceed some rate of growth, there will be an AD policy stance and a corresponding rate of employment that cannot be exceeded. The constraint is relative rather than absolute because it is partly activities elsewhere, especially rates of inflation, that will influence domestic AD policy and the unemployment rate.

If the political constraint is encountered at higher rates of unemployment than the payments constraint, the payments constraint is irrelevant and the country may well run an external surplus. If the payments constraint corresponds to the higher rate of unemployment, the political constraint is irrelevant. In other words, the effective constraint is the one with the higher unemployment rate. Further, if the rate of unemployment at which a constraint becomes operative is higher than the FE rate of unemployment, the latter ceases to be a policy goal.

One final matter of terminology: a sufficient condition for restricting AD to levels generating less than FE is a foreseen or experienced unacceptable rate of inflation at FE. Earlier remarks asserted that during the post-war period there was a growing tendency for *potentially* strong inflationary pressures to develop at FE everywhere. In the absence of additional policy measures (to be referred to as the ability to implement a successful long-run incomes policy) such potential pressures either result in or are thought to result in unacceptable rates of inflation at FE. In this case, an economy will be said to suffer from an inflationary bias. As a result, in economies that have failed to develop incomes policies, a political constraint will take hold before FE is attained because of this bias.

It should be noted that a political or a payments constraint may take hold in the absence of strong inflationary pressures. However, before the late 1960s most OECD economies were able to achieve FE because neither a political nor a payments constraint was operative at rates of unemployment greater than FE. Nevertheless, a key conclusion in this study is that since the late 1960s there has been an increased tendency for *actual* strong inflationary pressures to develop at FE and therefore for most economies to suffer from an inflationary bias. It is this trend more than anything else that dictates the incorporation of supply influences in an explanation of unemployment performance. The characteristics of those economies capable of realizing FE and those subject to an AD constraint are taken up next.

5 Macroeconomic Performance and Institutions

5.1 Introduction

In the previous chapter it was concluded that party control might well play a role in AD policy determination. However, whatever the political support for policy, the authorities in charge may be constrained by undesirable costs. The discussion is continued and extended in this chapter. It offers an institutional-analytical explanation of differences in unemployment and inflation performances within the OECD economies for approximately the quarter of a century following the Second World War. The end-point chosen is 1973 since it marks the peak year in economic activity in most economies.

This was a period of outstanding performance for modern capitalism. Never before in history have so many countries grown so rapidly under conditions of FE or near FE with acceptable rates of inflation and payments positions. Unfortunately, this phase was to last less than a quarter of a century. However, in this chapter there is less concern with celebrating the success of capitalism in the 1950s and 1960s, especially its ability to provide FE and safety nets for the economically and politically weaker elements of the society, than with explaining differences in the degree of success from one country to another. Following the framework outlined in chapter 4, differences in unemployment rates before 1974 are explained in terms of differences in political forces determining the demand for FE and in other institutional features constraining macropolicies during this period in different countries.

As always, an underlying assumption is that there is no automatic tendency toward FE in any of the capitalist economies, and certainly none toward FE without inflation or payments disequilibrium. AD policies do have output and employment effects, enabling the authorities to pursue FE should they so desire. However, while stimulative AD policies can reduce unemployment to FE rates when private demand is insufficient, such policies were not universally adopted even in the post-war period before 1974. This chapter explains why.

5.2 Party Control and Unemployment before the Breakdown

Party control, union power, and unemployment

Figure 5.1 gives the annual average rates of unemployment and price inflation for 18 OECD countries during the post-war period until 1974. The scatter of points indicates that the sample of countries depicted can be divided into two groups depending upon their unemployment performance during the period 1963–1973.[1] There are the high unemployment countries, that is, Canada, Ireland, Italy, and the United States, with an average rate of unemployment of 5 percent. The remaining countries qualify as low unemployment countries, although the United Kingdom raises some difficulties with an average unemployment rate of 3.2 percent. Leaving aside the United Kingdom, unemployment rates in the low unemployment economies ranged from a little over 2 percent (Belgium) to zero. While it is undoubtedly true that some involuntary unemployment exists even when unemployment rates are 2.3 percent or less, it will be assumed here that the overwhelming majority of the OECD economies considered experienced FE. Five did not.[2]

The party control or demand-determined theory of policy choice argues that unemployment rates will vary inversely with such variables as the strength of the trade union movement and the "leftist" composition of government. Figure 5.1 reveals that strong unionized countries with left-wing governments such as Austria, Norway, and Sweden experienced low rates of unemployment while countries with weak union movements and right-wing governments such as Canada, Italy, and the United States experienced high unemployment, supporting the party control hypothesis.[3] However, the Japanese and Swiss records

---

[1] See also table II.1.

[2] During this period it was widely accepted that "full employment" prevailed in countries like Canada and the United States when the unemployment rate fell to 3 or 4 percent. However, this convention was not derived from any careful analysis of the nature of unemployment at 3–4 percent. For example, the unemployment rate in the United States in 1969 was 3.4 percent. Yet it would be hard to argue that this unemployment was voluntary. Of all the weeks of unemployment experienced during 1969, 35 percent were experienced by people out of work for 26 weeks or more and 16 percent of these total weeks of unemployment were experienced by people out of work for 40 weeks or more. See K. Clark and L. Summers, "Labor market dynamics and unemployment: a reconsideration," *Brookings Papers on Economic Activity*, No. 1, 1979, table 4.

Implicitly, the conventional definition of FE in North America is based on a belief that any lower rate of unemployment would set off unacceptable rates of inflation. Since unemployment rates in the United Kingdom never fell below 3 percent after 1966 and averaged 3.6 percent from 1966 to 1973, the United Kingdom can be excluded from the FE group.

[3] See tables 2.6 and 2.7 for relevant data.

Figure 5.1 Average rate of increase of consumer prices and standardized unemployment rates for 18 OECD countries for the period 1963–1973: A, Australia; Au, Austria; B, Belgium; C, Canada; D, Denmark; Fin, Finland; F, France; G, Germany; Ir, Ireland; I, Italy; J, Japan; Ne, Netherlands; NZ, New Zealand; No, Norway; Su, Switzerland; S, Sweden; UK, United Kingdom; US, United States. *Source: The Revised OECD Data Set*, Centre for Labour Economics, London School of Economics

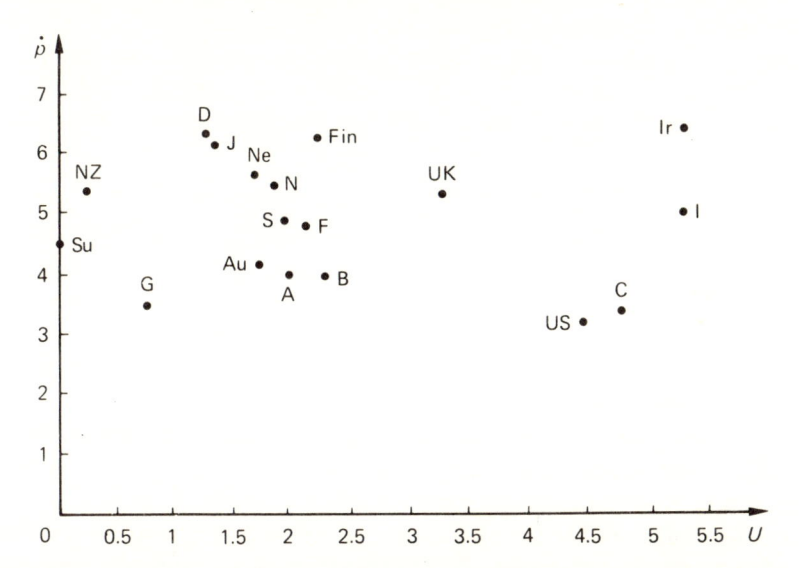

are particularly hard to reconcile with the demand-determined explanation of unemployment. Both countries had weak trade union movements and right-of-center pro-business governments, yet they experienced some of the lowest unemployment rates in the sample of countries. Clearly, strong union movements and left-of-center governments are at best only sufficient conditions for FE. Obviously other influences are at work here and, whatever impact demand factors may have had on policy, their importance can be determined only by introducing them explicitly.

Party control, union power, and inflation

Consider next the impact of demand influences on rates of inflation. Those economies with high union densities and leftist party control did not experience relatively higher rates of inflation than those with weak union movements, as a comparison of the Scandinavian and North American countries reveals. Yet the stronger bargaining power of labor in the countries with high union density would lead one to expect more explosive cost–push mechanisms, other things being equal. This would be maintained, for example, by writers concerned with "overloading" the economy. However, the data do not support this, suggesting that countries like Norway and Sweden were able to obtain the cooperation of labor unions and business in restraining wages and prices despite strong labor and booming demand conditions. Such an ability would overcome one possible constraint on the use of stimulative AD policies (or would lessen the need to apply restrictive policies), encouraging the authorities to supply (or allow) FE. Clearly, it is necessary to distinguish between potential and actual inflationary pressures.

The cross-country Phillips curve

These considerations are reflected in figure 5.1 in the lack of any cross-country tradeoff between unemployment and inflation rates during this period. The correlation between average rates of inflation and unemployment is $r = -0.06$.[4] The countries with high unemployment and low unionization such as Canada, Italy, and the United States did not experience more favorable inflation records than, say, Austria. Put another way, what is revealed is the success of the FE countries, especially those heavily unionized, in achieving relative price stability. Figure 5.1 also depicts appreciable differences in the "misery" or "discomfort" index, that is, the sum of the average rates of unemployment and inflation, between countries. Higher unemployment bought only greater misery; it did not bring reduced rates of inflation. Since differences in the misery index are almost entirely due to differences in unemployment rates, they also cannot be explained simply in terms of differences in party control or obvious economic divisions within the countries.

5.3 The Impact of Unions on Inflation

Potential versus actual use of union power at full employment

In order to begin to understand the lack of correlation between unemployment and inflation rates across countries, it is necessary to understand why inflation rates are not positively correlated with union strength and party control of government. After all, the more organized the labor movement, the greater should be the economic pressure it

[4] The correlation between average rates of inflation and unemployment for the same countries for the period 1951–73 is $r = -0.25$. The sample mean and variance for average rates of inflation for the period 1963–73 are 4.9 percent and 0.95 percent respectively, while the same statistics for unemployment rates for the same period were 2.3 percent and 2.6 percent respectively.

can mobilize behind wage demands and the greater the political strength behind its demands for FE policies. This requires a distinction between the market power conferred upon a unionized labor force under FE conditions and its actual use of such power. It will be argued that unions do give rise to potentially serious inflationary problems whenever the economy moves toward FE, because FE increases their power. However, whether or not this results in serious inflation actually developing depends upon the institutional features surrounding the labor market, particularly the manner in which collective bargaining is carried out.

Fairness considerations, unions, and the Phillips curve

The period of prolonged FE in the 25 years following the Second World War resulted in a shift in relative economic and political power of labor, allowing labor to introduce fairness considerations in wage settlements (and other aspects of the job). Fairness came to be defined increasingly in terms of protection and growth of real wages and protection of relative wages.[5] Under conditions of unrestricted collective bargaining, wage settlements are the result of a bilateral bargaining process between labor and management or a unilateral determination of wages by one or the other of the parties. There is no effort by either or by any third party to bring wage settlements into line with some common interest or national goal such as wage (and price) stability. Bargaining is to determine a fair wage and a fair relative wage through the adjustment of the money wage, with the behavior of the cost of living and wage settlements elsewhere being key considerations.

In these circumstances a negative relation between unemployment and rates of inflation within an economy emerges, other things being equal, as labor takes advantage of its increased economic power when labor markets tighten and management becomes more acquiescent when profit conditions improve. Moreover, this tradeoff between unemployment and inflation is likely to be most unfavorable in the sense that the Phillips curve will be badly positioned. In particular, inflation rates are liable to be high and even accelerating while appreciable amounts of involuntary unemployment remain. To see better why this is the case, it is helpful to reinterpret the inflationary mechanisms just discussed in a game theory framework as examples of a prisoner's dilemma.

[5]The concept of fairness was popularized by J. Hicks, *The Crisis in Keynesian Economics*, Basic Books, New York, 1974.

5.4 Inflation as a Prisoner's Dilemma

Price and wage stability as public goods

By definition public goods have two properties, joint consumption and nonexcludability: the benefits received by any one consumer do not reduce the benefits available to others, and once a public good exists no one can be excluded from enjoying its benefits.

The properties of a public good lead to free riding, that is, some individuals or groups benefiting from the good, for example, price and wage stability, are not contributing to the costs of providing it, in this case restraining wage demands and price increases. Going further, if free riders, in this case unions and business groups, can impose large external costs on others who also wish to benefit from the public good (and if there is limited opportunity for communication and collusion), the activities are then said to take on the characteristics of a prisoner's dilemma. These arise if each of a set of individuals or groups pursuing its own immediate self-interest brings about a result that is less favorable to everyone than could be realized if a different principle of behavior were to be adopted. Such market failures can arise in an economy with no central authority coordinating activities.

Free riders and wage–wage and wage–price inflation

Under a system of unrestricted collective bargaining wage–wage and wage–price inflationary mechanisms are activated whenever labor markets become tight. These mechanisms, which are easily modeled as examples of prisoner's dilemmas, do much to explain the negative relation between inflation and unemployment rates shown by individual country Phillips curves. The wage–wage mechanism is a case of a set of labor groups each trying to maintain or even improve their relative position in the wage structure. Under decentralized unrestricted collective bargaining, relative wage considerations will always motivate individual labor groups to push for wage increases. Such a strategy will be seen to be in their interest regardless of what other labor groups do. If others do not follow suit, a more aggressive labor group will increase its relative wage, while if all follow suit, its relative position will not have deteriorated. Since all labor groups are likely to reason in this way, and since such self-improvement efforts intensify and increase in incidence when labor markets tighten, wage–wage inflation will accelerate when unemployment rates fall. Overlapping labor contracts strengthen these tendencies.

The wage–price mechanism reveals an attempt by capital and labor to protect or increase profit margins and real wages respectively. Consider the likely behavior of labor. In a world of unrestricted (but not necessarily decentralized) collective bargaining, labor groups will tend to see it in their own immediate self-interest to push for higher money wages in an effort to improve real wages. If business does not respond by raising prices, real wages rise. If the cost increase is passed on by business, labor will reason that it is no worse off. Again, such self-improvement efforts by labor can be assumed to intensify and increase as labor markets tighten, and therefore the wage–price inflation process will gather momentum as unemployment rates fall.

Free riders and the prisoner's dilemma

Efforts to improve a group's position in the wage structure or to shift the distribution of income cannot be successful for everyone or even for most groups. Even so, they do cause inflation rates to accelerate. However, the results are much more costly than this, as recent experience has shown, because the response of governments to accelerating rates of inflation has been to impose restrictive AD policies, leading to increased rates of unemployment and to low or negative rates of growth of productivity, real wages, and profits. Hence a principle of action different from immediate self-interest is required to contain the potentially strong inflationary forces that develop at FE—one that still protects real and relative wages. Without such a principle, FE without strong inflation is unlikely. Note that if fairness considerations were not important factors in wage settlements (as they were not before unions), neither inflationary mechanism would operate. In a world of weak labor, inflation need not be modeled as a prisoner's dilemma.

Summary

The essential point that emerges from all this is that countries in which inflation can be modeled as a prisoner's dilemma will be faced with an inflationary bias, that is, a tendency for inflation rates to increase strongly or even accelerate as the economy approaches FE. This tendency arises when unionized labor groups strive to realize real wage and relative wage targets by continuously exploiting their market power to the fullest. As a result, the growth of money wage demands and settlements accelerate when labor markets tighten and restrictive policies are then introduced. When this occurs labor market behavior is suboptimal in the sense that another form of behavior could lead to results in which everyone is better off. Therefore the achievement of low rates of inflation at low rates of unemployment lies in the ability to motivate labor to seek fairness by other means than unrestricted collective bargaining. Moreover, such behavior, if adopted, will likely lead to a more rapid growth of real wages.

The kinds of institutions and policies that so motivate labor and reduce prisoner's dilemma problems, thereby allowing a flatter or a more favorably placed Phillips curve, are the subject of the remainder of this chapter.[6] The discussion now shifts to the institutional features of an economy that do much to determine whether or not free riding with respect to the public good of price and wage stability is a serious problem, that is, whether or not potentially strong inflationary forces at FE are contained. The presence or absence of these features goes far to explain why there was no correlation across countries between unemployment and inflation rates.

5.5 Why Phillips Curves Differ

Beyond the Phillips curve

The appreciable differences in unemployment rates and misery indices shown in figure 5.1 would be "explained" by many economists as simply due to differences in Phillips curves, each country observation in the diagram representing one point on its own Phillips curve.[7] Countries with high rates of unemployment have been forced to restrict AD in order to keep inflation rates down to rates experienced by countries faced with a more favorably placed Phillips curve. Unfortunately, this explanation is of little help to policy-makers intent upon improving the performance of the economy. Modeling inflation as a prisoner's dilemma was meant to suggest a means for probing deeper. Market behavior in economies in which fairness would be imposed by labor in wage settlements must be modified if inflationary pressures at FE are to be reduced. This leads straight to an analysis of what policies, rewards and punishments, and institutional frameworks support and en-

---

[6]It is often said that the purpose of an incomes policy is to make the Phillips curve steeper, not flatter. It would be more correct to say that when the authorities intend to fight inflation by increasing unemployment, a steep Phillips curve reduces the costs of restrictive AD policies. However, if the aim is to reduce unemployment, an incomes policy must aim to flatten the Phillips curve as the task of AD is then to stimulate the economy.

[7]For comparative studies incorporating institutional influences see Bruno and Sachs, *The Economics of Worldwide Stagflation*, chs. 10 and 11, and C. Bean, P. Layard, and S. Nickell, "Rise in unemployment."

force a more social form of conduct, that is, to a discussion of social bargains or incomes policies and the conditions required for their success. The conclusions, based on a country by country analysis, are qualitative in nature.

Two kinds of social bargains

At the center of any social bargain is the continuous functioning in the labor market of some kind of agreement, with both explicit and implicit elements which are embodied in convention and law, that outlines rewards and punishments to induce compliance with some wage (and price) goal or target. For example, labor would have the right to expect FE and additional welfare benefits if they restrain their wage demands and would face restrictive AD measures if they fail to live up to their obligations. Rewards and punishments to induce good conduct would also be available and known to employers.

The nature of the bargain need not be and was not identical across countries during this post-war period. Simplifying only moderately, it is helpful to think of all bargains falling into one of two pure types depending upon certain institutional features of an economy. On the one hand, there were those countries in which the labor movement was so strong that pro-labor governments were able to gain power for an appreciable part of the time. In these economies the bargain included the promise of FE, the introduction of welfare programs to enhance the "social wage" of labor, and tax schemes to reduce inequalities in the distribution of incomes. The main thrust of such bargains was first to cause centralized labor, because of its encompassing nature, to internalize the inflation costs of its wage demands, and second to transfer the distributional conflicts of the society from the labor market to the political sphere.

In contrast, there were economies in which the trade union movement had never been strong (but in which labor unions were accepted by management and government), the welfare state was never extensively developed (although the tax structure was relatively progressive), and pro-labor parties never governed alone, if at all, at the national level. In this type of environment, employers and government sought to convince labor that wage settlements must be influenced by their impact on, for example, export success or the profitability of the firm. In exchange for restraining their wage demands in this way, workers would receive various rewards, for example, bonus payments, good working conditions, acceptable grievance procedures, a share of productivity gains, and continuous employment. If successful, relatively moderate wage and price developments at the firm level aggregated into respectable overall inflation performances.

Some conditions for success

The post-war period is replete with examples of unsuccessful attempts to restrain inflation at FE. However, whichever of the two types of bargains is being considered, success (to be defined presently), when it was achieved, depended upon several conditions being met. First, only in those economies in which it was widely understood and accepted by government, labor, and employers that unrestricted collective bargaining was incompatible with FE and acceptable rates of inflation was it possible to realize these latter two goals (as well as external equilibrium) simultaneously for any period of time. Rejection of an uncritical belief in the curative powers of "market forces," "countervailing powers," or "invisible hands" has been a necessary condition for superior macroperformance, for only in these economies has it been clear that a constant effort on the part of government and others was necessary to make individual wage settlements consistent with some national goal of wage and price stability, that is, to make a permanent income policy work.

Second, in both cases bargains took place within an industrial relations system (IRS) that could be characterized as cooperative; labor-management relations started from a position of trust and cooperation, believing that there are always important areas of common agreement that must be preserved by continuous compromise and consultation.

Third, in both cases there was common agreement that the key to wage and price stability was wage stability. This was based on a realization that many prices cannot be influenced directly by policy, for example, imports, whereas most wages are set in domestic markets. In addition, the tendency of firms to set price using a relatively stable long-run percentage markup allowed for a relatively predictable indirect control of prices through an influence on wages.

Fourth, in both cases governments were prepared to provide in one form or another the kinds of leadership needed to bring wage and price settings into line with national goals. This need not have involved open intervention in collective bargaining. It did involve the introduction of supplementary policies to increase the likelihood of success of the bargain, for example, manpower policies to reduce labor market frictions and special programs for the long-term unemployed. However, in neither case was government prepared to engage in "union bashing."

Fifth, both kinds of bargains were structured to convince labor that restraint was in their long-run self-interest. Sixth, pronounced after-tax differences in incomes were prevented, at least compared with economies unable to work out a successful social bargain. On this reading, those economies in which a successful bargain could not be achieved faced much stronger inflationary pressures at every rate of unemployment. For some assumed level of demand for FE, policy-makers in these economies were less willing to supply it. The result was higher rates of unemployment.

5.6 Corporatism

Corporatist policy-making

The structures of policy-making that were operative during the period 1963–73 (and today), enabling both relatively low rates of inflation and low rates of unemployment, need elaboration. Some additional definitions are useful. The term corporatism has meant different things to different people, but in the present context it is most usefully referred to as an institutionalized pattern of economic policy-making. Large interest group organizations cooperate with each other and with public authorities, not only in the discussion of policies, in this case how to restrain wages and prices under FE conditions, but also in their implementation and monitoring. The term necessarily implies an ideology of social and political partnership (rather than class politics) that in varying degrees guides routine politics and industrial relations. In many cases the partnership and cooperation involve representatives of large highly centralized organizations ("peak organizations") which are encouraged by the state, granting the private groups a representational monopoly in decision-making. In all cases, however, the cooperative partnership element is seen as an important feature affecting behavior in the labor market.

As already suggested by the discussion of two types of bargains, corporatist policy-making operates within different kinds of institutional frameworks, depending upon such critical factors as (a) the coalitions that control the government, for example, whether it is dominated by business or labor groups, and (b) the nature of the political institutions and channels of influence available to the state and private groups. In particular, these "policy networks" will determine the degree to which representatives of unions, employers, and other organized interest groups are integrated into and cooperate with government agencies. As a result, the social bargain or system of rewards and punishments for compliance with general goals would vary.

Indices of corporatism

Social scientists (including economists more recently) have become interested in corporatist forms of policy-making because it has appeared to lead to more successful economic performance, for example, a lower rate of inflation at some unemployment rate and a reduction of industrial disputes as indicated by strike activity. To further establish this connection, indices have been developed that allow a ranking of capitalist economies in terms of their degree of corporatism.[8] A cross-country comparison is then made between the index and various measures of macroperformance to establish the relationship. From the total institutional framework these indices extract and measure differences between countries in those institutions that are considered most relevant in generating successful corporatist policies that overcome the problems of the prisoner's dilemma, thereby reducing if not eliminating an actual inflationary bias. As will become clear in the examples below, this requires institutional arrangements in which labor uses means other than maximum exploitation of their market power to protect their real and relative wages.

A successful bargain or incomes policy

Quite naturally, this effort to alter behavior has varied in intensity, as has success in containing inflation. Unfortunately, many economists have incorrectly designated those periods when an obvious effort was made to induce wage restraint, such as when statutory measures were introduced, as the periods when an incomes policy was in effect. Such short-run "shock" measures are then often found to be unsuccessful, for example, a decline in inflation rates during the implementation period is followed by a catch-up period. However, success of an incomes policy or social bargain and therefore superior macroperformance can be more sensibly defined as achieving FE with politically acceptable rates of inflation and with external equilibrium in some long-run sense.[9] Success will be so defined throughout this study since

[8] See Crouch, "Conditions for trade union wage restraint." Crouch's index was deleted from his final draft but was made available to others through the circulation of preliminary drafts.
[9] See R. Flanagan, D. Soskice, and L. Ulman, *Unionism, Economic Stabilization, and Incomes Policies: European Experience*, Brookings Institution, Washington, DC, 1983, for a treatment of incomes policies in the manner adopted here.

such an incomes policy relieves the authorities of both the constraints on AD policy discussed in the last chapter.[10]

5.7 Social Democratic Corporatism

One of the more popular indices defines and measures corporatism in terms of institutional characteristics of the union movement, the employer associations, and decision-making on the factory floor. For example, a country is assigned a high corporatist value if (a) unions belong to a limited number of federations in which collective bargaining is conducted by federation officials who also control union dues, (b) there is little shop-floor autonomy, with the rank and file having little say in wage bargaining or strikes, (c) there is cooperation and coordination of plans between employers, particularly if wage bargaining is centralized, and (d) institutions of codetermination, in which there is consultation and joint decision-making between management and the workers, are widespread at the plant level.[11]

High values for this corporatism index are earned by the Scandinavian countries, for example. These are countries with large highly centralized and powerful trade union movements that have, nonetheless, enjoyed rates of wage and price inflation no higher than, say, the two North American economies in which trade unions are weak and rates of unemployment were much higher. In these circumstances collective bargaining can be carried out through peak organizations that internalize the costs of their actions in such a way that money wage settlements are more easily made consistent with overall national goals of wage and price stability.[12]

The likelihood of success in countries with high index values is increased as they tend to develop a corporatist form of policy formulation and implementation, in which capital, labor, and pro-labor govern-

[10]This same criterion is captured in the "Scandinavian" model of inflation which requires that the rate of inflation in the "tradable" or "exposed" sector does not move too far out of line with inflation rates in the same sector of a country's trading partners; otherwise, under a fixed-rate regime, the country's competitiveness will suffer, either through rising relative prices or through a profit squeeze and reduced investment. For the early formulation see O. Aukrust, "PRIM I: a model of price and income distribution of an open economy," *Review of Income and Wealth*, 16, March 1970, 51–78.

[11]This index, developed by Crouch, is used by McCallum, "Inflation and social consensus," and Bruno and Sachs, *Economics of Worldwide Stagflation*, in their regressions, and in chapter 6 below.

[12]It has been argued that under a highly centralized union movement, it is more likely that a FE real wage will be chosen by the union. As argued in chapter 3, the money wage is what is determined in the labor market. See Jackman, "Wage formation in the Nordic countries."

ment each take an active part. Under these arrangements, policy networks develop that act to mediate and reconcile the demands of potentially competing organized interest groups. Such policy networks are especially important for the long-run success of an incomes policy. The term social democratic corporatism (SDC) is used to describe this system of policy-making and institutions aimed at reducing inflation at FE.

However, there are additional measures that support wage and price stability as the discussion of social bargains suggests. The SDC group of countries are characterized by large welfare programs; parliamentary decisions on the distributions of national output have been noticeably substituted for market-determined distributions. In this set of circumstances not only is the demand for FE likely to be strong, but the authorities will find themselves in a position to supply it since at least one possible adverse side effect, that is, severe inflation, is less likely. To be sure, a powerful centralized union movement may not cooperate in the interests of wage restraint, but centralized bargaining, pro-labor governments, and other features such as manpower programs would increase the likelihood of the success of a voluntary (consensus) incomes policy. A low rate of unemployment is one reward for cooperation. Austria, Denmark, Finland, Germany, The Netherlands, Norway, Sweden, and Switzerland have been described as countries with institutions and policy networks that satisfy this description. Others have treated Switzerland (and The Netherlands, Germany, and Belgium) somewhat differently. This alternative form of corporatism is considered in sections 5.10 and 5.11.[13]

5.8 Pluralist Economies

Unfortunately, the usefulness of the index of corporatism outlined in section 5.17 is weakened by its registering low values for countries with different policy networks, bargains, and party control but nonetheless with successful corporatist policy formation. This will be considered further in the next three sections. Such indices fare quite well, however, in predicting performances in what will be called pluralist economies. Thus, in sharp contrast with the SDC framework, consider

---

[13]See Crouch, "Conditions for trade union wage restraint," for the former treatment of Switzerland (and other countries); and P. Katzenstein, "Capitalism in one country?: Switzerland in the international economy," *International Organization*, 34, Autumn 1980, 507–40, for a different view.

a country with a decentralized low density trade union movement and an absence of any employers' federation so that collective bargaining takes place at the firm or even the plant level. Allow further that the IRS is adversarial in the sense that business and labor start from the position that economic relations are dominated by areas of conflicting interests, that the welfare state is poorly developed, and that the governing party is pro-business. Finally assume that government has consistently failed to play an active leadership role in reconciling sectoral differences in the interests of national goals and in reducing structural unemployment problems. Either "invisible hands," "market forces," and "countervailing powers" are assigned these tasks or, as in the case of a country like Italy, government intervention has been in support of one side of the market.

Taken together, such institutional characteristics define pluralist economies and would generate a low to zero value on any corporatist scale. More importantly, they describe a configuration of institutions that leads to labor's seeking its "fair share" in what it considers to be the only way possible, through pressing its market power to the limit. In this case, money wage demands will intensify as unemployment falls and as the kinds of prisoner's dilemmas just described become more operative, generating strong inflationary pressures at FE or even before it is reached. As a result of these institutional and political factors, governments in these countries are forced to adopt a less than FE policy stance, given their concern with inflation. Canada, Ireland, Italy, and the United States can be cited as countries that fit this description. In all four countries both the demand for and the supply of FE would be weak. The case of the United Kingdom is somewhat different and is discussed below.

5.9 Bourgeois Democratic Corporatism

There is much to be said for an institutional-party control explanation of unemployment rates and Phillips curves and their differences across countries that singles out and contrasts SDC and pluralist countries. However, social scientists who see successful economic performance as the outcome of the social democratic form of corporatism and poor performance as due to pluralist institutions have a tendency to overemphasize the importance of the centralization of the labor movement and to downplay the importance of other kinds of political coalitions and policy networks that have achieved favorable economic performance.[14]

The performances of Japan and Switzerland show that this association between the degree of centralization of key institutions, union density, party control, and the size of the welfare state on the one hand, and unemployment policy and performance on the other, is not as clear cut as some writers have argued. Both countries have weak decentralized trade union movements, undeveloped welfare states, and party control has been dominated by right-of-center parties.[15] Yet their unemployment and inflation (and strike) records are exemplary. Clearly left-of-center party control, a developed welfare state, and strong centrally organized trade union movements are not necessary conditions for the achievement of FE with acceptable rates of inflation. Something is missing in the SDC–pluralist dichotomy as an explanation of the relative demand for FE and the ability or inability to supply it. In particular, there is a neglect of alternative institutions, rewards systems, and bargains for inducing socially beneficial forms of economic behavior.[16]

Social scientists who have been aware of these alternative paths to FE often have been forced to fall back on descriptive phrases such as the "dominant sociocultural political norms," "paternalistic capitalism," or "corporatism without unions" to indicate the overriding force that allows FE to be supplied.[17] What these expressions suggest are institutional, historical, and political developments that have led not only to a strong desire on the part of the authorities to supply FE, but also to an ability to do so without sizable adverse side effects. Thus it has been argued that in both countries historical developments have fostered the growth of institutions of cooperation and trust between

[14]See A. Newell and J. Symons, "Corporatism, laissez-faire and the rise in unemployment," *European Economic Review*, 31 (3), 1987, 567–601. While allowing that Japan somehow became corporatist in the 1970s, the critical feature of corporatism to these authors is centralized wage settings. As the text makes clear, wage setting in Japan is anything but centralized.
  Furthermore, the authors err in their assertion that corporatism operates against the interests of workers because in the absence of a successful corporatist policy, while unemployment would be higher, real wages of the employed would be greater. On the contrary, a successful income policy leads to FE and FE leads to higher rates of growth of productivity and real wages for all workers. In contrast, high unemployment rates lead to reduced rates of growth of productivity of employed workers, and therefore reduced rates of growth of their real wages.
[15]The lack of a developed welfare state is compensated somewhat in Switzerland by widespread private pension schemes. See Katzenstein, "Capitalism in one country?"
[16]In many studies that stress the influence of corporatism on macroperformance, Japan and Switzerland are either ignored or given slight attention.
[17]See M. Schmidt, "The politics of unemployment: rates of unemployment and labour market policy," *West European Politics*, 7, July 1984, 5–24.

workers and employers, leading to a highly cooperative IRS. This is revealed most dramatically in the low strike records and in the willingness of workers to reduce their wage demands when their company has experienced a decline in profits and sales or when such declines are predicted. Money wages (or at least their rates of growth) have proved to be flexible downward in these conditions, allowing companies to regain their profitability as inflation rates fall.[18] The result is that the cost of FE policies in terms of inflation or loss of export markets is low. All this can be put more concretely by considering separately the institutions and policy networks that have contributed to the commendable macroperformance in these two economies.

5.10 Alternative Forms of Corporatism—Switzerland

The uniqueness of the Swiss form of economic policy-making is expressed in the term consociational—a form of governing in which policy-making is carried out within a society with several political parties, each having a loyal constituency (usually with a religious or ethnic basis) but none commanding a majority. The result is a long tradition of coalition governments and political and economic compromise. These coalitions have included labor as part of the governing coalition despite its weak support at the polls and the dominant position of internationally minded capital in the economy.

Certain other features impart a special character to coalition governments in Switzerland: they are lasting, encompassing, and rather noninnovative. These features have been attributed largely to the importance of direct democracy in Switzerland. Legislative decisions are subject to mandatory referenda and the constitutional right of popular initiative exists. As a result, to prevent challenges to legislative decisions, coalitions are formed that are encompassing enough to have a safe chance of winning both parliamentary and popular votes.[19] To ensure this, an elaborate system of advisory committees and expert commissions has been established that allows proportional representation for the large number of diversified groups that make up the special interest group structure of Switzerland. This allows all potentially ef-

---

[18]See R. Kastli, "The new economic environment in the 1970s: market and policy response in Switzerland," in M. de Cecco (ed.), *International Economic Adjustment: Small Countries and the European Monetary System*, St. Martin's Press, New York, 1982.

[19]See P. Katzenstein, *Corporatism and Change: Austria, Switzerland and the Politics of Industry*, Cornell University Press, Ithaca, NY, 1984. As mentioned in section 5.7 in important ways. Belgium, The Netherlands, and Germany contain similar institutional features.

fective sources of opposition to find a way of having their views heard, leading to a consensus on important proposed legislation.[20] Naturally these kinds of pre-parliamentary forms of bargaining give most groups a feeling of participation and give them actual governance in a form of corporatist policy-making.

The inclusion of organized labor in advisory groups and government is considered to be particularly critical in inducing socially beneficial behavior in the labor market. It is seen by labor as an indication of a general acceptance of unions by government and business in contrast to the attitudes taken by these groups in, say, North America. However, in addition, and in a manner similar to the SDC countries, labor representatives play a role in making, administering, and monitoring policies.[21]

This spirit of compromise and trust which permeates Swiss society and politics naturally spills over to the economy and to the labor market in particular. In fact, labor and management voluntarily agree annually to resolve labor conflicts through negotiations first and, if that fails, to use binding arbitration. Strikes, lockouts, and boycotts are outlawed in these agreements which cover approximately 90 percent of the private sector. Compromise at the enterprise level is also reflected in wage and unemployment decisions. Shortfalls in demand are shared by workers and management. Workers have shown a willingness to take wage cuts in such circumstances and employers have responded by reducing profit margins and dividends. Work sharing rather than layoffs for the indigenous labor force and the absence of automatic wage indexation are also characteristics of Swiss labor markets.[22] The overall result is that labor sees itself as having a stake in wage restraint and industrial harmony and, in so doing, achieving FE and rising living standards.

5.11 Alternative Forms of Corporatism—Japan

The Japanese system of economic policy-making has often been referred to as corporatism without unions. Unlike Switzerland, labor par-

---

[20]Katzenstein, ibid., states that economic policy making is largely in the hands of five groups rather than political parties.

[21]One writer (Crouch, "Conditions for trade union restraint") has even concluded that inclusion in a coalition government achieves the same results that would be forthcoming under labor party rule under the SDC model. As mentioned earlier, Crouch also finds traces of consociational forms of governance in The Netherlands, Austria, and Belgium.

[22]See J. Danthine and J. Lambelet, "The Swiss recipe: conservative policies aren't enough," *Economic Policy*, 2 (5), 1987.

ties have never been brought into any coalition government (let alone governed by themselves). Policy-making can be described as corporatist, however, as representatives of big business and agricultural interests have been treated as partners along with government in the making and implementation of policies. Policy networks have developed in which all major industries in Japan have been organized into powerful trade associations with representatives appointed with the authority to act on behalf of the firms composing the industry. These representatives deal directly with government bureaus or departments (the Ministry of Trade and Industry, or MITI, in the case of most economic policy-making) in developing and implementing policies.[23]

The Japanese trade union movement is composed of hundreds of autonomous trade unions organized at the company level (as in Switzerland) with collective bargaining activities in any one labor market only loosely coordinated with developments in others.[24] With labor excluded from policy-making at the national level and little in the way of a welfare state to provide it with a high social wage, strong wage–wage and wage–price inflation at FE would seem likely. Yet the evidence clearly indicates that inflationary pressures under FE conditions have been contained as well as in most other economies, and when inflation did get out of hand it was quickly brought under control without drastic increases in unemployment rates. This suggests that some other form of bargain was struck to reduce wage–wage and wage–price inflationary pressures at FE under a decentralized union structure.

The key institutions in understanding this are the development of institutions of cooperation or codetermination at the company level (as in Switzerland) and a system of pay very much influenced by the actual performance of the company, that is, the bonus system. As has become well known, the large modern Japanese corporation is part of the Japanese worker's extended family. The performance of the company reflects not only on management but on the worker's own sense of self-esteem. However, a large reservoir of trust between management and workers also exists within the Japanese company, so much so that when management stresses the need for wage restraint during negotiations to protect profits and export markets, such statements are

---
[23]See T. Pempel and K. Tsunekawa, "Corporatism without labour? The Japanese anomaly," in P. Schmitter and G. Lehmbruch (eds.), *Trends Towards Corporatist Intermediation*, Sage Publications, Beverly Hills, CA, 1979.

[24]Collective bargaining is synchronized, however, with consultation between union leaders before settlement.

106 *Framework*

believed. To a large extent this trust arises out of the terms of employment that give workers something like lifetime tenure, various large nonpecuniary benefits, and an ability to participate as junior partners in shop-floor decision-making.[25] The result is a form of bargain that, among other things, acts to reduce inflationary pressures. For example, when export markets are thought to be endangered by foreign price competition, management has been able to induce workers to restrain their contractual wage demands.

On average, however, a large share of wages in the modern Japanese company is the result of a bonus system whereby payments are made on the basis of the recent profitability of the company. This not only leads to a less rapid increase in labor costs for any particular company that is suffering from low profits, but also enables the authorities to induce wage and therefore price restraint through threatened or actual restrictive AD policies since the latter will lead to reduced sales and profits. The willingness of Japanese companies to maintain employment and allow dividends to fall in these circumstances aids in achieving workers' cooperation. This automatic stabilizer, together with a willingness of Japanese workers to accept reduced contractual pay increases, was most apparent in the mid-1970s when the rate of wage and price inflation in Japan was drastically reduced without large increases in unemployment. Together these institutions work to contain inflationary pressures at FE in most circumstances or, as in the early 1970s when inflation rates soared, to allow the authorities to rapidly reduce inflation rates without high unemployment costs.[26]

5.12 Why the Cross-country Phillips Curve is Horizontal

The structure of full employment economies

The structure of the union movements and collective bargaining, the politics of the ruling parties, the policy networks, the development of the welfare state, and the power of labor in the SDC economies varied greatly from Japan and Switzerland. However, these two share important common features with the SDC economies. In all these economies the IRS could be characterized as cooperative. Labor and management develop a strong feeling of mutual trust that is quite distinct from attitudes in the high unemployment pluralist countries. The low strike

[25]See Cornwall, *Conditions for Economic Recovery*, pp. 304–7.
[26]Ibid., p. 264–67, and R. Freeman and M. Weitzman, "Bonuses and employment in Japan," *NBER Working Papers Series*, No. 1878, April 1986.

record in the two nonpluralist subgroups is but one manifestation of the important similarities between two otherwise quite diverse groups of countries.[27]

The mechanisms or policy networks used to achieve success differed because the industrial *structure* of the countries making up the two groups differed, as did the relative power of capital and labor. However, compared with the mechanisms of conflict resolution in the high unemployment countries, the similarities in matters of significance, that is, the industrial *relations* systems of these countries, were apparent. As a result, while the demand for FE might vary between these two groups because of differences in political power, the supply of FE was forthcoming because the nature of the IRS helped remove an important supply constraint. To put it differently, there was little reason *not* to supply FE in these countries.

The high unemployment countries

The poor employment records of the two North American countries and of Ireland and Italy have already been discussed. The argument can be rephrased in terms of the demand for and supply of FE. Thus the demand for FE was low in Canada, Ireland, Italy, and the United States largely because of the weak position of the trade unions and weakness or lack of left-of-center political parties. The willingness of governments to supply FE was also weak for several reasons. A fear of inflation that could not be controlled if unemployment was reduced to rates similar to the low unemployment countries was the most pressing. Related to this was an unwillingness in all four countries to introduce labor market policies that would reduce structural unemployment at every unemployment rate and a greater independence of the central banks compared with many of the low unemployment countries.[28] Finally, a desire by governments largely

---

[27]McCallum's index of strike volume gives mean value of 3.5 for a group of OECD countries comprised of SDC countries plus Japan and Switzerland. The remaining OECD countries in his sample have a mean value of 4.9 for this index. See McCallum, "Unemployment in the OECD countries," table 4, and table 6.1 below.

[28]See Woolley, "Monetary policy instrumentation." It is always possible to fall back on "structural" explanations of high unemployment in these cases. According to this alternative view, imperfections in the labor market prevented the ready absorption of the unemployed. While this view has force, it is largely neglected in this study, partly because the greater structural problems in some economies could have been combated by private and government-run policies should the authorities have wished to introduce them. We have only to think of German entrepreneurs seeking out, hiring, and retraining Turkish peasant women to work in Germany to see the weakness of the structural explanations of high unemployment.

108 *Framework*

unsympathetic to labor to reduce the power of labor in these countries should be considered.

The performance in the United Kingdom has still to be accounted for. Here the trade union movement was decentralized, the industrial relations system was highly adversarial, and there was no strong tradition of government providing leadership in reconciling competing economic demands, that is, in pursuing corporatist policies. On the basis of what has just been said, it would be expected that the United Kingdom would have been faced with a poorly positioned Phillips curve and therefore would have experienced a rather poor combined unemployment and inflation rate, that is, a high misery index. Instead the 1963–73 record reveals a moderate rate of unemployment and inflation rates no higher than average for the sample.

An explanation of this anomaly is available. The demand for FE would be relatively strong because the trade union movement is strong when measured in numbers. Other things being equal, this would lead to low unemployment rates. However, the trade union movement is decentralized and decentralized decision-making in an adversarial environment leads to strong wage–price and wage–wage inflationary pressures at FE. The result of these two institutional characteristics of the British labor force was an upward trend in both inflation and unemployment rates during the period 1963–73. The former trend would have contributed importantly to the persistent payments problems, thereby reinforcing the latter trend.

5.13 Conclusion

As will be apparent in the next chapter, any attempt to measure the relative importance of the strength of the demand for and supply of FE and to use such measures to predict performance is fraught with dangers and difficulties. The data are crude and our ignorance of these matters is very great. However, none of this should detract or subtract from the truth of the message of this chapter. Successful macroperformance is intimately tied up with the institutional setting in which the authorities must operate. Inheriting an institutional framework that is not of their making, some policy-makers would have had to implement much more radical policies than they did if the performance of their economies was to match others. The required policy-induced institutional changes were not forthcoming.

6 Econometric Tests of Institutional Influences

6.1 Introduction

Having considered several different kinds of economies differentiated by their modes of conflict resolution, that is, whether attempts were made to work out a social bargain between labor, management, and government and, if so, what kind of bargain, some general conclusions were reached with respect to the relative strengths of the demand for and supply of FE and the impact of these influences on policy and performance. Even conceding the point that explaining macroeconomic performance in terms of institutional forces does not lend itself to exact causal connections and definite conclusions, there is much to be gained by formalizing the analysis somewhat and even employing standard econometric tests of such a theory.

The main task to be performed in this chapter is to account quantitatively for important differences in the macroeconomic performances of the OECD countries in the period before 1974. Attempts to explain why growth rates differ have become fairly commonplace in applied macroeconomics.[1] Here the analysis considers why unemployment rates and misery indices differed across countries and does so within a demand and supply framework. This is done by selecting and quantifying those features of an economy thought to represent the demand for FE and the ability and willingness of the authorities to supply FE.

6.2 Measures of Social Bargains

Crouch's corporatist index

Previous studies stress the importance of wage setting and the manner in which it is carried out as a key determinant of success in controlling

---

[1]For example, E. Denison, *Why Growth Rates Differ: Postwar Experience in Nine Countries*, Brookings Institution, Washington, DC, 1967; and J. Cornwall, *Modern Capitalism: Its Growth and Transformation*, Blackwell, Oxford, 1977.

inflation at FE. As noted in chapter 5, Crouch singles out four characteristics of an industrial relations system as critical in this regard.

1. How centralized is the union side in collective bargaining?
2. How centralized is the employer's association?
3. How much rank and file autonomy is allowed in collective bargaining decisions?
4. How widespread are institutions of codetermination or cooperation throughout the IRS?

Trade union movements with highly centralized collective bargaining structures facing centralized employers' associations receive two points in his corporatist index with additional points obtained if there is little rank and file autonomy and if institutions of codetermination are widespread. Maximum values of four are achieved by Austria, Germany, The Netherlands, Norway, and Sweden.

There is much to applaud in this heroic effort to abstract a few key features critical for success from the institutional framework. This index rightly stresses the importance of encompassing organizations as they assist in internalizing social costs. It implicitly rejects the concept of an invisible hand; instead, it emphasizes the value of a spirit of cooperation in the labor market. It does not include a measure of the size of the welfare state, efforts to redistribute income through progressive taxation, manpower programs, or the importance of party control. However, since left-wing governments, highly progressive tax systems, and well-developed welfare states tend to coexist in countries with highly centralized trade union movements, these other influences are picked up to some extent in the index.

What the index fails to account for are other types of social bargains that, according to the earlier analysis, also lead to superior macroperformance.[2] What chapter 5 emphasized is that there are other configurations of institutions that are and have been conducive to wage restraint under FE conditions. Thus, even without highly centralized peak organizations, it is clear that in some economies a bargain was reached in which labor sought its fair share of income through means other than maximum exertion of its market power, that is, through the maximum short-run increase in money wages that the market would bear. In order to allow for the possibility of two distinct kinds of social

---

[2]For example, Switzerland, Japan, and Belgium scored low on Crouch's index with corporatist values of 2.0, 1.5, and 0.5 respectively. See McCallum, "Unemployment in the OECD countries."

bargain (arising out of two quite different industrial relations and power structures), different variables reflecting the likelihood of success must be used. Some measure of strike activity has been used in other studies and is adopted here.[3]

Strike volume

The general rationale of the approach can be put in two ways. First, strikes are a manifestation of conflict in the labor market between capital and labor. Those economies with high levels of strike activity will also be subject to relatively high levels of money wage demands and settlements at any level of unemployment but especially at FE. Second, in a world of uncertainty, labor at the firm level must rely largely on the information provided by management with regard to the economic condition of the firm, especially its current and future competitiveness. Most important is the alleged size of wage increases consistent with the preservation of the firm and the jobs it provides. The greater is the degree of trust on the part of the workers in response to such pronouncements by management, the less likely will be the aims of the two sides to diverge in a wage dispute and therefore the less likely will there be excessive wage settlements and strikes. If this carries over to the national level, then again a low level of strike activity nationwide will reflect a labor market climate leading to success.[4] According to the view advocated here, the higher the strike activity in a country, other things being equal, the higher will be the rate of wage and therefore price inflation at any level of unemployment, that is, the more poorly positioned will be the Phillips curve, and the higher therefore will be the rate of unemployment permitted by the authorities.[5]

Strike records

Table 6.1 records the average strike volume, that is, the number of mandays lost per 1,000 workers, for 18 OECD economies for selected postwar periods. While strike activity within each country varied appreciably

---
[3]See, for example, McCallum, ibid.

[4]McCallum, "Inflation and social consensus," discusses these points and the relevant background literature. See also M. Paldam, "Industrial conflict and the Phillips curve—an international perspective," *Memo 80–4/5, Institute of Economics,* Aarhus University, pp. 1–37, 1980.

[5]Note that the emphasis of the text is on causation running from strikes to inflation. There is a theory that reverses this causation, arguing that it is inflation that causes strikes. However, work by Paldam strongly supports the position that conflict or strikes lead the wage–price increases. See M. Paldam, ibid. Furthermore, this reverse causation is a time-dependent relationship whereas the regressions in the text are cross-country.

112   *Framework*

Table 6.1   Average volume of strike activity for 18 OECD economies for selected periods

	1955–62	1963–73	1974–79	1980–88
Italy	412	870	1067	465
Canada	284	590	878	444
Ireland	139	464	620	316
USA	435	464	312	106
Australia	228	297	601	302
UK	185	296	491	333
Finland	63[a]	351	350	372
Belgium	282	146	193	60[b]
France	116	162	160	57
Denmark	282	171	71	169
Sweden	1	37	25	176
Japan	121	76	78	8
New Zealand	47	128	279	384
Norway	150	24	55	97
Germany	25	27	42	26
The Netherlands	30	26	21	14
Austria	66	16	1	14
Switzerland	0	3	2	0

[a] 1958–62.
[b] 1980.

Source: ILO, *Yearbook of Labour Statistics*, Geneva, various issues.

over time, differences across country in every period were substantial and even more dramatic. For example, in 1963–73 the average number of man-days lost per 1,000 workers varied from 870 in Italy to 3 in Switzerland. These differences are interpreted as reflecting differences in cooperativeness within the industrial relations system. Drawing a horizontal line across the table in such a way as to separate Finland from Belgium strongly suggests a bimodal distribution of strike activity. For example, taking the period 1963–79, the mean value of strike activity from the countries above and below this dividing line is 527 and 87 man-days lost respectively, with standard deviations of 280 and 65 respectively.

6.3 Simple Correlations

As a preliminary to more elaborate multiple regression analysis, simple correlations between different measures of strike volume and macroperformance were computed. Table 6.2 presents correlation coefficients for either the average volume or the logarithm of the average volume of strike activity and average rates of unemployment and val-

Table 6.2 Simple correlations between unemployment rates/misery indices U/MI and average volume of strike activity S for selected periods

	U/MI (1963–73)	U/MI (1974–9)	U/MI (1980–4)
S (1955–73)	0.82^a/0.66^a	–	–
S (1963–73)	0.87^a/0.74^a	–	–
log S (1950–69)	0.70^a/0.67^a	–	–
S (1963–79)	–	0.70^a/0.80^a	–
S (1974–9)	–	0.64^a/0.78^a	–
S (1974–84)	–	–	0.46^b/0.70^a
S (1980–4)	–	–	0.38^b/0.69^a
log S (1950–78)	–	0.70^a/0.82^a	0.56^b/0.68^a

[a] Significant at the 99 percent level.
[b] Significant at the 95 percent level.

ues of the misery index, that is, the sum of unemployment and inflation rates, for selected periods. Account is taken of the possibility that the relevant years determining the cooperativeness in the labor market may sometimes precede as well as correspond to the performance period.

In all three periods, but especially 1963–73 and 1974–79, the simple correlations between both the unemployment rate and the misery index and the average volume of strikes are high. For example, average strike volume in 1963–73 correlates highly with the average unemployment rate ($r = 0.87$) and the misery index ($r = 0.74$) for 1963–73. Other measures of strike volume give similar results. The relationship is maintained in the period 1974–79 with the volume of strikes in 1963–79, 1974–79, and the logarithm of strike volume in 1950–78 all correlated with performance for 1974–79 at a highly significant level. By the 1980s the relationship has weakened somewhat but still remains high, especially for the misery index. While no a priori justification for the use of any particular measure of the strike variable is available, the mere fact that a number of measures of cooperativeness in the labor market and the likely success of social bargains are significantly correlated with performance is supportive of the approach adopted here (and in other studies).

6.4 Unemployment Rates, 1963–1973

The variables

Cross-country regressions of unemployment rates, wage and price inflation rates, and the misery index were run for 18 OECD countries covering the period 1963–73, using standardized unemployment rates available from the LSE data set.[6] This represented a period

[6] *The Revised OECD Data Set*, Centre for Labour Economics, London School of Economics.

of sustained boom throughout the OECD before the full impact of the first oil shock. It was assumed that external conditions facing each economy were similar enough that the impact of domestic institutional forces could be isolated. In chapter 7 regression analysis is employed to cover a much more extended period of time.

In the regression analysis for the period 1963–73, the dependent variables were regressed against various political and economic institutional variables as well as more conventional economic variables applying ordinary least-squares techniques. Proxies used to measure the presence or absence of those institutional features that allow FE at acceptable rates of inflation included Crouch's corporatist index C_j and the average volume of strike activity S_j in a country for either 1955–62, 1955–73, and 1963–73 or the logarithm of strike volume for 1950–69.[7] Both the corporatist and strike variables are used as measures of the degree of cooperation between employers and workers, not merely with respect to shop-floor activities but also cooperation between these two and government in furthering wage and price stability.[8] Accordingly, both variables are hypothesized to influence the position of the Phillips curve and therefore the inflation costs of any unemployment rate. A high strike volume would lead to a badly positioned curve while a high degree of corporatism would lead to a favorable tradeoff.

The political or party control variables tested were votes for left-of-center parties in any country on average for 1946–76, the share of cabinet posts held by left-of-center parties in 1965–81, and the average percentage of the labor force unionized in 1946–76. It was hypothesized, for example, that if two countries had similar strike records (and therefore similar inflation rates at any unemployment rate), the country with the stronger leftist vote would have the lower unemployment record. These variables representing the demand for FE were meant to test whether a prolonged period of, say, pro-left voting sentiments or strong union power generated a political attitude which was conducive to a low unemployment policy.[9] Additional predetermined variables included the average rate of price inflation in a previous period and the

---

[7]At this stage it was not considered feasible to experiment with other time periods for the simple reason that so little work has been done that would indicate the appropriate intervals to use. The same remarks apply to the adopted demand for FE variables.

[8]They are highly correlated with $r = -0.74$.

[9]See Rothschild, " 'Left' and 'right' in Federal Europe." The cross-country approach overcomes problems associated with lags, while holding external influences on policy outcomes constant.

Table 6.3 Cross-country regressions for unemployment rates U, wage inflation rates $\dot{w}$, and misery indices MI in 18 OECD countries for 1963–73

		$\bar{R}^2$
1	$U_j = 0.94 + 6.05 S_j^a$ $(0.22)\ \ (0.73)$	0.77
2	$U_j = 3.68 - 0.71 C_j^a$ $(0.47)\ \ (0.20)$	0.33
3	$U_j = 2.00 + 5.32 S_j^a - 0.03 L_j$ $(0.62)\ \ (0.79)\ \ \ \ (0.02)$	0.80
4	$U_j = 4.86 - 0.53 C_j^a - 0.05 L_j$ $(0.74)\ \ (0.22)\ \ \ \ (0.03)$	0.46
5	$U_j = 2.28 + 5.94 S_j^a - 0.04 L_j^b$ $(0.66)\ \ (0.99)\ \ \ \ (0.02)$	0.75
6	$U_j = 0.86 + 0.72 S_j^a - 0.07 L_j^a$ $(1.1)\ \ \ (0.16)\ \ \ \ (0.02)$	0.65
7	$\dot{w}_j = 4.75 + 1.27 \dot{q}_j^a$ $\phantom{\dot{w}_j = }(0.89)\ \ (0.21)$	0.65
8	$\mathrm{MI}_j = 5.83 + 6.40 S_j^a$ $\phantom{\mathrm{MI}_j = }(0.29)\ \ (0.99)$	0.62
9	$\mathrm{MI}_j = 2.88 + 0.90 S_j^a$ $\phantom{\mathrm{MI}_j = }(1.3)\ \ \ (0.25)$	0.42

The dependent variables U, $\dot{w}$, and MI are respectively the average rates of unemployment and wage inflation and the sum of the rates of price inflation and unemployment (the misery index) for 1963–73; S is a measure of strike volume. In regressions 1, 3, and 8 the average strike volume for 1963–73 is used. Regressions 6 and 9 use the logarithm of strike volume for 1950–69, and regression 5 uses the volume of strikes for 1955–62. L is the percentage of left votes for 1946–76, $\dot{q}$ is the average rate of growth of labor productivity for 1963–73, and C is Crouch's index of corporatism.

The data for the dependent variables are taken from the LSE data bank; the strike and corporatist data have been constructed from International Labor Organization sources or are taken from McCallum, "Inflation and social consensus." The voting data are taken from Korpi, *The Democratic Class Struggle*, Routledge and Kegan Paul, London, 1983, p. 38, and the productivity data are taken from *Historical Statistics*, OECD, Paris, various issues.

The subscript values in parentheses are standard errors. The $\bar{R}^2$ values are corrected for degrees of freedom.

[a] Significant at the 5 percent level.
[b] Significant at the 10 percent level.

rate of growth of productivity during the period. Neither was ever significant.

The regression results

Table 6.3 summarizes the regression results. What stands out clearly in the regressions is the importance of the strike variable in explaining differences in unemployment across countries and its superiority to the corporatist variable. This is true whatever strike measure is used, further attesting to the robustness of the variable. As seen in regressions 1 and 2 in table 6.3, each variable when entered separately has the correct sign but the (adjusted) R^2 value is substantially higher for the regressions with the strike variable. When they appear together in the same regression, the corporatist variable is nonsignificant. Depending on the strike variable used, the R^2 value varies from 0.46 to 0.77, with the average strike volume 1963–73 giving the best result.

Strike volume measures the number of man-days lost from strikes per 1,000 workers. The coefficient for the volume of strike variable in regression 1 reveals, for example, that for every extra 100 man-days lost by strikes per thousand workers, the unemployment rate rises by 0.605 percent. Similarly, regression 1 predicts that the higher strike volume in Italy relative to Switzerland, 870 compared with 3 man-days lost, should result in an Italian unemployment rate 5.24 (= 6.05 × 0.867) percent higher than in Switzerland. The actual unemployment rate difference was 5.3 percent. The explanation of unemployment differences is as follows. The higher the volume of strike activity, the greater will be the degree of conflict in the labor market over the distribution of income and the farther from the origin will be the Phillips curve. Therefore the higher will be the inflation costs of any unemployment rate, the more restrictive will be AD policy, and the higher will be the rate of unemployment.

Party control or demand variables were also included on the right-hand side of the right-hand side of the regressions. The percentage of votes L_j for left-of-center parties always gave better statistical results than the percentage of the labor force unionized or the share of leftist cabinet posts, and neither of the latter was significant when either variable was used in the same regression equation as the leftist vote variable. The inclusion of a demand for FE variable with either a strike or corporatist variable very much increased R^2 (whatever strike variable was used) and was significant at the 5 percent and 10 percent levels respectively, when the logarithm of the volume of strikes in 1950–69 (regression 6) and the volume of strikes in 1955–62 (regression 5) were used.

6.5 Unemployment Accounting

The discussion earlier pointed out that the party control explanation of cross-country differences in unemployment rates could not explain

Table 6.4 Estimated sources of differences in unemployment rates U between the United States and Switzerland, 1963–73, implicit in table 6.3, regression 6

Actual difference in U	Predicted difference in U	Sources of Difference	
		S	L
4.50	4.65	3.46	1.19

why such countries as Japan and Switzerland, with weak trade union movements and right-of-center pro-business governments, experienced low unemployment rates. Rather than reject the party control explanation of policy choice and unemployment outcomes out of hand, it was suggested that additional influences on unemployment rates needed to be considered in order to determine whether such political influences were important.

Including the strike (or corporatist) variable in the regressions along with a political control demand variable illustrates this strategy, as the former is intended to hold constant some portion of the inflation cost of unemployment. As regressions 3–6 make clear, once this is done the political demand variable enters with the right sign and increases R^2 substantially. What must not be lost sight of, however, is that the strike variable alone is capable of explaining up to 77 percent of the variation in unemployment rates across economies. Regression 6 in table 6.3 can be used to bring out other implications of the approach. The coefficient of the logarithm of strike volume variable indicates that a 1 percent increase in the volume of strikes leads to an increase of approximately 0.75 percent in unemployment rates. However, the coefficient for the "party control" variable reveals that a 1 percent increase in left-of-center votes leads to a reduction of approximately 0.07 percent in the unemployment rate because of the greater demand for low unemployment.

Consider further the implications set out in table 6.4. The average values of the logarithm of strike volume for Switzerland and the United States for 1950–69 were 1.4 and 6.2, while average unemployment rates for 1963–73 were zero and 4.5 percent respectively. Of this difference of 4.5 percent in unemployment rates, 3.46 (= 0.72 × 4.8) percent can be accounted for by a more favorably placed Phillips curve and therefore a lower cost of unemployment according to regression 6.

Party control as represented by the percentage of left-of-center votes cast in national elections in 1946–76 was on average 18 percent in

118 *Framework*

Switzerland and 1 percent in the United States. Thus the 17 percentage point difference in the demand for FE variable leads to a 1.19 (= 0.07 x 17) percent difference in unemployment rates in Switzerland compared with the United States. Together the stronger demand for FE and the greater willingness to supply FE in Switzerland accounted for a 4.65 (= 3.46 + 1.19) percent difference in predicted unemployment rates between the two countries.

6.6 Cross-country Differences in the Misery Index, Price Inflation, and Wage Inflation, 1963–1973

The regressions undertaken to explain price inflation rates were unsuccessful.[10] This very much suggests that the authorities were attempting to keep the rate of inflation in their own country in line with their major trading partners or some key country, for example, the United States, as outlined in the Scandinavian models of inflation.

Variables such as strike activity and leftist votes also proved unsatisfactory in explaining cross-country differences in rates of wage inflation. What did prove to be significant were differences in rates of growth of labor productively $\dot{q}$ as seen in regression 7. Almost two thirds of the cross-country differences in rates of wage inflation can be explained by cross-country differences in productivity growth alone.

Finally, several regressions with the misery index as the dependent variable were tried. Regressions 8 and 9 set out typical results. The volume of strikes in 1963–73 and the logarithm of strike volume in 1950–69 are each highly significant, especially the former as seen by regression 8. Both regressions reveal the impact of the relative success of a social bargain as measured by strike volume on overall inflation and unemployment performance. For example, in regression 8 an increase in the average volume of strikes by 100 man-days per 1,000 workers increases the misery index by 0.64 (= 6.4 x 0.1) percent.

A comparison of the predictions for the United States and Switzerland is again useful. In 1963–73, the average values of the misery index in the United States and Switzerland were 8.1 percent and 4.5 percent respectively, and as seen in table 6.1 the average volume of strikes was 464 man-days and 3 man-days lost per 1,000 workers in

---

[10]As already indicated, the sample mean and variance for the average rate of inflation in 1963–73 are 4.9 and 0.95 respectively. The lack of variability of inflation rates across countries during this period contrasts greatly with subsequent periods. The sample means and variances for the average rates of inflation are 10.2 percent and 12.6 percent respectively in 1974–79, and 8.8 percent and 12.0 percent respectively in 1980–84.

the same two countries. Of this difference of 3.6 percent in the misery indices, 2.95 (= 6.4 × 0.461) is accounted for by differences in strike volume.

6.7 Tarantelli's Study

The significance of the regression results become clearer if a comparison is made with another similar study. Consider Tarantelli's attempt to explain differences across countries in the misery index for three different post-war periods in terms of an index of "neocorporatism"—a measure of certain institutional features that are alleged to lead to a favorably placed Phillips curve.[11] Although the index is not clearly defined, it is constructed in such a way that (a) the greater is the degree of cooperation of unions and employers' representatives with government, (b) the greater is the degree of centralization of collective bargaining, and (c) the more cooperative is the industrial relations system, the greater is the index of neocorporatism. It is then hypothesized that the greater is the degree of neocorporatism, the less will be the sum of the rates of inflation and unemployment because such institutional characteristics lead to greater wage restraint at any rate of unemployment.

Estimates of the relation between the misery index MI and the degree of neocorporatism N are given in table 6.5. In each period a negative relation was found indicating roughly that the greater the degree of centralization of collective bargaining and the greater the degree of social consensus, that is, mutual trust and cooperation between business, labor, and government, the better was the macroeconomic performance of a country as measured by the sum of the rates of inflation and unemployment. For example, the country with the highest degree of neocorporatism, Austria, consistently had one of the lowest combined rates of inflation and unemployment, while Italy, a country with a low degree of neocorporatism, was consistently near the top in terms of the misery index. The results also indicate that neocorporatism became more important over time as revealed by the increasing slope coefficients.

Such studies are very much in keeping with the desire in this study to relate inflation and unemployment rates to institutional features of

[11]The countries in his sample consisted of those listed in table 2.8 with the exceptions of Ireland and Switzerland. See E. Tarantelli, "The regulation of inflation and unemployment," *Industrial Relations*, 25, Winter 1986, 1–15. Unfortunately Tarantelli died before he could complete a longer study in which a detailed analysis of the construction of the index was to be given. Many more elements were evidently included in his index than suggested in the text.

Table 6.5 Cross-country regressions for the misery index in 16 OECD economies for selected periods

$MI_j = 18.9 - 0.38N_j$ $(0.87)\ (0.084)$	1968–73	$R^2 = 0.565$
$MI_j = 26.2 - 1.2N_j$ $(2.02)\ (0.19)$	1974–9	$R^2 = 0.70$
$MI_j = 31.2 - 1.49N_j$ $(2.29)\ (0.22)$	1980–3	$R^2 = 0.75$

The subscript values in parentheses are standard errors.

Source: Tarantelli, "Regulation of inflation."

the economy. The underlying assumption in Tarantelli's study is that when neocorporatist institutions are prevalent and strong, a country is faced with a favorably placed Phillips curve. AD can therefore be highly stimulative without generating a high misery index.

One important difference between the present work and Tarantelli's study is the use of the volume of strikes as an independent variable rather than the more complex (but poorly defined) neocorporatist index. Another important difference is Tarantelli's failure to consider demand variables and therefore to isolate demand and supply forces. For example, it is possible for two countries to be faced with identical Phillips curves and yet experience different values of the misery index because different demands for FE will put them at different points on the Phillips curve.

However, differences in the values of the misery index between countries can also reflect differences in Phillips curves. For example, demand factors may lead to identical unemployment rates in two countries, yet their misery indices may be very different because their Phillips curves are quite different. Unlike this study, Tarantelli's study is unable to discriminate between differences in values of the misery index resulting from differences in Phillips curves and those resulting from differences in the demand for FE.

6.8 An Evaluation

Admittedly the statistical results of this study are not as strong as would be liked and the data used are often crude. The chief difficulty is that so little is known about the way in which to introduce and measure the relative demand and supply forces underling AD policies. By necessity the political control variables are averages over a number of years and strive to pick up the political climate or the center and outer limits of the political spectrum. Yet very little is known about the correct number of years over which to average the political control variables in order to determine this climate. Furthermore, since the usual case is that changes in party control within a country shift the political agenda only slightly to the left or right of center, radical shifts in unemployment goals such as those associated with Thatcherism cannot be picked up at all well in this manner. Further refinement of the political variables is clearly required.

The same can be said for the impact of institutions on the position of the Phillips curve. There is ample evidence by now that strike activity strongly reflects important characteristics of a country's industrial relations system—characteristics that very much influence the likelihood of wage restraint under FE conditions. But again the correct time interval over which to average strike activity in order to best represent these characteristics is not well known. Nor can a sharp sudden improvement or deterioration in the conditions leading to wage restraint be handled.

However, there are some things to be said in favor of the approach. At the very least, the attempt at quantifying the influence of institutional forces on economic outcomes can be seen as an advance over the more common approach in applied econometrics which falls back on dummy variables to pick up such influences.[12] In addition, the results appear to be largely insensitive to different contending definitions of the institutional variables, suggesting that while the appropriate variables may not be known with great precision, the importance of the institutional influence is clear. Third, the results of this study compare favorably with other similar studies.

Finally, while the institutional-analytical explanation of unemployment and inflation advanced in this study may on first reading appear somewhat removed from the traditional economist's approach, the policy model outlined in chapter 7, appendix A, indicates a less radical interpretation, for what that appendix makes clear is that the familiar Phillips curve found in the textbooks is but a simplified version of the kind of Phillips curve underlying regressions 3–6 in table 6.3. Institutional influences have been added here. These regressions can be looked upon as reduced forms of a system of structural equations in which unemployment and inflation rates are determined simultaneously.

[12]"Hasn't econometric theory come up with something better [than dummy variables]? If not, don't we need to start looking for independent measures of 'content–discontent' to use, however feeble a representation of the relevant elements they might be?" G. Ackley, "Comments and discussion," *Brookings Papers on Economic Activity*, No. 2, 1975, p. 440.

6.9 What Can We Learn from the Experience before the Breakdown?

With this in mind, it bears repeating that macroeconomic performance varied substantially across countries in the period 1963–73, from an unemployment rate low of zero (Switzerland) to a high of 5.3 percent (Ireland and Italy), yet rates of inflation differed little. As emphasized in chapter 5, all modern capitalist economies are subject to potentially strong inflationary pressures at FE. But even in those economies in which it might be expected that actual inflation would be the strongest at FE, that is, the heavily unionized countries with pro-labor governments, FE without relatively high rates of inflation was evident. The simple models estimated in this chapter support the earlier conclusions: a strong potential inflationary bias need not result in high rates of inflation at FE even in heavily unionized economies if a social bargain can be struck with labor. Given the right collection of institutions, as proxied here by a low strike volume, superior macroperformance resulted. In contrast, a poor performance was obtained in those high strike activity economies described earlier as pluralist, that is, Canada, Ireland, Italy, the United Kingdom, and the United States, which are trapped by history with an adversarial IRS.

Several other important messages emerge. Contrary to the beliefs of those espousing the party control theory of policy choice, a strong union movement or pro-labor party control is not a necessary condition for FE policies and outcomes. Low unemployment (and low misery index values) were found in both strongly unionized and weakly unionized economies and in countries with left- and right-controlled governments as long as strike activity was low. However, other things being equal, leftist control did reduce unemployment rates.

Since the rise of unemployment rates in the early 1970s, a number of writers have fostered the argument that strongly unionized economies with extensive welfare states have been largely responsible for increased rigidities in the labor market—rigidities that lead to real wages above their market-clearing levels and therefore to classical unemployment. In varying degrees, depending upon the writer, the prolonged period of mass unemployment since the early 1970s has been attributed to an unwillingness of labor to permit the reduced rate of growth of real wages that would allow the labor market to clear and eliminate most of the unemployment.

It should be clear that, whatever the impact of strong unionization and extensive welfare states, these did not lead to the kinds of problems that would constrain AD policies and therefore generate high unemployment in the period before 1974. Among the low unemployment countries of this period were Austria, Belgium, Denmark, Norway, and Sweden—countries with the highest union densities and extensive welfare states as well.[13]

6.10 Why Were Unemployment Rates So Low in the OECD?

The average (unweighted) rate of unemployment in the OECD for 1963–73 was 2.3 percent. As table II.1 reveals, in the post-1973 period average OECD unemployment rates almost doubled in the remaining years of the 1970s and almost tripled in the 1980s. Of the 18 OECD countries considered in table II.1, 13 experienced unemployment rates of 2.3 percent or less on average in 1963–73, with an average unemployment rate for the group of 1.5 percent. The important question is why so many economies were relieved of any constraint on their AD policies during 1963–73.

Consider first the relative inflation records of the OECD economies during the pre-1974 period. In the 18 countries listed in table II.1, the sample mean and variance for the average rates of inflation in 1963–73 are 4.9 percent and 0.95 percent respectively. Given the large dispersion of unemployment rates (a sample mean and variance of 2.3 percent and 2.6 percent respectively), a low correlation between cross-country inflation and unemployment rates is predictable, that is, the horizontal cross-country Phillips curve discussed in the previous chapter is obtained.

Note next that for most of the period 1963–73 a relatively fixed exchange rate system prevailed, forcing inflation discipline upon the authorities in the various countries. This would lead to a strong desire on the part of the authorities to achieve a targeted rate of domestic inflation equal to that of their trading partners, especially the United States.[14] Because of the success of the kinds of social bargains or incomes policies discussed in chapter 5, such a targeted rate of inflation was achieved and was consistent with FE in the overwhelming majority of the countries.

However, an AD stance generating FE cannot be maintained in the long run unless it is also consistent with an acceptable payments position and trade flows depend upon more than relative import and export

[13]See table 2.6 for data on union density.
[14]More correctly, the authorities would aim to achieve a rate of inflation of traded goods equal to their competitors. This discipline is captured in the Scandinavian model of inflation.

prices. For the OECD as a whole, both the balance of trade and payments were in surplus in 1963–73, with the surplus of the larger economies more than offsetting the deficits of the smaller OECD countries. In most of the deficit economies, the size of the payments deficit relative to output was small and the growth of exports substantial, both facilitating a continuous acceptance by lenders of the net deficit position of the borrowers and a willingness of the borrowers to accumulate indebtedness. The rapid expansion of exports therefore played a key role in the ability and willingness of the authorities to keep unemployment rates low as it relieved most economies of any payments constraint.

There were several factors at work leading to the rapid expansion of exports. The United States played a major role in this period, both politically and economically. With the dollar a much desired currency, the large current account deficits of the United States were accepted. While this international liquidity was injected into the system, the liberalization of international trade enabled the economies to greatly expand their export markets. These were certainly important factors behind the expansion of world trade.

Outside the United States, growth in exports was aided by extended periods of an overpriced dollar, but more fundamental influences were also at work. The argument can be summarized as follows.[15] An important determinant of the rapid growth of exports almost everywhere was the rapid growth of productivity.[16] This could, in turn, be largely attributed to the "late start" in industrialization outside the United States, together with dynamic economies of scale. The late start gave other OECD economies a potentially large productivity bonus in the form of an ability to borrow technology from the industrially more advanced economies, especially from the United States. In fact, this potential bonus was realized as the OECD economies borrowed the most advanced technologies through licensing arrangements and implemented and diffused them rapidly through high rates of investment.

All this generated relatively rapid productivity growth when combined with dynamic scale economies (Verdoorn's law) and can ac-

---

[15] For a fuller treatment see Cornwall, *Modern Capitalism*, chapters. 6, 9, and 10, and *Conditions for Economic Recovery*, chapter 13.

[16] Rates of growth of productivity in manufacturing and export success have been found to be highly correlated in several studies. See G. Ray, "Labour costs and international competitiveness," *National Institute Economic Review*, 61, August 1972, 53–58; R. Gross and M. Keating, "An empirical analysis of exports and domestic markets," *Economic Outlook Occasional Studies*, OECD, Paris, December 1980; and F. Cripps and R. Tarling, *Cumulative Causation in the Growth of Manufacturing Industries*, Department of Applied Economics, University of Cambridge, Cambridge, June 1975.

count for much of the "catching up" to the United States in incomes and technology. Furthermore, relatively rapid rates of growth of productivity would lead to superior cost performance, other things being equal, and would enhance export success in these economies. Rapid productivity growth would also generate rapid growth in real wages, thereby lessening labor's efforts to improve conditions through excessive money wage demands.

However, in an age of affluence, export success also depends on product quality, and the link between productivity growth and product improvement is less obvious than the tie between productivity growth and rates of increase of labor costs and product prices. Therefore consider the following. Efforts to produce high quality goods reduce costs through a strong emphasis on quality control. Second, high rates of growth of productivity lead to rapid growth of profits and cash flows allowing greater expenditures on product improvement and marketing. Finally, once superior quality has been established, cumulative forces lead to sustained export success. As incomes rise, consumption of high quality goods will spread to middle income groups and the growth of sales will accelerate. Given dynamic economies of scale, the accelerated productivity growth will further improve cost competitiveness, product quality, and marketing abilities.

Suffice it to say that whatever the underlying causes, rapid growth of exports played a key role in relieving economies of a payment constraint and helped greatly in reducing unemployment rates. However, separating causes from effects is anything but simple in what must be described as an era in which a virtuous circle operated. As will be apparent when the period of breakdown is considered in later chapters, low rates of unemployment throughout the OECD in the pre-1974 era greatly reduced the inflation costs of FE for any country. In turn, these reduced costs allowed the authorities almost everywhere to maintain stimulative AD conditions. The breakdown of the Bretton Woods agreement, the oil shocks, and certain internal structural changes in many of the economies were more than sufficient to bring an end to this phase of rapid growth of productivity and exports, low inflation and unemployment rates, and ultimately relief from any AD constraint.

6.11 Conclusions

What has been argued in the first half of this study is that the traumas of the Great Depression and the Second World War, the steady extension of suffrage and free education, and the growth of unionization prior to the Second World War led to an enormous post-war policy response in the OECD countries. At the very least, restrictive AD policies were avoided and the welfare state was steadily extended almost everywhere. However, as argued and discussed more fully below, these policies of the first 25 years following the Second World War did not merely reduce unemployment and provide safety nets for most citizens. They induced important institutional changes, especially in the industrial relations systems and labor markets of the economies—an illustration of the remaining link in the causal chain shown in figure 1.2.

The most important economic impact of these induced institutional changes was the development of potentially strong inflationary forces whenever the economy approached FE. In many economies these potential pressures were contained by concerted efforts during most of the 1950s and 1960s, and often in economies with strong union movements. The policies did not necessarily reduce inflation rates to zero but they resulted in rates of inflation that were not appreciably higher than those experienced in the high unemployment economies. In some cases inflation rates were lower. Judged by this most important criterion, the containment of such potentially explosive inflationary pressures should be seen as the workings of a successful long-run incomes policy.

In the less successful economies, the potential inflationary bias could only be controlled by restraining AD. However, as events of the late 1960s and early 1970s were to prove, neither of these policies was sufficient to prevent a series of shocks from setting off the latent inflationary forces everywhere. The AD policy response was rather muted, at least until the first oil shock, as on average the payments positions were little affected. As a result unemployment rates increased only moderately throughout the OECD before 1974. Only with the oil shock of 1973–74, the further acceleration of inflation rates, and the deterioration in the balance-of-payments positions did AD policies become noticeably restrictive. While the second half of the 1980s saw some recovery, especially in the United Kingdom and the United States, in retrospect this confirmed the existence of an economic breakdown and signaled the beginning of the phase of mass unemployment.

PART II

Breakdown

Introduction II: Breakdown

II.1 Introduction

Looking back

Capitalism's finest hour was described in chapters 5 and 6. Never before had so many economies grown so rapidly for such a sustained period. Full employment conditions prevailed for almost a quarter of a century in most of the developed capitalist economies. Partly as a result of FE conditions but also because rapid growth allowed the expansion of the welfare state, a marked reduction of the rates of deprivation and poverty also took place. A future of secular stagnation and reserve armies of the unemployed was far from the minds of the authorities, the public, or the economics profession.

During this period the mainstream explanation of the favorable unemployment performance proceeded along Keynesian lines. According to this view, strong investment and export demand (together with periodic adjustments of AD policies) enabled most countries to realize low unemployment rates. Some countries, it was true, accepted the need to keep unemployment rates relatively high to prevent politically unacceptable rates of inflation from developing or to bring the external account into balance. But the extent to which it was considered necessary to restrict AD was not enough to prevent the majority of the OECD economies from reducing unemployment to very low levels. Seen in terms of the causal chain of chapter 1, a distribution of power and an institutional framework existed that encouraged FE performances.

Differences in performance across countries recorded in tables 6.1 and II.1 suggest that the OECD economies could be divided into two groups: a strike-prone group with high unemployment and a high misery index, and a more successful group. The results of simple but suggestive econometric tests of a theory developed to explain differences in unemployment records and misery indices between countries during the period 1963–73 were reported in chapter 6. These tests

Table II.1 Annual average standardized unemployment rates U, rates of inflation of consumer prices $\dot{p}$, and misery indices MI in 18 OECD countries

	1960–73			1974–79			1980–83			1984–91		
	U (%)	$\dot{p}$ (%)	MI (%)	U (%)	$\dot{p}$ (%)	MI (%)	U (%)	$\dot{p}$ (%)	MI (%)	U (%)	$\dot{p}$ (%)	MI (%)
Low unemployment economies												
Austria	1.4	4.2	5.6	1.5	6.3	7.8	2.6	5.5	8.1	3.5	2.9	6.4
Japan	1.3	6.2	7.5	1.9	9.9	11.8	2.3	4.3	6.6	2.5	1.8	4.3
Norway	1.9	5.1	7.0	1.8	8.7	10.5	2.4	11.1	13.5	3.6	5.8	9.4
Sweden	1.5	4.6	6.1	1.5	9.8	11.3	2.3	10.8	13.1	2.0	7.0	9.0
Switzerland	0.1	4.2	4.3	1.0	4.0	5.0	1.2	4.8	6.0	2.4	3.1	5.5
Average[a]	1.2	4.9	6.1	1.5	7.7	9.3	2.2	7.3	9.5	2.8	4.1	6.9
High unemployment economies												
Canada	5.0	3.2	8.2	7.2	4.6	11.8	9.4	9.8	19.2	9.2	4.5	13.7
Ireland	5.2	5.9	11.1	7.6	15.0	22.6	10.7	16.6	27.3	16.2	4.2	20.4
Italy	3.9	3.3	7.2	4.6	16.1	20.7	6.1	17.5	23.6	8.0	6.9	14.9
USA	4.8	3.2	8.0	6.7	8.5	15.2	8.4	8.3	16.7	6.3	4.0	10.3
Average[a]	4.7	3.9	8.6	6.5	11.1	17.6	8.7	13.1	21.7	9.9	4.9	14.8
Low–high unemployment economies												
Australia	2.1	3.5	5.6	5.0	12.1	17.1	7.2	10.3	17.5	7.9	6.7	14.6
Belgium	2.4	3.6	6.0	6.3	8.4	14.7	11.1	7.6	18.7	9.8	3.1	12.9
Denmark	1.8	6.2	8.0	5.5	10.8	16.3	9.1	10.3	19.4	9.1	4.1	13.2
Finland	2.0	5.7	7.7	4.4	12.8	17.2	5.0	10.4	15.4	4.9	5.2	10.2
France	2.0	4.6	6.6	4.5	10.7	15.2	7.5	12.1	19.6	9.8	4.0	13.8
Germany	0.8	3.4	4.2	3.2	4.7	7.9	5.4	5.1	10.5	6.0	1.9	7.9
Netherlands	1.5	4.9	6.4	5.1	7.2	12.3	9.5	5.5	15.0	9.5	1.7	11.2
New Zealand	0.2	4.9	5.1	0.8	13.8	14.6	3.8	14.0	17.8	5.9	8.9	14.8
UK	2.9	5.1	8.0	5.1	15.6	20.7	10.0	10.8	20.8	9.4	5.8	15.2
Average[a]	1.7	4.7	6.4	4.4	10.7	15.1	7.6	9.6	17.2	8.0	4.6	12.6
Overall Average[a]	2.3	4.5	6.8	4.1	9.9	14.0	6.3	9.7	16.0	7.0	4.5	11.5

[a] All averages are unweighted.

Sources: OECD, *Economic Outlook*, OECD, Paris, June 1992, tables 50, R18, R19; OECD, *Historical Statistics, 1960–1990*, OECD, Paris, 1992, table 811; R. Layard et al., *Unemployment: Macroeconomic Performance and the Labour Market*, Oxford University Press, Oxford, 1991, table A3.

illustrated one of the main assigned tasks of this study—to relate differences in macroperformances to basic institutional differences.

The year 1973 marked a high point in economic activity in the majority of the OECD economies. Beginning in 1974 or shortly thereafter, growth rates of GDP, productivity, and per capita incomes fell, often resulting in absolute declines in the levels of overall economic activity for the first time since the early 1950s. These falls were accompanied by large increases in unemployment rates which have continued until the present.

Three patterns of unemployment

Table II.1 gives annual average rates of unemployment and price inflation and average values of the misery index for 18 OECD countries during four periods beginning in 1960. First, there is the thirteen-year period leading up to the general collapse of the post-war boom which began in most countries late in 1973. The second period, from 1974 to 1979, ends with the second oil shock. During these years most governments still felt that a return to FE with low rates of price and wage inflation was likely in the near future. During the third period, 1980–83, strong restrictive policies were implemented almost everywhere. The final period comprises the most recent past when hopes for an early return to "normalcy" were no longer widespread. For the OECD as a whole the average (unweighted) unemployment rates rose from 2.3 percent in 1960–73 to 4.1 percent in 1974–79 and 6.8 percent in 1980–91. Over the same time span, the variance of unemployment rates rose from 2.64 percent to 5.39 and 10.9 percent.

Considering the years following 1973, it is clear from table II.1 that unemployment rates increased markedly in most countries. The reactions of governments to the events of the early 1970s were such as to give rise to three different patterns of unemployment, taking the postwar period as a whole. First, there were those countries that achieved a creditable unemployment record in the earlier period and maintained low rates of unemployment in the more recent period, that is, unemployment rates less than 5 percent (Austria, New Zealand, Norway, Sweden, Switzerland, and Japan). Second, there were those that matched their high unemployment performances of the earlier period with high unemployment after 1973 (Canada, Ireland, Italy, and the United States). Third, there were a number of countries which experienced low unemployment rates in the first period but allowed unemployment to rise more recently (Australia, Belgium, Denmark, Finland, France, Germany, New Zealand, The Netherlands, and the United

Kingdom). These three groups are designated as low, high, and low–high unemployment countries respectively in table II.1.

An important question is why some countries that had pursued FE goals until the early 1970s radically altered their policies after that, so much so that the average rate of unemployment for the 18 OECD countries in 1974–79 and 1980–91 was about double and triple, respectively, the average rate of the period 1960–73. Explaining cross-country differences since 1973, as well as the forces leading to an increase in the average rates of unemployment in individual countries and in the OECD as a whole, is the key task of the remainder of the book. The assumption that there are no automatic FE tendencies under capitalism and that there is a role for discretionary AD policies is retained and supported.

II.2 Stability Downward—Instability Upward

In order to understand this general collapse of the advanced capitalist economies, it is necessary to disentangle many of the developments that occurred in the period preceding 1974. In particular, it must be stressed that the period of stagnation and stagflation since 1974 is intimately related to the period of accelerating rates of inflation of the late 1960s and early 1970s. Furthermore, these developments preceding 1974 are themselves very much the product of an even earlier post-war period. Thus, throughout the pre-1974 period, institutional and structural changes, induced by the prolonged period of FE following the Second World War, were taking place that would shape the course of events to follow.

It can be said that even in the first year or two of the 1970s all the OECD governments were prepared to take action to stimulate economic activity should unemployment rates show any indication of rising appreciably above their post-war average values. Hence, until then the likelihood of a serious recession anywhere was slight. However, given the changing structure of labor markets throughout the OECD as well as the commitment to maintain FE in most of them, by the late 1960s rapidly accelerating rates of inflation had become a distinct possibility. The danger was that a series of outside disturbances could activate the inflationary mechanisms that were potentially strong everywhere and thereby disturb the economies from their low unemployment–moderate inflation growth paths. As a result of over two decades of affluence, the capitalist economies could be described as moving along a low unemployment growth path that was stable downward but unstable upward. This is discussed at some length in chapter 9.

II.3 Instability Downward—Stability Upward

Whether shocks or structural changes were the primary cause, it is the inflation of the late 1960s and early 1970s that provides the link between the period of rising promise and affluence of the 1950s and 1960s and the mass unemployment of today. The downturn of 1973–74 was due largely to restrictive AD policies initiated in response to the previous acceleration of inflation rates and developing payments problems. The authorities were no longer willing to supply FE because the inflation and payments costs were too high, and they have continued to restrict AD since. Consequently, it is useful to think of the current situation as one in which most capitalist economies are moving along a high unemployment path that is stable upward but unstable downward.

The high unemployment can be traced ultimately to a "poor institutional–policy fit."[1] The institutional framework that had evolved over the post-war period was unable to accommodate strong AD policies after the early 1970s. Disturbances leading to increases in AD are unlikely to ignite strong inflationary pressures (because of restrictive AD policy responses), but those leading to decreases in AD can lead to strong downward movements of the real sector. This is also discussed in chapter 9.

II.4 A Misdirected Research Program

More than anything else, an acceptance of the theory that the long-run Phillips curve is vertical and that there exists a unique equilibrium unemployment rate has been responsible for the belief that the critical mystery or macropuzzle of recent times is why unemployment rates have been high and persistent. According to VPC analysis, the explanation cannot be a simple Keynesian one of too little AD, otherwise inflation rate would not be high and persistent but would be experiencing a free fall. Other explanations must be found.

As should be apparent from the discussion in chapter 3, the immediate cause of persistent high rates of unemployment throughout the capitalist world since 1973 can be explained quite well in terms of

[1] See chapter 1 for a discussion.

insufficient AD. AD has been deficient not because stimulative AD policies would be ineffective in reducing unemployment, but because the costs of FE policies were considered to be too high—a prediction supported by the explosive behavior of inflation rates in the late 1960s and early 1970s and their sluggish behavior more recently despite high unemployment. What needs to be explained, and what a properly designed research agenda would have focused on since the mid-1970s, is why inflation rates have remained so high while policy-induced involuntary unemployment has risen to post-war highs. As will be clear from chapter 8, the existence of high and persistent rates of inflation tells us nothing about the nature of the prevailing unemployment.[2] Explaining the persistence of high inflation despite high unemployment is another key task of this part of the study.

---

[2]It is often said that Switzerland has so little unemployment simply because it can be exported by sending foreign workers home. This misses completely the real question of interest about Switzerland: how can rates of inflation be so low when labor markets are so tight?

7 Unemployment Performance since the Breakdown

7.1 A Look at the Record

Introduction

It was asserted in Introduction II that the shift to restrictive AD policies in the early 1970s was the result of higher inflation costs, especially at FE. This assertion will be supported in the remaining chapters. This chapter undertakes a more detailed analysis of the performance of the different OECD economies since 1973 and again reports the results of simple econometric tests. The results aid in understanding intertemporal developments. As before, the regression models explain differences in unemployment in terms of some variables seldom used by economists. Nevertheless, the relevance and force of the results are established in the appendix to the chapter, which indicates how the regression models are derived from more conventional Phillips curve models.

Causal empiricism

Consider the Eurosclerosis explanation of rising unemployment. Like one of the key arguments of this study, it maintains that the causes of today's difficulties arise out of developments of an earlier period. The Eurosclerosis position argues that across countries the more powerful is the trade union movement and the more extensive is the welfare state, the greater are the real wage gap and the classical unemployment problem. In addition, the less effective will be stimulative AD policy, and, in general, the more poorly will an economy perform, other things being equal. This naturally suggests that the rise in unemployment and inflation shown in table II.1 and the deterioration in macroperformance everywhere can be traced to the rising power of labor and the extension of the welfare state.[1]

---

[1] Consider the following: "In this light, the more widespread and intensive influence of unions in Europe than in the United States may help explain the drastically different product wage

Even a casual look at the record reveals the shortcomings of this position. As already shown in chapters 5 and 6, economies with powerful trade unions and extended welfare states were among the best performers in the period 1963–73. The Eurosclerosis hypothesis would therefore have to predict a clear deterioration in the unemployment and inflation records of these kinds of economies and a noticeable relative improvement in performances in economies such as Canada and the United States which have weak union movements and relatively limited welfare states. In short, it would predict the best performers of the past to be the worst more recently and vice versa.

Table II.1 provides a useful point of departure. It shows that in both 1974–79 and 1980–91, some economies with strong union movements and extended welfare states performed comparatively well (for example, Austria, Norway, and Sweden). In contrast, some economies with weak unions and limited welfare states, that is, the high unemployment economies, performed rather badly.[2] The same is true if comparisons are made of changes in the unemployment rate or the misery index from 1960–73 to 1974–91. This suggests that, whatever it is that determines relative performance, it is not the extent of the welfare state or the strength of the trade union movement.

Intertemporal correlations

There is related evidence disputing the Eurosclerosis thesis. Table 7.1 records very high correlation coefficients between cross-country unemployment rates, inflation rates, and misery indices from one sub-period of the post-war period to the next. From 1960–73 to 1974–79 and from 1974–79 to 1980–88 not only did the rankings of economies, according to their unemployment, inflation, and misery index records, change little, but the deviations of the performances of the various countries from the mean of all 18 countries follow a (positive) linear relation over time.[3] For example, the intertemporal correlation coefficients for cross-country unemployment rates, inflation rates, and misery indices in the 18 OECD countries between 1960–73 and 1974–79

trajectories in these two parts of world and Europe's comparative lack of success in reducing its unemployment after the recession of the early 1980s." A. Lindbeck and D. Snower, "Union activity, unemployment persistence and wage–employment ratchets," *European Economic Review*, 31 (1–2), February–March 1987, p. 165.

[2] A comparison of unemployment rates and misery index values 1980–91 in Canada and the United States with those for Austria, Norway, and Sweden reveals that the latter three economies experienced the three lowest unemployment rates and misery indices. See table II.1.

[3] The intertemporal correlation between rates of price inflation in 1960–73 and 1974–79 is lower than the other correlations, but these periods cover a shift in exchange rate regimes.

Table 7.1 Intertemporal correlations between unemployment rates U, inflation rates $\dot{p}$, and misery indices MI for 18 OECD economies for the periods 1960–1973, 1974–1979, and 1974–1979, 1980–1988

		1960–73			1974–79		
		U	$\dot{p}$	MI	U	$\dot{p}$	MI
1974–79	U	0.79[a]					
	$\dot{p}$		0.45[b]				
	MI			0.80[a]			
1980–88	U				0.89[a]		
	$\dot{p}$					0.79[a]	
	MI						0.90[a]

[a] Significant at the 99 percent level.
[b] Significant at the 95 percent level.

are 0.79, 0.45, and 0.80, respectively, with an even stronger correlation between periods 1974–79 and 1980–88 for all three variables.[4] Whether the economy was strongly unionized with an extensive welfare state or not, if it performed well (poorly) before the breakdown, it has very likely behaved the same way since. This certainly suggests that the determinants of relative performances have not changed appreciably over time. Since the ability to implement a successful incomes policy (as proxied by the strike variable) explained much of the relative success of a country in the period 1963–73, the

[4]Calmfors and Driffill chose the changes in unemployment rather than the level of unemployment as one of the important performance variables to study. It is difficult to see a justification for this. For example, table II.1 reveals an increase in unemployment rates of only 2.2 percent in the United States from 1960–73 to 1980–91, while unemployment increased by 5.0 percent in Germany between these periods. This is hardly grounds for assigning higher marks to the American performance. The fact remains that only 95.2 percent and 93.0 percent of the American labor force was employed in the periods 1960–73 and 1980–91, respectively, while the corresponding figures for Germany were 99.2 percent and 94.2 percent. Indeed, if levels of performance rather than changes in levels of performance are the criteria for evaluation, then even when Japan and Switzerland are included in the same group as strike-prone Canada, Italy, and the United States, this group of "decentralized economies" comprises the worst performers according to the misery (= Okun) index.

However, there is a more serious shortcoming in their study, concerning their treatment of Japan and Switzerland. Their conclusion that economies with decentralized union movements, that is, those that most closely resemble the competitive model, perform better than economies intermediate in terms of union structure, is dependent upon the inclusion of Japan and Switzerland in the former group. When they are dropped, the group is dominated by high strike economies. As a result, according to the level of the three performance indicators they use, decentralized economies (minus the two low strike economies) do the worst and this is true for the change in the Okun index. See I. Calmfors and J. Driffill, "Bargaining structure, corporatism and macroeconomic performance," *Economic Policy* 3, April 1988, 13–62.

continued relative success can be attributed to continued favorable industrial relations. Indeed, this is the case as regression analysis makes clear.[5]

7.2 Regression Analysis: Unemployment in the Post-war Period

Pooled cross section–time series regressions

Chapter 6 used cross section analysis to establish the importance of institutions in explaining differences in unemployment records between countries before the breakdown. While the econometric results described in this section reaffirm the important role of institutions in explaining these cross-country differences both before and after the early 1970s, the main interest is in intertemporal developments.

To this end, pooled cross section–time series regression analysis was undertaken to test a theory of the determinants of unemployment covering the period 1960–88 for the same 18 OECD economies considered in chapter 6.[6] Four time series data points were used for each country, 1960–67, 1968–73, 1974–79, and 1980–88, the end points being those adopted by the OECD in order to reduce the effect of cyclical movements on the results.

As in chapter 6, variables representing the demand for FE and the willingness to supply FE, what were considered the basic determinants of unemployment performance, were highlighted as explanatory variables. However, in these regressions for each country, each period, only lagged values of strike variables and left-of-center votes variables were used in order to eliminate potential simultaneous relations problems. In addition a cumulative measure of left-of-center votes was used following Korpi's theory that this gives a better measure of the demand forces influencing unemployment.[7] As before it was hypothesized that: 1) the larger the volume of strikes, the more badly positioned would be the Phillips curve, the less the willingness to supply FE and, therefore, the higher the rate of

---

[5]See table 6.2 for additional evidence.
[6]Correlation and regression analysis using more recent data available after completion of the final draft of this chapter gave very similar results.
[7]See Korpi, W., "Political and economic explanations for unemployment: A cross-national and long-term analysis," *British Journal of Political Science*, July 1991. Vol. 21 (3), pp. 315–348. Left-of-center vote data are from Mackie, T. and R. Rose, *The International Almanac of Electoral History*, Macmillan, London, 1991. For the 1960–67 period average strike volume for the period 1950–59 was used.

unemployment; and 2) the larger the percent of left-of-center votes, the greater the demand for FE and, therefore, the lower the unemployment rate.

The cross section regression analysis of chapter 6 allowed a comparison of the impact of institutional differences on macroperformance while holding external developments constant. Since the primary interest here is in explaining changes over time, additional RHS variables thought important in explaining intertemporal changes were introduced. Initially, four additional explanatory variables were tested: for each country, each period, the annual average rate of inflation in the previous period; the "world unemployment rate" in the current period, that is, the weighted average rate of unemployment in the remaining countries scaled by its ratio of exports to GDP; the rate of inflation of import prices scaled by the ratio of imports to GDP for the period; and the annual average rate of productivity growth for the period. The results are shown as regressions 1–4 in table 7.2.[8]

The regressions were estimated using OLS, and following Hendry's specification approach, Hocking's Sp test was used to determine whether a RHS variable could be dropped from the model. Simple observation of the effects on the adjusted R-square and t-statistics in regressions 2 and 3 suggests that productivity growth and the import price variable are of little explanatory value. The results of the Sp tests indicate that these variables can be dropped from the equation and attention confined to regression 3. The four remaining variables, strikes, left-of-center votes, lagged inflation rates and world unemployment rates, were interpreted as the basic determinants of unemployment rates and differences across countries and over time.

The interpretation of the results of regression 3 are straightforward. For every 1 percent increase in lagged strike volume, unemployment is predicted to rise by a little more than .9 percent. Any shift to the left in voting patterns of 1 percent leads to a reduction of unemployment of .071 percent and a 1 percent increase in lagged rates of inflation generates a little less than a .25 percent increase in unemployment rates. The world unemployment variable is included in recognition of the interdependence among open economies and captures changing export demand conditions on local unemployment directly or indirectly through

[8] These data were obtained from the LSE Centre for Economic Performance data set, updated using the latest OECD *Historical Statistics*. Some early data (prior to 1964) were obtained from the LSE Centre for Labour Economics data set.

Table 7.2 Pooled cross section–time series regressions for unemployment rates in 18 OECD economies for 1960–1988

					Sp test
				R^2	$F \leq$ Critical F
1) $U_{jt} = \begin{array}{c}5.889\\(7.298)\end{array} + \begin{array}{c}0.997S_{jt-1}\\(7.580)\end{array} - \begin{array}{c}0.068I_{jt-1}\\(5.385)\end{array} + \begin{array}{c}0.216\dot{p}_{jt-1}\\(3.301)\end{array} + \begin{array}{c}1.612U^w_j\\(6.493)\end{array} - \begin{array}{c}0.192\dot{p}^I_j\\(1.746)\end{array} - \begin{array}{c}0.071\dot{q}\\(0.629)\end{array}$				.773	—
2) $U_{jt} = \begin{array}{c}5.607\\(9.499)\end{array} + \begin{array}{c}0.987S_{jt-1}\\(7.596)\end{array} - \begin{array}{c}0.069I_{jt-1}\\(5.525)\end{array} + \begin{array}{c}0.226\dot{p}_{jt-1}\\(3.511)\end{array} + \begin{array}{c}1.633U^w_j\\(6.666)\end{array} - \begin{array}{c}0.185\dot{p}^I_j\\(1.695)\end{array}$				.775	.4116 < 2.308
3) $U_{jt} = \begin{array}{c}5.417\\(9.219)\end{array} + \begin{array}{c}0.925S_{jt-1}\\(7.317)\end{array} - \begin{array}{c}0.071L_{jt-1}\\(5.607)\end{array} + \begin{array}{c}0.224\dot{p}_{jt-1}\\(3.438)\end{array} + \begin{array}{c}1.486U^w_j\\(6.398)\end{array}$				.768	1.6463 < 2.0462
4) $U_{jt} = \begin{array}{c}5.371\\(7.256)\end{array} + \begin{array}{c}0.608S_{jt-1}\\(4.955)\end{array} - \begin{array}{c}0.075L_{jt-1}\\(4.718)\end{array} + \begin{array}{c}0.483\dot{p}_{jt-1}\\(7.489)\end{array}$				.633	15.2081 > 2.0615

Absolute values of t-statistics in parentheses.

The RHS variables are log of average strike volume lagged one period S_{t-1}, average percentage left of center votes lagged one period L_{t-1}, average annual rate of inflation for previous period $\dot{p}_{t-1}$, average unemployment rate for the period of the 17 other countries weighted by exports/GDP U^w, and average rate of import price inflation for the period weighted by imports/GDP $\dot{p}^I$, and average productivity growth for the period $\dot{q}$. Data were obtained from the LSE Centre for Economic Performance, updated using the latest OECD *Historical Statistics*. Some early data (prior to 1964) were obtained from the LSE Centre for Labour Economics.

Table 7.3 Estimated sources of differences in unemployment rates from 1960–1973 to 1974–1988 in four large economies implicit in table 7.2 regression 3

	Actual differences in U	Predicted differences in U	U^w	$\dot{p}$	S	L
UK	5.02	3.84	1.59	1.05	1.08	.11
Italy	2.93	3.04	1.40	.88	1.23	–.47
Canada	3.43	2.91	1.55	.67	.74	–.06
USA	2.32	1.17	.56	.76	–.09	–.05

inflationary effects. Since it is scaled by each country's ratio of exports to GDP, it permits different effects across countries as well as through time. For example, in the 1960–73 period the scaled world unemployment rate varied from a low of .123 for the United States to 1.359 for Belgium, rising in the 1974–88 period to .497 and 4.125, respectively. It is clearly of considerable importance in explaining unemployment, as its exclusion in regression 4 reveals, a result consistent with McCallum's findings.[9]

Unemployment accounting

From 1960–73 to 1974–88 every economy in the sample experienced a substantial rise in world unemployment rates and lagged rates of inflation. Increases in these two variables contributed substantially to the rise in every country's unemployment rate, suggesting that the authorities responded to tightened political and payments constraints and a greater inflationary bias by restricting AD.[10] Over time, the lagged strike volume variable changed noticeably in several economies and usually in such a way as to play an important role in increasing unemployment rates. There were no noticeable intertemporal shifts in cumulative left-of-center votes in either direction. As a result this variable contributed little to intertemporal changes in unemployment in the different economies.

The four economies considered in table 7.3 summarize these points. In each, the rise in world unemployment rates accounts for approximately 40–50 percent of the predicted rise in unemployment rates. The impact of increasing rates of lagged inflation was not as strong but still an important cause of rising unemployment rates everywhere. Table 7.3 includes three of the seven economies experi-

[9] See McCallum, "Unemployment in the OECD countries."
[10] See section 4.11.

encing a large rise in lagged strike volume as detailed in table 6.1 and in these cases the impact on unemployment was substantial.

7.3 Why Did Some Succeed?

The depressed state of world demand puts extreme strain upon the institutions of any country should it strive to restimulate AD unilaterally. This immediately raises two questions. First, as the critical difference between the pre- and post-1974 world economic environment is the higher average rate of unemployment in the current period, why have the developed economies not undertaken coordinated restimulation? Second, why, despite the pronounced increase in the average rate of unemployment across the OECD, have five economies been able to minimize the rise in unemployment until the 1990s?

The beneficial effects of a coordinated program have been studied by any number of writers. These efforts have frequently been formulated in game-theoretical terms. International prosperity, like low rates of inflation, is a public good. While it is desired by all, any country has an incentive to share the benefits of stimulative policies elsewhere while avoiding any costs associated with a stimulative policy at home. The outcome is then suboptimal as none reflate.[11] As will be shown in chapter 10, the problems and difficulties of world reflation are even more pronounced than this. Even if all economies were to engage simultaneously in a program of restimulation, such a program would be short lived.

The second question needs further discussion here. Table II.1 reveals that, while the overall average rate of unemployment rose from 2.3 percent in the period 1960–73 to 7.0 percent in 1980–91, there were substantial differences between the three groups of countries. In the low–high and high unemployment economies, the average unemployment rate rose by 6.3 percent and 5.2 percent, respectively. In contrast, in the low unemployment economies the average increase was 1.6 percent. Three of these economies—Austria, Norway, and Sweden—display the characteristics of SDC economies in their most extreme form. Japan and Switzerland were characterized earlier as bourgeois democratic corporatist economies. What needs to be discussed are the characteristics of these economies that allowed them to minimize the rise in unemployment rates despite depressed world conditions.

---

[11] This difficulty can be described as a vicious circle. Mass unemployment has raised the inflation costs of FE for any country, and the increased costs of FE in every country have led to restrictive AD policies almost everywhere.

Of the five, only Japan and Switzerland have shown on average a surplus on current account since 1973.[12] Export growth was rapid in both countries despite the deterioration in their relative competitive positions.[13] With a rapid expansion in exports, a strong payments position, and inflation brought under control (by 1976 in Switzerland and by 1978 in Japan) there would be little reason for the authorities to allow unemployment rates to rise appreciably. Although growth of productivity and real wages slowed in these two countries, a "second generation of incomes policies" did not require a decline in exchange rates and real wages.

Conditions were quite different in Austria, Norway, and Sweden. All, especially Norway, ran substantial payments deficits on average during the post-1973 period until the 1980s. A notable improvement in the payments position did not occur until the early 1980s, yet all were unwilling to allow unemployment rates to rise substantially. In addition, all, particularly Norway and Sweden, were willing to accept inflation rates higher than those of Japan and Switzerland. The greater willingness to sacrifice relative price stability for lower unemployment is to be expected, given the earlier findings. These three SDC countries are among those with the highest union densities, the largest leftist vote, and the most centralized union structures.[14] It would be expected that the demand for FE would be relatively strong in these economies.

The issue comes down to a willingness of the authorities to supply FE during the period before the payments position improved. This has two aspects: whether the central bank could operate independently of the legislative and executive powers, and whether the costs of FE would be unacceptably high. With respect to the former point, Woolley's comparative study reveals a lack of such independence of the monetary authority in Austria and Sweden (Norway is not included in his study) in contrast with Germany and the United States.[15] As a result, in Austria and Sweden the ruling party could count on the cooperation of the central bank in determining a unified AD policy. As the record makes clear, this was not the case in Germany or the United States.

[12]Switzerland ran a surplus each year from 1974 to 1990 with the exception of 1980, with an average surplus of 4.0 percent of GDP. Japan ran a surplus of 1.5 percent of GNP on average in the period 1974–90. The corresponding figures for Austria, Norway, and Sweden were –0.8 percent, –2.2 percent, and –1.4 percent respectively. See OECD, *Economic Outlook*, December 1992, table R21.

[13]Ibid., chart M and table R9.

[14]See tables 2.6 and 2.7 and Calmfors and Driffill, "Bargaining structure." The huge payments deficits in Norway in the mid-1970s did not inhibit the authorities since North Sea oil was projected to yield huge surpluses by the end of the 1970s. See Flanagan et al., *Unionism, Economic Stabilization and Incomes Policies*, pp. 164–65.

[15]Woolley, "Monetary policy instrumentation."

The problems facing the authorities in these SDC economies should they try to improve their payments position while maintaining near FE in the face of restrictive AD policies elsewhere are considered in section 9.6. Among the possible difficulties is an inability to reduce the real exchange rate. Achieving increased competitiveness is a necessary condition for success of policy. During much of the post-1973 period Sweden, and to a lesser extent Norway, pursued the soft-currency option, allowing their effective exchange rates to decline, while Austria followed a hard-currency strategy. From 1974 to 1987 the effective exchange rate rose by approximately 40 percent in Austria and fell by approximately 13 percent and 30 percent in Norway and Sweden respectively. Nevertheless, according to various measures of a country's relative competitive position, all three economies can be said to have satisfied this condition from 1977 on.[16]

In one sense this ability to contain the costs of FE should not be too surprising. Data on strike volume in table 6.1 show that Austria, Norway, and Sweden, along with Japan and Switzerland, were among the seven countries with the most favorable strike records from 1963–73 on. It would therefore be expected that these SDC economies would be among the most successful in concluding a social bargain to contain inflation at FE despite worsening world economic conditions. Certainly much can be attributed to the long experience with the social bargain approach to incomes policy in these countries with highly centralized collective bargaining. Incomes policy institutions have existed since early in the post-war period, and the authorities would have been able to take advantage of the encompassing nature of collective bargaining in directing the attention of the bargainers to some national wage and price goals. All of this experience would have made it easier for labor in these countries to realize that, despite the reduced growth of real wages after 1973, an acceleration of money wage settlements would be counterproductive.[17]

[16]OECD, *Economic Outlook*, chart M. Among other things this requires that wages rise less in the country pursuing a hard-currency option than they do in countries following a soft-currency option. From 1975 to 1984 the rate of increase in hourly earnings in manufacturing in Austria, Norway, and Sweden was 6.5 percent, 9.5 percent, and 9.5 percent respectively. See OECD, *Economic Outlook*, June 1988, table 20.

[17]In Austria the top officials of the union movement are isolated from the kind of rank and file pressure that led to the breakdown of incomes policies in many economies in the late 1960s. The rank and file vote directly for representatives in their own firms who then elect the high union officials. Flanagan et al, also emphasize the importance of only a few participants taking part in a consensus policy. See Flanagan et al., *Unionism, Economic Stabilization and Incomes Policies*, pp. 52, 79.

Two final points should be noted. There is little in the way of indexation of wages in Austria and Sweden, and the Norwegian system contains lags and flexibilities that have facilitated union consultation with government.[18] Second, the problem of capital flight is much reduced in these three SDC economies because of exchange controls and poorly developed capital markets during much of the period.

7.4 Conclusions

The cross-country regression results of chapter 6 covering the 1963–73 period revealed that differences in unemployment records could be explained to a large extent in terms of an ability to strike a bargain that permits low rates of unemployment together with acceptable rates of inflation and payments positions. The high intertemporal correlations between inflation and unemployment rates and the misery index shown in table 7.1 suggested that the determinants of relative performance have remained fairly constant throughout the post-war period. The regression results of table 7.2 confirm these conclusions.

The rise in world unemployment rates and past rates of inflation accounted for most of the rise in unemployment in each country. Changes in strike volume were important in several economies but not universally so. Intertemporal changes in the political distribution of votes was never large enough to affect unemployment rates with anything like the impact of the other three RHS variables. Nevertheless the cumulative left-of-center votes variable was statistically significant in the regressions and can be viewed as an important influence on the average level of unemployment in an economy throughout the 1960–88 period, as well as explain differences between countries at any point in time.

In the appendix it will be shown that the regressions of table 7.2 can be treated as reduced forms of a familiar structural relation, the textbook short-run Phillips curve. Chapter 8 and 9 will then trace out how changes in three of the four basic determinants of unemployment, that is, the RHS variables in regression 3, table 7.2, affect the position of the Phillips curve with special emphasis on the manner in which these shifts lead to a greater inflation bias.

---

[18]However, some Swedish agreements have allowed contracts to be reopened when inflation exceeds some threshold. See Flanagan et al., ibid., pp. 170, 357. In contrast, the Belgian form of indexation was so complete that reduction of the real exchange rate through devaluation was seen to be quite unlikely. See J. Dreze and F. Modigliani, "The trade-off between real wages and employment in an open economy (Belgium)," *European Economic Review*, 15 (1), 1981, 1–40.

Appendix A: A Formal Analysis of the Immediate and Basic Determinants of Unemployment and Inflation

A1 A flexible exchange rate policy model

In this appendix the regression results of table 7.2 are shown to be reduced forms of structural equations describing more familiar types of Phillips curves and a social preference function.

A simple policy model can be written as follows:

$$\dot{p}_j = f_1(U_j, S_j, U_j^w, \dot{p}_{j_{t-1}}) \tag{7.1}$$

$$U_j = f_2(\dot{p}_j, L_j) \tag{7.2}$$

Equation (7.1) is a modified short-run Phillips curve for price inflation found by substituting a short-run Phillips curve for wage inflation into a markup pricing equation.[19] The unemployment rate appears on the right-hand side along with the world unemployment rate U_j^w, the lagged rate of inflation $\dot{p}_{j_{t-1}}$, and the strike variable S_j. The latter three variables affect the position of the Phillips curve. For example, according to the analysis of chapter 6 (and chapters 8 and 9) the higher is the strike volume or the world unemployment rate, other things being equal, the less favorably placed will be the Phillips curve and the higher will be the rate of inflation associated with any rate of unemployment. The analysis is easily expanded to incorporate other factors influencing inflation, such as unemployment insurance and the demographic composition of the labor force.

Equation (7.2) gives the socially optimal level of unemployment, describing the various demand and supply forces determining the desired unemployment rate. It is based on a social preference function to be described in the next section. The current rate of inflation is expected to have a positive influence on the desired unemployment rate, as it measures a cost of any AD or unemployment policy. For example, the higher is the current rate of inflation, the more restrictive will AD policy be and therefore the higher the rate of unemployment, other things being equal. L_j is a measure of party control and affects the demand for FE. As already determined, when L_j represents the percentage of leftist votes case in recent elections, it has a negative influence on unemployment rates. The lagged rate of inflation could also be included as an explanatory variable to reveal a willingness or unwillingness (positive or negative coefficient) to live with inflation.[20]

---
[19]See section 8.3, equations (8.4)–(8.6).
[20]See McCallum, "Unemployment in the OECD countries."

Figure 7.1 The social preference function

[Figure: axes $\dot{p}$ vs U, two concave indifference curves labeled IC_1 and IC_2]

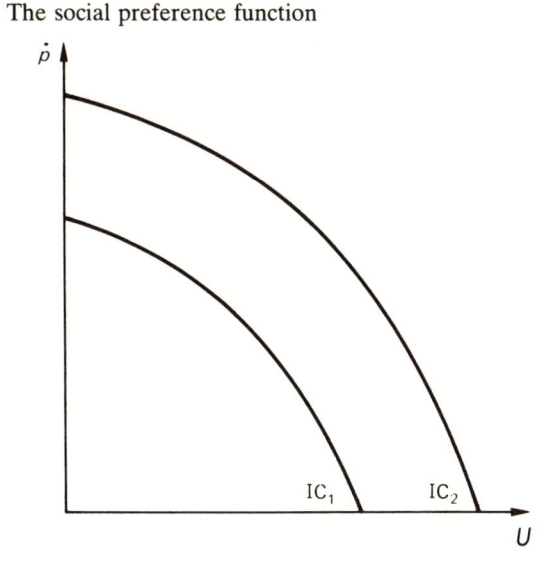

Together these two equations determine the two endogenous variables $\dot{p}_j$ and U_j, which can be written as functions of the predetermined variables S_j, $\dot{p}_{jt-1}$, U_j^w, and L_j. Note that the unemployment rate is treated as an endogenous variable in this analysis. This is quite proper even if most econometric studies treat it as exogenous. In truth, it is the variable that the authorities influence through their choice of AD policy and this choice will, in turn, be influenced by the likely inflation costs as well as by other factors. Therefore, it is an endogenous variable, as is the rate of inflation. Over an extended period of time, it can be expected that on average the authorities can be fairly successful in regulating AD and that actual unemployment rates will reflect their preferences.

The two structural equations, (7.1) and (7.2), written in linear form and taking account of the expected sign of the slope coefficients, become

$$\dot{p}_j = a_0 - a_1 U_j + a_2 S_j + a_3 U_j^w + a_4 \dot{p}_{jt-1} \tag{7.3}$$

$$U_j = b_0 + b_1 \dot{p}_j - b_2 L_j \tag{7.4}$$

A2 The preference function

Changes in the Phillips curve

The derivation of equation (7.4) and the relation between this structural equation and the reduced-form estimates given in table 7.2 can be seen with the help of figure 7.1. Two social indifference curves are drawn, each indicating combinations of inflation and unemployment rates, that is, values of the mis-

148 Breakdown

Figure 7.2 The social preference function and the Phillips curve

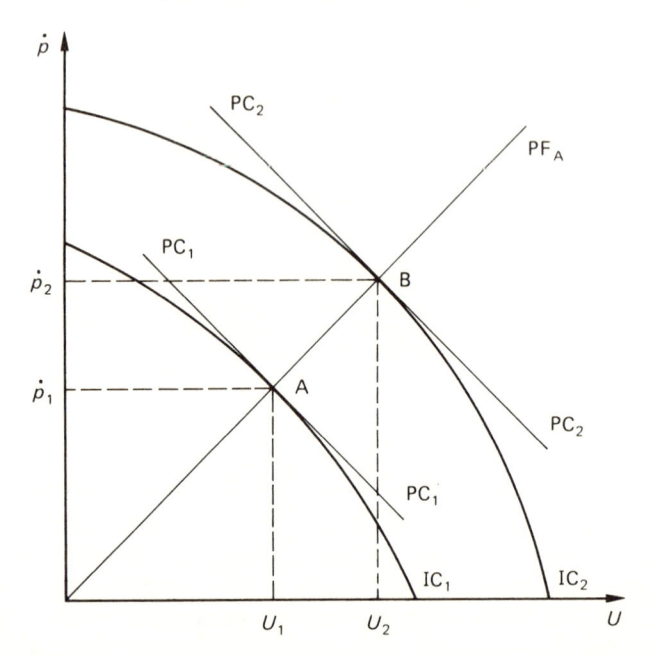

ery index, between which the authorities and the voters are indifferent. Since it is assumed that both inflation and unemployment involve costs, the closer the indifference curve is to the origin, the more it is preferred. The curves are drawn convex to the origin, indicating that higher rates of unemployment must be accompanied by increasingly lower rates of inflation if the authorities are to remain indifferent. In drawing this social preference map some fixed value of the measure of the strength of left-of-center votes, L_j, is assumed since it measures the "taste" for inflation and unemployment. If political power varies in either direction, this will result in a new set of indifference curves.

Figure 7.2 combines the social preference function with Phillips curves giving different possible objective tradeoffs. The Phillips curves, for example PC_1, are drawn as straight lines, although the more common curvilinear form could be used. Each corresponds to given values of S_j, U_j^w, and $\dot{p}_{jt-1}$. Assume initially that PC_1 gives the combination of unemployment and inflation rates open to the economy. The optimal policy is denoted by the tangency point A, with $\dot{p} = \dot{p}_1$ and $U = U_1$. Consider next the same preference map but with a higher strike volume and a second Phillips curve PC_2. The new point of tangency of PC_2 with the difference curve nearest the origin is B with $\dot{p} = \dot{p}_2 > \dot{p}_1$ and $U = U_2 > U_1$. If points A and B and tangency points for other indifference and Phillips curves are connected, line PF_A in figure 7.2 is obtained which plots equation (7.4) for some given value of L_j, the demand

Figure 7.3 The demand for full employment and the social preference function

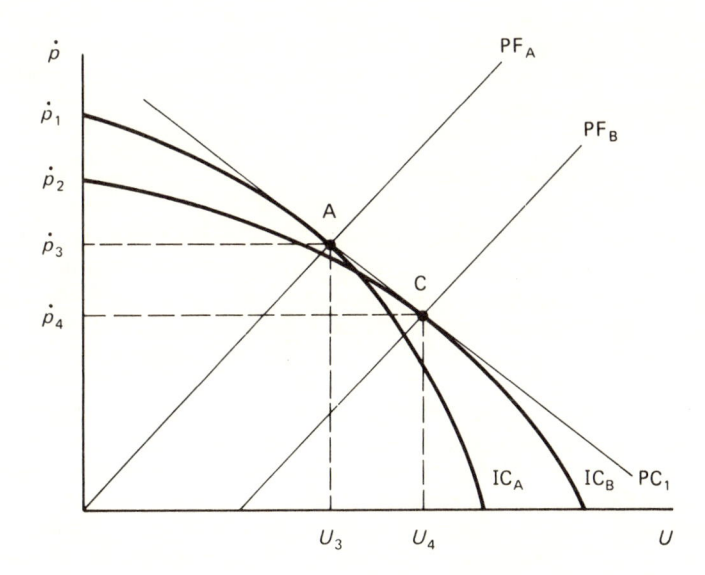

influence on unemployment policy. All optimum policy choices will lie on PF$_A$, the exact equilibrium point determined by the Phillips curve constraining policy choice. Finally, note that the steeper is the Phillips curve, the lower is the rate of inflation and the higher is the rate of unemployment at any point of tangency and the further to right is the preference function or tangency line.

Changes in the preference function

In figure 7.3 two quite different indifference curves are shown together with the Phillips curve PC$_1$. Let IC$_A$ be one of a set of social indifference curves representing community preference for country A. Clearly point A represents the optimum policy stance for country A. Consider next line ICB representing one of a set of social indifference curves in a country with a different distribution of political power. Note that ICB is drawn so that the zero unemployment option is associated with a lower rate of inflation than is ICA, that is, $\dot{p}_2$ rather than $\dot{p}_1$. Further, with ICB the authorities in country B are indifferent to a sizable rise in unemployment even if inflation is reduced only slightly. In contrast, given the distribution of preferences in country A, inflation rates would have to fall more substantially to result in a new point of indifference. A movement to the right until inflation has fallen to zero reveals the same strong relative preference for price stability in country B.

150 *Breakdown*

For convenience, assume that countries A and B are faced with the same Phillips curve PC_1. Figure 7.3 reveals two points of tangency; point A represents a "left-wing" policy choice and point C represents the policy choice in a country with more "right-wing" sentiments. Given identical Phillips curves, the left-leaning country chooses high inflation and low unemployment, $\dot{p}_3$ and U_3, compared with the low inflation–high unemployment choice, $\dot{p}_4$ and U_4, of the right-wing country.

A3 The workings of the model

If figure 7.3 is expanded to include additional social indifference curves for each country, one indicating left-wing and the other right-wing political strength, two tangency lines can be determined by allowing the Phillips curves to shift. These are shown in figure 7.3 by PF_A and PF_B respectively. In general, the steeper are the indifference curves, the further to the left is the tangency line.

Equation (7.4), the tangency line, and equation (7.3), the Phillips curve, are two equations in the endogenous variables U and $\dot{p}$ and can be solved for their equilibrium values. They are shown graphically in figure 7.4. Assuming some value for the predetermined variables S_j, U_j^w, and $\dot{p}_{jt-1}$, we can determine the Phillips curve PC_A for country A. Similarly, if a value is assigned to L_j, a tangency line PF_A can be drawn giving the tangency points for all possible Phillips curves and the social indifference curves. As drawn, PF_A intersects the Phillips curve PC_A at $U = U_2$ and $\dot{p} = p_2$ which are the equilibrium rates given the assigned values of the predetermined variables S_j, U_j^w, p_{jt-1}, and L_j. A similar procedure can be carried out for country B.

Figure 7.4 can also be used to show the impact of differences in any of the predetermined variables or what were earlier referred to as the basic determinants of unemployment (and inflation). Consider first country B with a political spectrum further to the "right" than that of country A, measured in this model by a lower percentage L_j of leftist votes. This results in a preference function curve PF_B further downward and to the right. Allow also that country B is more strike ridden than A, resulting in a Phillips curve PC_B further from the origin. The tangency line PF_B and the Phillips curve PC_B together determine an equilibrium in country B of higher rates of unemployment and inflation, that is, $U = U_1$ and $\dot{p} = \dot{p}_1$, than in country A. Country A has all the earmarks of an SDC economy and country B those of a pluralist economy.

A4 The reduced forms and the structural equations

In their reduced form equations (7.3) and (7.4) can be written

$$\dot{p}_j = \frac{1}{1+a_1b_1}(a_0 - a_1b_0 + a_1b_2L_j + a_2S_j + a_3U_j^w + a_4\dot{p}_{jt-1}) \qquad (7.5)$$

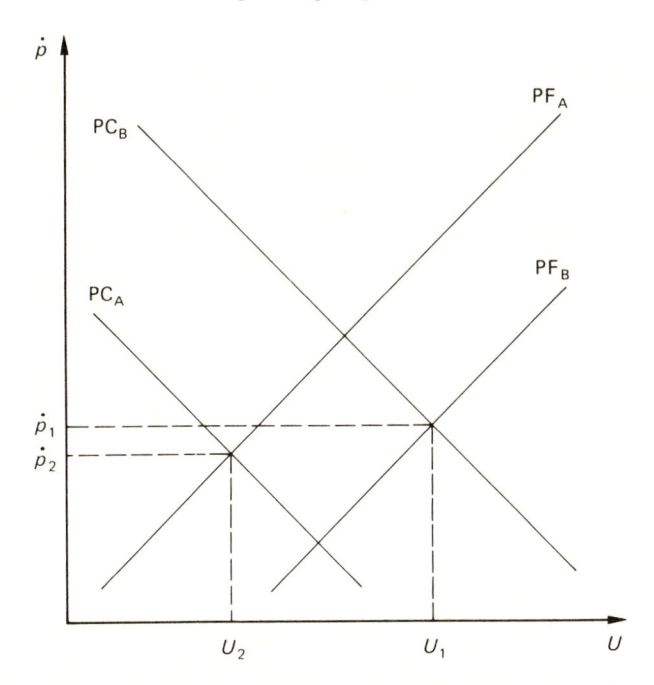

Figure 7.4 A flexible exchange rate policy model

$$U_j = \frac{1}{1 + a_1 b_1} (b_0 + a_0 b_1 - b_2 L_j + a_2 b_2 S_j + a_3 b_1 U_j^w + a_4 b_1 \dot{p}_{j-1}) \quad (7.6)$$

Equations (7.5) and (7.6) express the rates of inflation and unemployment as functions of their "basic" determinants. Ultimately, the rates of both inflation and unemployment depend upon institutional forces that influence the position of the Phillips curve, together with the lagged rate of inflation and the world unemployment rate, and the strength of demand for FE. Both equations can be estimated directly since all elements of simultaneity have been eliminated. Regression 3 in table 7.2 is an estimate of equation (7.6). Chapter 8 considers more complicated structural equations explaining wage and price inflation.

8 High Inflation and Policy-induced High Unemployment

8.1 Starting Over

Having argued in chapter 3 that the existence of long-run high rates of unemployment can be largely explained by insufficient AD, chapter 8 develops a framework to explain the rising inflation costs over time of any unemployment goal. What is to be proposed is a useful way of modeling not only the higher costs of FE in the 1980s and the 1990s but also the inflation of the late 1960s and early 1970s, the acceleration of inflation rates following the second oil shock, and the high unemployment–high inflation between these periods. In addition, the model gives insights into likely future developments, as current unemployment policies are linked to institutional changes which have long-lasting implications. At the center of the analysis is a variable-coefficient model of inflation combined with hysteresis effects and certain institutional influences.

To make these points, the unreality of the symmetry assumption of NAIRU analysis will be discussed first. Even if it is allowed that there is some minimum rate of unemployment below which stimulative AD policies are ineffective in reducing unemployment further but cause inflation rates to accelerate, it is quite another thing to argue that any rate of unemployment greater than this minimum can only be maintained by continuously decelerating rates of inflation. Once the symmetrical knife-edge concept can be purged from inflation and unemployment analysis, the case against some kind of unique automatic equilibrium unemployment rate independent of policy and ultimately institutions is further strengthened. The rejection of the symmetry assumption does not necessarily imply that the whole concept of vertical long-run Phillips curves must be discarded. For example, it need not disallow real wage bargaining at low rates of unemployment. However, what must be recognized is that the extent to which workers actively seek to protect their real wage through money wage demands varies with economic conditions, for example, the unemployment rate or the expected rate of inflation.

8.2 The Variable-coefficient Phillips Curve

Prior to the post-war period, wage settlements were often devoid of fairness influences, that is, of any adjustment in money wage settlements to protect real and relative wages.[1] The inferior bargaining position of labor allowed employers to present a "take it or leave it" money wage offer, with wage fluctuations largely reflecting overall economic conditions. With the rising power of labor in the period following the Second World War, settlements that protected real and relative wages became important goals of labor and were recognized as a legitimate part of wage negotiations by employers. The inclusion of the expected rate of inflation in the money wage equation is a recognition of this legitimacy.[2] However, it is reasonable to assume that fairness considerations are less enforceable in wage settlements when labor markets are slack.

Consider next a logical implication of NAIRU models—the alpha strand. Even if it is determined that the NAIRU has increased to, say, 20 or 30 percent, wage bargaining is still in real terms even if most unemployment is now involuntary. A little reflection suggests that this is a rather strange assumption. Most Phillips curve models, for example those that use the reciprocal of the unemployment rate as an explanatory variable, make the response of current wage inflation to changes in the unemployment rate depend upon the level of unemployment. This is true of NAIRU analysis. However, it is a notable feature of NAIRU analysis that when relating wage inflation to the expected rate of price inflation, the response of rates of wage inflation to changes in the expected rate of price inflation is assumed to be independent of the level of p_t^e, that is it is always equal to unity.

Surely if there is any involuntary unemployment, by definition these workers will accept a job for which they are qualified at the going real wage or less if such jobs become available. As the result of an increase in AD, the formerly unemployed will be quite willing to accept a

---

[1] See section 5.3.
[2] The text interpretation of p^e in the wage equation is that, although real wages are the ultimate concern, wage settlements are in money terms and therefore labor must seek its goal through money wage settlements. The expected rate of inflation variable is not included in the wage equation to indicate that labor supply is defined in terms of p^e. See G. Perry, "Determinants of wage inflation around the world," *Brookings Papers on Economic Activity*, No. 2, 1975, p. 408.
A mathematical treatment of fairness is given in appendix A, section A1.

154 Breakdown

money wage that does not incorporate complete compensation for expected rates of price inflation.[3] However, even in the case of employed workers, it is unlikely that wage bargaining will be conducted in real terms irrespective of the state of the economy. For example, at high rates of unemployment, both actual and expected rates of inflation are likely to be low. In this case, it can be anticipated that employed workers will be less fearful that their money demands will be inadequate to protect real wages than if inflation rates were high. As a result, it can be expected that the response of wages to expected rates of inflation will be smaller in the former case. In addition, employed workers will be quite mindful of the relative lack of alternative jobs should they become unemployed when unemployment rates are high. This should also reduce their wage response to expected inflation rates.

However, as unemployment falls and actual and expected inflation rates rise, at the higher expected rates of inflation workers will become more concerned that "normal" money wage settlements will not protect their real wages. It can also be assumed that, with the improvement in alternative job prospects, their demands for real wage protection will increase. As a result, the response of money wage demands to the expected rate of price inflation will increase with $\dot{p}_t^e$.

Together, these points lead to the conclusion that, while labor has been able to gain acceptance of fairness considerations in wage negotiations, the extent to which it is able and will seek to protect real wages in this manner will vary. The coefficient of the price expectations variable (which has been proxied by the lagged price inflation variable in all the models so far) cannot be realistically treated as a fixed parameter. In the remainder of this chapter models of the Phillips curve are developed that are applicable to an economy in which no successful incomes policy has been implemented, that is, one in which collective bargaining is unrestricted. They will apply to pluralist economies and to economies in which a previously successful incomes policy has broken down.

[3]In one attempt to avoid this difficulty it is argued that entrants to the labor force may find that non-union firms are not able to absorb them because of legal restrictions preventing competition between non-union and union firms. However, this can only be true (if it is true) if public employment is ruled out. With involuntarily unemployed workers, the creation of job openings through government-sponsored projects will lead to permanent reduction in unemployment with newly employed workers accepting work at something less than the going real wage. It is difficult to see how the real wage could become stuck in this case.

8.3 Fairness and the Dynamics of Inflation

The wage–price spiral

It is useful in formalizing the variable impact of fairness on wage settlements to begin with a simple model incorporating fairness and then introduce the mechanism governing its variable effect. Consider a period before widespread development of the trade union movement when management had the upper hand in wage settlements and real wages were not protected. In such circumstances the Phillips curve could be written simply as

$$\dot{w}_t = a_0 + a_1 U_t^{-1} \tag{8.1}$$

or with some more complicated lag structure for the unemployment rate. However, when wage settlements come to reflect the protection of real wages, this change can only be captured if the Phillips curve is expanded to include price inflation variables. Whether wage settlements are based on the expected or actual rates of price inflation, the price variable is meant to represent the importance of fairness in wage settlements. For example, write

$$\dot{w}_t = b_0 + b_1 U_t^{-1} + b_2 \dot{p}_t^e \tag{8.2}$$

where $\dot{p}_t^e$ represents the expected rate of inflation in period t. For simplicity assume that expectations are adaptive, that is,

$$\dot{p}_t^e = \dot{p}_{t-1}^e + c\,(\dot{p}_{t-1} - \dot{p}_{t-1}^e) \tag{8.3}$$

If $c = 1$, equation (8.2) can be written

$$\dot{w}_t = b_0 + b_1 U_t^{-1} + b_2 \dot{p}_{t-1} \tag{8.4}$$

Given some simplifying assumptions, for example, markup pricing, constant income shares, and no change in nonlabor costs, price inflation is given by

$$\dot{p}_t = \dot{w}_t - \dot{q} \tag{8.5}$$

where $\dot{q}$ is a fixed rate of growth of labor productivity. Equation (8.4) illustrates quite clearly that, once the price variable is incorporated in the wage equation, a feedback effect from prices to wages must be considered along with the pass-through effect from wages to prices contained in equation (8.5). Together the two effects gen-

156 Breakdown

erate an interaction between rates of wage and price inflation—the wage–price spiral.

Short-run and long-run Phillips curves

The wage–price spiral gives rise to the well-known distinction between short-run and long-run Phillips curves. The former is given by equation (8.4) for wage inflation; substituting equation (8.4) into (8.5) gives

$$\dot{p}_t = b_0 - \dot{q} + b_1 U_t^{-1} + b_2 \dot{p}_{t-1} \tag{8.6}$$

which is the short-run Phillips curve for price inflation. In the short run the wage-price interaction is capable of generating an acceleration or deceleration of inflation rates. However, if it is assumed that $0 < b_2 < 1$, as is done in this section, the interactions between wage and price inflation work themselves out eventually, with each converging on a constant rate given by

$$\dot{w}^* = \frac{b_0 - b_2 \dot{q} + b_1 U^{-1}}{1 - b_2} \tag{8.7}$$

and

$$\dot{p}^* = \frac{b_0 - \dot{q} + b_1 U^{-1}}{1 - b_2} \tag{8.8}$$

respectively.[4] Equations (8.7) and (8.8) are the long-run counterparts to equations (8.4) and (8.6). As should be clear, the long-run curves are steeper than their short-run counterparts because $b_1/(1 - b_2) > b_1$.[5]

There is no long-run counterpart to equation (8.1) for wage inflation before fairness considerations and unionization, because the feedback effect from price inflation to wage inflation is absent. The wage–price spiral is a modern phenomenon, resulting from fairness considerations in wage settlements enforced by unions.

Equations (8.7) and (8.8) represent two long-run Phillips curves in the sense that they define all those combinations of unemployment and wage or price inflation rates at which the rate of inflation is constant.[6]

---

[4] See appendix A, section A1.

[5] The wage–wage inflationary mechanism is easily grafted onto the text model (in principle), leading to an even more explosive inflationary situation after unionization.

[6] What is clearly missing in the model is the inclusion of prices of imported goods. In certain periods, such as the early 1970s, accelerating and decelerating rates of inflation of prices of imports were a dominating force in the overall inflation.

All points on each long-run curve are equilibrium points in this sense. Simple as this model may be, it is sufficient to indicate how critical the assumption of real wage bargaining, that is, $b_2 = 1$, is for the uniqueness of equilibrium.

8.4 Variable-coefficient Models of Inflation

The variable-coefficient model of inflation can take different forms.[7] The basic idea asserts that the coefficient of the price expectations variable varies depending upon the state of the economy, for example, unemployment or the expected rate of inflation itself. Two examples of the latter are discussed here.

Write as before the simplest expectations-augmented Phillips curve

$$\dot{w}_t = b_0 + b_1 U_t^{-1} + b_2 \dot{p}_t^e$$

Again, assume for convenience that $\dot{p}_t^e = \dot{p}_{t-1}$. An early example allowed b_2 to vary continuously with the state of the economy by assuming $b_2 = b_5 \dot{p}_{t-1}$, $b_5 > 0$, giving

$$\dot{w}_t = b_0 + b_1 U_t^{-1} + b_5(\dot{p}_{t-1})\dot{p}_{t-1} \tag{8.9}$$

In this case

$$\frac{\partial \dot{w}_t}{\partial \dot{p}_{t-1}} = 2b_5 \dot{p}_{t-1}$$

indicates the variable impact of past inflation, and therefore expected inflation rates, on wage bargaining.[8]

In traditional Phillips curve analysis, low rates of unemployment are associated with higher rates of inflation because labor bargains harder, management is less resistant to higher money wage demands, and greater excess demand pushes up wages in flexprice markets—hence the negative slope to the Phillips curve. The variable-coefficient Phil-

---

[7] See O. Eckstein and R. Brinner, *The inflation process in the United States: A study prepared for the Joint Economic Committee*, U.S. Congress, U.S. Government Printing Office, Washington, DC, February 1972; R. J. Gordon, "Wage–price controls and the shifting Phillips curve," *Brookings Papers on Economic Activity*, No. 2, 1972; D. Hamermesh, "Wage bargains, threshold effects and the Phillips curve," *Quarterly Journal of Economics*, 84, August 1970, 501-17; and M. Kirby, "A variable expectations coefficient model of the Australian Phillips Curve," *Australian Economic Papers*, 20, December 1981, 351-58.

[8] See Gordon, "Wage–price controls."

lips curve (VCPC) retains this assumption but also assumes that, whatever the unemployment rate, the higher is the expected rate of inflation, the greater is the response of money wages to this expectation because of a greater concern that real wages will not be protected otherwise. More specifically, $\partial \dot{w}/\partial \dot{p}_{t-1} = 1$ if $\dot{p}_{t-1} = {}_{1/2}b_5$. When, in fact, $\dot{p}_{t-1} < 1/2b_5$, workers do not demand a money wage adjustment equal to the past rate of price inflation. However, as past rates of inflation rise, concern for the real wage develops and the response of wage inflation to any given change in past (= expected) rates of price inflation increases.[9] Note that such growing concerns are self-fulfilling. Finally, the larger is b_5, the lower is the past (= expected) rate of inflation needed to generate real wage bargaining.

8.5 The Eckstein-Brinner Model of Inflation

The inflation severity factor

Useful as the above model may be, a different formulation of considerable merit is the VCPC model of inflation adopted here. In this model the expectations coefficient is made a function of $\dot{p}_t^e$ (which, again, is assumed equal to $\dot{p}_{t-1}$ for expositional purposes) but a discontinuity is introduced in the manner in which the level of past (and therefore expected) rates of inflation affect the expectations coefficient. Write

$$\dot{w}_t = g_0 + g_1 \dot{p}_{t-1} + g_2(\dot{p}_{t-1} - g_3) + g_4 U_t^{-1} \tag{8.10}$$

and

$$\dot{p}_t = \dot{w}_t - \dot{q} + h_0 \tag{8.11}$$

so that

$$\dot{p}_t = (g_0 + h_0) + g_1 \dot{p}_{t-1} + g_2(\dot{p}_{t-1} - g_3) + g_4 U_t^{-1} - \dot{q} \tag{8.12}$$

where (a) $0 < g_1 < 1$, (b) $g_2 = 0$ if $\dot{p}_{t-1} \leq g_3$, otherwise $g_2 = 1 - g_1$, and (c) $g_3, g_4 > 0$. h_0 is an additional influence on price inflation to be specified shortly and g_3 is defined as the threshold rate of inflation. All other variables have their previous meanings. Assumptions (a)–(c) are

---

[9]Note that the unemployment rate variable will not pick this up if forces other than the unemployment rate, for example, import prices, influence overall inflation rates.

given the following interpretations. There is incomplete sensitivity of money wages to moderate inflation, that is, when $\dot{p}_{t-1} \le g_3$, but when inflation is severe, that is, $\dot{p}_{t-1} > g_3$, there is complete sensitivity. At this higher rate of inflation expectations are affected such that any further increase in the rate of price inflation is completely transmitted to wage inflation with a one-period lag.[10] Estimates of the parameters of equation (8.10) are given in appendix B.

In addition to describing a dynamic wage–price inflationary mechanism, the model emphasizes that a qualitative change takes place in the nature of inflation when it exceeds the threshold rate, that is, when $\dot{p}_{t-1} > g_3$ percent. The nature of the long-run tradeoff between wage (and price) inflation and unemployment changes when inflation becomes "severe." Until the threshold is exceeded, inflation rates are considered of less consequence (and very likely unemployment rates are high), and price inflation is not completely built into wage demands as $\partial \dot{w}_t/\partial \dot{p}_{t-1} = g_1 < 1$. Call this segment of the long-run Phillips curve track I.

The long-run equilibrium rate of inflation in Track I

Track I has no unique equilibrium unemployment rate independent of AD policy. To see this, it is necessary to solve the model for the long-run equilibrium, that is, the constant rate of inflation associated with some given rate of unemployment. A long-run equilibrium solution exists for both wage and price inflation. To facilitate comparison with NAIRU analysis, the long-run rate of price inflation will be determined. In appendix A, section A2, it is revealed how similar the results are if the long-run rate of wage inflation is found.

The long-run equilibrium rate when inflation is moderate, that is, $\dot{p}_{t-1} \le g_3$, implies that $g_2 = 0$. In this case the long-run Phillips curve for price inflation can be written

$$\dot{p}^* = \frac{g_0 + h_0 - \dot{q} + g_4 U^{-1}}{1 - g_1} \qquad (8.13)$$

Since $0 < g_1 < 1$, $1 - g_1 > 0$ and the division on the right-hand side of equation (8.13) is appropriate. Thus there is a tradeoff between unemployment and inflation over that range of unemployment rates corresponding to rates of price inflation equal to or less than g_3 per-

---

[10]See Eckstein and Brinner, "Inflation process in the United States." The text model is a simplified version of the original model but nothing essential has been altered.

cent. The authorities may pick any rate in this range without fear of ever-accelerating or ever-decelerating rates of inflation.

The long-run equilibrium orate of inflation in Track II

Assume now that the average rate of inflation in the last period exceeds g_3 and therefore $g_2 = 1 - g_1$. As equation (8.12) includes the inflation severity factor $\dot{p}_{t-1} - g_3$, any attempt to solve for the long-run Phillips curve by setting $\dot{p}_t = \dot{p}_{t-1} = \dot{p}^*$ gives the expression[11]

$$\{1 - (g_1 + g_2)\}\dot{p}^* = g_0 + h_0 - \dot{q} - g_2 g_3 + g_4 U^{-1} \qquad (8.14)$$

Since, however, $1 - (g_1 + g_2) = 0$ by assumption (b), there is no longer a tradeoff between the rates of price inflation and unemployment. The inflation term drops out and the remaining expression is solved for U_0 as in NAIRU analysis giving

$$U_0 = \frac{g_4}{\dot{q} + g_2 g_3 - g_0 - h_0} \qquad (8.15)$$

Call this segment of the long-run Phillips curve track II. Figure 8.1 illustrates these results.

8.6 The Workings of the Model

Track I

Starting from a rate of unemployment greater than U_0, say U_1, introduce stimulative demand policies to reduce the rate of unemployment. The long-run Phillips curve LPC₁ indicates that, as long as unemployment rates remain in excess of U_0, the associated rate of price inflation will not exceed the threshold rate of g_3 percent. As unemployment rates fall, but remain greater than U_0, the short-run wage–price interactions given by equations (8.4) and (8.5) (not shown) take hold. The track I nonvertical segment of LPC₁ in figure 8.1 gives the long-run equilibrium rate of inflation that would result at each unemployment rate if that rate were maintained long enough for the wage–price interactions to work themselves out. In these cases the inflationary process is no different from that modeled in section 8.3 except that wage rather than price inflation was considered there.[12] Over the entire range of unemploy-

---
[11]See appendix A for a fuller treatment of equations (8.13) and (8.14).
[12]Compare the analysis in appendix A, sections A1 and A2.

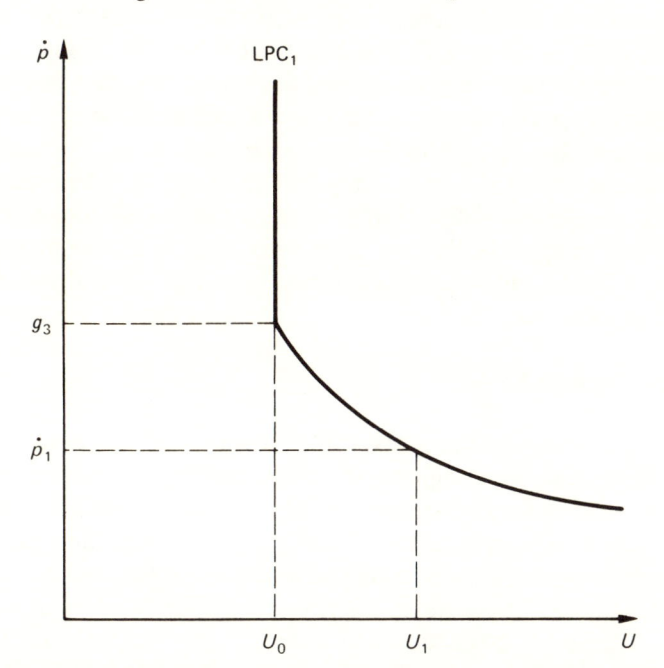

Figure 8.1   The long-run variable-coefficient Phillips curve

ment rates that cover track I, changes in AD affect both unemployment and inflation rates in the long run. Any unemployment rate equal to or greater than U_0 is a potential equilibrium unemployment rate.

Track II

At $U = U_0$ the economy is on the vertical segment of the long-run Phillips curve and further stimulative AD policy gives the usual NAIRU results as this shifts the economy to the second track. At unemployment rates less than U_0 the resulting inflation is considered severe, and labor, concerned lest its real wage should decline, responds by building price inflation completely into wage demands. This causes wage inflation to accelerate so rapidly that, taking accounts of the pass-through effects on price inflation and subsequent feedback effects on wage demands, wage and price inflation rates accelerate without limit.

Multiple equilibria

Two points must be emphasized. First, as mentioned earlier, in this model there is no equilibrium unemployment rate independent of the stance of AD policy. Second, and related, the two-track model of inflation discards the symmetry assumption of NAIRU and NRH analysis. Starting from $U = U_0$ in figure 8.1, if AD is reduced and unemployment rises above U_0 to U_1, say, and is maintained there through policy, this does not require a continuous decline in the rates of growth of the money supply and inflation; the rate of inflation declines, but only to $\dot{p}_1$. The economy is not teetering on a knife-edge. Only in VPC analysis, when the rate of inflation decelerates without limit whenever actual unemployment exceeds some unique NAIRU, are there no acceptable policy options. With the VCPC, the limit to the decline in $\dot{p}$ at any $U > U_0$ allows policymakers an opportunity to pick any point on the nonvertical segment.[13]

8.7 Are Workers Fooled?

Before discussing the many favorable properties of the model, a possible criticism can be anticipated and answered. Over the segment of the Phillips curve in which the response of wages to past price increases is incompletely sensitive, that is, $U \geq U_0$, workers are often said to be fooled or suffering from a money illusion, since the money wage response to price increases is allegedly insufficient to maintain real wages. The latter response is said to require $g_1 = 1$ at all times. However, if pricing is on a markup basis, as in equation (8.5), this is a rather superficial conclusion because the behavior of real wages is completely independent of the size of g_1.

Thus, although not essential, if all costs other than labor are ignored and h_0 is assumed to be zero, from equation (8.5) $\dot{p}_t = \dot{w}_t - \dot{q}$ or $\dot{w}_1 - \dot{p}_t = \dot{q}$. The rate of growth of real wages, far from declining if $g_1 < 1$, actually rises in step with the growth of labor productivity. What is critical is the behavior of employers, not employees. If the former are content to maintain profit margins and merely pass through labor cost increases, nobody is "fooled." When price inflation is proceeding at a rate that is of little concern to workers, the growth of real wages will take care of itself, thus justifying the lack of concern by labor.

8.8 The Shifting Long-run Variable-coefficient Phillips Curve

A rise in import prices

The instability of the NAIRU was discussed in chapter 3. The likely instability of the long-run VCPC must also be recognized and can be

[13] See chapter 3, appendix B, for a related point.

related to hysteresis effects. Before that, however, it is helpful simply to derive the consequences of parameter changes on the VCPC.

Recall from equation (8.15) that the long-run Phillips curve becomes vertical at

$$U_0 = \frac{g_4}{\dot{q} + g_2 g_3 - g_0 - h_0} \tag{8.15}$$

Further, from equation (8.13), the asymptote of the Phillips curve is given by $(g0 + h0 - \dot{q})/(1 - g1)$. Then changes in either of the intercepts of equations (8.10) and (8.11), that is, g_0 or h_0, or the rate of growth of productivity $\dot{q}$ will shift both the vertical segment and the asymptote of any long-run Phillips curve, while changes in the threshold rate of inflation g3 will shift the vertical segment but not the asymptote.

Consider first a once-over increase in h_0 to h'_0. This can be interpreted as an increase in the rate of growth of import prices $\dot{p}^1$ due to either an increase in foreign prices at given exchange rates or a depreciation of the currency with foreign prices remaining unchanged.[14] This shifts the long-run Phillips curve from LPC$_1$ to LPC$_2$ as indicated in figure 8.2, thereby increasing the inflation costs of any unemployment target. If unemployment was initially at U_2 and remains there, the inflation rate rises from $\dot{p}_1$ to $\dot{p}_2$. However, if the initial unemployment rate was U_0 or U_1, and is maintained through policy, inflation rates accelerate without limit. Similarly, if the rate of inflation of imported goods returns to its original rate, the long-run Phillips curve shifts back to LPC$_1$.

The acceleration of prices in international commodity markets was an outstanding feature of the inflations of the late 1960s–early 1970s and again in 1979–80, and the subsequent decelerations of inflation rates in these markets had much to do with the declines in overall rates of inflation. Depreciation has been forced on countries because of a rise in world unemployment rates, i.e., U^w, when the country chose not to achieve external balance by restricting AD.

The breakdown of an incomes policy

An increase in g_0 (or a decline in $\dot{q}$) is easily seen to have similar effects on the costs of unemployment goals. The intercept g_0 can be given alternative interpretations. For example, it could represent the

[14] Recall from chapter 3 that, in discussing the alpha strand of VPC analysis, an increase in $\dot{p}^1$ shifted the VPC to the right.

164 Breakdown

Figure 8.2 The impact of rising import prices on the variable-coefficient Phillips curve

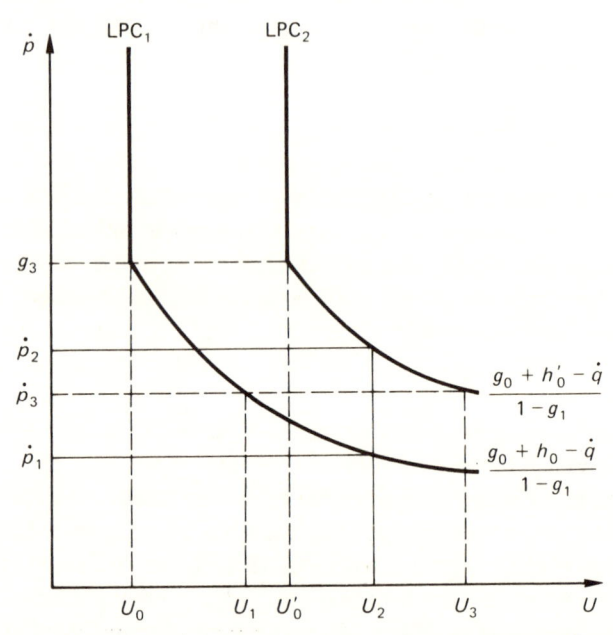

[Figure 8.2: Graph with vertical axis $\dot{p}$ and horizontal axis U. Two long-run Phillips curves LPC₁ and LPC₂ are shown as vertical lines. Horizontal dashed lines mark levels g_3, $\dot{p}_2$, $\dot{p}_3$, $\dot{p}_1$. Vertical dashed lines mark U_0, U_1, U_0', U_2, U_3. Two downward-sloping curves are labeled $\dfrac{g_0 + h_0' - \dot{q}}{1 - g_1}$ and $\dfrac{g_0 + h_0 - \dot{q}}{1 - g_1}$.]

real wage target $\dot{q}^T$ demanded by labor that was treated as a factor influencing the NAIRU in chapter 3. An increase in $\dot{q}^T$ can then be interpreted as representing more aggressive behavior on the part of labor in its wage demands, or as indicating the breakdown of an incomes policy.[15]

A slight re-interpretation of figure 8.2 brings out the implications of a higher target rate of growth of real wages. Assume that the unemployment rate is initially at U_2. Let the shift in the long-run Phillips curve from LPC₁ to LPC₂ reflect an increase in $\dot{q}^T$. If the unemployment rate remains at U_2, the rate of inflation rises from $\dot{p}_1$ to $\dot{p}_2$. Allow next that the authorities consider an inflation rate of $\dot{p}_2$ unacceptably high and respond by reducing AD enough to increase unemployment to U_3 and to reduce the rate of inflation to $\dot{p}_3$.

It is common in VPC literature to ascribe the persistence of high unemployment, say U_3, to workers targeting too high a real wage since

---

[15] In much of the Eurosclerosis literature a rise in $\dot{q}^T$ relative to $\dot{q}$ is alleged to increase the real wage gap. In this study, such an increase is to be interpreted as real wage resistance, as the real wage is determined in the product market. See Bruno and Sachs, *Economics of Worldwide Stagflation*, pp. 174–6, for the former view.

the authorities have no choice but to restrict AD when the NAIRU shifts to the right. However, once it is allowed that there is no unique equilibrium unemployment rate, even in the absence of hysteresis, a very different interpretation of events is required. In the present example, if the authorities had not chosen to reduce AD, the unemployment rate would have remained at U_2, but they did not choose this option because they considered an inflation rate of $\dot{p}_2$ unacceptably high. The important macroquestion is why inflation rates are so high at U_2 (and why the demand for low unemployment rates is so weak) since this is what has led to the restrictive AD policies and the higher unemployment rate U_3.[16] The incorporation of hysteresis effects in the next section strengthens the argument.

The breakdown of an incomes policy and its inflationary consequences can be discussed in somewhat different terms. Strike variables were treated in part I as proxies for institutional arrangements that advance or retard a social bargain. When industrial relations deteriorate and social bargains break down within a country, a rise in strike volume is likely. Thus in the late 1960s and early 1970s several countries experienced "wage explosions" attributed to a breakdown in labor relations which were accompanied by substantial increases in strike activity. If, then, g_0 is assumed to represent strike activity, an increase in strike volume will also cause an outward shift of the long-run Phillips curve in figure 8.2.[17]

A self-fulfilling prophecy

A decline in the threshold rate of inflation g_3 also causes the Phillips curve to shift outward as can be seen from inspection of equation (8.15). Assume initially that the critical threshold level for g, is 5 percent and the (previous period) inflation rate is 4 percent. Since the actual inflation rate is below the threshold, complete compensation for price inflation is not built into wage demands. However, assume that some unexplained event causes workers to be more concerned about protecting their real wages and therefore to lower the threshold rate to 3 percent. Now any expected rate of inflation (= $\dot{p}_{t-1}$) greater than 3 percent leads to real wage bargaining. In figure 8.3 this is shown by a

---

[16] The policy implications of inflation persistence are very different from those flowing from VPC analysis. See chapter 11.

[17] For studies that treat strikes in this way see Paldam, "Industrial conflict", 1980; and D. Hibbs, *The Political Economy of Industrial Democracies*, Harvard University Press, Cambridge, MA, 1987, chapter 3.

166 Breakdown

Figure 8.3 The impact of reduction in inflation thresholds on the variable-coefficient Phillips curve

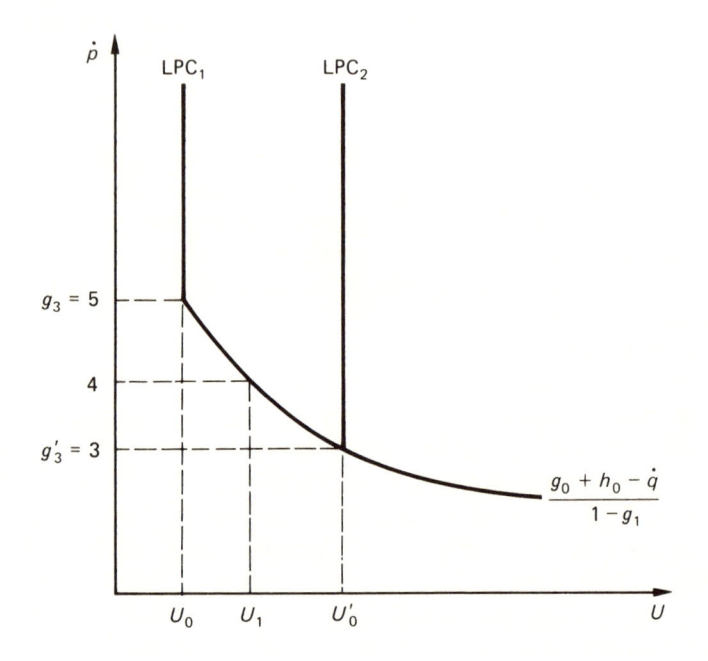

decline in the threshold rate of inflation from g_3 to g'_3. However, this decline also causes the unemployment rate corresponding to the vertical segment to increase from U_0 to U'_0 with a corresponding decrease in the length of the track I segment. If, initially, the unemployment was greater than U_0 but less than U'_0, say U_1, and is maintained, then after the threshold rate has been lowered, inflation rates accelerate without limit.

Unfortunately, expectations that real wages might be endangered can be a self-fulfilling prophecy. Assume again an unemployment rate of U_1 with $g_3 = 5$ percent and suppose that the threshold rate falls to $g'_3 = 3$ percent because workers become more concerned about the ability of their money wage demands to protect real wages. This concern will cause actual inflation rates to accelerate and restrictive AD policies to be introduced. But anything that leads the authorities to restrict AD, such as accelerating inflation rates, is liable to reduce the rate of growth of productivity and therefore real wages. Note also that such a sequence of events well describes a collapse of a hitherto successful incomes policy and the loss of one of the chief benefits of restrained money wage growth, that is, rapid growth of real wages.

8.9 Hysteresis and the Variable-coefficient Phillips Curve

Performance and the position of the variable-coefficient Phillips curve

It was pointed out in chapter 3 that many of the alleged determinants of the NAIRU are very likely influenced by the actual performance of the economy, which depends on AD policies. The parallel story to be told now merely requires a recognition that with hysteresis effects or path dependence, the past and current performance of the economy affects the position of the VCPC (including its vertical segment). In particular, periods of high and rising unemployment lead to outward shifts in the VCPC (including its vertical segment). In particular, periods of high and rising unemployment lead to outward shifts in the VCPC, while tight labor markets and boom conditions generate shifts in the opposite direction. The former shift makes persistent inflation a distinct possibility.

Consider one of the conclusions of chapter 3. It was argued that the performance of the economy affects, among other things, the rates of growth of actual and expected productivity, prices of traded goods, attitudes toward employment rather than leisure, union strength, and unemployment benefits. Some of these induced, largely institutional, effects are explicitly included in the VCPC model of section 8.5, for example, the rate of growth of productivity $\dot{q}$. Others can easily be incorporated, as the treatment of changes in the equation intercepts have just made clear. All that is being added here is the recognition that these parameters are actually functions of performance.

Performance and productivity growth

The issues are easily demonstrated by analyzing induced changes in productivity growth. As discussed in chapter 3, believers in hysteresis effects argue that prolonged periods of restrictive AD and high and rising rates of unemployment lead to reduced rates of physical investment, particularly innovative investment, the atrophy of labor skills, and the loss of labor's work ethic and management's innovative drive. This amounts to an induced reduction in the rate of growth of labor productivity $\dot{q}$.

Consider the following sequence of events traced out in figure 8.4. Assume that the economy is initially at point A on some long-run Phillips curve (not drawn) experiencing an unemployment rate of U_1 and an acceptable rate of inflation, say $\dot{p}_1$, when h_0 increases owing to a run-up of oil prices. This sets in motion the wage–price mechanism, which results in the inflation rate rising to $\dot{p}_2$ as the long-run Phillips

Figure 8.4 Hysteresis and the variable-coefficient Phillips curve

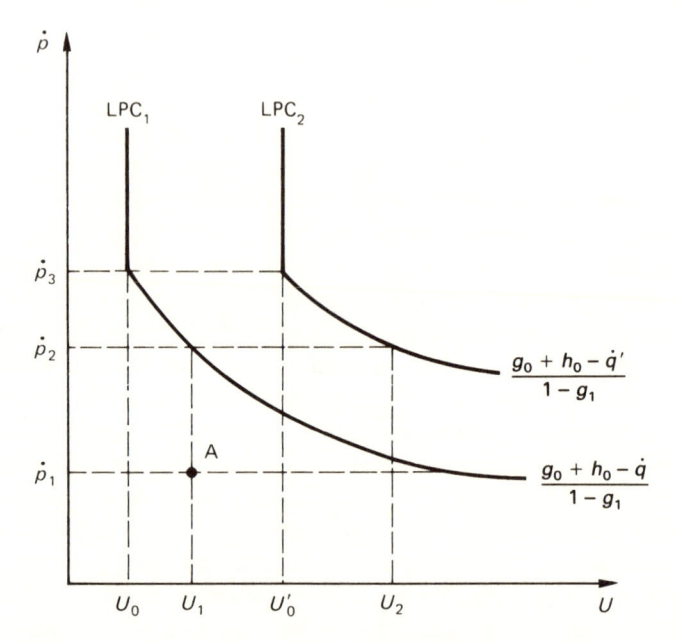

curve shifts to LPC$_1$. Assume that this is considered to be an unacceptably high rate of inflation. In response, the authorities sharply reduce AD and allow unemployment rates to increase to U_2.

The existence of hysteresis in this context means that the restrictive policy response to higher inflation causes a second outward shift of the Phillips curve to, say, LPC$_2$ in figure 8.4 because of the induced decline in the rate of growth of labor productivity from $\dot{q}$ to $\dot{q}'$. Over time, the unemployment rate has risen from U_1 to U_2 while the rate of inflation remains at $\dot{p}_2$. The increase in unemployment from U_1 to U_2 can be directly attributed to the reduction in AD. The persistence of high rates of inflation is indirectly related to AD policy because the position of the Phillips curve (including its vertical segment) depends on attempts to curb inflation, that is, hysteresis, and because an unwillingness of the authorities to push unemployment rates above U_2 does not permit a reduction in the rate of inflation.[18] U_2 is the new (policy-determined) equilibrium unemployment rate.

---

[18] Hargreaves Heap, "Choosing the wrong natural rate," indicates how hysteresis generates curvature to the long-run Phillips curve even if it is assumed that the expectations coefficient is unity.

Performance and wage bargaining

The impact of restrictive AD policies on employment and inflation is similar when the labor market is not treated as an integrated whole but divided into segments according to "membership rules" (for example, which workers are to be considered in some collective agreement) or according to unemployment experience (for example, long term or short term). For example, depending upon how expectations are generated in insider–outsider models of the labor market, a decrease in AD may have no effect on rates of inflation of money wages and prices and only affect employment when workers with seniority—the remaining insiders—are unconcerned about the unemployment of the recently hired. Formally, this can be represented by an increase in the intercept, g_0 in equation (8.10) and an outward shift of the VCPC in figure 8.4 in response to a decline in AD, as higher rates of inflation are now associated with every rate of unemployment along track I.

An alternative source of hysteresis arises when restrictive AD policies are long lasting and lead to long-term unemployment. In such cases skills and work habits atrophy, leading to less intensive job search. On the employers' side the long-term nature of the unemployment may act as a screening device. Considering both sides of the market, the long-term unemployed then have little influence on wage settlements and, as a result, any given unemployment rate is again associated with a higher rate of wage, and therefore price, inflation. Like the induced negative effect of restrictive AD policies on productivity growth, these examples can generate rising unemployment and persistent high rates of inflation.[19]

8.10 Conclusions

An end to "fine tuning"

Hysteresis effects raise serious practical problems for discretionary AD policy. As an example, assume that the authorities have in mind some social preference function revealing the utility of different combinations of inflation and unemployment. Their aim is to maximize this utility function subject to a Phillips curve constraint.[20] Allow further

---

[19] See O. Blanchard and L. Summers, "Hysteresis in unemployment," *European Economic Review*, 31 (1–2), 1987, 288–95; and A. Lindbeck and D. Snower, "Wage setting, unemployment, and insider–outsider relations," *American Economic Review, Papers and Proceedings*, 76, May 1986, 235–9.

[20] See chapter 7, appendix A.

that restrictive AD policies result not merely in a movement down a given Phillips curve but also in a shift away from the origin of the curve because of induced decreases in the rate of growth of productivity $\dot{q}$

In this case, a successful targeting of the inflation–unemployment goal requires that this shift be taken into account in setting policy. In the case of restrictive AD policies, a given increase in unemployment will be accompanied by a smaller reduction in inflation than if hysteresis effects were absent. In general, rates of inflation are less sensitive to changes in the unemployment rate once path dependence is recognized. Naturally, AD policies induce other effects but the point is that once hysteresis effects are introduced, discretionary policy has additional difficulties in realizing its targets.

Going for an incomes policy

There are other policy messages implicit in what has been said. First, just as a decrease in AD which increases the unemployment rate from U_1 to U_2 leads to a shift to the right of the long-run Phillips curve in figure 8.4, an increase in AD reverses the process. This immediately suggests a program for ending mass unemployment—"going for growth." However, while recognition of the symmetry of hysteresis effects reaffirms the Keynesian symmetry and the effectiveness of stimulative AD policies, it does not necessarily imply that substantial stimulative AD policies are complete solutions to the current difficulties. As discussed in introduction I, economic recovery today is not analogous to dentistry. Increases in AD do lead to reductions in unemployment when there are involuntarily unemployed resources and they induce such results as an increase in productivity growth and a reduction in long-term unemployment. But the discussion of long-term unemployment in the last section indicates that any recovery policy would also have to include additional programs such as long-run retraining programs to replace lost human capital and, of course, a social bargain. Furthermore, there are additional induced effects of stimulative AD policies which are likely to unleash serious inflationary problems; for example, foreign repercussions of the unilateral adoption of stimulative AD policies may well have inflationary results. This discussion will be left for chapter 9.

Second, the two-track model of inflation reveals how difficult is the containment of inflation at FE in an economy which makes no concerted continuous effort to achieve wage restraint. For example, a reduction in the threshold rate of inflation g_3 is enough to generate accelerating rates of inflation, and when cumulative price increases arising out of movements in international commodity markets or changes in the exchange rate are introduced, the instability of the Phillips curve and the potential explosiveness of inflation are highlighted.

This is not said as an argument for discarding Phillips curve analysis. Other things being equal, tighter labor markets increase inflationary pressures and it is difficult to explain recent events, including the policies adopted by the authorities, without emphasizing this negative Phillips curve relation. Rather, the remarks are meant to suggest how important it is to shift the Phillips curve inward permanently, thereby relieving the authorities of the need to be constantly adjusting AD policies. This involves constructing a recovery program based on a set of institutions that aim specifically to restrain wages and prices at FE whatever the behavior of the "other things."

Hysteresis, the persistence of inflation, and the causal chain

Much of the hysteresis literature seeks to explain the persistence of unemployment.[21] What is emphasized here is that hysteresis effects are better viewed as sources of inflation persistence. Prolonged high rates of unemployment can be explained quite adequately by long-run policies of restricted AD. An outward shift of the VCPC increases the rate of inflation associated with any unemployment rate as the various examples of path dependence in this chapter make clear. If one of the sources of this outward shift is a restrictive AD policy, inflation rates will be sluggish downward as unemployment rates rise.

This misdirection of the macroresearch agenda arises out of the long-standing acceptance of the vertical long-run Phillips curve and a unique equilibrium unemployment rate to which the economy rapidly and automatically converges. Within this framework a shock-induced rise in unemployment is supposed to set in motion falling prices and Pigou effects that return the economy to the NAIRU. The

[21]See Blanchard and Summers, "Hysteresis in unemployment"; C. Pissarides, "Unemployment and macroeconomics: an inaugural address," *Centre for Labour Economics Discussion Paper*, No. 304, London School of Economics, March 1988; and G. Alogoskoufis and A. Manning, "Unemployment persistence," *Economic Policy*, 3 (2) October, 1988, 427–69.

failure of inflation rates to fall markedly when unemployment rates rise sharply must then be attributed to an increase in the NAIRU. Why the NAIRU has increased becomes the main interest.

Even in the absence of hysteresis effects, multiple equilibria occur in VCPC analysis and indeed in any framework that allows for a long-run tradeoff between inflation and unemployment. As a result, equilibrium unemployment and inflation rates are determined by the stance of AD policy, certainly along the track I segment of the VCPC. In this context, the concluding remarks of chapter 3 should be updated. When hysteresis effects are introduced, the relevance of any kind of analysis that defines equilibrium independently of policy (and performance) is doubly suspect. A framework that sets as one of its tasks the explanation of why an AD policy is chosen provides a framework for dealing with path dependence as well as explaining macroperformance.

Appendix A: Analytical Solutions

A1 Model A

In section 8.3 a simple model of wage–price dynamics was written as

$$\dot{w}_t = b_0 + b_1 U_t^{-1} + b_2 \dot{p}_{t-1} \tag{8.4}$$

and

$$\dot{p}_t = \dot{w}_t - \dot{q} = b_0 - \dot{q} + b_1 U_t^{-1} + b_2 \dot{p}_{t-1} \quad 0 < b_2 < 1 \tag{8.6}$$

where $\dot{w}$, U, $\dot{p}$, and $\dot{q}$ are the rates of wage inflation, unemployment, price inflation, and productivity growth respectively, with the time subscripts indicating the lag structure.

Standard procedures for deriving analytical solutions are applied, and the particular solution is found by setting $\dot{p}^* = \dot{p}_t = \dot{p}_{t-1}$ in equation (8.6) and solving for

$$\dot{p}^* = \frac{b_0 + b_1 U^{-1} - \dot{q}}{1 - b_2} \tag{8.8}$$

which is the long-run Phillips curve LPC. Next let $\dot{p}_t = Ad^t$ and write equation (8.6) as

$$\dot{p}_t - b_2 \dot{p}_{t-1} = b_0 + b_1 U_t^{-1} - \dot{q} \tag{8.6'}$$

Then the homogeneous form can be written as

$$Ad^t - b_2 Ad^{t-1} = 0$$

and

$$d - b_2 = 0 \text{ or } d = b_2 \text{ and } \dot{p}_c = A(b_2)^t$$

for the complementary function.

To find the constant A, let $\dot{p}_t = \dot{p}_0$ when $t = 0$. Then

$$\dot{p}_0 = \dot{p}_c + \dot{p}^* = A + \frac{b_0 + b_1 U^{-1} - \dot{q}}{1 - b_2}$$

The complete solution of the model is

$$\dot{p}_t = \left(\dot{p}_0 - \frac{b_0 + b_1 U^{-1} - \dot{q}}{1 - b_2} \right)(b_2)^t + \dot{p}^* \tag{8.16}$$

Equation (8.16) reveals that, for any permanently maintained U, there will be a corresponding long-run rate of inflation $\dot{p}^*$, illustrating the large number of unemployment rates at which inflation rates do not accelerate

174 Breakdown

when $0 < b_2 < 1$. Following any disturbances, the inflation rate may deviate from this long-run value as such shocks "activate" the term in parentheses. However, the impact will be temporary since $\dot{p}_t$ always converges on $\dot{p}^*$ if $0 < b_2 < 1$.

Equations (8.4) and (8.6) can also be solved for the long-run Phillips curve for wage inflation. Substituting equation (8.6) lagged one period into equation (8.4) and setting $\dot{w}^* = \dot{w}_t = \dot{w}_{t-1}$ gives

$$\dot{w}^* = \frac{b_0 - b_2\dot{q} + b_1 U^{-1}}{1-b_2} \tag{8.17}$$

for the particular solution. As the complementary function of the solution for wage inflation is derived in the same way as that for price inflation, the complete solution need not be derived but simply given as

$$\dot{w}_t = \left(\dot{w}_0 - \frac{b_0 + b_1 U^{-1} - b_2\dot{q}}{1-b_2}\right)(b_2)^t + \dot{w}^* \tag{8.18}$$

Since $\dot{w}_t$ converges on $\dot{w}^*$ if $0 < b_2 < 1$, equation (8.17) is the long-run Phillips curve for wage inflation. The long-run rate of growth of real wages is found by subtracting equation (8.8) from equation (8.17), giving $\dot{w}^* - \dot{p}^* = \dot{q}$, the rate of growth of productivity. As pointed out in section 8.7, the behavior of real wages depends only on the behavior of productivity and is independent of the size of b_2. This is true in the short run as well.

A2 The two-track model: Track I

The two-track model of inflation in section 8.5 was written

$$\dot{w}_t = g_0 + g_1\dot{p}_{t-1} + g_2(\dot{p}_{t-1} - g_3) + g_4 U_t^{-1} \tag{8.10}$$

and

$$\dot{p}_t = \dot{w}_t - \dot{q} + h_0 \tag{8.11}$$

or

$$\dot{p}_t = (g_0 + h_0) + g_1\dot{p}_{t-1} + g_2(\dot{p}_{t-1} - g_3) + g_4 U_t^{-1} - \dot{q} \tag{8.12}$$

The particular solution of the track I part of the model (i.e. $g_2 = 0$ when $\dot{p}_{t-1} \leq g_3$) for price inflation is found in the same way as the particular solution of model A and is

$$\dot{p}^* = \frac{g_0 + h_0 - \dot{q} + g_4 U^{-1}}{1-g_1} \tag{8.13}$$

The complete solution is

High Inflation and High Unemployment 175

$$\dot{p}_t = \left(\dot{p}_0 - \frac{g_0 + g_4 U^{-1} - \dot{q} + h_0}{1-g_1} \right) (g_1)^t + \dot{p}^* \tag{8.19}$$

which only differs from the solution to model A by the inclusion of the constant term h_0 in the numerator of both parts of the complete solution. Since by assumption $0 < g_1 < 1$, the dynamic properties of track I are virtually identical with those of model A.

The complete solution of the model of wage inflation is

$$\dot{w}_t = \left(\dot{w}_0 - \frac{g_0 + g_4 U^{-1} - g_1 \dot{q} + g_1 h_0}{1-g_1} \right) (g_1)^t + \dot{w}^* \tag{8.20}$$

where

$$\dot{w}^* = \frac{g_0 + g_4 U^{-1} - g_1 \dot{q} + g_1 h_0}{1-g_1} \tag{8.21}$$

A3 The two-track model: Track II

When $\dot{p}_{t-1} > g_3$, $g_2 \neq 0$ and past rates of inflation are built into wage settlements completely. As a result equation (8.12) must be written differently. Write it as

$$\dot{p}_t - (g_1 + g_2)\dot{p}_{t-1} = g_0 + h_0 - g_2 g_3 + g_4 U_t^{-1} - \dot{q} \tag{8.12'}$$

Since $g_1+g_2 = 1$, $\dot{p}^* = \dot{p}_t = \dot{p}_{t-1}$ is not satisfactory as a long-run equilibrium solution since the left-hand side of

$$\{1-(g_1+g_2)\}\dot{p}^* = g_0 + h_0 - g_2 g_3 + g_4 U^{-1} - \dot{q} \tag{8.14}$$

is zero.

Instead try

$$\dot{p}^* = kt \tag{8.22}$$

or

$$kt - (g_1+g_2)k(t-1) = g_0 + h_0 - g_2 g_3 + g_4 U^{-1} - \dot{q} \tag{8.23}$$

giving

$$k(1-g_1-g_2)t + (g_1+g_2)k = g_0 + h_0 - g_2 g_3 + g_4 U^{-1} - \dot{q} \tag{8.24}$$

Since $g_1 + g_2 = 1$, this gives

$$k = g_0 + h_0 - g_2 g_3 + g_4 U^{-1} - \dot{q} \tag{8.25}$$

or

$$\dot{p}^* = (g_0 + h_0 - g_2 g_3 + g_4 U^{-1} - \dot{q})t \tag{8.26}$$

for the particular solution.

176 Breakdown

Next, let $\dot{p}_t = Ab^t$ as before and write the homogeneous form of track II as

$$Ab^t - (g_1 + g_2) Ab^{t-1} = 0$$

and

$$b - (g_1 + g_2) = 0$$

or

$$b = g_1 + g_2 = 1$$

implying

$$\dot{p}_c = A$$

for the complementary function. To find A, let $\dot{p}_t = \dot{p}_{00}$ when $t = 0$. Then

$$\dot{p}_{00} = \dot{p}_c + \dot{p}^* = A + (g_0 + h_0 - g_2 g_3 + g_4 U^{-1} - \dot{q})t = A \quad \text{for } t = 0$$

The complete solution is

$$\dot{p}_t = \dot{p}_{00} + (g_0 + h_0 - g_2 g_3 + g_4 U^{-1} - \dot{q})t \quad \dot{p}_{00} > g_3 \quad (8.27)$$

Setting equation (8.14) equal to zero gives the unemployment rate U_0 corresponding to the vertical segment of track II as

$$U_0 = \frac{g_4}{\dot{q} + g_2 g_3 - g_0 - h_0} \quad (8.15)$$

Inspection of equation (8.27) reveals that any unemployment rate less than U_0 makes the expression in parentheses positive and inflation rates accelerate without limit, as in the NAIRU analysis of chapter 3. However, for any unemployment rate equal to or greater than U_0, and hence any inflation rates equal to or less than g_3, the long-run rate of inflation is given by equation (8.13). All such unemployment rates generate nonaccelerating long-run rates of inflation.

A4 The shifting variable-coefficient Phillips curve

For convenience equations (8.13) and (8.15) are repeated:

$$\dot{p}^* = \frac{g_0 + h_0 - \dot{q} + g_4 U^{-1}}{1 - g_1} \quad (8.13)$$

$$U_0 = \frac{g_4}{\dot{q} + g_2 g_3 - g_0 - h_0} \quad (8.15)$$

Together these two relations indicate the impact of changes in parameters on both the vertical and downward-sloping positions of the VCPC. Increases in g_0 and h_0 and decreases in $\dot{q}$ shift the vertical segment to the right and the downward-sloping segment upward and to the right as shown in figures 8.2 and 8.4. In the concluding section of the text, the symmetry of the hysteresis effect was cited as another support for the effectiveness of stimulative AD policies. Clearly, inspection of equations (8.13) and (8.15) indicated that decreases in g_0 and h_0 and increases in $\dot{q}$ shift the entire curve to the left and lower the downward-sloping portion. Changes in the threshold rate of inflation g_3 affect only the vertical segment as shown in figure 8.3.

Appendix B: Regression Analysis

Estimates of the Eckstein-Brinner VCPC for Canada were undertaken using ordinary least-squares methods. The VCPC model estimated was

$$\dot{w}_t = g_0 + g_1 \dot{p}_{t-1} + g_2(\dot{p}_t^e - g_3) + g_4 U_t + e_t$$

where $\dot{w}$ is the annual rate of wage inflation quarter by quarter computed as $(w_t - w_{t-4})/w_{t-4}$, $\dot{p}_{t-1}$ is the annual rate of increase of the consumer price index lagged one quarter similarly computed quarter by quarter as $(p_{t-1} - p_{t-5})/p_{t-5}$, U_t is an annual unemployment rate computed quarter by quarter as a four-quarter moving average, $\dot{p}_t^e$ is the expected rate of inflation in period t (variously defined) and similarly computed, g_3 is the inflation threshold, and e_t is the error term. The period covered was from 1961 IV to 1983 IV.

Let $\dot{p}_t^e - g_3$ be defined as the inflation severity factor, ISF_t. The data series was generated in the following manner. Some value for g_3, and some distributed lag function of the form $\dot{p}_t^e = (\dot{p}_{t-1} + \dot{p}_{t-2} + \dot{p}_{t-3} + \dot{p}_{t-4} + \dot{p}_{t-5})/5$ was assumed. If in any period $\dot{p}_t^e \leq g_3$, ISF_t was assumed to take a value of zero. If $\dot{p}_t^e > g_3$, ISF_t was assumed to be given by the excess of $\dot{p}_t^e$ over g_3.[22]

The underlying economic rationale for this procedure was as follows. When inflation is low, labor merely looks back one period in determining a fair real wage. Given the costs of acquiring information, workers seek out more information when inflation is high. Alternatively, workers show less concern about protecting their real wages through money wage settlements when inflation is low. As indicated in the text and appendix A, during periods of prosperity real wages grow in line with productivity growth justifying their lack of concern. When $\dot{p}_t^e > g_3$ a greater concern is shown for real wage protection. In order to make the best guess possible of current inflation rates, workers look back several periods to better formulate their expectations.[23]

It will be noted that annual rates of price inflation are computed for any quarter as a change in the price index since the same quarter in the previous year divided by the price index of the earlier quarter. This means, for example, that if the expected rate of price inflation in period t is generated by a moving average of annual rates over the five previous quarters, expectations are in fact generated over a time space covering two years, that is, from period $t-1$ to period $t-9$.

By varying the length of time over which expectations are determined, various numbers of early observations were dropped. It became clear from the

---

[22]This is essentially the manner in which Eckstein and Brinner generated values for the independent variable ISF_t. See Eckstein and Brinner, "Inflation process in the United States," p. 4.

[23]There is also a statistical reason for using two different independent variables $\dot{p}_{t-1}$ and $\dot{p}_t^e$ (variously defined) in defining the track I and track II money wage responses. If $\dot{p}_t^e$ is used instead of $\dot{p}_{t-1}$, severe multicollinearity arises at both low and high threshold levels.

ordinary expectations-augmented Phillips curve estimates that this strongly affected the coefficient of the price variable $\dot{p}_{t-1}$. For example, the more observations from the early 1960s that were excluded, the larger was the price coefficient. This kind of structural instability was also found by Eckstein and Brinner, suggesting the need to use the variable-coefficient approach.

Given the fact that union contracts in Canada typically last for two to three years, it was felt that something like a five-quarter moving average was appropriate. Various regressions were tried using alternative distributive lag functions defining $\dot{p}_t^e$.

Various values for g_3 were assumed and estimates of the coefficients were obtained for each g_3 together with different alternative expectations-generating functions. Two wage series were used, one for hourly earnings in manufacturing and the other for weekly earnings in all industries. The best R^2 results were obtained when $g_3 = 0.06$ in the manufacturing regressions and $g_3 = 0.07$ for the industry regression and when $\dot{p}_t^e$ was generated as a moving average over the previous five quarters whether the unemployment rate or its reciprocal was used. These are shown in table 8.1 along with estimates of ordinary expectations-augmented Phillips curves.

The sense of the manufacturing regression using U_t as an independent variable is as follows. When the expected rate of inflation is 6 percent or less, the rate of hourly earnings is adjusted upward by a little less than one-half of the change in the expected rate of inflation. When $\dot{p}_t^e$ exceeds 6 percent, there is complete sensitivity to expected inflation.[24] The all-industries regression is to be interpreted similarly. When $\dot{p}_t^e$ is 7 percent or less, the rate of weekly earnings is adjusted upward by one-quarter of the change in the expected rate of inflation, but $\dot{p}_t^e$ greater than 7 percent results in complete sensitivity. The lower threshold level for manufacturing than for all industries can be explained by better information and organization of more unionized wage bargainers.

The ordinary expectations-augmented Phillips curve regressions for manufacturing gives a coefficient close to unity for the price expectations variable. According to VCPC analysis, this model is an incorrect specification of the Phillips curve. The estimated coefficient value should be interpreted as an average of a small coefficient when $\dot{p}_t^e$ is low and a higher coefficient when $\dot{p}_t^e$ exceeds the threshold g_3.

---

[24] By the usual β test, the sum of the estimates for g_1 and g_2 were not significantly different from unity.

180 Breakdown

Table 8.1 Wage inflation in Canadian manufacturing and all industries, 1961–1983

Ordinary expectations-augmented Phillips curve
$$\dot{p}_t^e = (\dot{p}_{t-1} + \dot{p}_{t-2} + \dot{p}_{t-3} + \dot{p}_{t-4} + \dot{p}_{t-5})/5$$

	Constant term	U_t	$\dot{p}_t^e$	$\bar{R}^2$	DW
Manufacturing	0.079 (0.018)	−0.830[a] (0.268)	0.974[a] (0.166)	0.921	1.80
All industries	0.080 (0.017)	−0.709[a] (0.235)	0.725[a] (0.151)	0.923	1.60

	Constant term	$1/U_t$	$\dot{p}_t^e$	$\bar{R}^2$	DW
Manufacturing	−0.014 (0.29)	0.0026[a] (0.0013)	0.892[a] (0.191)	0.916	1.76
All industries	−0.052 (0.025)	0.0019[b] (0.0011)	0.645[a] (0.171)	0.918	1.53

Variable-coefficient Phillips curve
$$\dot{p}_t^e = (\dot{p}_{t-1} + \dot{p}_{t-2} + \dot{p}_{t-3} + \dot{p}_{t-4} + \dot{p}_{t-5})/5$$

	Constant term	U_t	$\dot{p}_{t-1}$	$(\dot{p}_t^e - g_3) = \text{ISF}_t$	$\bar{R}^2$	DW
Manufacturing	0.084 (0.021)	−0.697[a] (0.276)	0.477[a] (0.170)	0.692[a] (0.313)	0.925	1.64
All industries	0.091 (0.020)	−0.614[a] (0.238)	0.250[b] (0.136)	0.827[a] (0.269)	0.929	1.66

	Constant term	$1/U_t$	$\dot{p}_{t-1}$	$(\dot{p}_t^e - g_3) = \text{ISF}_t$	$\bar{R}^2$	DW
Manufacturing	0.0091 (0.0025)	0.0019 (0.0013)	0.493[a] (0.169)	0.709[a] (0.339)	0.922	1.61
All industries	0.001 (0.022)	0.0017 (0.0012)	0.814[a] (0.281)	0.243[b] (0.143)	0.925	1.62

Two wage series are used: the seasonally unadjusted average weekly industrial composite earnings and the average hourly earnings in manufacturing. The price series is the consumer price index (all items). Annual rates of wage and price inflation for each quarter are computed as the change in earnings or the price index since the same quarter in the previous year divided by the level of earnings or the price index of the earlier period. Annual unemployment rates are computed as simple four-quarter moving averages.
The numbers in parentheses are standard errors. The $\bar{R}^2$ values are adjusted for degrees of freedom.
[a] Coefficient significant at the 5 percent level.
[b] Coefficient significant at the 10 percent level.

Source: *Canadian Statistical Review*, various issues

9 Explaining the Breakdown

9.1 Introduction

Macrodevelopments following capitalism's golden years have been dominated by (1) the acceleration of inflation rates in the late 1960s and early 1970s and again during the period 1979–80, (b) the higher and rising rates of unemployment for two decades beginning in 1974, and (c) the failure of inflation rates to fall to levels usually associated with such high rates of unemployment.

An explanation of the rising unemployment throughout the OECD was provided in chapter 3. Chapter 8 described how the inflation costs of any AD policy could rise over time in response to certain key events, for example, a decline in productivity, a rise in import prices, or the breakdown of an incomes policy. In this chapter intertemporal developments, especially the persistence of inflation, are analyzed in terms of the framework developed in these earlier chapters. The main focus will be on the period of prolonged mass unemployment and high rates of inflation since 1974. However, the acceleration of inflation rates in the late 1960s and early 1970s requires consideration because the acceleration of inflation was responsible for the drastic policy response, followed by the large increase in unemployment in the period since 1973.[1] Together with chapter 10, this chapter makes clear the causes of the perverse macrodevelopments since the late 1960s.

Moreover, serious inflation will almost certainly provoke similar policy responses in the future. Inflation and high unemployment are linked in the sense that a predictable government response to serious inflation is part of the endogenous chain of events in many capitalist economies. Understanding the causes of high rates of inflation aids in developing preventive measures. At the very least it should help ex-

[1]The acceleration of inflation rates in 1979–80 and their subsequent deceleration can be largely explained in a manner similar to the acceleration of inflation rates in the 1960s–1970s and will not be treated in any detail.

plain why restrictive AD policies have become the routine anti-inflation weapon despite their lack of success.

9.2 The "Great Post-war Inflation"

The OECD report of the experts

The influential OECD report of the mid-1970s, the so-called McCracken Report, correctly attributed the inflation of the late 1960s and early 1970s to a variety of causes.[2] First, the prolonged prosperity of the 1950s and 1960s led to growing expectations and aspirations on the part of the labor force which increased the intensity of cost-push inflationary pressures. Second, the synchronization of booms in the various OECD economies in 1972–73 led to a rapid run-up of commodity prices which was further intensified by a speculative boom in these markets. Third, various shocks and errors of policy occurred during the early 1970s that added to the inflation, for example, the run-up of oil prices and the collapse of the Bretton Woods exchange rate regime. In the view of the OECD experts these causes underlying the acceleration of inflation rates were best interpreted as a number of unfavorable shocks occurring in a short period of time that were not likely to recur. Growth, price stability, and FE would resume following a program of gradual and carefully planned recovery according to this unfortunately incorrect prognosis.

An alternative interpretation

To others the shocks and their aftermath merely revealed a more basic underlying fact: in the absence of successful policies for coordinating collective bargaining with the national goal of wage and price stability, an inflationary bias had developed and become widespread. Wage and price inflation under these conditions could be expected to reach unacceptable rates at FE. According to this second view, events revealed just how explosive the endogenous wage–price and wage–wage inflationary mechanisms had become and how inflation prone were the economies. Even countries that had hitherto been able to control inflationary pressures by means of favorable institutional arrangements were unable to do so under the new circumstances. This was evident before the occurrence of such "supply shocks" as the phenomenal rise in prices of internationally traded commodities.

[2]OECD, *Towards Full Employment and Price Stability*, OECD, Paris, 1978.

This second interpretation of the inflation is emphasized here as it incorporates examples of long-run path dependence or hysteresis discussed in section 8.9. It is also in keeping with the McCracken Report's finding that rising expectations and aspirations arising out of the prolonged period of prosperity beginning in the 1950s contributed to inflationary pressures. But the present study considers this path dependence to be more profound and to lead to an endogenous inflationary mechanism that is unstable upward when subject to shocks. This is a basic feature of the explanation of events of the late 1960s and early 1970s.

9.3 Stages of the "Great Inflation"

An outline

Considering the period of the late 1960s and early 1970s as a whole, formalized versions of the OECD explanation that analyze the Great Inflation in terms of stages are helpful in understanding the events of the time.[3] This is a class of theories that explains inflation as an interaction between the wage–wage and wage–price mechanisms that comprise the endogenous core of any inflation process plus shocks that serve to displace inflation rates from some kind of long-run path.[4]

Stage 1 of the inflationary process can be described as the result of the wage explosion in many of the OECD countries together with highly stimulative AD policies in North America. Stage 2 coincides with the amplification of these disturbances by endogenous mechanisms already in place in the noncorporatist economies and by similar mechanisms brought into play following the collapse of social bargains in countries that had previously been able to contain inflation under FE conditions. Stage 3 is the period of the synchronized boom throughout the OECD in 1972–73, which added more fuel to the ongoing high inflation. Finally, stage 4 takes account of the rapid acceleration in the prices of internationally traded commodities—for food and raw materials in late 1972 and then for oil in late 1973—and their impact on the endogenous forces.

The initiating forces

The early phases of the acceleration of inflation rates in the 1960s can be traced in the North American economies to increasingly tighter

---

[3]See A. Blinder, *Economic Policy and the Great Stagflation*, Academic Press, New York, 1981, chapter 5, for an alternative stage analysis.
[4]Since this argument has been developed rather fully elsewhere, it will only be summarized here. See Cornwall, *Conditions for Economic Recovery*, chapter 7.

labor markets in response to steadily increasing AD expansion associated with the Vietnam War. The economy simply moved up the track I segment of the Phillips curve as unemployment rates fell and inflation rates rose.

In many European economies, several of which could be described as economies with explicit or implicit bargains leading to wage restraint in the past, distributional issues became paramount. These concerns operated in the first instance as shocks disturbing a fairly long period of wage restraint. Detailed analysis on a country-by-country basis during the second half of the 1960s found that in several countries labor, especially the rank and file, was dissatisfied with real wages and other aspects of employment and made strong efforts to remedy conditions by pushing for higher money wage demands.[5] But, more fundamentally, the increased concern with distributional issues caused a marked change in the process of wage determination. Rather than wage setting's being strongly influenced by the kinds of bargains described in chapter 5, the cost–push mechanisms became operative. Potential inflationary biases became actual with the breakdown of the "first generation" of incomes policies.[6]

Strike activity

This explanation of the initial acceleration in rates of wage inflation relies on causes of the political institutional type stressed in earlier chapters. In many countries the Phillips curve could be said to have shifted outward to the right. In the cross-country analysis of chapters 5 and 6, differences in the volume of strike activity across countries were assumed to be a proxy for differences in Phillips curves. Along these lines it would be expected that any outward shift in a country's Phillips curve over time would be reflected partly in an increase in strike activity in that country, as outlined in section 8.8.

Intertemporal studies of strike activity in the OECD economies clearly reveal that a rapid increase in strike activity was a common event in the late 1960s and early 1970s, with the increase in wage inflation lagging behind the increase in strike activity by approxi-

---

[5] See D. Soskice, "Strike waves and wage explosions, 1968–1970: an economic interpretation," in C. Crouch and A. Pizzarno (eds.), *The Resurgence of Class Conflict in Western Europe since 1969*, vol. 2, Holmes and Meir, New York, 1978; Perry, "Determinants of wage inflation," especially the "Comments"; and Flanagan et al., *Unionism, Economic Stabilization and Incomes Policies*, chapter 1.

[6] The expression is from Flanagan et al., ibid. See section 8.8 for a Phillips curve analysis.

mately a year.[7] This is certainly reflected in trends in strike volume. The average volume of strikes in the 18 countries increased from 152 man-days lost per 1,000 workers in 1963–67 to 295 in 1968–72. The occurrence of both higher strike activity and an acceleration in the rate of wage inflation within such a short period of time, rather than just an increase in strike activity, has been cited as evidence of increased worker discontent and aggressiveness rather than, say, employer discontent.[8]

The endogenous mechanisms

Whatever the country, additional disturbances, emanating largely from international commodity markets, followed and led to rapid increases in prices of imported goods, which naturally fed through to the cost of living.[9] As labor became even more concerned with its real wage, this fed back to money wages, passed through to product prices, etc. It might also be expected that the threshold level of inflation would have fallen, thus intensifying the process.[10]

Much has been written about the importance of disturbances on the supply side in the Great Inflation of the late 1960s and early 1970s and the acceleration of inflation rates in 1979–80.[11] As important as the wage explosion and the acceleration of commodity prices were, it is essential not to lose sight of the endogenous mechanisms stressed in chapter 8 which were magnifying the force of these disturbances. When fairness considerations prevail and collective bargaining is unre-

[7] See Paldam, "Industrial conflict," Paldam and Rasmusen, "Date for industrial conflicts"; and D. Grubb, "Topics in the OECD Phillips curve," *Economic Journal*, 96, March 1986, 55–79. See also table 6.1.
[8] See Paldam, "Industrial conflict." The acceleration of rates of inflation in 1974 despite rising unemployment was seen by many as evidence that Keynesian theory was no longer applicable. However, convincing explanations of the continued acceleration of inflation, all consistent with Keynesian views on the role of aggregate AD, are available. The simplest involves recognizing that, following a period of accelerating inflation partly induced by rising commodity prices, there is likely to be an acceleration in rates of price inflation in excess of any previous acceleration in rates of wage inflation. As a result real wages will suffer if the rate of growth of money wages does not also accelerate as it did in a majority of countries in 1975. See Perry, "Determinants of wage inflation," table 1.
[9] See Grubb, "Topics in the OECD Phillips curve," figure 2.
[10] See section 8.8.
[11] For this view see W. Beckerman and T. Jenkinson, "What stopped the inflation? Unemployment or commodity prices?" *Economic Journal*, 96, March 1986, 39–54. The authors use pooled cross-section and time series data covering the period of 1963–83 to estimate a short-run Phillips curve for wage inflation for 12 OECD economies. Their chief interest lies in determining the relative impact of unemployment and import price changes on wages. The latter impact is found to dominate, while the text stresses the importance of both influences in the long run.

stricted, the feedback effect from price inflation to wage inflation must be combined with the pass-through effect from wages to prices. This in itself makes the inflationary process more explosive, as the earlier distinction between the long-run and short-run Phillips curves demonstrates. Reductions in unemployment or merely disturbances that push up wages or prices initiate wage–price and wage–wage spirals that can be substantial. When both of these reactions are operative along with threshold effects, a powerful mechanisms is available that further prolongs and amplifies the inflationary impact of adverse shocks. Their continued and widespread operation beginning in the late 1960s ensured the explosion of prices, both in the late 1960s–early 1970s and in the late 1970s–early 1980s.

9.4 Breakdown

The policy response to inflation

During the period 1968–73 unemployment rates rose slightly. A more rapid deterioration in the employment picture then followed. Table II.1 gives average rates of unemployment for the period between the two oil shocks. Despite some fluctuations in unemployment rates, especially in the United States and Germany, inflation rates had so accelerated by 1974 that the authorities permitted a rise in average OECD unemployment rates in the period 1974–79 to approximately double the 1960–73 averages. The resolve of the authorities to combat the inflation through restrictive AD policies dominates macropolicy after 1973. There were some reversals of policy but, with few exceptions, policy-makers were reluctant to push their economies towards the low unemployment rates of the pre-1974 period.[12]

The rapid run-up of oil prices in 1973–74 not only contributed to this inflation but also contributed heavily to a shift in the balance of payments of the OECD from an average surplus of 0.3 percent of GDP in 1963–73 to an average deficit of almost 0.7 percent in 1974. Given the strong dependence upon energy imports and their low price elasticity of demand, the resulting payments difficulties in so many countries intensified the resolve of the authorities. The difficulties of the early

---

[12]For an analysis of the role of restrictive AD policies from 1974 onward, see S. Fischer, "Monetary policy and performance in the U.S., Japan and Europe, 1973–86," *NBER Working Paper Series*, No. 2475, December 1987; Bruno and Sachs, *Economics of Worldwide Stagflation*, chapters 8 and 10; McCallum, "Unemployment in the OECD countries"; and A. Boltho, "Economic policy and performance in Europe since the second oil shock," in M. Emerson (ed.), *Europe's Stagflation*, Clarendon Press, Oxford, 1984.

phases of the decline were then increased by widely adopted "beggar your neighbor" policies throughout the post-1973 period, contributing to the substantial decline in the growth of exports. The oil shock of 1979–80 added to the pressures for restrictive policies.[13]

The inflation response to policy

Even though commodity prices responded strongly to the decline in world demand following both oil shocks, wage and price inflation did not return to the rates usually associated with the unemployment rates that prevailed in the remainder of the 1970s and into the 1980s. They remained stuck on a new higher plateau. Figure 9.1 shows the worsening inflation–unemployment developments. Moving from left to right, the average rates of inflation and unemployment for the periods 1960–73, 1974–79, 1980–83, and 1984–91 are plotted for 18 OECD economies and three subgroups. The subgroups were designated earlier as the low, high, and low–high unemployment economies. Unemployment rates rise in all three groups of economies from one period to the next, but despite the rise in unemployment rates, inflation rates in the 1980s were on average higher than in the period 1960–73. Comparing the figures for 1960–73 with those for 1980–91 for the 18 OECD economies as a group shows a rise in average rates of unemployment from 2.3 to 6.8 percent while inflation rates increased from an average of 4.5 to 6.2 percent.

Several explanations for why inflation rates could fail to decline during the periods between the two oil shocks and throughout the 1980s to levels usually associated with the high unemployment of these periods and why a potential inflationary bias could become an actual one in most economies are provided in chapter 8. Three causes are of particular relevance during these two periods. First, the events of the late 1960s discussed in sections 9.3 and 9.4 above signaled an end to social bargains in several economies, and little in the way of a "second generation" of income policies has since been attempted. In addition, however, two new factors have contributed to problems in the various economies (and a constraint on AD policies)—policy-induced hysteresis effects and the general nature of the breakdown in a highly interdependent world economy, itself partly induced by the collapse of social bargains. All three have increased the cost of reducing unem-

---

[13]See references cited in the previous note. McCallum's study is particularly useful since it indicates the relative impacts of "world demand" and domestic policies on unemployment.

188 *Breakdown*

Figure 9.1 Inflation and unemployment patterns for three groups of OECD economies in the periods 1960–1973, 1974–1979, 1980–1983, 1984–1991. Data from Table II.1

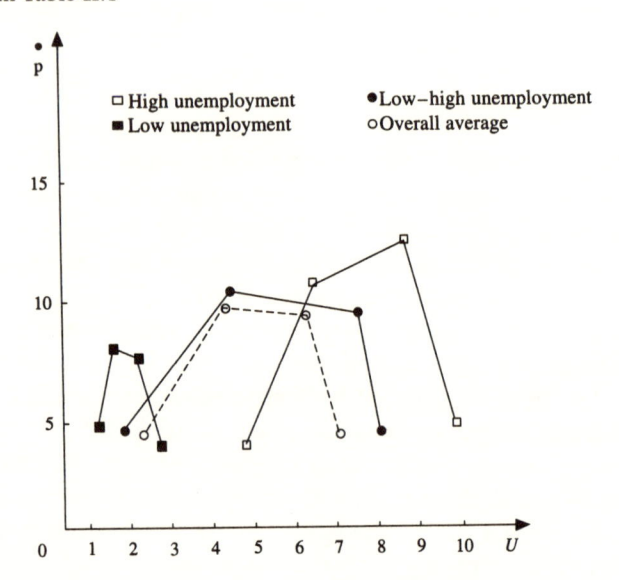

ployment and have led to a more widespread inflationary bias throughout the OECD.

9.5 The Rising Inflation Costs

Internal factors—pre–1974

Notice has already been taken of certain structural changes that occurred in the pre–1974 period and were reflected in higher strike activity in 1968–73. Some of the underlying structural changes have been treated in great detail in a case study of nine European economies by Flanagan et al.[14] The study focuses on the many causes leading to the breakdown of the first generation of incomes policies in the late 1960s described in section 9.3. By their continued presence they remain factors raising the costs of any employment policy in the post–1974 period. The findings need only be summarized here.

The most critical structural change behind the breakdown in many Western European countries was the challenge by the rank and file to

---
[14]Flanagan et al., *Unionism, Economic Stabilization and Incomes Policies*. Additional detail for a number of countries is provided by Soskice, "Strike waves and wage explosions."

union authority, which diminished the ability of the union leaders to implement and sustain the social bargains in operation earlier. This challenge to authority is partially traced to rising aspirations and expectations brought about by prolonged FE—a point cited in the McCracken Report summarized in section 9.2 and emphasized here. One result was an increased emphasis on unrestricted collective bargaining as the union leaders, fearful of losing the support of their rank and file, were and continue to be less willing to enter into social bargains.

In addition, the rise of public employee unions was found to accelerate wage–wage and wage–price inflation at any unemployment rate in several countries, while the splintering of political parties led to coalition governments that could not implement successful consensus policies in others, for example, Denmark. Considering these influences in total, it must be emphasized that even if unemployment rates had not risen elsewhere, changes were occurring in several countries, some even before the 1970s, that were to increase the costs of any unemployment policy thereafter.

Internal factors—post–1973

In section 8.9, it was maintained that, other things being equal, restrictive AD policies shift the VCPC to the right by reducing productivity growth and increasing labor market segmentation. Both these influences have been found to be operative in the post-1973 period.[15] Since the period preceding the breakdown was one of steady growth in productivity and per capita incomes, from 1974 on new domestic considerations enter, increasing the costs of any unemployment policy. This is the widespread sentiment among labor that its money wage demands eventually have to be sufficient to generate a "catch-up" in real wages that had failed to grow sufficiently since 1974. In addition, throughout the OECD the prevailing labor view is that it has been made to bear the main cost of fighting inflation and therefore accelerated money wage demands are a means of "getting even."[16] As in chapter 8, such beliefs can be described in terms of an increase in the target rate of growth of real wages $\dot{q}^T$. In this chapter these influences

[15]See, for example, R. Boyer and P. Petit, "Employment and productivity growth in the EEC," *Cambridge Journal of Economics*, 5, March 1981, 47–58; and R. Gregory, "Wage policy and unemployment in Australia," *Economica* (Supplement), 53, 1986, S53-S54.

[16]The head of the United Auto Workers of Canada announced on national television that, while a settlement during the early 1980s contained a wage clause unsatisfactory to the union, this would be remedied at a future date when economic conditions had improved.

190   Breakdown

are viewed as two additional examples of path dependence and should be included among other examples of hysteresis effects induced by restrictive AD policies. They operate with special force under low unemployment conditions.

The external environment

If the structural changes within a country that lead to higher inflation costs of any unemployment policy are common to many countries, more restrictive AD policies will generally be adopted. Thus at least part of the increase in average unemployment rates in the OECD after 1973 can be attributed to several economies reacting in unison to these higher costs. Naturally, these depressing influences on AD would have been magnified by the reactions of the adversely affected trading partners. As a result, the rate of growth of the volume of OECD exports would and did decline sharply.

In addition, as documented in table 2.9, a deterioration in the payments position of the OECD economics followed each oil shock, reinforcing the desire of the authorities to restrict AD.[17] Comparing the 1963–73 averages with 1980, the shift in the OECD from surpluses to current accounts deficits occurred at the same time as an increase in average OECD unemployment rates from 2.3 to 4.7 percent. This suggests how serious payments problems would be on average if unemployment rates were reduced everywhere to pre-1974 rates, even if the internal factors just discussed were absent. More to the point, the ability and willingness of any one country to implement a more stimulative AD is also very much reduced when world demand conditions deteriorate. In this case mass unemployment will have so raised the inflation costs of reducing unemployment, should any individual country attempt to return to FE on its own, that unemployment will remain high almost everywhere.[18] This is now taken up.

9.6 The Ineffectiveness of Traditional Payments Policies

Introduction

If the reasonable assumption is made that no country can borrow to cover a deficit that exceeds some percentage of its GNP for more than

---

[17]See tables 2.9 and II.1. The rate of growth of OECD exports by volume fell from an average rate of 9.2 percent in 1968–73 to an average rate of 5.0 percent in 1979–90. See OECD, *Historical Statistics, 1960–90*, Paris, 1992, table 4.8.

[18]See section 8.8, especially the discussion of figure 8.2.

a short period (except perhaps the United States), then the return to FE (or merely maintaining FE while others implement restrictive AD policies) requires policies that lead to expenditure switching. Exports must be stimulated or imports curtailed or both. The traditional macroinstrument for inducing this kind of behavior is the exchange rate. Unfortunately, because of certain institutional and structural changes during the period following the Second World War, the exchange rate has become an ineffective instrument for correcting balance-of-payments difficulties when world demand conditions are depressed if stimulative AD policies are introduced simultaneously or merely maintained. The problem is that reductions in the exchange rate have relatively large price effects and relatively small output effects.[19]

Three post-war trends

At least three difficulties stand in the way of success should any country wish to unilaterally increase AD relative to its trading partners and to overcome a payments constraint through depreciation (or devaluation). These are the possibilities of low price elasticities of demand for exports and imports, real wage resistance, and speculative capital outflows. All these difficulties became more acute after 1973.

A traditional argument that depreciation will be unsuccessful in correcting a payments deficit is framed in terms of the Marshall–Lerner conditions. Assuming infinite supply elasticities, if the sum of the price elasticities of demand for a country's exports and imports is less than unity in absolute value, a depreciation of the currency will actually lead to a deterioration of the payments position. A large number of econometric estimates of the value of the elasticities leads to no definite conclusions. Depending on the country and the time period, the evidence can be either favorable or unfavorable for the use of exchange rate policy. Furthermore, it is widely recognized that elasticities vary depending on the time frame adopted. The so-called *J*-curve effects attempt to capture this distinction. Short-term impacts may lead to a worsening of the payments position while long-term impacts may lead to a correction.

What is not debatable is the increasing trend in international trade toward more highly fabricated goods that are desired for their nonprice

---

[19]In contrast, it has been argued in chapters 3 and 8 that restrictive AD policies generally induce output effects. Current policies in most countries are thus examples of, at best, an inefficient application of instruments to targets.

The Australian policy of allowing the nominal exchange rate to rise while reducing the real exchange rate through restraining money wage increases is not considered here.

qualities, for example, design, durability, reliability, delivery dates, etc.[20] This in itself results in a downward trend in price elasticities of traded goods, making it increasingly unlikely that the Marshall–Lerner conditions will be satisfied. There is also the dynamic argument claiming that attempts to correct payments deficiencies by depreciation push the country into greater production of goods that are relatively price sensitive, that is, the "down-market" type of good that experiences slow worldwide growth of demand. As a result, if depreciation helps to correct the payments deficit, it may do so only temporarily as income effects will eventually dominate price effects.

Real wage resistance

Yet another argument made against the successful use of the exchange rate as an instrument for relieving a payments constraint in these circumstances is the existence of real wage resistance. A cheapening of exports relative to imports following depreciation will likely lead to a decline in real wages. Under FE conditions organized labor can be expected to press for higher money wage increases in an effort to protect their real wages following depreciation. Only in the event that the depreciation policy has the prior approval of the trade unions is this likely to be averted.[21] A resulting wage–price inflation can lead to the real exchange rate's return to its previous level. This inflationary bias finds its roots in the rising power of labor under FE conditions as stressed throughout this study. By general agreement, complete resistance to real wage reductions through accelerated money wage demands takes time so that some reduction of the real exchange rate in the short run is usually allowed. But recall that, also by general agreement, price elasticities are smaller in the short run and only become larger later when this inflationary impact of depreciation is likely to be large. Again, there is the distinct possibility that depreciation will be unable to bring the current account into balance.

Why real wage resistance can be so much of a problem even in the corporatist economies can be seen as follows. In the pre-1973 post-war period of booming world trade and high levels of employment, union support of voluntary incomes policies, including the acceptance of

---

[20] See A. Maizels, *Growth and Trade,* Cambridge University Press, Cambridge, 1970, chapter 3.

[21] In this case a willingness to forgo real wage resistance can lead to the decline in real wages, but this is not to adopt the Eurosclerosis argument that the real wage is always set in the labor market and that real wage resistance and a real wage gap are the same thing.

some kind of wage norm, was reinforced by a strong steady upward trend in real wages as well as by FE. When restrictive policies are in effect in a large bloc of countries elsewhere and world trade is growing at a reduced rate, stimulative AD policies and a depreciation of the currency may well require a substantial decline in real wages, certainly in the short run, for their success and this would lead to noncompliance with the incomes policy. Any previous agreement to coordinate wage demands with some national goal will be terminated as unions seek to restore real wages through accelerated money wage demands. The inflation costs of FE then become excessive.

Capital flight

If the reduction in real wages could be limited, real wage resistance might be avoided. However, there is a third difficulty to consider that makes it likely that any country that wishes to permanently reflate unilaterally can expect to run into serious difficulties in controlling its exchange rate and inflation. The international interdependence of capital markets is even more apparent than the increased importance of trade. So efficiently and effectively does this system of markets work that the authorities in any country may have little control over the magnitude of the actual depreciation of the exchange rate compared with what was planned. Whether reflation is to be implemented by fiscal or monetary policy (but especially the latter), if a deliberate decrease in the exchange rate is engineered at the same time as stimulative AD policies are implemented, exchange rate speculation can be very destabilizing, at least from the local authorities' point of view.

In these circumstances stimulative AD policies generate fears of accelerated inflation in the minds of managers of exceedingly large and mobile capital funds. This leads to a withdrawal of funds from the country, a further depreciation of the currency, and greater fears of inflation. As the experiences of several countries in the recent past show, governments are soon forced to reverse their AD policies in order to protect the exchange rate.

The point is that there is an asymmetry here in the way in which the world financial community affects the ability of governments to achieve macropolicy goals. The example of capital flight illustrates quite clearly the ability of managers of mobile capital funds to force a government to abandon a policy of AD stimulation. Restrictive policies, by moving the current account toward surplus, attract foreign capital, thereby reinforcing the restrictive policy in contrast.[22]

Summary

Low price elasticities of demand reduce the effectiveness of reductions in the real exchange rate in correcting balance-of-payments difficulties. Real wage resistance and capital flight make it far more likely that reductions of the nominal exchange rate, undertaken simultaneously with expansionary AD policies, will increase the inflation costs of FE without achieving external balance. Trends in the post-war period have increased the likelihood that the problems of low price elasticities, real wage resistance, and capital flight will occur. Even in the absence of those adverse internal changes that have increased the costs of FE, the readiness to move back to and maintain FE has been reduced. When these internal structural changes are considered together with depressed external conditions, the unwillingness of most governments to supply FE and the mass unemployment of the 1980s are understandable. Those few economies that continued to maintain low rates of unemployment were discussed in section 7.3.

9.7 Conclusions

Comparing the periods before and after the earlier 1970s, the performance on average has greatly deteriorated. As pointed out in chapter 2, it would be difficult to maintain that this rise in unemployment can be traced to a shift in political power to the right. Notwithstanding the advent of Thatcherism and Reaganism, if anything political power has not shifted markedly, comparing the periods before and after the breakdown. The main responsibility for the intertemporal decline in employment must be attributed to the rise in the inflation costs of any employment policy almost everywhere. Most OECD economies now face a less favorable tradeoff between inflation and unemployment and an inflationary bias.

Nowhere is this deterioration in the inflation/unemployment choices available to governments better revealed than in latter years of the 1980s boom. Table 9.1 details the inflation/unemployment records of the seven largest OECD economies and those of the United States and

[22]See M. Steward, *Controlling the Economic Future*, Wheatsheaf, Brighton, 1983, chapters 5 and 6.

Table 9.1 Unemployment and inflation rates for the G7, the United Kingdom, and the United States 1979 to 1991

		1979–80[a]	1981–83[a]	1984	1985	1986	1987	1988	1989	1990	1991
G7	U	5.2	7.4	7.3	7.2	7.1	6.7	6.1	5.7	5.6	6.3
	$\dot{p}$	11.3	7.4	4.7	4.0	2.1	2.9	3.4	4.5	5.0	4.3
USA	U	6.4	8.8	7.4	7.1	6.9	6.1	5.4	5.2	5.4	6.6
	$\dot{p}$	12.4	6.5	4.3	3.5	1.9	3.7	4.1	4.8	5.4	4.2
UK	U	5.7	11.2	11.7	11.2	11.2	10.3	8.6	7.1	6.8	8.9
	$\dot{p}$	15.7	8.4	5.0	6.1	3.4	4.1	4.9	7.8	9.5	5.9

[a] Annual average.

Sources: OECD *Historical Statistics*, 1960–1990, OECD Paris, 1992, table 8.11; and OECD, *Economic Outlook*, OECD, Paris, June 1992, tables 50 and R18.

the United Kingdom. The high 1979–80 figures for inflation in each case partly reflect the direct and indirect impact of the second oil shock. The rise in unemployment rates and the fall in inflation rates in 1981–83 reflect the policy responses to the acceleration of inflation rates of 1979–80 and inflation response to these extremely tight restrictive AD policies, respectively.

What is of more immediate interest is the behavior of unemployment and inflation in the remainder of the 1980s decade. For the G7 as a group, that is, the seven largest OECD economies, as well as the United Kingdom and the United States, inflation rates reached a trough in 1986 and then increased steadily until 1990. But in all three examples inflation rates began to accelerate while unemployment rates were comparatively high. For example, inflation rates in the G7 averaged 2.9 percent in the 1960–68 period, the 1987 average in table 9.1, but the average unemployment rate for the G7 during this earlier period was only 2.8 percent compared to 6.7 percent in 1987. Only the rapid rise in unemployment rates in the 1990s recession (double digit rates in the majority of the G7 economies in 1992) reduced inflation enough by 1992 (not shown) to allow the authorities to declare the war against inflation finally "won."

The inflationary bias depicted in table 9.1 is traced to the breakdown of incomes policies in several countries and the widespread depressed state of AD. But it is also traced to causes induced by restrictive AD policies themselves.[23] While restrictive AD policies may have worked to reduce inflation rates to some extent, inflation rates remain high, given the mass unemployment. In chapter 10 it is concluded that without radical policy-induced institutional changes, these conditions will persist indefinitely.

[23]Evidence collected by the OECD and others strongly indicates that the rise in costs of any employment goal in the 1980s cannot be attributed to an increase in labor-market mismatch. See OECD, *Economic Outlook*, OECD, Paris, December 1988, pp. 35–40. Government budgetary deficits at high rates of unemployment also act to constrain AD policies, but since higher deficits are thought to lead to inflation this influence is neglected in the text.

10 A Model of Long-run Mass Unemployment

10.1 Weak and Strong Corporatist and Pluralist Economies

Pluralist economies

A chain of events covering over two decades was traced out in chapter 9. In this chapter a model of long-run mass unemployment based on these events is developed. Among other things, it is shown that, even if the economies of the developed world could be transported miraculously to FE through some sort of coordinated AD policy, the inflation that this would soon entail would again lead to breakdown. Further, it is argued that, without radical changes in certain key institutions, the current economic breakdown will continue indefinitely and will be general throughout the OECD. Restrictive AD policies are shown to be incapable of eliminating the mechanisms generating long-run mass unemployment. Initially, to keep matters simple, any possible impact on the payments positions of the OECD economies through import penetration from newly industrializing countries (NICs) will be ignored. Section 10.4 allows for this possibility.

The model is as follows. High and rising rates of inflation lead in the first instance to mass unemployment because when inflation cannot be brought under control by any other means, governments respond by implementing restrictive AD policies. Such responses do not succeed in eliminating the inflationary bias but lead, as they have done since the early 1970s, to continued breakdown.

However, the mechanism by which inflation leads to mass unemployment under existing institutions is rather more complicated. This is made clear by a recognition that some economies, which in the past were quite capable of controlling inflation at FE, are quite incapable of achieving these goals simultaneously under current economic conditions. Thus, in studying the causes of breakdown in the capitalist economies, it is useful to adopt a framework that focuses on three different kinds of economies. First, there are those economies that experience, or in which the authorities anticipate, unacceptably high or even accelerating rates of inflation under conditions of sustained FE. AD policies will be subject to an AD constraint as discussed in chapter 4 because of an inflationary bias. Moreover, AD policies are constrained whatever the state of the world economy, in particular whether the rest of the world is at FE or not, because of domestic or internal conditions.

Because of their existing institutional framework, no successful incomes policy allowing acceptable rates of inflation while involuntary unemployment is reduced to a minimum can be implemented in these economies. As a result, they will pursue AD policies that are restrictive enough to restrain inflation. The fear that stimulative policies will lead to greater budget deficits and the fear of the greater power of labor under FE conditions, partly because it is believed that each causes inflation rates to accelerate, will reinforce this trend towards restrictive AD policies.[1]

In the first group of economies belong those referred to earlier as pluralist economies. The institutional features that prevented realization of FE without serious inflation before 1974 and that have led to a more widespread inflationary bias today were discussed in chapters 5 and 9. The countries whose institutional features most clearly reflect these unfortunate institutional arrangements today need not be specified with any great deal of exactness. It is helpful, nevertheless, to think of several developed English-speaking economies, for example, Canada, Ireland, the United Kingdom, and the United States, as the core members of this group.

However, because of institutional changes in some of the economies that could be described as corporatist before the late 1960s, for example, more rank and file autonomy in the unions, other economies now suffer from an inflationary bias because of the conditions within their economies and must be included in the first group.[2] With the breakdown of the first generation of incomes policies, this first group must be considered much larger compared with the pre-1974 period.

[1] For example, the restrictive AD policies pursued by Mrs. Thatcher's government were likely motivated by both a fear of inflation and a desire to reduce the power of the unions, and large budgetary deficits, such as those experienced in the United States and Canada in the 1980s, certainly act as constraints on the use of stimulative fiscal policies.

[2] See Flanagan et al., *Unionism, Economic Stabilization and Incomes Policies*.

Weak and strong corporatist economies

There is, in contrast, a second group of economies which, because of favorable institutional arrangements, could realize FE without accelerating rates of inflation *if restrictive policies were not adopted by the first group of economies*. These countries would likely adopt FE policies if expansionary policies were in force elsewhere, and did so in the pre-1974 period. Because they are not in force, this second group of economies is subject to an AD constraint. They too are now obliged to pursue restrictive AD policies, albeit for quite different reasons. Their AD policies are constrained by an inflationary bias ultimately due to depressed world economic conditions induced by the restrictive AD policies of the first group. Stimulative policies together with a depreciation of the currency generate unacceptable rates of inflation, not FE and external balance.

The second group of economies will be referred to as weak corporatist economies. Their key features were also described in chapter 5. They would be able to implement FE policies today, provided that restrictive AD policies were not being followed by the expanded pluralist group of countries. Unfortunately, given the high degree of economic interdependence, many of those economies that were best able to achieve external balance and to contain inflation at FE in the past are not, with a few possible exceptions, able to pursue FE policies under current conditions.[3] The importance of the pluralist group guarantees that, by restricting AD, depressed AD conditions will be exported to other countries in the form of significantly decreased demand for their exports. Given the inability to correct matters through depreciation, FE cannot be maintained.[4]

Together these two groups comprise the vast majority of the OECD countries. The remaining group of economies is made up of those able to realize near FE with manageable payments positions and acceptable rates of inflation despite depressed world economic conditions. This is largely a matter of being able to contain the potentially strong inflationary pressures through a successful second-generation incomes policy following a decline in world economic activity. This group will be referred to as the strong corporatist group. They were singled out for discussion in section 7.3.

---

[3] Japan, Sweden, Switzerland, Norway, and Austria are possible exceptions as noted in chapter 7.
[4] See A. Thirlwall and M. Hussain, "The balance of payments constraint, capital flows and growth rate differences between developing countries," *Oxford Economic Papers*, 34, November 1982, 498–510.

10.2 Exporting Unemployment

Implicit in this classification is the assumption that, in the face of depressed demand conditions in the pluralist bloc, any weak corporatist economy acting alone is not able to offset the adverse effects of FE policies on the payments position through exchange rate policies. As argued in chapter 9, in most cases depreciation of the exchange rate is not sufficient to induce the kind of expenditure switching needed to bring the current account of the economy into balance at FE when there is worldwide depressed demand and export growth is declining, but it does lead to high rates of inflation. The result is that, as long as the pluralist group restricts AD because of internal circumstances, less than FE conditions are imposed upon most of the rest of the world. An inflationary bias in the pluralist group, that is, a tendency for unacceptable rates of inflation at or before FE, leads not only to breakdown in those countries but to mass unemployment throughout the developed capitalist world.

It is useful for analytical reasons to divide the demand constrained capitalist economies into two mutually exclusive groups—pluralist and weak corporatist—even if it is not always obvious to which group a country belongs. What is essential to this explanation of mass unemployment is that there exists a bloc of weak corporatist as well as pluralist economies. It then follows that the stagnating capitalist economies can be considered to fall into one or another of two groups: those in which restrictive AD policies would be employed even if these economies were isolated from outside influences because they would be faced with unacceptable inflation at FE, and those forced to adopt these policies because of the actions of others. With this simplifying assumption, the causal mechanism at work today generating economic breakdown is better illuminated.

10.3 A Coordinated Stimulative Policy is Not Sufficient for World Recovery

The stress on two explanations of depressed AD policies is obviously a simplification of current conditions in which so many countries have sacrificed the FE goal. Restrictive AD policies in a country may be the result of a set of problems, rather than a single cause, and the reasons for restricting AD can vary over time. Despite this, nothing critical is overlooked when applying the dual explanation of restrictive AD policies nor in considering what must be done to correct these conditions.

What is emphasized is the overwhelming nature of the strain that depressed world economic conditions put on economies that, under better circumstances, could perform well.

The value of this explanation of mass unemployment is evident when it is used to evaluate a widely advocated program for ending breakdown—a coordinated and simultaneous restimulation of AD in the OECD economies, the so-called "locomotive." In order to bring out the critical issues, it will be assumed that the economic performance of the less developed countries (LDCs) will vary directly with that of the overall performance of the developed capitalist world.

Thus, suppose that in every OECD economy a stimulative monetary or fiscal policy is introduced with the aim of returning to FE. In the pluralist economies this could mean that the authorities, who hitherto had been unwilling to move the economy to FE because of an inflationary bias, are now persuaded that the bias has been eliminated as a result of past restrictive policies. Since the programs are being implemented everywhere, payments difficulties will be minimized as the economies move toward FE since exports in the different countries will expand along with the induced growth of imports. Some individual adjustments in exchange rates will obviously be necessary as export performance and import penetration will vary across countries, but for the sake of argument assume that this is of little consequence. The question is: what are the prospects of long-run success of this joint effort?

Since the expansions in the individual countries are in phase, there is a strong possibility that the run-up of prices in international commodity markets (including oil) experienced in the early 1970s will repeat itself. But, again for the sake of argument, assume that this problem has been resolved. Unfortunately, even under these favorable conditions, the boom will be short lived. For if an inflationary bias exists in some countries, whatever the state of world demand, it can be expected that unacceptable rates of inflation will set in soon after unemployment rates have begun to fall in the pluralist group. This will lead to a reimposition of restrictive AD policies in these countries. The impact of these policies on the rest of the developed economies (and the LDC group) will depend upon the importance of the inflation-prone group of countries to world trade. When this bloc is sizable, its restrictive AD policies will be exported to the weak corporatist group and to the rest of the world.

As the example of the locomotive indicates, altering the state of world demand, although it acts to relieve the constraint on AD policies in the weak corporatist group, is not the key to world recovery. Critical to this explanation (and in the real world) is the constraint operating in the pluralist economies on the use of AD policies, for unacceptable rates of inflation at FE will lead them to adopt restrictive AD policies. Given the inability of exchange rate policies to induce sufficient expenditure switching and the importance of the demands of the pluralist economies for the exports of the weak corporatist economies, under existing institutions the latter group of countries will also be forced to sacrifice the FE target.

To put the issue in its most general form, what matters is whether there exists a bloc of economies that limits its imports to something less than the FE level through restrictive AD policies even if AD is not depressed in the rest of the world. A fear of increased government deficits or a desire to reduce the power of labor in the pluralist group will generate the same result as "inflation fighting."[5]

10.4 Looking to the Future

If this predicted failure of the locomotive to bring recovery seems unduly pessimistic, there is an even more gloomy possibility: the pluralist economies might never participate in a coordinated reflationary program. As a result even the short-lived recovery just outlined will never be realized. The behavior of the capitalist economies since the second oil shock would seem to confirm the more pessimistic scenario of uninterrupted mass unemployment. What the data reveal is a rising trend in unemployment rates in the OECD, attenuated slightly by a limited recovery in employment in some economies in 1984–89. Forecasts for the 1990s reveal a deterioration in the unemployment picture.

Much has been made of the 1980s boom in the United States. As already discussed in introduction I, what tends to be overlooked in the discussion of rising rates of employment and output is the poor recovery in unemployment. By 1989 unemployment rates had fallen, but only to a value that was considered to be normal for the bottom of the business cycle in the 1950s and 1960s. Even this limited recovery required continued massive budgetary deficits, a rapid growth of indebtedness relative to incomes by households, and large payments deficits, none of which could be maintained indefinitely. In other words,

---

[5] The OPEC countries restrict their imports because of an inability to absorb an amount equal to their exports. The resulting surplus also has a depressing influence on world trade.

while the American recovery may have appeared substantial when measured by the increase in output from the trough of the cycle in the early 1980s, measured in terms of the movement of unemployment rates it has been a nonsustainable "recessionary boom."[6]

The relatively poor record of the United States in recent times, compared with its unemployment performance in earlier periods, has been paralleled by the records of Canada and the United Kingdom. Moreover, looking to the future, the concern with inflation and deficits expressed by the authorities in these economies in the early 1990s, even when unemployment rates remain high by pre-1974 standards, suggests a continued unwillingness to supply strong stimulative policies in the future. Given the absence of strong and sustainable AD policies in the United States and other English-speaking economies, the unemployment policies of these pluralist economies and others will continue to spill over to the rest of the world.[7]

This spillover has been reinforced by the behavior of the authorities in Germany since the early 1970s. From 1963 to 1973 Germany had one of the most creditable unemployment (and inflation) records, yet throughout the 1970s and early 1980s unemployment rates increased steadily until 1983 and remained high throughout the 1980s. Analysis of statements of both the central bank and the central government indicate that an overriding fear of inflation has been the chief cause of restrictive policies throughout most of the period since the early 1970s.[8] Rightly or wrongly, the German authorities since the early 1970s have assumed that FE and acceptable rates of inflation were no longer compatible and have proceeded to restrict AD policies despite a strong payments position. More recently, problems associated with reunification have served to intensify the concern with inflation.

If successful incomes policies could be introduced in the pluralist bloc, FE could be exported to the rest of the world.[9] The failure to develop and implement such policies is at the root of today's difficulties. As the discussion in chapters 5 and 6 made clear, this will entail a

---

[6] In chapter 11 this is expressed as, in effect, a transfer of spending from the 1990s to the 1980s.

[7] Together Canada, the United Kingdom, and the United States purchased 28 percent of the exports of the remaining industrial countries in 1981. If Germany is included, the figure rises to 52 percent. See IMF, *Direction of Trade Statistics,* IMF, Washington, DC, 1981.

[8] See F. Scharpf, "Economic and institutional constraints."

[9] If all the corporatist economies would reflate simultaneously, the beneficial effects would also be substantial. Nevertheless, worldwide recovery would not be complete if the pluralist economies were still constrained.

radical policy-induced restructuring of institutions, especially the industrial relations system.

Allow finally for an additional difficulty with recovery in the OECD, increased import penetration by the NICs. Recall that the period of the 1950s and 1960s was one of widescale borrowing of technology (primarily from the United States), a realization of dynamic economies of scale and booming exports throughout the OECD. More recently, several NICs have experienced similar benefits from technology transfer and scale economies and have increased their sales penetration of OECD markets. As a result, in formulating a model of mass unemployment, say, for the 1990s it is inappropriate to assume that the payments position of the OECD will be as favorable as it was in the pre-1974 period. Rather the likelihood that most OECD economies will encounter a payments ceiling before achieving FE in the absence of counter-acting policies must be considered.

The point is that in addition to the adoption of social bargains in the pluralist economies to counter a potential inflationary bias, new export-led industrial policies will be required to eliminate payments ceilings. If such policies cannot be developed, a third constraint on AD policies must be incorporated in the model. To put it otherwise even if social bargains are successfully implemented throughout the OECD restraining inflation tendencies at FE, payments constraints may make recovery impossible throughout the OECD.

10.5 Why Restrictive Aggregate Demand Policies Are So Costly

A summary of the argument

An alternative position holds that a failure to eliminate the inflationary bias must be attributed to a failure of the authorities to adopt a credible restrictive policy response to the inflationary pressures since the early 1970s. According to this view, a correctly designed restrictive AD policy would so alter the behavior of labor that the inflationary bias in the pluralist world could be rooted out. Once this has been done, a coordinated program of stimulation can bring an end to the unemployment problem. The charge here is that efforts to make FE consistent with price stability through restrictive policies will fail in the sense that they will be very costly in the short run and completely ineffective in the long run. Such policies, designed to reduce an inflationary bias, will in fact intensify inflationary difficulties.

To state the argument very briefly, first it is clear from the record of the 1970s and 1980s that in most capitalist economies restrictive policies must be applied in such a way that unemployment rises to double-digit rates before rates of price and wage inflation are affected appreciably.[10] They are thus extremely costly in the short run. Second, whether periods of policy-induced unemployment are short with a sharp increase of unemployment rates or prolonged with a gradual rise in unemployment in order to reduce inflation, any attempt to reflate the economy following a "successful" anti-inflation period will lead to unacceptable rates of inflation long before involuntary unemployment has been appreciably reduced. In this sense, such policies are therefore ineffective in the long run.

Why wages and prices are so unresponsive

The view that depressed AD conditions will quickly, and with little pain, reduce inflation is usually based on a microtheory of "flexprice" markets. In these markets the reduction of AD leads to a downward shift of demand curves in individual product and labor markets followed by an induced downward shift in individual supply curves. Employment need hardly be affected (if at all) as inflation rates come down. The behavior of wages and prices since the early 1970s indicates the irrelevance of this view of markets.

However, even when it is conceded that markets are "fixprice" and that quantity rather than price adjustments are the immediate and dominant response to excess supply situations, arguments supporting restrictive AD policies as an inflation cure are available. According to this version, the restriction of AD and the creation of excess supply conditions in labor markets would lead labor to reduce its wage demands which, because of markup pricing, will pass through to prices and reduce price inflation. The early versions of cost–push inflation envisaged this kind of wage–price spiral and its reversal as the basis of the Phillips curve.

This point can certainly be granted, but the immediate issue is how much unemployment must be created and for how long before wage demands are reduced sufficiently. Much of the earlier discussion in chapter 5 is relevant here, especially that dealing with two characteristics of the IRS in most pluralist economies. First, collective bargaining is not industry-wide or nationwide or synchronized, but is carried out in a decentralized manner leading to overlapping contracts. Second, the

---

[10]See table II.1 and figure 9.1.

IRS is highly adversarial, so that labor and management consider conflict to be a natural part of their relationship. Under these circumstances restrictive AD policies must be both severe and prolonged before an appreciable impact can be made on rates of wage inflation. Labor locked in an adversarial relation with management will treat any lessening of wage demands as an opportunity for management to increase profits. In addition, the decentralized nature of bargaining and the concern with relative wages will lead labor groups to resist reductions in wage demands lest other labor groups do not follow suit. As discussed in chapter 5, these examples of the prisoner's dilemma generate strong inflationary pressures. Both factors work to keep the rate of wage inflation from falling as unemployment rates rise. Only when unemployment rates have been greatly increased and maintained will senior workers feel that their jobs are insecure. At that point wage demands and settlements can be affected.

Credible restrictive policies

As is apparent, the actual unemployment costs of the restrictive AD policies of the 1970s and 1980s were enormous. Unemployment rates were forced up for over a decade before inflation rates were brought down substantially, and this involved increasing unemployment eventually to double-digit rates in many countries. This would seem to indicate that at the very least the costs of unemployment are not small and short-lived.

However, advocates of the credibility hypothesis would have it that if the (monetary) authorities would only carry out their restrictive policies in such a way as to convince the public that (a) there is no other way in which to permanently eliminate inflation and (b) they will persist at their task regardless of the unemployment cost, inflation will come down quickly and with little unemployment cost. This they failed to do in the recent period, so the argument goes. "Gradualist" restrictive policies were applied when what was needed for credibility were more extreme policies that would lead to a rapid and pronounced rise in unemployment rates. In this manner inflation rates would have come down quickly and dramatically, and policy could have soon been reversed.[11]

[11] For an early statement of the credibility hypothesis see W. Fellner, "The valid core of the rationality hypothesis in the theory of expectations," *Journal of Money, Credit and Banking*, 12, November 1980, 763–87. An argument for sharp severe doses of restriction is found in J. You, "Is taxed-based incomes policy an answer?" *Canadian Public Policy*, 8, Winter 1982, 95–101.

10.6 Why Restrictive Aggregate Demand Policies Are Ineffective in the Long Run

It is difficult to devise a test that would either support or reject the credibility hypothesis. Fortunately, there is a means to finesse the short-run issue. Thus, even if the resulting unemployment increase was short-lived because inflation rates were brought down quickly, the costs would still be high if attempts to restimulate the economy should lead to accelerating rates of inflation before involuntary unemployment had been appreciably reduced. In other words, the crucial test of any restrictive AD policy is not whether it can reduce inflation. Recent events in many of the capitalist economies indicate quite clearly that if unemployment rates are increased enough, inflation rates will come down. Rather, the crucial test of such policies is what happens if and when the authorities decide to restimulate the economy following a period when inflation has been brought down.

A good deal of insight into the likely result of an eventual restimulation of the economy is possible if two points just made in another context are recalled. First, collective bargaining in most of the pluralist economies is decentralized and unsynchronized. Second, the industrial relations system is decidedly adversarial. These factors have made a workable voluntary incomes policy impossible in the past and will continue to do so under FE conditions at any future time. But following a period of policy-induced recession and high unemployment, there will be at least two additional factors, cited in chapter 9, leading to a renewal of strong inflationary pressures if a stimulative AD policy is ever implemented. First, labor in the pluralist economies will have interpreted the restrictive policies as an attempt to weaken its power. Second, prolonged periods of slack lead to prolonged periods of low (and even negative) rates of growth of real wages. As a result, labor will seize any opportunity to try and regain these "lost" real wages and will do so through the only means available—accelerated money wage demands. Under these conditions it is difficult to see how a period of harsh restrictive measures, during which inflation rates come down because unemployment has become sufficiently large, followed by the introduction of stimulative policies can be thought to lead to wage and price stability.[12]

---

[12] One way of interpreting the credibility hypothesis is that the fear of unemployment, actual and possible, has been made so strong through past restrictive AD policies that workers (and management) will internalize the costs of their wage-setting (and price-setting) behavior during the boom. High wage demands (and high price markups) will be avoided according to this

Following the commencement of a policy of restimulation, labor rightly or wrongly will feel that it has been punished in the past and will be aware that even for those who remained employed real incomes have not risen. Labor groups will press their new advantage (tighter labor markets) to the full, hoping through accelerating money wage demands to recapture their "rightful" share of income. If their resentment over past events is not enough, the decentralized nature of collective bargaining will act to build up inflationary pressures as tighter labor markets set in motion an intensified wage–wage inflationary process.

The point to be emphasized is that in some economies affluence and the rising power of labor interact with existing institutions leading to more than just an inflationary bias and the unworkability of an incomes policy. These conditions also lead to the failure of restrictive AD policies to induce behavior that will eventually permit FE without inflation. All things considered, even an optimist would have his doubts that restrictive AD policies are sufficient to permanently reduce let alone eliminate inflation in the pluralist economies under FE conditions. The conclusion seems inescapable: restrictive AD policies, that is, incomes policies based on fear, are not a means of breaking out of the high unemployment trap described in the first half of the chapter.

10.7 Conclusions

The year 1973 marked the end of the most widespread and sustained boom in the history of capitalism. For the OECD as a whole unemployment rates in the early 1990s are projected to remain over three times their 1960–73 average with no immediate prospects of improvement, while productivity growth rates are projected to continue at less than half their earlier rate.[13]

Various competing theories have been offered to explain this breakdown which is now into its third decade. This chapter has singled out the collapse of AD everywhere, with the imposition of restrictive AD policies by government after government. A major distinction between the explanation here and others that emphasize a lack of effective demand has been the stress on three possible constraints limiting AD

---

doctrine out of fear that the authorities will repeat or intensify their policies. As a result wage and price settlements will become coordinated with the national goals of overall wage price stability. This is nothing more than a voluntary incomes policy based on fear.

[13] See OECD, *Economic Outlook*, OECD, Paris, June 1992, table 2 and June 1993, table 53.

policies in the different countries: the first generated by internal conditions in the pluralist economies, the second attributable to the depressed state of world demand and relevant for the weak corporatist group, and the third due to growing competition from the NICs. The first and third constraints dominate in the sense that even if the second constraint were eliminated, but not the others, overall recovery in the OECD would still be impossible. In contrast, if economies could eliminate their inflationary bias and payment constraints, coordinated stimulative policies (given some control of commodity prices) are likely to be successful.

More will be said on the payments constraint in chapter 12. In conclusion, consider only the difficulties involved in eliminating the inflation constraint on AD policies. Unfortunately, some basic structural and institutional changes in the pluralist economies are required before these economies can ever achieve FE with acceptable inflation rates. "Temporarily" creating unemployment will not achieve this goal because it will not eliminate the conditions creating the inflationary bias. The only available means for achieving FE and acceptable inflation is to alter the institutions that give rise to the bias. The adversarial nature of industrial relations together with the decentralized nature of the union movement and the absence of a tradition of government intervention in the interests of reconciling competing demands are among the institutional causes of an inflationary bias. A different conception of the role of the state, the introduction of a cooperative industrial relations system, and possibly centralized bargaining would clear the way for the implementation of an incomes policy that had some chance of success. Regrettably, it has not been well recognized that such radical institutional changes are needed in societies where so much lip service is given to invisible hands and the value of laissez-faire government policies.[14] Various policies that would take some account of these institutional constraints in the pluralist countries have been advocated by economists. Tax-based incomes policies (TIPs), in their many variants, are a good example.[15] The arguments just presented suggest that additional and more radical change is required if FE without unacceptable inflation is to be realized.

A second program for recovery involve sacrificing the goal of worldwide recovery and settling for recovery outside the pluralist bloc.

---

[14] This lip service to a policy of nonintervention is not to be confused with the actual behavior and practice of these governments.

[15] See H. Wallich and S. Weintraub, "A tax-based incomes policy," *Journal of Economic Issues*, 5, June 1971, 1–19, for one of the earliest studies.

This could take the form of a coordinated AD policy by the weak and strong corporatist economies. In addition, coordinated trade and lending policies that discriminate against the pluralist bloc could be introduced to ease a possible payments constraint.[16] The key to success here involves the implementation of a second-generation incomes policy in Germany, which is the largest European economy in the OECD.

There are other possibilities, some involving a smaller group of economies or even an individual country. But however much they may differ, they will share one thing in common: all will require radical changes in key institutions. Without these adaptations, the model of long-run mass unemployment sketched in the first half of the chapter will be applicable. Regrettably, everything is in place for continued mass unemployment in the 1990s.

---

[16]See F. Cripps, "Causes of growth and recession in world trade," *Economic Policy Review*, 4, March 1978, 37–43. Cripps advocates discriminating against those OPEC countries that run a trade surplus. This can be generalized to discriminating against any country that restricts imports to something less than their FE levels for reasons other than the depressed state of world demand.

A program for dealing with reflation by a subset of OECD economies has been given by J. Dreze and C. Wyplosz, "Autonomy through cooperation," *European Economic Review*, 32(2–3) 1988, 353–62.

PART III

Recovery

Introduction III: Recovery

> "[In the United States] it is almost inconceivable what rubbish a public man has to utter today if he is to keep respectability."*

III:1 Introduction

The period since the mid-1970s can be considered as serious an economic breakdown as the Great Depression. While the decline in activity and the rise in unemployment rates has not been as pronounced as during the 1930s, the period of high unemployment and stagnation has lasted twice as long. Given the severity of the depression, monetary policy was correctly seen by Keynes as ineffective. Recovery from the Great Depression required a strong stimulative fiscal policy involving deficit financing. Yet recovery had to await the stimulative fiscal measures associated with rearmament and the Second World War. Given the ideological climate of the times, deficit spending in peacetime on non-defense projects was unacceptable and remained so until after the Second World War.

This raises the question of the likelihood of recovery in the 1990s. The concluding sections of chapters 9 and 10 give no reason for optimism. It was pointed out in the final section of chapter 9 that the inflationary bias in the capitalist world has if anything become more pronounced. Inflation rates began to accelerate on a wide scale in the second half of the 1980s even while unemployment rates remained high. This can only strengthen the future resolve of the authorities in favor of policies of restraint. In Chapter 10 it was maintained that the key to recovery was the widespread adoption of social bargains by economies of the OECD. This involved the adoption of a "second generation" of incomes policies in many economies that at one time had adopted social bargain strategies to contain potentially strong inflationary forces. For others, such as the

---

Collected Works of John Maynard Keynes, Vol. xxi, p. 45, Cambridge University Press, Cambridge, 1982.

English-speaking economies, this required the substitution of social bargain strategies for what was termed in chapter 5 market-power strategies.

Support for such measures today is not strong. The mood of the 1990s throughout the developed capitalist world can only be described as one of pessimism. Absent is the optimism of the period between the two oil shocks when studies such as the McCracken Report could envisage a recovery by 1980, provided a limited and reasonable number of conditions were met. This pessimism has certainly been reinforced by events of the 1980s. During the early 1980s the authorities in most of the OECD economies pursued the most highly restrictive policies of the post–Second World War era. Inflation rates were greatly reduced but, as just mentioned, even though unemployment remained high, in the second half of the 1980s inflation rates again accelerated. Overall, events since the breakdown of the early 1970s have lent support to Kalecki's theory of the political business cycle in which capitalism must maintain a reserve army of the unemployed[1].

III.2 Outline of Part III

Is this pessimism justified? Certainly recovery by means of a rearmament program, whether it involves the establishment of a command economy such as Nazi Germany or something less sinister, can hardly be accepted as a solution. Part III of this study offers an alternative solution to the unemployment problem based on the findings of the first two parts of the study, by considering policies for recovery in the largest of the pluralist economies. Recovery in the United States is a pre-condition for worldwide recovery and, in addition, similar policies will be required for recovery in other OECD economies. Before discussing a recovery program, Chapter 11 discusses the 1980s boom in the United States because it was a very special kind of boom leading to a very special kind of aftermath. Chapter 12 then outlines a program for recovery in the United States. It emphasizes the means of creating the right ideological climate for implementing a more concrete recovery program.

Discussion of paradigms and the historical record is undertaken first, in order to remind the reader once again that there are respectable ways of interpreting capitalist development other than the time-honored mainstream view. These sections also serve to suggest that the

[1] See Section I.1

mistaken macroeconomic policies of the last two decades are based not just on erroneous economic theories, but can be traced ultimately to an incorrect basic view of the workings of capitalism.

The concluding chapter briefly discusses and compares alternative programs with a somewhat detailed analysis of a "market" solution to today's difficulties that would prove even more harmful than those currently in effect. The chapter concludes with a recapitulation of the implications of current policies in a path-dependent world; performance during the rest of this century will be determined by our decisions today.

11 The Boom of the 1980s and its Aftermath

11.1 Introduction

As discussed in chapters 9 and 10, the 1970s outward shifts of the Phillips curve have increased the inflation costs of low unemployment. Even during the rather mild recovery in employment rates in the second half of the 1980s, inflation rates rose above their pre-1974 rates, while unemployment rates remained double to triple those of the earlier period.

This chapter also considers developments of the 1980s but the focus is on the nature of the boom from 1982 until 1990 in the United States for two reasons. The United States is the most mature of the developed capitalist economies in the sense that the distribution of output and the structure of the technology have evolved to a state that other economies will likely achieve only after their income levels have risen further. Developments in the United States provide possible clues to future patterns of development elsewhere. Second, as argued in chapter 10, world recovery requires basic structural changes in the pluralist economies and recent events in the largest pluralist economy can also provide clues for structuring the required worldwide recovery program. As will be maintained, because of the special features of the boom of the 1980s, e.g. debt overhang, excess stock of housing and commercial real estate and revenue-strapped state and local governments, a return to low unemployment in the 1990s has been made more difficult.

11.2 The Booms of the 1960s and 1980s

The special features of the 1982–90 boom are revealed by a comparison with the earlier 1959–69 boom.[1] Table 11.1 records rates of growth

---

[1] The boom of the 1960s probably begins in 1958 but revised constant dollar estimates begin only in 1959. Following the usual convention, a level of GDP is designated a peak (trough) in GDP if it is followed by at least two quarters of negative (positive) growth in GDP. The one-quarter declines in GDP in 1959, 1960, and 1970 are therefore ignored. Unless otherwise indicated national income data are taken from U.S. Department of Commerce, *Survey of Current Business*, September, 1992 tables 2 and 1.2, and January, 1993, table 1.2.

Table 11.1 Annual average rates of growth of GDP and selected components in the 1959–1969 and 1982–1990 booms and the 1969–1973 mini-boom in the United States and various subperiods

	1959–69 (%)	1959–64 (%)	1964–69 (%)	1969–73 (%)	1982–90 (%)	1982–86 (%)	1986–90 (%)
$\dot{Q}$	4.1	3.9	4.2	3.3	3.3	4.0	2.6
$\dot{I}^F$	4.5	4.6	4.4	6.4	4.0	8.0	0.1
$\dot{I}^B$	6.0	5.3	6.7	4.8	2.7	3.6	1.8
$\dot{I}^P$	5.2	5.2	5.2	2.2	–0.2	–0.7	0.2
$\dot{I}^E$	6.7	5.4	7.9	6.5	4.9	6.4	3.5
$\dot{I}^H$	1.8	3.9	–0.3	8.8	5.8	16.2	–3.7
$\dot{C}^d$	5.2	4.2	6.3	6.6	6.6	11.2	2.2
$\dot{G}$	3.7	2.9	4.4	–1.4	3.2	4.3	2.1
$\dot{G}^F$	2.5	1.2	3.8	–6.0	2.9	5.1	0.7
$\dot{G}^{S+L}$	5.0	5.0	5.0	2.6	3.4	3.7	3.2

$\dot{Q}$ is the rate if growth of GDP. $\dot{I}^F, \dot{I}^B, \dot{I}^P, \dot{I}^E$, and $\dot{I}^H$ are the rates of growth of total fixed, business fixed, plant, equipment, and housing investment, respectively. $\dot{C}^d$ is the rate of growth of expenditures on consumer durables. $\dot{G}, \dot{G}^F$ and $\dot{G}^{S+L}$ are the rates of growth of total, federal, and state and local government expenditures, respectively.

Sources: U.S. Department of Commerce, *Survey of Current Business*, September 1992, table 2; and *Economic Report of the President*, February 1992, table B–2.

of GDP and different components of final demand over the entire length of each boom, as well as for selected subperiods. Besides the greater length (10 versus 8 years) and strength of the earlier boom (4.1 percent annual growth in GDP compared to 3.3 percent), what stands out in table 11.1 is the much more rapid and sustained rate of growth of business fixed investment spending in the earlier period (6.0 versus 2.7 percent) and the higher rate of growth of consumer investment, that is, the sum of residential housing construction and consumer durable goods expenditures, in the 1980s. It has often been asserted that the boom of the 1980s was the longest peacetime expansion in postwar history. As just detailed, in spite of the rapid growth of federal government spending connected with national defense in the 1980s boom, the Reagan boom was shorter and the growth rate lower than the boom of the 1960s.[2]

More important than the differences in lengths of the two booms was the shifting importance of the final expenditures categories during

---

[2]The rate of growth of GDP in the 1982–90 boom was also much lower than that of the shorter boom of 1975–79. In the latter boom GDP grew steadily at an annual rate of 4.2 percent, generated primarily by a strong boom in both business in fixed investment and residential construction. Government outlays were virtually unchanged during this period.

the course of each as revealed in table 11.1. In the early stages of the 1960s boom, 1959–64, business fixed investment, outlays by state and local governments, and consumer investment expenditures surged, with the first two types of spending remaining strong through the remainder of the 1960s, while consumer investment leveled off beginning in the mid-1960s as residential construction stagnated. The overall growth of the economy remained high until 1969 due partly to a rapid increase in federal government outlays related to the escalation of the war in Vietnam. GDP peaked in 1969(III) and fell until 1970(II).

In the boom of the 1980s, business fixed investment, government outlays (this time related to national defense), and consumer investment outlays again provided the stimulus to aggregate demand in the first half of the boom, 1982–86. As in the earlier boom, after growing for a few years, residential housing outlays leveled off, but unlike the second half of the earlier boom, this was accompanied by a noticeable decline in the growth rate of business fixed investment, which dropped to 1.8 percent in 1986–90 (compared to 6.7 percent in 1964–69), largely due to the weakness of business outlays on structures. The rate of growth of overall activity turned negative in the third quarter of 1990, initiating a three-quarter-long recession.

The recoveries following the two recessions were (and continue to be) also noticeably different. A mini-boom began in the first half of 1970 and GDP grew steadily until 1973. The force behind the recovery of the early 1970s was consumer investment, with residential construction and consumer durable goods expenditures growing at an annual rate of 8.8 and 6.6 percent, respectively. In contrast the recovery following the recession of 1990 was anemic. There was no upsurge in consumer investment generating any kind of mini-boom such as that of the early 1970s, only stagnation, at least until 1992(III).

The key questions are why the American economy turned around so quickly after the 1969–70 recession and then grew at an annual rate of over 3 percent for three more years, and why the boom of the 1980s was followed by over two years of stagnation. In this regard, it is helpful to divide the economy into household, business, and government sectors, the foreign sector being omitted for convenience, and to introduce a new spending category. The expression "consumer investment" was earlier defined as the sum of outlays on consumer durables and residential construction, an investment category to be contrasted with investment by the business and government sectors. A related term, "household-related expenditures," will be used to indicate non-consumption expenditures that provide services directly connected with and related to the place of residence. These investment expenditures can be undertaken by households, businesses, and governments and would include, for example, new residential construction and what has been termed "house-connected" investment: household investment in household furnishings and equipment, business investment in stores, restaurants, and garages, and, in the public sector, public housing and sewer and water systems, to name a few. While the focus will be on residential construction when discussing cyclical fluctuations, it is important to keep in mind that booms and slumps in residential housing investment will be accompanied by similar movements in other non-consumption outlays that qualify as household-related.

11.3 A Non-linear Model of the Cycle

Consider next a cyclical mechanism at work in the post–Second World War period generating the kinds of booms and recessions just detailed, one that can at the same time account for the sectoral shifts in outlays over the course of each boom.[3] Basically the mechanism is comprised of interaction of the kinds of endogenous variables emphasized in Keynesian cyclical models subject to two kinds of constraints or "ceilings," a ceiling in the capital goods industry and what will be termed a "monetary ceiling."[4]

The capital goods industry consists of firms producing equipment and structures for the economy. Based on earlier studies, it can assumed as an acceptable approximation that the production of new capital goods for sale to government and to business is always to order and not for inventory.[5] In contrast, production of new capital goods for households (consumer investment viewed from the supply side), whether they be residences or household furnishings and equipment, may be to order—for example, custom built houses—but are largely

---

[3] For a fuller account see J. Cornwall *Growth and Stability in a Mature Economy*, Martin Robertson, London, 1972, chapter X; and "Stability and stabilization of mature economies," in K. Velupillai (ed.), *Nonlinearities, Disequilibria and Simulation: Essays in Honour of Bjorn Thalberg*, Macmillan, London, 1992.

[4] Earlier versions of such a model are found in R. Goodwin "The nonlinear accelerator and the persistence of business cycles," *Econometrica*, Vol. 19, 1951, pp. 1–17; and B.Thalberg "Stabilization policy and the nonlinear theory of the trade cycle," *Swedish Journal of Economics*, Vol. 3, 1971, pp. 294–310.

[5] See V. Zarnowitz, "Unfilled Orders, price changes and business fluctuations," *The Review of Economics and Statistics*, November, Vol XLIV, No. 4, pp. 367–394.

for inventory—for example, speculative housing and washing machines.

During strong booms, orders by business for new capital goods will be large relative to the output capacity of the capital goods industry, restraining actual business investment expenditures and causing backlogs of demand to build up as long as new orders exceed production. Also of importance, many of the larger construction firms in the capital goods industry can and do produce either for the household sector in the form of residential construction, or for the business sector in the form of new structures or plant. Their orientation will depend upon relative profitability. The available evidence indicates profit rates are higher in business construction projects so that when the demand is there, the larger construction firms shift resources in order to satisfy this demand.[6]

Next consider the monetary ceiling. It is often argued that when monetary policy is conducted through the use of "quantitative" controls, policy is "neutral" in the sense that credit is said to be rationed solely on the basis of its cost. However, until the period of deregulation in the 1980s monetary policy had been especially biased, acting to curtail mortgage lending and therefore residential construction during booms and to expand both during recessions.

Assume a strong boom in overall activity that has been under way long enough for the authorities to become concerned about inflation, leading the central bank to tighten credit conditions by reducing the growth of bank reserves. This causes interest rates on new debt instruments, including mortgages, to increase. However, interest rates on mortgages rise more slowly than rates on more marketable securities, for example, corporate and government bonds, causing lenders to back away from the mortgage market.

In addition, "thrift institutions"—for example, mutual savings banks and savings and loan associations in the United States, trust and mortgage loan companies in Canada, and building societies in England—traditionally have matched mortgage loans with deposits. During a period of rising interest rates on marketable securities, rates that thrift institutions can pay on their deposits rise relatively slowly because they can only raise mortgage rates (to finance higher deposit rates) on new mortgages and these are only a small part of their total mortgage holdings. The result is "disintermediation," the by-passing of financial

[6]This assumption is supported in unpublished studies by the Federal Reserve Bank of Boston in the 1960s.

intermediaries by potential depositors during the middle and late stages of the boom and the direct placement of their funds in the capital market where rates of interest have risen relatively. Since mortgage dealings are largely carried out through financial intermediaries in economies such as the United States, residential construction and other forms of household-related expenditures are cut back. The argument is symmetrical. During recessions and early stages of the boom, the monetary ceiling ceases to operate and just the opposite "intermediation" process occurs, stimulating mortgage lending and residential construction and other forms of household-related expenditures.

11.4 The Relationship between Booms and Slumps

Based on the post–Second World War experience, in the absence of important changes in the defense budget, business investment expenditures largely determine the shape of fluctuations in overall activity. Thus when *demand* by business for new investment goods is strong, the increase of business investment *expenditures* will be large, relative to the case when business demand for investment goods is weak. In addition the duration of the investment expenditure boom will be longer relative to a case of weak business investment demand, as production to order results in larger backlogs of demand that take time to work themselves off.

This translates into a strong boom in GDP of long duration and has additional ramifications. When business investment booms are large in amplitude and long in duration, subsequent recessions tend to be mild and of short duration. On the other hand, other things remaining equal, weak booms in business investment demand, while generating mild booms in business investment expenditures and in overall activity, lead to recessions that are sharper and of longer duration or at least to weak recoveries. Cyclical movements as well as long-term developments are history dependent.

This causal interrelationship between the phases of the business cycle is the result of the operation (or the failure to operate) of the ceiling in the capital goods industry and the monetary ceiling just discussed. For example, consider the case of a boom driven by strong business investment demands and expenditures. The stronger and longer is this investment boom, the stronger and longer will be the boom in GDP and the milder will be the following recession for three reasons. First, the stronger is the boom in business demand for new construction, the greater will be the shift of resources to satisfy business demands, the more will residential construction and other types of household-related expenditures be cut back, and the greater will be the deferred demand for household-related expenditure that can only be satisfied in the subsequent recession.

Second, the stronger is the business investment boom, the larger will be the backlog of unfilled business orders for both new plant and equipment when the boom comes to an end. Other things being equal, this will lead to a more moderate and a slower decline in business investment outlays during the subsequent recession, as the larger stock of deferred business demand is worked off. This is crucial because once the recession sets in, the turnaround in overall economic activity will require a smaller increase in residential construction and other forms of household-related expenditure to offset the smaller and less rapid downturn in business investment.

Third, the stronger is the business investment and GDP boom, the tighter monetary policy will become once the boom is under way. This leads to greater disintermediation as interest rates on marketable securities rise relative to rates on deposits at thrift institutions, causing depositors to withdraw their funds in larger amounts and place them directly in the capital market. The result is a drying up of mortgage funds and a postponement of consumer investment in housing and other household-related expenditures until the recession.

In effect, to the extent that the two ceilings operate in the boom, recessions will be bounded from below by the counter-cyclical movement in household-related expenditures.[7] Mild recessions of the type experienced in the United States in the 1950s and 1960s are examples of this kind of history-dependence. To the extent that the two ceilings fail to operate in the boom, the subsequent recession will be more severe. The Great Depression of the 1930s was a most extreme example of the failure of the constraints to operate in the previous boom. Differences between the boom of the 1960s, the subsequent short recession and the recovery of the early 1970s, and the boom of the 1980s and today's stagnation can to a large extent be explained in terms of the operation of the two constraints in the 1960s boom and their failure to operate in the 1980s.

---

[7]Until the recession of 1990, growth of state and local government expenditures also played an important role in turning the economy around following a short and mild downturn.

11.5 Path Dependence in the 1959–73 and 1982–92 Periods

The booms

The boom of the 1960s proceeded at a more rapid rate of growth and had a longer duration than that of the 1980s. Differences in the behavior of business fixed investment had much to do with this. As mentioned, defense expenditures played an important role in the second half of the 1960s boom and the first half of the 1980s boom. As shown in table 11.1, both business investment and government outlays grew more rapidly in the 1960s period. Their combined average rate of growth (not shown) was 4.3 percent in the 1960s compared to 3 percent in the boom of the 1980s. Differences in the behavior of business fixed investment in the two booms is of particular importance because of its effect on the subsequent recession and recovery. The milder recession and the much stronger recovery following the 1969–70 downturn was very much related to the greater strength of the 1960s boom, particularly the greater strength of the business investment boom. When business investment booms are strong a ceiling in the capital goods industry becomes operative and disintermediation increases. This is shown in table 11.1 in the relatively slow growth of housing investment throughout the 1960s (1.8 percent), especially in the second half of the 1960s (–0.3 percent).

Lest this be interpreted as a decline in the demand for housing, data on residential housing vacancy rates in table 11.2 lead to a different interpretation. These fell throughout the 1960s both for rental and owner-occupied housing, indicating a building up over the 1960s of a backlog of demand for new housing (and other household-related expenditures). When monetary policy shifted to ease early in the 1970s following the weakening of the economy, the backlog of demand combined with easier terms of credit and the shift in deposits to thrift institutions resulted in a strong household-related spending boom.[8]

Housing investment outlays also grew rapidly in the first half of the 1980s boom and then turned down, tracing out a pattern similar to that of the 1960s boom. This would again suggest the operation of the two ceilings. However, other considerations lead to a different conclusion. First, business fixed investment outlays were very weak during the 1982–90 boom compared to the 1960s boom (and also the mini-boom of 1975–79). As a result, construction firms would not be moving out

[8]See J. Cornwall, *Growth and Stability*.

Table 11.2 Rental and home-owner vacancy rates in the United States in 1959–1969[a] and 1982–1992

	1959	1960	1961	1962	1963	1964	1965	1966	1967	1968	1969
Total rental units	6.1	7.2	8.0	7.7	7.2	7.3	7.7	7.5	6.6	5.5	5.0
Total home-owner units	1.0	1.1	1.2	1.2	1.4	1.3	1.5	1.4	1.3	1.0	0.9

	1982	1983	1984	1985	1986	1987	1988	1989	1990	1991	1992
Total rental units	5.3	5.7	5.9	6.5	7.3	7.7	7.7	7.1	7.2[b]	7.3[b]	7.3[c]
Total home-owner units	1.5	1.5	1.7	1.7	1.6	1.7	1.6	1.6	1.7	1.6[b]	1.6[c]

[a] First quarter
[b] Fourth quarter
[c] Third quarter

Sources: U.S Department of Commerce, *Statistical Abstract of the United States*, various issues; and U.S. Department of Commerce, Office of Business Analysis, *Economic Bulletin Board*, November 1992.

of residential construction to the degree they did in the second half of the 1960s and would be meeting the demand for new housing to a greater extent if the demand were there. In addition, the backlogs of demand for both business equipment and structures would be relatively low when the economy turned down, leading to a sharper decline in GDP. Second, table 11.2 indicates that the demand for new housing relative to the housing stock was weak during the 1980s boom, as vacancy rates rose during the period. As a result when monetary policy eventually eased, it would not be expected that outlays for new housing and household equipment and furnishings would pick up as they had in the early 1970s and they did not.[9]

The recessions and recoveries

The recession following the boom of the 1960s lasted from 1969(IV) until 1970(II), although the decline in GDP was less than 1 percent and was followed by a relatively strong recovery in GDP in the first half of 1970. Measured on a quarterly basis, GDP achieved its previous 1969(III) peak level in 1970(III).[10] The recession marking the end of the 1980s boom was also short and mild, although sharper than that of 1969–70. GDP fell by a little over 2 percent from a peak in 1990(II) to the 1991(I) trough. More important, unlike the 1970 recovery, the recovery of 1991–92 was weak. After three quarters of decline and six of "recovery," GDP in 1992(III) was still only .5 percent higher than its 1990(II) peak. After a spurt in overall activity in 1992(IV), ten quarters after the previous peak in GDP, GDP surpassed the 1990(II) high by only 1.5 percent. In comparison, ten quarters after the 1969(III) peak, GDP was 5.3 percent higher.

Housing investment outlays declined steadily throughout 1990 and remained depressed until mid-1991 when a modest increase took place. The high vacancy rates in both rental and home-owner housing up through 1992 detailed in table 11.2 would explain the weakness of the recovery in housing investment. In effect the kinds of expenditures that in the 1960s boom were postponed until the early 1970s, in the later boom were moved up from the 1990s to the 1980s.

Furthermore, difficulties in the way of recovery from the 1990 re-

---

[9]Rates of growth of all fixed investment expenditures, including expenditures on consumer durables and housing, were more similar in the two booms, but as outlined in the text this had much to do with the failure of the 1980s boom to be followed by a spurt in family-related investment similar to that of the early 1970s.

[10]On an annual basis GDP did not decline until 1974.

226 *Recovery*

Figure 11.1 Index of residential construction plus state and local government expenditures, 1969 (III)–1972 (I) and 1990 (II)–1992 (IV), 1969 (III) and 1990 (II)=100

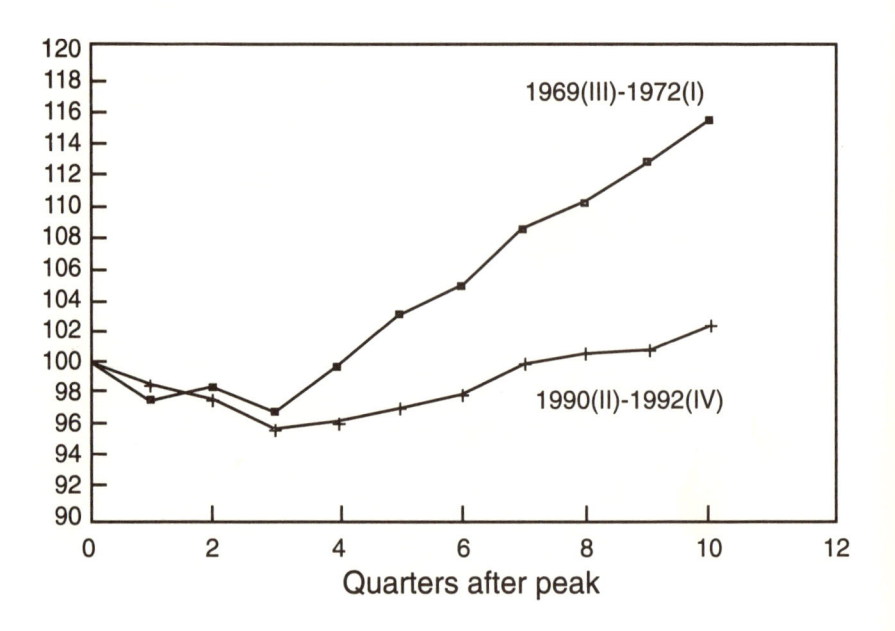

Sources: U.S. Department of Commerce. *Survey of Current Business.* September 1992, Table 2; January 1993, table 1.2; and U.S. Department of Commerce, Office of Business Analysis, *Economic Bulletin Board,* November, 1992.

cession were compounded by the failure of state and local government expenditures to grow as rapidly as they had in the early 1970s. Figure 11.1 contrasts the behavior of the sum of residential construction and state and local government expenditures from the peak quarters of the 1960s and 1980s booms in GDP until ten quarters later. As mentioned, until the 1990s, growth in these two types of expenditures had been key factors in pulling the economy out of a recession and initiating a recovery. Ten quarters after the 1969(III) peak in GDP these two types of expenditures were 16 percent higher than their 1969(III) level. In contrast by 1992(IV), ten quarters after the 1990(II) peak in GDP, they were less than 3 per cent above their 1990 (II) level. Differences in the behavior of these two spending categories in the two recessions and recoveries help explain the differences not only in the overall recoveries of the economy, but also in the nature of the preceding booms.

11.6 The Aftermath

During the second half of the weak 1980s boom inflation rates began to accelerate even when unemployment rates remained high. This in itself would contribute to the weakness of the current recovery in output and employment and help explain why short term OECD forecasts are not overly optimistic.[11] With the economies indicating an inflationary bias even at high rates of unemployment, the authorities would have been rather cautious and slow to switch their priorities from containing inflation to stimulating the economy and would continue to be so, at least in the short run.

The central point of this chapter has been that there were endogenous factors at work in the United States that have contributed to the weakness of the recovery in the early 1990s. Unfortunately these and other considerations make it more unlikely that stimulative AD policies can or will be used to engineer a strong recovery in the rest of the decade. Two of the more unfortunate legacies of the 1980s boom are the increased ineffectiveness of stimulative monetary policy and the increased constraint on the use of stimulative fiscal policy.

Consider first consumer investment in housing and consumer durables, especially those related to household formation, and other forms of household-related expenditures. A shift to an easier monetary policy before deregulation had fairly predictable effects, such as increased intermediation, mortgage lending and housing investment. With deregulation the close relation between intermediation and availability of mortgage funds has been weakened. However, because of the peculiar nature of the 1980s boom and its aftermath, it is possible to assess the resulting impact of easier monetary policy on housing, at least in general terms. Thus whatever the increase in size of the pool of mortgage funds available for mortgage lending, the data on vacancy rates recorded in table 11.2 indicate that up through 1992 there was still a substantial excess stock of housing to be worked off before a boom in residential construction comparable to those of the recent past is likely to occur.

An additional adverse legacy of the 1980s has been the growth of indebtedness of the household sector. To cite but one statistic, gross interest payments plus scheduled principle payments as a share of disposable income rose from a 1983 low of approximately 14 percent to an approximate high in the early 1990s of 18 percent. This ratio was

---

[11]See OECD, *Economic Outlook,* OECD, Paris, December 1992, table 49.

reduced to 16 percent in 1992 but still remains historically high.[12] Until this debt burden is substantially reduced, the negative impact on borrowing by the household sector for whatever purpose will act as a drag on recovery.

Concerning expenditure patterns of state and local government, in earlier post– Second World War cycles state and local governments tended to postpone capital expenditures during the boom and waited for the subsequent recession to enter the capital markets in order to take advantage of lower interest rates. After a lag this led to an increase in government outlays in time to give the economy a needed boost. Figure 11.1 reveals all too clearly the usual boost to the economy by state and local government spending has not been forthcoming in the current period.

Basically the problem can be traced to serious budget gaps beginning in late 1986 and reflecting structural deficits, that is, deficits under FE conditions, in state and local government budgets and poor economic conditions. The forces generating deficits even at FE include a cut back in federal grants in aid and (spending) mandates imposed by the federal government and the courts. The important effect has been to severely restrain state and local government spending. This is likely to be especially noticeable during times of recessions when their budget deficits have risen sharply.[13] Easier monetary policy is less effective in this case.

Forecasters with an optimistic view of the workings of capitalist systems are given to refer to the "natural turnaround of the economy" when predicting recoveries. Although the forces responsible for this turnaround are seldom spelled out in detail, the forces that have in fact initiated recoveries in the past are, at the time of this writing (April 1993), unable to perform their stabilizing role. This is but to say that stimulative monetary policies have become less effective in the current period than in earlier postwar periods of stagnation. This conclusion is given added force by the recognition that suppliers of credit have tightened their lending terms in the 1990s, to a large extent because of the over-relaxation of credit standards in the 1980s boom.

---

[12]See OECD, *Economic Outlook*, OECD, Paris, June 1982, figure F and *Economic Report of the President*, U.S. Government Printing Office, Washington DC, 1993, pp. 87–88 and chart 3–5. Similar increases in this ratio were found for Canada and the United Kingdom. For a further study of the problem of household debt burden see J. Sargent "Deregulation, debt, and downturn in the UK Economy," *National Institute Economic Review*, No. 137, pp. 75–98, August 1992.

[13]See L. Rubin "The state and local government sector: long-term trends and recent fiscal pressures," *Federal Reserve Bulletin*, December, Vol. 78, No. 12, pp. 892–901, 1992.

Among the various possible sources of recovery, exports, business investment, and federal budget policy have yet to be discussed. Given the worldwide nature of the current recession, an export-led boom in the United States seems most unlikely. Nor is it likely that the business sector will spontaneously undertake a strong investment program. The boom of the 1980s led to an overbuilding in commercial buildings as well as in residential housing. Not only have the high vacancy rates acted to reduce new commercial construction, so has the fall in prices of the existing stock. In addition, capital utilization rates in manufacturing are low, business debt overhang is high, and trends in the 1960s and 1970s suggest that the trend of business investment as a share of GDP is, if anything, downward.[14]

This leaves the federal government as a possible initiator of recovery, as was the case in the first term of the Reagan administration. Discussion of this important point will be undertaken in detail in chapter 12. Suffice it to say at this point that events today resemble conditions of the 1930s in two important respects. Not only is monetary policy a weakened tool for regulating AD, but fiscal policy is limited in the role it can play by the same kinds of ideological constraints that prevented acceptance of Keynes' program in *The General Theory*. In addition there is the impact of the huge federal government deficits of the 1980s on the willingness to undertake deficit financing in the 1990s.

[14]See Section 11.2.

12 A Program for Economic Recovery in the United States

12.1 Introduction

In chapter 10 it was concluded that world recovery required the elimination of the inflationary bias in the pluralist economies. In these economies, inflation now rises to politically unacceptable rates long before unemployment rates reach FE levels. Under such circumstances the authorities in the pluralist economies will not permit unemployment rates to fall to anything like those of the 1960s, and their high unemployment is exported to the other OECD economies.

Chapter 11 discussed some additional obstacles in the way of a return to low rates of unemployment in the United States.[1] Rising indebtedness in the consumer, business, and government sectors during the 1980s, overbuilding in the construction industry, and "budget gaps" have all contributed to the slow and weak recovery from the 1990 trough and have reduced the ability of monetary policy to forcefully stimulate the economy, should the authorities desire to do so.

In the case of the federal government, the sustained large budget deficits and the resulting growth of debt in the 1980s have generated strong sentiments in favor of reducing federal deficits, especially through government spending cuts. Together these events have created a situation in the 1990s similar to that which policymakers faced in the 1930s, a reduced role for monetary policy and political constraints on the use of fiscal instruments in stimulating the economy. This raises serious problems for the future. The United States has consistently been a high unemployment economy and the average rate of unemployment during the 1982–90 GDP boom was almost one-third higher than its 1960–73 average. As maintained throughout the study, recovery is first and foremost a permanent reduction in unemployment. Without a radical change in attitudes and policies, future performance will remain poor.

[1] Similar obstacles have developed in Canada and the United Kingdom.

In spite of difficulties facing the authorities, a feasible program for recovery is available, although it differs substantially from those tried and widely advocated in the past in the United States. This chapter outlines a program for recovery in the 1990s for the United States, the largest and most influential of the pluralist group. While there are important institutional and historical differences between the United States and Canada and the United Kingdom, there are enough basic similarities between the institutional frameworks of all three economies to consider the recovery program of this chapter as especially relevant for improving conditions in all three economies. In addition, important parts of the program, especially those dealing with export policies, are relevant for recovery in all of the OECD economies.

It is also important to note that a successful recovery program in the three pluralist economies will remove one of the basic obstacles standing in the way of a successful coordinated stimulative policy throughout the OECD. It is useful, therefore, to assume throughout this chapter that the recovery program discussed here is part of a coordinated OECD program of stimulation.[2] Before outlining the program, a contrast between two widely differing views of the workings of capitalism and an inspection of the long-run unemployment records in the United States and other capitalist economies provides some useful background.

12.2 Paradigms and Recovery Programs

Sociologists have pointed to an important difference between members of that profession and economists in their perceptions of the workings of capitalism. Most economists view capitalist economies either as self-regulating systems with markets that clear rapidly, if not instantaneously, or as economies capable of being stabilized through the application of the traditional monetary and fiscal instruments of policy.[3] Shocks, including mistaken efforts at policy intervention, may lead to deviations from a FE growth path, but these deviations are seen as short-lived because of the inherent self-regulating properties. Sociologists, on the other hand, see capitalism as a system capable of generating economic and political conflict and other basic structural changes as part of its natural evolution, which can lead to lengthy periods of poor as well as superior performance.

---

[2]See sections 10.3 and 10.7.
[3]See J. Goldthorpe "The current inflation: towards a sociological account," in F. Hirsch and J. Goldthorpe (eds.), *The Political Economy of Inflation*, Harvard University Press, Cambridge, MA, 1978. See the Preface to the 1993 addition for a brief discussion of paradigms.

Advocates of restrictive AD policies as the critical first step in a program for recovery are especially prone to base their policies on a view of capitalism as an inherently stable, self-regulating system (in the absence of errors by policymakers, at least). This is certainly true of the variations on this theme summarized in earlier chapters.

The McCracken Report, published in the mid-1970s, optimistically foresaw an early return to low unemployment following a short period of restrictive AD policies.[4] The Great Inflation of the late 1960s–early 1970s was partly attributable to institutional changes, that is, the rise in aspirations and expectations induced by two decades of high employment and prosperity. However, in its policy recommendations the Report concluded that in the final analysis the difficulties were caused by a series of shocks occurring in a short period to an otherwise stable system and were unlikely ever to be repeated. By making sure that the recovery program did not proceed too rapidly, a return to conditions of the Golden Age was thought possible by 1980.

In a similar vein, when the unemployment costs of the restrictive policies of the 1980s proved to be high, believers in the credibility doctrine did not assign these costs to basic structural changes in the institutions of capitalism. Rather these high costs were seen as the result of human error, that is, of the inability of those in charge of policy to convince the public of their desire and intent to rid inflation from the system at any cost.

In both of these cases, the programs for recovery are seen as a "technical" solution to the economic breakdown; the authorities need only to correctly put into force the available policy instruments, for example, either a slow engineered recovery of AD allowing inflationary expectations to decline or a more believable implementation of a restrictive AD policy.

Consider in contrast some of the implications of the sociologist's appraisal of capitalism as a system capable of inducing harmful as well as beneficial structural changes as an inherent part of its evolution. From this perspective when economic performance deteriorates, rather than attribute this to "outside influences," there is a strong inclination to look for the structural changes responsible. Institutions and institutional change must form a key part of the analysis. In this case the solution to poor performance and instability cannot be considered merely technical, but requires further changes in some of the institutions of the society. If successful, these policy-induced changes may

---

[4]See section 9.2.

permit the more familiar policy instrument to be used once again to achieve the desired goals, such as a stimulative AD policy to reduce unemployment.[5]

Certainly we know that over time institutions change in important ways and that these changes are often induced by economic performance. The findings of chapter 5 also indicate that institutions differ substantially between countries and institutions matter in the sense that they importantly affect economic performance. It is but a slight "inductive leap" from these two considerations and a look at the historical record to the position that over time institutions may evolve in an unfavorable way and that if these changes are not offset through policy, economic performance will deteriorate. Certainly this is the message of earlier chapters; it is also the central conclusion of this chapter. More particularly, the American economy and the other pluralist economies have been subject to an historically new form of market failure in the post–Second World War period and will continue to malfunction in the 1990s unless a major program for recovery is undertaken, one requiring policy-induced changes in institutions.

12.3 The Unemployment Record in the Twentieth Century

Consider next the unemployment records. Largely as a result of two decades of prosperity, interests among macroeconomists, including those who would consider themselves "Keynesian," shifted from the short run and Keynesian problems of insufficient AD to the long run, with growing acceptance of the view that capitalism in the long run was indeed a self-regulating system.[6] In this new view, in the short run the economy may operate at less than its FE level but, because of mechanisms such as the Pigou effect, in the long run AD will automatically adjust and the economy will return to a FE level of output determined by exogenous supply forces.

There is a certain amount of difficulty in verifying or refuting this position by an appeal to the historical record. It has never been made clear what is meant by the long run and the short run, and for how long and how often over, say, the course of a 10-, 50-, or 100-year period the economy must remain at or achieve FE before the self-regulating assumption is supported. However, there are unemployment data for a number of economies covering approximately three-quarters of a cen-

---

[5] The institutional-policy fit solution described first in chapter 1.
[6] See references in footnotes 5–7 in chapter 3.

Table 12.1 Average annual standardized unemployment rates U and number of years annual unemployment rates exceeded 3 and 6 percent for selected periods in Canada, Sweden, the United Kingdom, and the United States

(a)

Annual average rate of unemployment

	1920–38	1950–73	1974–91	1980–91	1950–91	1920–91*
Canada**	8.4	4.7	8.6	9.3	6.3	6.9
Sweden	4.3	1.9	2.2	2.4	2.0	2.7
UK	9.4	2.7	8.1	9.6	5.0	6.4
USA	9.3	4.6	6.9	7.0	5.6	6.8

(b)

Number of years annual unemployment rate exceeded 3 and 6 percent

	3 percent rate		6 percent rate	
	1920–38	1950–91	1920–38	1950–91
Canada**	14 of 18	39 of 42	9 of 18	22 of 42
Sweden	11 of 19	3 of 42	5 of 19	0 of 42
UK	18 of 19	23 of 42	19 of 19	12 of 42
USA	17 of 19	38 of 42	11 of 19	15 of 42

* Excludes 1939–49
** Excludes 1920
Sources: A. Maddison, *Phases of Capitalist Development*, Oxford University Press, Oxford, 1982; D. Gubb, *The OECD Data Set*, Working Paper No. 615, Centre for Labour Economics, London School of Economics, March 1984; and *Economic Outlook*, No. 51, Paris, 1992, table R18.

tury. Table 12.1 summarizes the unemployment record for Canada, the United Kingdom, and the United States along with that of Sweden for comparison.

Reading across the rows of Panel (a), it is clear that there have been large variations in unemployment rates over time. Given any reasonable definition of FE, it is also clear that the three English-speaking economies experienced unemployment rates greater than the FE rate on average during the 1920–38 and 1974–91 periods, together more than half the years of the total period.

Reading down the columns reveals large differences in unemployment rates between Sweden and the other three economies whatever period is chosen. With the increased acceptance of vertical Phillips curve analysis and the NAIRU, differences in unemployment rates between economies (and over time) have often been explained in terms of differences in the NAIRU. However, as argued in chapter 3 the fact that high unemployment has persisted since the mid-1970s has lead even believers to recognize that the NAIRU may be substantially greater than the rate of unemployment at which all unemployment is voluntary or largely so. In other words, the FE rate of unemployment must be defined in terms of the nature of unemployment at any rate of unemployment and not in terms of the behavior of prices.

This recognition suggests that in evaluating unemployment records in terms of the ability or lack of ability to achieve FE, some benchmark rate of unemployment must be adopted as the FE rate. Figures in table II.1 suggest a benchmark of 2.3 percent, the average unemployment rate for the 18 OECD economies in the 1960–73 period (which falls to a little less than 2 percent when Canada and the United States are excluded). Instead in panel (b) comparisons are made between annual unemployment rates in a country and the unemployment rates of 3 and 6 percent. The 3 percent figure can be justified as a conservative benchmark rate; it is the average rate of unemployment for the seven largest OECD economies in the 1950–73 period. Additional justification is the recognition that there are large numbers of involuntarily unemployed workers at 3 percent in any economy.[7]

With this in mind, the comparison of records between the economies listed in Panel (b) indicates not only the inability of the English-speaking economies to attain FE in a long-run sense, but the vastly superior performance of Sweden. Over a period covering approximately three-quarters of a century, but excluding the Second World War period, Sweden experienced unemployment rates greater than 3 percent in only 14 years and unemployment rates greater than 6 percent in only 5 years. In contrast during the same 61 years, the comparable figures for the United States were 55 and 26 years, respectively. If it is assumed that the FE rate of unemployment in the United States is 3 percent, then over a period covering three-quarters of a century, FE was achieved in only one year out of ten. Similarly, if 4 and 5 percent are chosen as the FE rate of unemployment, FE is realized in approximately one year out of five and one year out of three (not shown), respectively. Only by choosing 6 percent as the FE rate of unemployment does the American economy succeed in attaining FE approximately half of the time. Similar figures apply to Canada and the United Kingdom.

[7] As pointed out in footnote 2 of chapter 5, in 1969 unemployment in the United States was 3.4 percent. Of all the weeks of unemployment experienced in that year, 35 percent was experienced by workers out of work for 26 weeks or more and 16 percent of the weeks of unemployment were experienced by workers out of work for 40 weeks or more. This hardly suggests the absence of involuntary unemployment at 3.4 percent.

These and additional calculations indicate that high average rates of unemployment over the entire 1920–91 period cannot be attributed simply to the high rates of unemployment in the 1930s. Moreover it must be emphasized that the years of high unemployment resulting from anti-inflation policies in the period since the mid-1970s should be included along with the 1930s in adding up the years of poor performances. They too reflect the absence of a self-regulating mechanism, for in a self-regulating economy of flexprice markets, restrictive AD policies should have powerful and rapid effects on inflation. For example, when unacceptable inflation has been the result of policy errors, past mistakes should be fairly easy to correct by simply reversing policy. This will initiate the quick price and wage responses that bring down inflation with little increase in unemployment in a self-regulating system. The fact that the record since the mid-1970s reveals that there were huge unemployment costs involved in reducing inflation was earlier attributed to the numerous market imperfections that describe an economy lacking in self-regulating mechanisms.[8]

Clearly the record does not suggest automatic FE tendencies at work in the three English-speaking countries in the twentieth century, even in the long run. History, that is, the invisible hand, has not been so generous as to pass economies like the United States from one golden age on to the next with a minimum of delay. Rather it is less benevolent, tracing out a pattern of economic development more in keeping with the sociologist's paradigm of capitalism generating both good times and bad as it evolves.

12.4 An Outline of the Program

The ideological climate and the implementation of the program

Chapter 10 offered arguments why the restrictive AD policies tried since the early 1970s would not lead to their expressed long-run goals of low unemployment *and* low rates of inflation. In this sense they are not *sufficient* for recovery. Fortunately, as the earlier chapters have indicated, they are not *necessary*; some economies have been able to contain inflation and still keep unemployment low by means of other policy instruments. Recovery in the United States requires the adoption of a modified version of these policies.

It is useful to divide the program into two parts, in which the first

[8]See section 10.5.

part lays the groundwork and is an essential precondition for the acceptance of the second part. In essence the first stage in a recovery program is to create a political and economic climate in which certain institutional changes are seen to be essential, if the agreed upon policy goals are to be achieved, and therefore acceptable in principle by the polity. This new ideological climate involves a recognition that new modes of economic and political behavior and a new understanding of the workings of a modern capitalist economy are essential for recovery.[9]

The second part of the program involves determining in detail the more immediate policies required for realizing the macroeconomic goals, such as whether to stimulate AD through current or capital government outlays, and implementing them in the most efficient and politically acceptable ways.

The concluding sections of the chapter will take up rather briefly some of these issues within the context of the program outlined by the Clinton administration.

Most of this chapter will be concerned with ideological foundations of the program. This can be defended in several ways. First, as was made clear in chapter 5, the economies that performed successfully before the breakdown, while in general agreement over such matters as the proper role of the state in the economy, the importance of trust and feelings of fairness and the kinds of market behavior essential for achieving the goals of FE, low rates of inflation and external balance, did so within political and institutional frameworks that otherwise differed, such as the distribution of political and economic power, the structure of the trade union movement. However, largely by trial and error, additional country-specific institutional changes were brought about that enabled these economies to develop and implement the policy instruments leading directly to the desired goals. In a somewhat similar manner, if in the United States an ideological climate can be created that is conducive to the acceptance of a similar set of basic institutional prerequisites, then by trial and error the exact form of the additional adaptations will be found.

Second, as stated earlier, recovery is not simply a "technical" matter of specifying the goals of policy and the policies for achieving these goals. Before any kind of practical measure can be successfully introduced, the general public and especially their political leaders must understand its underlying rationale. Third, the centers of economic and

---

[9]Chapter 5 summarized the kinds of institutions that were so successful before the early 1970s in other economies and which in some modified form must be created in pluralist economies for successful performance.

political power are especially hostile to the kinds of institutions that have proved so successful in other economies in facilitating superior performance. The "received wisdom" in the United States is that capitalist economies work best in a laissez-faire, "free" market, deregulated environment. Unfortunately, these economic views still form the basis of and a justification for the continuation of counter-productive programs, like Thatcherism and Reaganism. Success involves the acceptance of new views and the discarding of old views. Before considering this in detail, some comments on the formal structure of the program are helpful.

The structure of the program

The program necessary for recovery in the United States, like the programs that have succeeded in other economies in the past, must be envisaged in terms of the realization of several goals simultaneously, which together constitute a hierarchy of policy goals. For example, economic recovery requires more than a simple use of stimulative AD policies as might have been the case in the 1930s. Several goals of policy must be realized simultaneously and, as will become clear, this will also involve policy-induced institutional changes. Thus an important feature of the program is the simultaneous realization of the goals of FE and politically acceptable rates of inflation.[10] This is essential, as the willingness of groups to enter into a social bargain to restrain inflation will not be forthcoming unless FE is part of the reward. As well, the willingness of the authorities to increase AD to a level consistent with FE is conditional on the ability to successfully implement a social bargain.

In addition it is necessary to treat the macroeconomic policy goals in a hierarchical context in which the realization of lower priority goals provides the instruments of policy for achieving intermediate goals. The latter, in turn, provides the means necessary for realizing the ultimate goals of policy, in this case FE and acceptable rates of inflation. Partly because of this and partly because success requires prior policy-induced changes in attitudes and behavior, that is, a new ideological climate, there is no "quick fix" for the current difficulties.

In general terms the thrust of the argument can be made clearer by thinking of the new ideology in terms of an acceptance of three basic propositions, a format helpful in establishing the connection between policy goals and instruments of the program. Each proposition will be

[10]See sections 4.11 and 5.10 for a definition of a politically acceptable rate of inflation.

stated simply, to be followed by an elaboration in terms of related views and detailed comments or references to earlier comments in the study.

Bearing this in mind, the first part of the program involves creating an ideological climate that will lead to the acceptance in principle of (a) the central policy message of *The General Theory*, that is, AD policies, especially fiscal policies, are required periodically to achieve the unemployment target and (b) a social bargain strategy in the labor market as a key element in the program, that is, labor must seek fair treatment through a "cooperative solution." Together the acceptance of these views implies the acceptance of (c) an expanded role for government.

12.5 Creating the Ideological Climate—Keynes Reborn, Part One

Creating the ideological climate that will lead to the acceptance of discretionary AD policies in general and stimulative fiscal policies in particular is essential for the successful implementation of the program. The task can be broken down into an acceptance of four related views; the first two summarize positions supported earlier and the second two are supported in the next section.

1. Capitalism is not an automatic self-regulating system. Left to itself, the performance of the private sector will generate the kind of unemployment record summarized in Table 12.1.
2. Stimulative AD policies can reduce unemployment and increase output when there are involuntary unemployment resources. Crowding out is a FE phenomenon.

The radical and correct message of *The General Theory* was Keynes's belief that the private sector lacked a self-regulating mechanism capable of automatically bringing the system to a FE equilibrium, certainly in some short-run sense. Active intervention through the use of discretionary AD policies could and should be used to offset the worst part of any instability in the private sector and to revive its "animal spirits." Until the 1970s there was strong support within the economics profession that unless the authorities were prepared to actively intervene, recurring recessions and even serious downturns of the 1930s variety could not be ruled out. Support for this view has greatly declined since the early 1970s with some traces of a Keynesian "revival" in the 1990s.

In chapter 1 it was maintained that the welfare costs of the prolonged period of malfunctioning now lasting over two decades are best measured by the high levels of unemployment and that the reduction of unemployment is the main goal of a recovery program. Renewed support for Keynes's position is therefore essential. Moreover the discussion in chapter 11 makes clear that fiscal policy will be the essential AD policy instrument for initiating and possibly sustaining a strong recovery. Additional factors, to be discussed shortly, indicate that over at least the medium term additional fiscal measures will also be required to achieve other goals in the recovery program.

The prevailing ideology in the United States has it that neither lower taxes or higher government spending leads to reduction of unemployment but instead crowds out investment (or exports) by diverting real resources from producing new capital goods. These and other arguments asserting the ineffectiveness of AD policy were rejected in chapter 3 as incorrect, but unfortunately widespread acceptance of these incorrect views provides an ideological obstacle and constraint on the use of stimulative fiscal policies for recovery. What must be made clear is that the FE rate of unemployment is neither the lowest rate of unemployment actually achieved in the past nor the average unemployment rate in the 1960–73 period nor the rate of unemployment at which the rate of inflation becomes politically unacceptable. Under current conditions of mass unemployment, stimulative AD policies need not lead to a diversion of real resources, that is, capital and labor, from new investment projects.

12.6 Creating the Ideological Climate— Keynes Reborn, Part Two

Acceptance of Keynes's central message implies the acceptance of two other views.

3 The federal and general government budget deficits are largely the result of the recession. Structural budget deficits are appreciably smaller. Reducing deficits requires economic recovery.[11]
4 Stimulative fiscal measures will be necessary to initiate the strong recovery and this may require budget deficits under FE conditions.

[11]The structural deficit of the federal government is calculated by assuming existing tax rates and programs and typically an unemployment rate of something like 6 percent. See R. Gordon, *Macroeconomics*, 6th ed., Harper Collins, New York, 1993, Figure 5–4. The latter assumption is both arbitrary and very misleading factually. See footnote 7 of this chapter. Obviously at a rate of unemployment more closely resembling FE, the structural budget deficit would be lower. It could even disappear.

Even if deficits must be run indefinitely, they are "sustainable," that is, a constant debt to GDP ratio is achievable, provided the growth at FE they ensure revives the "animal spirits" of the private sector sufficiently.

A different constraint on fiscal policy, also reminiscent of views espoused in the 1930s, arises from the belief that deficits and the resulting increase in debt are harmful and dangerous in an almost unlimited number of ways—for example, deficits are inflationary and debt places an unjust burden upon future generations. In this case, even if it were accepted that (a) increased budget deficits may be necessary to achieve FE and that (b) AD policies are effective in reducing unemployment when there is involuntary unemployment, the use of stimulative fiscal policies that increase deficits may be severely constrained, especially given the size of the current national debt. Since these beliefs are largely erroneous but widespread and held with such passionate intensity, some forgotten truths must be reaffirmed.

The charge that deficits are harmful because they are inflationary need not be of concern here. The implementation of a stimulative AD policy is conditional upon the successful implementation of a social bargain. More relevant is the assertion that any deficit-financed stimulative policy adds to the national debt, and therefore should be avoided because it will cause a reduction of living standards in future generations. The argument can be summarized in the following way. Assume some government spending project is undertaken in a closed economy and is financed by bonds instead of taxes. This increase in the deficit raises interest rates and thereby crowds out private investment. In an open economy the resulting higher interest rates may also lead to a crowding out of net exports as they attract foreign funds and lead to a rise in the exchange rate and a loss of competitiveness.

In the closed economy example, the decrease in the rate of private capital formation reduces the level of the growth path of per capita income. Future generations therefore suffer. In the open economy example, current account deficits lead to an increase in foreign indebtedness and larger interest payments for foreigners, thereby reducing the disposable income of Americans.[12]

---

[12] The story can be complicated by distinguishing between debt financed capital projects or increased government consumption, but this is not particularly helpful in analyzing the current situation of high unemployment. For a summary of the standard neoclassical FE analysis of deficit financing see J. Yellen, "Symposium on the budget deficit," *Journal of Economic Perspectives*, Spring 1989.

Whatever the merits of these arguments in a FE setting, they are certainly of little relevance today, with unemployment rates averaging over 7 percent in 1993 in the United States (and double digit rates in Canada and the UK). With *large scale involuntary unemployment* and with a *social bargain in place*, deficit financing in order to reduce unemployment generates a rather different scenario. Thus with inflation rates constrained, an accommodating monetary policy is available to keep interest rates from rising if needed. In this case, the stimulative fiscal policy reduces unemployment and increases output as well as government expenditures without reducing investment.[13] Moreover, even if interest rates are allowed to rise for whatever reason, investment need not decline. Contrary to overly simple IS–LM type models, in fact investment is related to other influences such as the level and growth of output and profits, and fiscal stimulation of the economy will likely lead to higher investment all things considered. If the additional interest payments are paid to nationals, there is a pure gain for Americans; if they must be paid to foreigners, they can be "paid for" out of the higher output.[14] Surely a failure to expand employment, output, profits, and investment is more harmful than any possible adverse side effects of the higher debt even in this latter case.

However, the choice being currently offered in the United States and elsewhere is not between discretionary measures of fiscal stimulation or using the built-in stabilizers to contain the downturn while they permit a passive rise in the deficit. Instead governments at all levels are opting for policies of reducing the deficit through restrictive AD policies and the results have been quite devastating. The budget deficits of today are primarily the result of the recession; their reduction requires economic recovery. Unfortunately, efforts to reduce deficits through reducing government expenditures and raising taxes not only worsen the recession by removing important built-in stabilizers from the system, they are unlikely to lead to serious reductions in the deficits.

12.7 Budget Dynamics and the Interaction of the Budget and the Economy

However, all of this neglects the long-run dynamics of the matter in two important ways. It fails to consider the medium- to long-run re-

---

[13]Note the added benefit when interest rates are not allowed to rise: interest payments on government and private debt are kept from rising.
[14]For a fuller description see the articles in J. Rock (ed.), *Debt and the Twin Deficits Debate*, Mayfield Publishing Co., Mountain View, CA, 1991.

sponse of the economy to the recovery program, such as the impact of continuous FE on the rate of growth of the economy and, equally critical, the medium- to long-run impact of growth on the economy on the budgetary requirements of continuous FE, such as the impact of any induced growth effects of the FE policy on the budgetary requirements of FE levels of output.

The so-called budget constraint or identity can be written

$$d(D/Q)/dt = G/Q + Tr/Q - T/Q + iD/Q \qquad (1)$$

where D/Q, G/Q, Tr/Q, and T/Q are the ratios of the national debt, government spending, transfer payments net of interest and tax receipts as a ratio of GDP, respectively. All variables are measured in real terms, and i is the rate of interest. Manipulation of equation (1) leads to a long-run dynamic expression of the budget constraint

$$d(D/Q)/dt = [G/Q + Tr/Q - T/Q] + [ir - \dot{Q}] (D/Q) \qquad (2)$$

where ir is the real rate of interest, $\dot{Q}$ is the rate of growth of real GDP and all other variables have their previous meaning.

Much thought has been given by economists to the question of whether or not a deficit is too large and, therefore, harmful in terms of its "sustainability." For purposes at hand sustainability will be defined as whether or not a deficit fiscal policy leads over time to a situation in which the ratio of debt to income, D/Q, converges to a fixed ratio. If it does, the national debt and GDP grow at the same rate and $d(D/Q)/dt = 0$.[15] It should be further noted that even if the expression in the first bracket of equation (2), the primary deficit, is positive, the policy can be sustained provided the rate of growth of real GDP exceeds the real rate of interest by the size of the primary deficit. If, on the other hand, the total expression on the RHS of equation (2) is positive, deficits in the long run lead to a rising debt/output ratio, and an increasing portion of the total deficit, that is, the primary deficit plus interest payments on the debt, will be accounted for by interest payments.

As should be clear, the sustainability criterion is merely a mathematical exercise and only establishes a framework within which to analyze the budgetary problems that might be associated with the recovery program. In this framework the primary deficit and the growth

---

[15]Note that the long-run sustainability criterion can allow for (hopefully) temporary increases in D/Q due to events such as the savings-and-loan bailout.

rate are exogenously given, whereas within the context of a recovery program, both are in fact endogenous. Thus the mere fact that the budget is set at a level capable of generating FE may increase the growth rate of total output. Alternatively at the same time as the FE part of the program is implemented, the authorities may choose to implement some kind of industrial policy in order to stimulate growth. In either case, the program may lead to a long-run reduction in D/Q and even a reduction in the primary budget deficit consistent with FE, making the budgetary aspects of the program politically more acceptable. The point is that in analyzing a recovery program (in contrast to doing a mathematical exercise), it will not do to assume that either the budget or the growth rate is given. This problem is taken up in section 12.9.

In this matter a simple practical point is worth mentioning. One estimate of the average primary budget deficits for the federal government 1990–94 was 1 percent of GDP and another estimate for the average primary budget deficit of all levels of government for 1990–93 was less than 1 percent. It is not unreasonable to assume that a return, say, to unemployment rates of 3–4 percent would generate primary budgetary surpluses.[16] The impact on real interest rates is less clear.

12.8 Creating the Ideological Climate—the Social Bargain

Creating the conditions that will lead to the acceptance of a social bargain in principle can also be broken down into that of four related views. Since supporting arguments have been made in chapters 5, 6, and 7, only references to the relevant earlier discussions need be given.

1. Unrestricted collective bargaining, that is, a situation under which labor groups vary their wage demands with the state of the labor market, low rates of unemployment and low rates of inflation cannot be achieved simultaneously. As discussed in chapter 5, collective bargaining in such conditions transforms a potential inflationary bias into an actual one.
2. Based on past experience, unless new policy instruments are found for containing inflation in the United States, the authorities will seek to contain inflation by the only means at their disposal, restrictive AD policies.[17] Given the existing inflationary bias, until the new instruments are developed and implemented, high rates of unem-

---

[16]See E. Gramlich in J. Rock (ed.), *Debt and the Twin Deficits Debate* and OECD, *Economic Outlook*, OECD, Paris, June 1992, table 39. See also remarks in footnote 11.

[17]See sections 5.12 and 9.4.

ployment, poverty, and bankruptcies, to name a few malfunctions, will continue indefinitely.
3. For reasons already made clear in chapter 10, restrictive AD policies will be costly in the short run and ineffective in the long run, that is, if and when the authorities allow the economy to move back towards FE. This remains true whether or not restrictive policies are credible. An incomes policy based on fear brings short-term pain for long-term pain.
4. Not only are the hardships imposed upon the American public by restrictive policies not sufficient to bring about recovery, such policies are not necessary. As chapters 5, 6, and 7 and the introduction to Part II have shown, other economies have succeeded in achieving acceptable rates of inflation without sacrificing the low unemployment goal by successfully implementing a social bargain. This was especially true before 1974, but even in the 1980s several economies performed well in this regard.

12.9 The Hierarchy of Policy Goals

Acceptance of the need for some kind of social bargain and some form of stimulative policy is but the first step in achieving goals of low unemployment and inflation. Unless rates of growth of GDP can be increased sufficiently in the process, the long-run dynamics of the budget constraint point to the possibility of an unacceptable growth in the national debt and a discontinuance of the recovery program. This potential problem serves to emphasize that there may be other policy goals in addition to FE and wage and price restraint that must be realized simultaneously as a condition of success. As indicated in sections 12.4 and 12.7, some of these additional goals must be seen as intermediate goals or conditions for the fulfillment of the more basic goals within a hierarchical framework. To keep matters as simple as possible without sacrificing essentials, consideration of additional policy goals will be limited to that of increasing the growth rate of the economy.

The importance of this additional goal can be seen from a second perspective, within the context of a highly interdependent world economy. Indeed it is because of the high degree of economic interdependence (and an inflationary bias) that economic recovery cannot be treated as simply a technical matter. Consider again the goal of FE. In a highly interdependent world economy, even the United States faces a limit to the size of current account deficits it can run. This balance of payments ceiling introduces an additional potential constraint on stimulative AD policies. This has two aspects. In the short to medium term, such a ceiling may be forced on the United States by the reactions of its trading partners and of speculators in the foreign exchange markets to what they consider excessive payments deficits. In a longer-term sense, even if deficit financing in the interest of reducing unemployment does not lead to a rising debt to output ratio, it could lead to a non-sustainable rise in foreign holding of debt to GDP. This indicates the importance of measures that do not merely keep the net export position from deteriorating, but actually improve it.

Various options are available in this regard, such as channeling government spending programs into those with a small direct import content. But the focus here is on policies that attack the sustainability problem at the same time as they operate to eliminate potential payments problems. This necessitates policies to increase the overall growth rate by stimulating the rate of growth of exports of manufactures. Such policies have several advantages, some of them relevant with respect to the sustainability issue and therefore the unemployment target. Higher rates of growth of exports of manufactured goods (and greater import substitution) stimulate the overall growth of GDP and labor productivity through important backward and forward linkage effects. A more direct favorable impact on growth can be seen in the following way. In the later stages of development, growth in a capitalist economy is dominated by the expansion of the industrial and service sectors. The industrial sector, in which manufacturing dominates, experiences substantially higher rates of growth of productivity than does the service sector. Even if it is assumed that domestic income elasticities of demand are approximately equal in the two sectors, other things being equal, the more rapid is the shift of labor into services the more the overall growth of productivity is reduced, because of lower *levels* of productivity in the service sector.[18]

However, provided the foreign income elasticity of demand for domestic manufactures is greater than the domestic income elasticity, expanding the growth of exports of manufactures will generate more rapid and prolonged growth of manufacturing output. Given its high

---

[18]See J. Cornwall and W. Cornwall, "Export-led growth: a new interpretation," in W. Milberg (ed.), *The Megacorp and Macrodynamics*, M. E. Sharpe, Armonk, NY, 1992.

rate of growth of productivity, export success will provide an important direct boost to the rate of growth of overall productivity and, therefore, to GDP.

Two favorable effects of such a successful industrial policy on efforts to achieve the low inflation goal also must be emphasized. First, the more rapid growth of productivity will increase the rate of growth of real wages. This increases the rewards to labor for adopting and complying with a social bargain policy. Second, to the extent that the growth rates of real wages and per capita incomes are increased, distributional issues will be lessened and wage and price restraint will be more likely.

12.10 A Diagrammatic Exposition

These considerations tie together important concluding remarks in chapter 10. As discussed, in the 1990s there are at least three likely constraints on AD policies facing the OECD economies, including a payments constraint because of growing competition from the NICs. Treating a recovery program as a hierarchy of policy goals that must be realized simultaneously brings out the interrelatedness of these constraints. In particular, it reveals that even those economies that had successfully implemented social bargains in the past may require policies to relieve a payments constraint in order to successfully implement a social bargain in the 1990s. The hierarchical structure of the policy goals of the program are diagrammed in figure 12.1. The FE and inflation control goals of policy are written above the dashed horizontal line. The fact that they must be realized together (and are therefore both basic) is indicated by the arrows drawn diagonally from each basic goal to the immediate instrument required for the realization of the other basic goal. Thus before a stimulative AD policy can be undertaken to reduce unemployment, acceptable inflation rates must be ensured in order to remove the inflation constraint. Similarly, before wage and price restraints will be acceptable even in principle, labor especially must be guaranteed FE.

Proceeding below the horizontal line, an arrow is drawn from the external balance goal to AD policy, stressing an additional possible constraint to stimulative AD policies that must be removed. There is also an arrow drawn from the high productivity growth goal to the social bargain goal indicating the additional reward, that is, rapid growth of real wages, that may be available and necessary for the

248 *Recovery*

Figure 12.1. The hierarchy of policy goals in an open economy with an inflationary bias

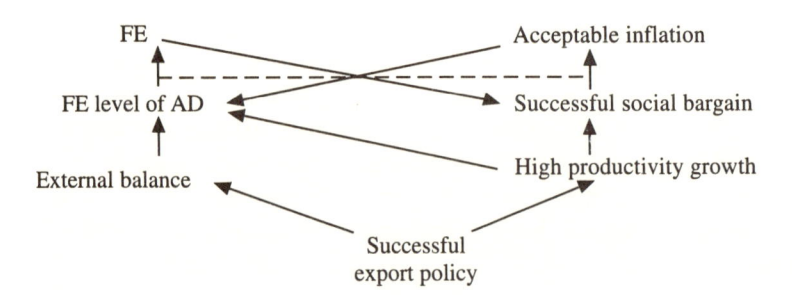

```
        FE                                  Acceptable inflation
         ↑  ↘                          ↗          ↑
    ─────┼──────────╲──────────╱──────────────────┼─
    FE level of AD   ◄────╳────►   Successful social bargain
         ↑              ╱   ╲              ↑
         │            ╱       ╲            │
    External balance ◄          ► High productivity growth
               ╲                      ╱
                 ╲                  ╱
                   Successful
                   export policy
```

Figure 12.2. Hierarchy of policy goals in an open economy with no inflationary bias

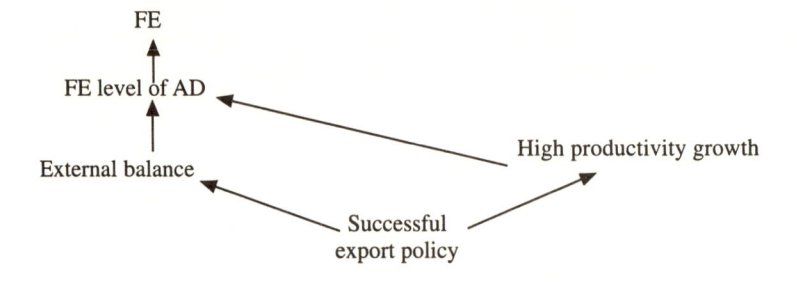

```
        FE
         ↑
    FE level of AD ◄──────────────
         ↑                        ╲
         │                         High productivity growth
    External balance ◄              ↗
               ╲   Successful    ╱
                   export policy
```

acceptance of a social bargain. Another is drawn from the high productivity goal to AD policies pointing up the favorable effect of higher productivity growth on relieving a budget constraint.

At the bottom of the diagram is an even lower link in the hierarchy, one introduced to show the need for a successful export policy in manufactures. As already discussed, any such success helps relieve a possible payments constraint and increases productivity growth, thereby in turn relieving the economy of constraints on AD policies and increasing the chances of acceptance of a social bargain. Figure 12.1, illustrates the importance of a successful export drive in manufactures in economic recovery. Not only is it the basis of economic growth, it is a key policy instrument in the realization of FE and acceptable rates of inflation.[19]

Figure 12.1 illustrates the complexity of the program of economic recovery.[20] It can be compared with Figure 12.2, depicting the interrelations of policy goals in an economy in which a social bargain is assumed not necessary because under FE conditions there is no inflationary bias. This was earlier described as a capitalist economy before the rise in power of labor and the importance of "fairness" in wage demands and settlements. Money wages were set by capital on a "take-it-or-leave-it" basis. Under FE conditions, money wages would be bid up by employers which would be "passed through" to prices, but there would be no feedback effect from higher prices to wages.[21]

Figure 12.2 does allow that FE is dependent upon export success and a rate of growth of the economy capable of sustaining any possible primary budget deficit. The contrast between figures 12.1 and 12.2 is meant to depict the greater difficulties in achieving the FE goal in a post–Second World War economy in which there is a more equal distribution of economic and political power between capital and labor and, therefore, a potentially greater inflationary bias.

12.11 The Clinton Program for Recovery

Given the acceptance in principle of the recovery program, there remains to consider what was designated in section 12.4 the second part of the program, determining in detail the policies needed to achieve the macro goals and the manner in which to go about implementing them.

A recovery program that must be structured as a hierarchy of goals

---

[19]The failure in the United Kingdom to achieve this kind of "export-led" growth can be seen as one of the chief causes of its economic decline, the other being its inability to implement a successful social bargain. There is also a message here with respect to globalization in general and the North American Free Trade Agreement (NAFTA) in particular. The free movement of goods and financial capital acts in effect to create a reserve army of the unemployed available to American firms, should they move their manufacturing operations. Advocates of NAFTA, while sometimes admitting the possibility of American manufacturing firms moving to Mexico, pin their hope for long-run American prosperity on newly affluent Mexicans increasing their demands for goods produced by the remaining American manufacturers. Surely more direct efforts to expand the manufacturing sector within the Unites States is a superior policy.

[20]Even so it is a simplification. Among the considerations missing from the diagram are the favorable impacts of higher AD on productivity growth and higher productivity on exports and inflation.

The text and figure reverse the usual textbook direction of causation from productivity growth to export success. When considering highly fabricated manufactures, non-price aspects of competition are very important. Superior quality generates rapid growth of sales and induces rapid rates of growth of productivity, another reason for the direction of causation assumed in the text and figure 12.1.

[21]See section 8.3.

(and instruments) requires the employment of a number of policies, all of which must be consistent with the ultimate goals of FE and acceptable rates of inflation.[22] In suggesting concrete policies for the United States, a useful point of departure is to consider policies and goals stressed by President Clinton and his advisors during the last presidential campaign. Simplifying somewhat, the Clinton program offers both short-run stimulative AD policies to initiate a recovery, with special emphasis on fiscal policy, and a longer-run package of spending and tax policies, constrained by a cumulative net deficit reduction program over a five-year period. Within the package of proposals are a number of policies which have an implicit stimulative AD effect but are essentially elements of an industrial policy.

With respect to the short run, it was argued in chapter 11 that a strong recovery would have to be initiated by fiscal policy, given the nature of the 1980s boom. Naturally whatever help can be gained from easier monetary policy is welcomed in the interests of deficit reduction.[23] The longer-run Clinton goals of rebuilding the infrastructure, investment in education and job training, and expansion of government employment conservation programs and a national service plan are consistent with the formal outline of a recovery program sketched in the previous sections, as is the program of federal support for key industries. The first three policies have little direct import content, and the industrial policy if correctly targeted and successful will lead to export expansion of manufactured goods and all the benefits noted in the previous sections. Moreover, rebuilding infrastructure and investment in human capital generate favorable productivity effects as well as sustaining AD.

12.12 What About the Demand Side?

There are several reasons why the Clinton program could fail to substantially reduce, let alone solve, the unemployment problem. For ex-

---

[22]For a detailed analysis of additional policies see chapter 12, "Incomes policies in English-speaking countries," in Cornwall, *The Conditions for Economic Recovery*. See also chapter 5 of this book.

[23]Some economists have argued for an AD policy that combines deficit reduction with easier monetary policy. In chapter 11 it was maintained that not much reliance should be placed on this kind of AD policy mix. See A. Blinder, "Is the national debt really—I mean really a burden?" in J. Rock (ed.), *Debt and the Twin Deficits Debate*.

The Clinton health care program, whatever its final form, will have an impact on AD and, therefore, unemployment. However, the design of the program is still uncertain and, important as it is, this program is not taken up in the text. Since the final draft of this chapter was completed, Congress has rejected the short-run stimulus part of the program.

ample, efforts to devise an industrial policy that leads to export-led growth in manufactures may fail. Ignoring this crucial condition for success, there are still two fundamental reasons why this program or some variant will fail to achieve a major reduction in unemployment rates, one related to its demand impact and the other to its supply effects.

With respect to the former, there is an underlying assumption that a short, quick injection of AD stimulus is enough to generate a boom, say, of the 1980s variety. Even without the implementation of a cumulative deficit reduction policy, with its substantial restrictive AD impact, a "jump start" is highly unlikely to generate an appreciable recovery in employment in the first half of the 1990s. The underlying causes of the weak recovery from the 1990 recession, detailed in chapter 11, would still be operative. When this recognition is combined with the fact that even the relatively weak Reagan boom of the 1980s required very large income tax cuts and very large increases in defense expenditures, it is difficult not to conclude that a much more powerful and sustained fiscal stimulation is required to noticeably stimulate the economy.[24]

It is true that the Clinton program contains policies to stimulate growth in productivity and output, but the positive effects of these industrial policies are likely to be forthcoming, if at all, in some longer run. If then a sizeable five-year cumulative deficit reduction policy is imposed upon an already stagnating economy (estimated at about $500 billion from currently projected levels), the effects will be highly depressing. A double-digit unemployment rate at the end of, say, a four-year term does not seem out of the question.

All of this is speculative to be sure. However, what does seem relatively certain is that the announced Clinton recovery program *if adhered to*, with its strong commitment to fiscal austerity will result in continued high unemployment and, because of this, low growth.

12.13 What About the Supply Side?

Even if the Clinton administration were to radically alter the AD aspects of its original program in order to emphasize the importance of reducing unemployment, the program would still fail to cure the unemployment problem. What is most lacking in the policy pronouncements

---

[24]Table 9.1 indicates just how modest was the recovery in unemployment rates following such a large fiscal stimulation package in the first half of the 1980s.

is a recognition that *any* efforts to reduce unemployment and stimulate economic growth may lead to politically unacceptable rates of inflation. The data in table 9.1 are a clear warning: even after a prolonged period of high unemployment, and even though unemployment rates fell only to modest levels in the second half of the 1980s, inflation rates began to accelerate. Under existing labor market institutions any attempt to reduce unemployment to rates even lower than those of the second half of the 1980s will lead to even more serious and unacceptable inflation. The implementation of a social bargain policy to reduce inflationary forces at low unemployment is therefore an absolutely essential part of any recovery efforts in the 1990s, yet it has received little attention.

The characteristics of those economies able to achieve low rates of unemployment and inflation through the successful implementation of a social bargain were discussed in chapter 5.[25] It is worth repeating some important similarities in the industrial relations systems of these economies cited earlier. In every case they could be described as having cooperative industrial relations systems, in which mutual trust rather than a "them" versus "us" atmosphere between labor and management dominated at both the micro and macro levels of the system. Underlying this trust was a widespread feeling that with respect to distributional issues, the economic (and social) system was essentially fair, certainly relative to attitudes prevailing in the pluralist economies. One of the most important results of this atmosphere of fairness, trust and cooperation was that labor was induced to shift from a market power to a social bargain strategy in its wage demands and settlements.

To repeat some other key points of chapter 5, at the heart of a social bargain is the continuous working in the labor market of some kind of agreement, with both explicit and implicit elements, which are embodied in customs, rules and laws. The agreement outlines the rewards and punishments used to induce compliance with any wage and price norms or goals set by the authorities. For reasons cited in chapter 5, this will primarily involve a wage norm and this puts special responsibility for success of the bargain on workers. But they will not accept this responsibility and the program will not succeed without a greater feeling of trust by labor toward business and government than exists today.

Given the long history of adversarial industrial relations in the United States, the requisite trust is contingent upon the average worker's belief in the basic fairness of the system. At this point in

[25] See sections 5.5–5.11.

American economic history, the average worker as well as the average citizen does not have a sense of receiving fair treatment from the economic system or from its government. To instill a sense of fairness and trust and thereby to induce labor to enter into a social bargain, rewards must be offered in exchange. A convincing argument must be made that anti-inflation AD policies always lead to poverty levels of incomes for the unemployed and to slow or even negative growth in real wages for the employed worker because of weak productivity growth. By restraining money wage demands, labor will be rewarded with full employment and accelerated real wage growth, and this must be made clear.

There are also perceived inequities that must be handled. A recovery program leading to full employment strengthens the relative power of labor and encourages the spread of unions. As the successful economies have demonstrated, working with the unions has benefits. Not only must "union bashing" be ended but unions must be treated at least as junior partners in the running of the firm. A more cooperative industrial relations system not only facilitates acceptance of a wage norm, it also leads to more rapid growth in productivity. Profit-sharing schemes strengthen these tendencies.

The recent period has been one in which the distribution of income has shifted to the advantage of the highest income earners, fostering a feeling of distributional unfairness in most Americans. As the low unemployment economies also demonstrate, a sense of fairness and trust is fostered by relatively equitable distributions of after tax and government transfer levels of incomes. Given the high degree of inequality in the after tax and transfer distribution of incomes in the United States, this requires a more progressive system of taxation and a rise in social expenditures aimed at increasing the "social wage" of the relatively low paid.

12.14 Conclusions

The long history of adversarial industrial relations reveals that so-called market forces or invisible hands have not driven out the inefficient institutions that have been the chief source of the macroeconomic difficulties. Success of a recovery program therefore necessitates an expanded role for government. This includes a willingness for the federal government to utilize deficit financing when necessary to achieve the low unemployment target, to encourage and aid export-led growth and to implement a social bargain to control inflation. In each case widespread acceptance of such policies is first necessary for their success, and this involves strong, intelligent, conciliatory political leadership. Note that this is not an unqualified endorsement of greater government intervention, but of interventions of a particular kind; government as well as labor and business must act in the public interest before it can be part of the solution.[26]

To illustrate the point, consider an alternative short-run stimulus package to the Clinton proposal, one that will have beneficial short-run effects and will increase the likelihood that the long-run goals of the Clinton program can be realized. In spite of the public rhetoric in favor of deficit reduction, there is little evidence that voters prefer a lower deficit to lower unemployment, the actual tradeoff. Unfortunately the Clinton policy of fiscal austerity reveals even in the short run a preference for deficit reduction, and at a time when the economy is weak. A policy of national sacrifice, albeit one of an "equitable" distribution of sacrifice, is to be adopted while economic hardship is widespread.

All of this is being advocated at a time when it is well recognized that the 1980s was a period when sacrifices and benefits were anything but fairly distributed. The gains in income and wealth during the Reagan boom were highly concentrated at the upper end of the income distribution, while a large segment of the lower income groups were made absolutely worse off.

Together these observations suggest an alternative short-run economic (and political) strategy similar to that adapted by the Japanese government in 1992–93, that at least offers some hope for recovery over the longer term.[27] This strategy proposes raising tax rates on the upper-income groups (as does Clinton's), allowing those who benefited so greatly from the policies of the two previous administrations to become the chief "deficit fighters" of the 1990s. Simultaneously the short-run fiscal stimulus would be increased through spending programs that would appreciably reduce unemployment, thereby partially compensating the less fortunate for their forbearance.

These measures will be at the expense of short-run deficit reduction, but they will give the economy a much-needed boost in aggregate demand at the same time as they increase the likelihood of a long-run

---

[26]What a social bargain entails is that market adjustments to excess supply and demand conditions require employment and output adjustments and not wage and price responses by firms, so that the latter are consistent with the inflation goal.

[27]See OECD, *Economic Outlook*, December 1992, p. 68, OECD, Paris.

cooperative solution to the inflation problem, that is, the likelihood of moving toward a social bargain. And as pointed out in section 12.7, these measures can pave the way for deficit reduction in the long run by initiating a recovery program of long-run growth.

The briefness of these remarks are not meant to suggest that shifting to a much more stimulative short-run policy would be politically easy. Rather it reflects the almost certain failure of the Clinton program to achieve any of its major goals, short or long run.

That said, it must be emphasized in conclusion that the costs of maintaining current policies are enormous and frightening. Given the tradition of independence that the Federal Reserve has enjoyed, it is difficult to believe that the goal of containing inflation will ever be sacrificed in the United States. This means that without radical changes in institutions and policies, a reserve army of the unemployed is what the American people can look forward to in the 1990s.

Even if unemployment rates remain steady at current rates, the social, political, and economic costs will rise, as these costs are to a large extent cumulative, increasing with the length of the high-unemployment period. Two examples, one very topical, are sufficient to make the point. Taking the first quarter of 1992 as a benchmark, the overall unemployment rate was 7.2 percent. However, during this same period, the unemployment rates among blacks and Hispanics was 13.9 and 11.5 percent, respectively, while unemployment rates for all 16- to 19-year-olds was 19.6 per cent and that for black 16- to 19-year-olds was 36.6 percent. With such a high proportion of 16- to 19-year-olds accustomed to continuous unemployment, lifestyles will develop that downplay the importance of work in the decade that is supposed to mark the beginning of America's renewal. Even more serious than the loss of the work ethic is the perpetuation of a permanent underclass in American cities. If urban riots tell us anything, it is that a necessary condition for long-run political and social stability in the United States is a radical reduction of minority group unemployment rates. Continued high overall unemployment makes this impossible. Meanwhile the cumulative effects of continued high unemployment further destabilizes the system.[28]

---

[28]Economists concerned about the political dangers of inflation are constantly citing the alleged connection between inflation and the rise of Hitler. What is overlooked in this analysis is that Germany experienced hyperinflation in the 1920s. The Nazis rose to power in the 1930s during a period of mass unemployment!

13 Choosing the Future

13.1 Policy Options

As argued in chapter 10, the key to ending mass unemployment throughout the developed capitalist economies is to eliminate the inflationary bias of the pluralistic bloc of economies. Only when FE has been made consistent with acceptable rates of inflation in these economies can it be expected that widespread stimulative AD policies will be reintroduced. Most programs proposed for eliminating this bias can be designated as one of the following: (a) policies that aim to change behavior through fear of unemployment; (b) policies designed to change behavior by reducing monopoly power; (c) policies designed to change behavior by working out a social bargain. While all three policies aim to eliminate the inflationary bias, the first two strive to do so by reducing the power of labor.

Policies that attempt to change behavior through fear of unemployment were discussed at some length in chapter 10 and require little further comment. The likelihood of success of this form of policy was found to be slight. To merely restate the earlier conclusion, attempts to alter behavior in the labor market through fear of unemployment will not lead to a return to FE because this class of policies will not eliminate the causes of an inflationary bias. It is the inability to work out a successful social bargain that has led to the bias and to the even greater difficulty of working out a bargain following a period of policy-induced high unemployment. A policy of fear can only permanently affect behavior by creating a permanent reserve army of the unemployed.

A more drastic attack on the inflationary bias in the pluralist economies would be to reduce the power of labor through legislation, for example, outlawing unions. In this way, something like nineteenth-century labor markets might be recreated in which fairness considerations no longer play a dominant role in wage settlements. This class of policies does not rely for its success on market participants internalizing the social costs of their behavior. Instead it aims to let the "price mechanism" accomplish this by breaking up organized interest groups and establishing competitive markets.[1]

The failure of current restrictive AD policies to reduce inflation more substantially has led many to advocate programs that change behavior through reducing market power. The private pursuit of self-interest is to remain the guiding principle of behavior. Advocates of the Eurosclerosis hypothesis and believers in an overloaded ungovernable economy often have such programs in mind. In addition to a decartelization program for labor, they advocate a reduction in the welfare state and in the progressivity of the tax structure. Because of its popularity but most importantly because its consequences are even more damaging than current policies, this alternative program requires further study.

13.2 Recreating the Nineteenth Century

Restoring competitive conditions

In one form or another these programs seek to create real economies that resemble the competitive textbook model. Some of the more important implications of a "decartelization" program include breaking up large corporations, the abandonment of any technology designed to take advantage of the economies of scale, and the abolition of unions. If carried far enough, decartelization would lead to a situation in which all demanders and suppliers are price-takers. In the extreme form of the program, Walrasian markets are envisaged in which atomistic competition is complemented by continuous and instantaneous market clearing. This supposedly leads to FE without inflation as long as the fiscal and monetary authorities behave themselves.

Would decartelization lead to flexprice markets?

It can be conceded in these circumstances that the kinds of problems described earlier in terms of a prisoner's dilemma and an inflationary bias would no longer exist. The private pursuit of private interests would no longer be inconsistent with price stability. However, advo-

---

[1] An early advocate of this program was Hayek. See, for example, F. Hayek, *Unemployment and the Unions* (2nd ed.), Institute of Economic Affairs, London, 1984. More recently the policy has been associated with Olson. See M. Olson, *The Rise and Decline of Nations*, Yale University Press, New Haven, CT, 1982; "The political economy and growth rates," in D. Mueller (ed.), *The Political Economy of Growth*, Yale University Press, New Haven, CT, 1983; and "Why nations rise and fall," *Challenge*, 27, March–April 1984, 15–23.

cates of market solutions to today's problems cannot simply stress a need to reduce the power of business and labor groups and establish a market system in which atomistic competition prevails. They must go further and argue for the need to establish a price mechanism with Walrasian markets that always clear because of their alleged optimality conditions including FE.[2] This part of their program is quite critical since it is a fairly well established point in economic theory that without market clearing even a competitive world is not likely to lead to FE.[3] Bearing this in mind, it is necessary to ask whether breaking up unions and large corporations will lead to a system of markets in which changes in wages and prices reflect shifting demand and supply curves and in which trading always takes place at intersection points.

By now there is a vast literature explaining why market clearing is most unlikely, especially in the labor market. A number of theories are available revealing that market behavior is greatly constrained, giving rise to non-market-clearing prices for good optimizing reasons. Many of these constraints would be operative in the absence of unions.[4] A general explanation of non-market-clearing can be expressed in terms of implicit contracts that define the rules and procedures governing transactions in many if not most markets. Here the analysis will be confined to labor markets, in particular why money wages tend to be rigid downward. However, the formulation is easily generalized to explain rigid money wages upwards and fixprice markets for goods in which prices tend to be rigid in both directions.[5]

Most firms in their dealings with labor have an interest in maintaining a continuous and harmonious labor–management relations. Because most jobs involve firm-specific tasks that require on-the-job training and substantial investment outlays in human capital, management has an interest in reducing turnover for purely cost-reducing reasons. Such continuity of the employment relationships is furthered by harmonious labor–management relations which are especially important under FE

---

[2] According to Olson, unions obtain wages above the competitive level by blocking mutually advantageous transactions, that is, those that would lead to market clearing. Because these wages are above market-clearing levels, unions prevent workers who would work for lower wages from obtaining work. Hence, eliminate unions and you will move towards FE. In addition, Keynesian AD policies are alleged to be ineffective in reducing unemployment in some long-run sense. See Olson, "Why nations rise and fall."

[3] See P. Korliras, "Disequilibrium theories and their policy implications: towards a synthetic disequilibrium approach," *Kyklos*, 33 (3), 1980, 449–74.

[4] See the references in chapter 3, note 11.

[5] See A. Okun, *Prices and Quantities: A Macroeconomic Analysis*, Brookings Institute, Washington, DC, 1981; and M. Wachter and O. Williamson, "Obligational markets and the mechanics of inflation," *Bell Journal of Economics*, 9, Autumn 1978, 549–71.

conditions. Harmonious relations are also needed in order to ensure that each worker accomplishes the tasks assigned to him, thereby promoting productivity growth.

However, in laying out a system of rules that outlines the tasks to be done and the means by which workers are to adapt to new tasks, it is impossible to establish a set of explicit enforceable rules to handle every contingency likely to occur on the shop-floor today or in the future. Even if this could be done, the transactions costs for management of implementing, monitoring, and enforcing such contracts would be enormous. For good profit-maximizing reasons management desires a system of general rules, often only implicit, that regulate the more important aspects of employment relations, for example, pay, promotion, layoffs, job content, and grievance procedures for settling unforeseen contingencies or simply differences of opinion. The concept of an "internal labor market" is meant to capture the flavor of this kind of governance system.

However, this governance system must be acceptable to labor and provide the inducements needed to obtain more than just a minimum of cooperation. The end result of all this is that, in order to minimize work-to-rule situations and strikes and to maximize productivity, certain rules and procedures have developed that foster consultation, cooperation, and continuity. For example, in the English-speaking economies an important practice is to keep money wages rigid in excess supply conditions except under exceptional circumstances such as the imminent bankruptcy of the firm. Labor in these countries has grown to consider wage cuts as unfair business practice since they are under the control of management.[6] Employers fear that workers will respond to wage cuts by reducing their productivity, especially after labor market conditions improve. In contrast, layoffs in response to declining sales are viewed as fair because the underlying cause is beyond the firm's control.

Fixprice markets would not necessarily disappear if unions were abolished, at least in democratic societies. In order to eliminate fixprice markets it would be necessary not only to break up unions but also to destroy implicit contract systems—governance systems that have improved efficiency in the past.

---

[6]In other countries with weak trade unions, such as Japan and Switzerland, wage cuts do occur and this is not interpreted by labor as an unfair practice. However, these are economies in which industrial relations are harmonious and in which labor trusts management.

Would flexprice markets lead to full employment?

However, even if a market system in which there were no monopoly powers and contracts systems had been eliminated could be imposed upon a modern capitalist society, this would not be sufficient to lead to continuous and rapid (let alone instantaneous) market clearing and FE. There are both economic and political considerations involved. Even assuming that there are no constraints on wage and price adjustments, there are strong economic reasons for believing that most markets would not clear. What is needed in addition to a lack of constraints are some very strong assumptions about information flows. Either it must be assumed that all traders in markets have perfect and costless knowledge of the equilibrium prices, or there must be some mechanism "unrelated to the trading process itself that would supply the needed information costlessly."[7] Only under these kinds of assumptions would the velocity of price adjustments in a market be infinite and markets clear instantly and continuously. Without this rapid price adjustment, quantity adjustments occur giving rise to the familiar multiplier process. This process is disturbance amplifying in that once a disturbance leads to excess demand or supply, the divergence from equilibrium widens. Thus FE is not guaranteed even if a decartelization program succeeds in eliminating any constraint on wage and price flexibility.[8]

However, there is no need to rely on rather abstract economic considerations to indicate the difficulties of a decartelization program. There are important political reasons why FE will not be realized even if constraints on price and wage movements could be removed. Thus, from a practical point of view, it is most unlikely that a program for altering institutions while continuing to encourage behavior motivated solely by self-interest would ever be applied to any group other than labor. In addition, the belief in the value of some kind of "free" market is strongest in the two North American economies and the United Kingdom, countries in which pro-business sentiments are most pro-

---

[7] See A. Leijonhufvud, *On Keynesian Economics and the Economics of Keynes*, Oxford University Press, New York, 1968, p. 69.

[8] A second economic consideration revolves around the nature of technology and its impact on competition. It has been shown that, even if all the other assumptions of the competitive model are fulfilled, if there are increasing returns to scale, competition breaks down in the sense that large-scale organizations with market power will develop. Under these conditions, there is no automatic tendency toward FE. Constant returns to scale are a necessary condition for FE (as are perfect capital markets) and a decartelization program would have to include measures to achieve this everywhere if the program is to achieve the goals it seeks. See M. Weitzman, "Increasing returns and the foundations of unemployment theory," *Economic Journal*, 92, December 1982, 787–804.

nounced and in which unions are relatively weak or anti-union sentiments are strongest or both. It seems reasonable, therefore, in evaluating this program for ending the current difficulties to treat it as a decartelization program for labor alone and to consider the impact of the program on labor relations.

Consider the likely effect of eliminating unions on worker attitudes toward management and on work conditions inside formerly unionized (and non-unionized) firms. Many important dimensions of a job are public goods and cannot be obtained without collective bargaining. Safety conditions on a job are prime examples. Without unions, measures to protect worker safety will be less frequently undertaken as the incentive for individual workers to improve safety conditions is very small and unlikely to lead to action. Nor can it be expected that management will be as concerned with safety as when unions are present. Finally, the kind of grievance system associated with unionization will undoubtedly atrophy in newly non-unionized firms. There will be no effective way for workers to express their discontent other than by changing jobs. Furthermore, without unions protesters can be easily dismissed—an experience all too likely, recalling nineteenth-century labor practices.[9]

Without unions and, more generally, without fair treatment, labor relations are bound to deteriorate drastically. The industrial workforces in today's economies are not composed of displaced migratory workers as was the case in the earlier stages of industrialization. Under FE conditions workers in an age of egalitarianism and universal suffrage will not tolerate conditions similar to those of the nineteenth century. If they are unable to reverse the program through legislation, they will respond by various forms of industrial disruption, for example, work to rule, wildcat strikes, industrial sabotage and civil disobedience. Only by creating widespread unemployment (or disregarding democratic rights) can it be expected that labor will comply in the face of such treatment.

For political reasons FE will not result from this program. Like the current program of restricting AD in the hope of changing behavior, a decartelization program may reduce inflation but it will also lead to continuous high rates of unemployment. Whether or not this program can result in flexprice markets and market-clearing prices is really beside the point. It will not only fail to cure the current difficulties, but it will also divide further any society in which it is tried, making it more difficult to handle any kind of economic and social problem.

[9]See R. Freeman and J. Medoff, *What Do Unions Do?* Basic Books, New York, 1984.

Post-Thatcher Britain stands as an example of some of the results that this kind of program will bring.

13.3 A Program for the Future

Neither a program of altering people's behavior through the fear of unemployment nor a program aimed at "unleashing the forces of the free market" leads to FE without inflation. Both programs, if pursued in earnest, will eliminate the kinds of prisoner's dilemma problems that give rise to serious cost–push inflation, but only by creating permanent mass unemployment. A third program for economic recovery proceeds in an entirely different manner. This policy includes proposals for working with unions. The thrust of this program is that an improvement in labor–management relations as part of a social bargain not only works to increase the chances of moving to FE with acceptable inflation but also increases productivity. Its correctness has been supported throughout this study.

The findings of chapter 3 provide a useful starting point for summarizing the program. A recurring theme—that it is important to distinguish between the costs of FE policies and their effectiveness—was initiated in this chapter. Stimulative AD policies do affect unemployment when there are involuntarily unemployed workers. However, it was acknowledge that such policies will lead to politically unacceptable rates of inflation and payments difficulties in many countries long before FE is achieved.

The distinction between the effectiveness and the costs of stimulative AD policies is important not merely because it leads to different explanations of why mass unemployment exists; it also highlights what have become the conflicting policy implications of the two positions. If unemployment today is primarily classical and therefore unresponsive to stimulative AD policies, one class of policy prescriptions for reducing unemployment will seem more reasonable, for example, reductions in the power of unions and the size of the welfare state. However, those who regard unemployment as essentially Keynesian, but are concerned that stimulative policies would lead to accelerating inflation rates, find the solution to the unemployment problem in a "second generation" of incomes policies, even while admitting the difficulty of realizing such a solution.

As stated, recovery throughout the OECD requires altering institutions in the pluralistic bloc of economies in such a way as to alter behavior, especially in the labor market. The required institutional changes are implicit in chapter 5 in the discussion of social bargains or permanent voluntary incomes policies and the conditions for their success. These findings were reinforced in later chapters. Both before the breakdown and after, the more able was an economy to develop the institutional conditions for a successful bargain, as reflected in the degree of industrial harmony, the lower tended to be unemployment rates and the misery index. The relatively successful economies in the post-war period have been those in which the authorities structure their policies so as to affect labor market behavior directly in a socially beneficial way, rather than indirectly by restricting AD or by giving the price mechanism a freer role to play. In these successful economies AD policies were largely relieved of their ineffectual and costly role of containing inflation—that role was assigned to the social bargain or incomes policy. This allowed AD policies to assume their natural and effective role of regulating unemployment, as Keynes rightly stressed.

The same point can be made somewhat differently. Keynes's program for curing unemployment is incomplete given current institutions. FE policies in an age of affluence, trade unions, and egalitarian beliefs must always be augmented with social bargains if unacceptable inflation is to be avoided. Supplementary supply-side policies are also required to counteract the adverse effects induced by past restrictive AD policies, for example, retraining programs for the long-term unemployed. To say this is but to restate the difficulties in implementing a program for recovery.

13.4 Studying Economic Breakdown

As stated at the beginning of this study, a period of accelerating inflation followed by a policy-induced period of mass unemployment and periodic high inflation with no end in sight can only be described as an economic breakdown. This judgment would remain true whether or not high rates of inflation are permanently purged from the economies by the restrictive policies. While unemployment rates have not reached the levels of the 1930s, the incidence of high unemployment has been wider and it has lasted longer.

This study has attempted to explain the breakdown using a framework that is somewhat unconventional. It stresses institutional developments, both as causes and effects of economic performance, along with an analytical form of analysis more familiar to economists. The value of such a procedure should by now be apparent. The causes of economic breakdown are rooted in basic changes in the institutional framework of affluent capitalism, themselves importantly related to past economic policies and performance. Only by first identifying and explaining these changes can events since the late 1960s be correctly understood. Nor can any successful program for recovery be formulated until the underlying causal chain of events is clear.

More concretely, the earlier chapters incorporate theories and findings of mainstream macroeconomics into a framework that emphasizes institutionalized political and economic power, on the one hand, and such influences as the structure of the labor market and methods of conflict resolution, on the other, in order to explain what were earlier termed the basic determinants of macropolicies and macroperformance. The rise in the relative power of unionized labor has been singled out for special attention because it is hard to conceive of a strong demand for FE (and the expansion of the welfare state) without this shift of power this century. However, in addition to this demand influence on policy and performance, institutions have acted as constraints limiting the scope of actions open to policy-makers. Desirable as FE may be, there have been numerous examples in the post-war period in which the authorities felt constrained in their use of AD policies. As a result, unemployment rates were allowed to exceed their FE levels. By the mid-1970s these constraints were so widespread and binding that unemployment rates rose everywhere throughout the developed capitalist world.

13.5 Path Dependence in Capitalist Development

The institutional-analytical framework emphasized not only the manner in which institutions constrain the actions of the authorities. It also stressed the importance of past actions by policy-makers in affecting the present institutional framework, and therefore current policy options, and the importance of current actions in influencing future institutions and options. To highlight the point in more conventional economic terms, if it can be said that an economy is moving toward some equilibrium, this equilibrium is determined by the path that the economy has taken and is currently taking, which is itself very much related to past and current policies.

Path or history dependence in capitalist development, first outlined in chapter 1, has been expressed in terms of a causal chain. This stress on the dynamics of constrained and limited policy options should be contrasted with the more conventional means–end optimizing framework of mainstream economics in which an almost infinite number of decisions of a marginal nature are possible. In reality, the choices available at any time are limited and constantly changing as the structure of the economy evolves. As a result, if actions and performances are to be understood, the analysis must emphasize the limited number of policy options, how they are changing, and the causes of these limitations. This is what has been attempted in the earlier chapters.

Two examples of path dependence or hysteresis have been featured, one giving rise to the breakdown of the early 1970s and a second, now in operation, reinforcing a tendency toward continued mass unemployment. It was argued that prolonged periods of FE and the rise of the welfare state significantly altered the manner in which labor markets function. These changes reinforced the redistribution of economic and political power initiated by the rising power of organized labor. As a result, potentially strong inflationary pressures developed at FE. These pressures were contained without sacrificing FE in most of the capitalist economies for almost two decades following the Second World War. But gradually the social bargains that held back these potentially destabilizing influences were undermined by rising challenges to the system in many economies—challenges that could to a large extent be traced to the prosperity and affluence of the 1950s and 1960s. This contributed importantly to the accelerating inflation in many countries in the late 1960s and early 1970s.

Path dependence was also illustrated by the restrictive policy responses to the accelerating rates of inflation beginning in the late 1960s and the responses to these policies. The general hope was that, by allowing unemployment to rise, the "inflationary psychology" that had developed in the early 1970s could be eliminated once and for all and a gradual restimulation of the economies would then follow. Unfortunately, inflation rates did not respond to the depressed AD conditions as expected, and mass unemployment has become a feature of the OECD economies.

One of the important reasons for this failure of restrictive AD policies is that the period of prolonged mass unemployment has induced structural and institutional changes that have increased the costs of any stimulative AD policy and have made it more difficult ever to return to FE. Some of the factors leading to these greater costs, for example, reduced productivity growth, more negative attitudes toward work and innovation, job discrimination against the long-term unemployed, and labor's desire to make up for the slow growth in real wages since the early 1970s and to "get even," were considered in chapters 8–10.

13.6 Choosing the Wrong Future

Seen in sequence, these two examples of hysteresis describe a prolonged period of post-war macrodevelopment dominated by history dependence. The desire to avoid the costs of another Great Depression ensured that the FE goal would be given a high priority following the Second World War. But in solving the unemployment problem the induced institutional impacts eventually created a new problem—an inflationary bias. Under FE conditions, inflation rates reached unacceptable levels and the policy response was restrictive AD policies. Thus the resolution of the unemployment problem was short-lived, lasting a little over two decades. Regrettably, the attempt to resolve the inflationary bias difficulty has merely induced additional problems.

To some, the conditions since the early 1970s mark a return to some kind of economic "normalcy"—the great boom of the 1950s and 1960s being merely an aberration. According to this view, unemployment may be high on average but recoveries alternate with recessions and governments come and go as in the past. Three responses are in order. First, as discussed in chapters 7 and 9, some economies have been able to maintain relatively low unemployment rates despite greatly depressed economic conditions elsewhere. Prolonged periods of high unemployment are not inevitable.

Second, even if it is assumed that the economic conditions of the 1980s and 1990s have been superior to those prior to the Second World War, the expectations and aspirations of the citizenry in the earlier period were certainly different from those held by post-war generations. One important result is that stimulative AD programs in the 1930s would very likely not have generated excessive money wage settlements (and did not in the early years following the recovery from the Second World War). The authorities were therefore in a position to choose FE policies (had they been ideologically inclined). No such options are available in the current period. Before stimulative AD policies can be introduced in the 1990s throughout the developed capitalist world, radical changes in institutions are required to remove an inflationary bias. Whatever view is taken of the relative levels of well-being, comparing the 1930s with the 1980s, the likelihood of any substantial improvement during the 1990s must be deemed considerably less than the prospects facing the average person looking toward the first post-war recovery decade.

This points up a related additional difference between the two periods, and that concerns the effects of the policies chosen to avoid a repeat of the Great Depression and those chosen to combat the Great Inflation. The commitment to FE following the Second World War did help solve the unemployment problem. The restrictive AD policies of the more recent period are supposedly necessary to eliminate serious inflation from the system, thereby allowing a return to FE. Unfortunately, present restrictive policies have not only created mass unemployment but are increasing rather than decreasing the likelihood of its continuance by increasing the costs of FE. If it is to be said that capitalism breaks down it is misleading to attribute the breakdown to too many demands on the state or to institutional rigidities generated by introduction of safety nets and the tolerance of unions. Rather, it breaks down because of an inability to implement a successful social bargain and, therefore, because of a need to control inflation by prolonged and continued high unemployment. Because of this, a continued future of economic breakdown is promised. Path dependence ensures it.

Bibliography

Ackley, G. "Comments and discussion," *Brookings Paper on Economic Activity,* No. 2, 1975.

Alogoskoufis, G. and Manning, A. "Unemployment persistence," *Economic Policy,* 3 (2), October 1988, 427–69.

Atkinson, A. In R. Dornbusch and R. Layard (eds.), *The Performance of the British Economy,* Clarendon Press, Oxford, 1987.

Aukrust, O. "PRIM I: a model of price and income distribution of an open economy," *Review of Income and Wealth,* 16, March 1970, 51–78.

Baily, M. "Stabilization policy and private economic behavior," *Brookings Papers on Economic Activity,* No. 2, 1978.

Baumol, W. and Blinder, A. *Economics: Principles and Policy* (2nd ed.), Harcourt Brace Jovanovich, New York, 1982.

Bean, C., Layard, P. and Nickell, S. "The rise in unemployment: a multi-country study," *Economica* (Supplement), 53, 1986, S1–S22.

Beckerman, W. and Jenkinson, T. "What stopped the inflation? Unemployment or commodity prices?" *Economic Journal,* 96, March 1986, 39–54.

Bernheim, B.D. "Ricardian equivalence: an evaluation of theory and evidence," *NBER Working Paper Series,* No. 2330, July 1987.

Blanchard, O. and Summers, L. "Beyond the natural rate hypothesis," *American Economic Review, Papers and Proceedings,* May 1988, 182–187.

Blanchard, O. and Summers, L. "Hysteresis and the European unemployment problem," *NBER Working Paper Series,* No. 1950, June 1986.

Blanchard, O. and Summers, L. "Hysteresis in unemployment," *European Economic Review,* 31 (1–2), 1987, 288–95.

Blinder, A. "The challenge of high unemployment," *American Economic Review, Papers and Proceedings,* 78, May 1988, 1–15.

Blinder, A. *Economic Policy and the Great Stagflation,* Academic Press, New York, 1981.

Blinder, A. "Is the national debt really—I mean *really* a burden?" in J. Rock (ed.), *Debt and the Twin Deficits Debate,* Mayfield Publishing Co., Mountain View, CA, 1991.

Boltho, A. "Economic policy and performance in Europe since the second oil shock," in M. Emerson (ed.), *Europe's Stagflation,* Clarendon Press, Oxford, 1984.

Boyer, R. and Petit, P. "Employment and productivity growth in the EEC," *Cambridge Journal of Economics,* 5, March 1981, 47–58.

Brittan, S. "The economic contradictions of democracy," *British Journal of Political Science,* 5, April 1975, 130–59.

Bibliography

Bruno, M. "Aggregate supply and demand factors in OECD unemployment: an update," *Economica* (Supplement), 53, 1986, S35–S52.

Bruno, M. and Sachs, J. *The Economics of Worldwide Stagflation*, Harvard University Press, Cambridge, MA, 1984.

Calmfors, L. and Driffill, J. "Bargaining structure, corporatism and macroeconomic performance," *Economic Policy*, 3, April 1988, 13–62.

Cameron, D. "The growth of government spending: the Canadian experience in comparative perspective," in K. Banting (ed.), *State and Society: Canada in Comparative Perspective*, University of Toronto Press, Toronto, 1986.

Cameron, D. "Social democracy, corporatism, labour quiescence and the representation of economic interest in advanced capitalist society," in J. Goldthorpe (ed.), *Order and Conflict in Contemporary Capitalism*, Clarendon Press, Oxford, 1984.

Castles, F. "Social expenditure and the political right: a methodological note," *European Journal of Political Research*, 14, 1986, 669–76.

Clark, K. and Summers, L. "Labor market dynamics and unemployment: a reconsideration," *Brookings Papers on Economic Activity*, No. 1, 1979.

Coe, D. and Gagliardi, F. "Nominal wage determination in ten OECD economies," in *OECD Working Papers*, OECD, Paris, March 1985.

The Collected Works of John Maynard Keynes. Vol. xxi, Cambridge University Press, Cambridge, 1982.

Cornwall, J. *The Conditions for Economic Recovery*, Blackwell, Oxford, 1983.

Cornwall, J. *Growth and Stability in a Mature Economy*, Martin Robertson, London, 1972.

Cornwall, J. *Modern Capitalism: Its Growth and Transformation*, Blackwell, Oxford, 1977.

Cornwall, J. "Stability and stabilization of mature economies," in K. Velupillai (ed.), *Nonlinearities, Disequilibria and Simulation: Essays in Honour of Björn Thalberg*, Macmillan, London, 1992.

Cornwall, J. and Cornwall, W. "Export-led growth: a new interpretation," in W. Milberg (ed.), *The Megacorp and Macrodynamics*, M. E. Sharpe, Armonk, NY, 1992.

Cripps, F. "Causes of growth and recession in world trade," *Economic Policy Review*, 4, March 1978, 37–43.

Cripps, F. and Tarling, R. *Cumulative Causation in the Growth of Manufacturing Industries*, Department of Applied Economics, University of Cambridge, Cambridge, June 1975.

Cross, R. (ed.). *Unemployment, Hysteresis and the Natural Rate Hypothesis*, Blackwell, Oxford, 1988.

Crouch, C. "The conditions for trade union wage restraint," in L. Lindberg and C. Maier (eds.), *The Politics of Inflation and Economic Stagnation*, Brookings Institution, Washington, DC, 1985.

Danthine, J. and Lambelet, J. "The Swiss recipe: conservative policies aren't enough," *Economic Policy*, 2 (5), 1987.

Denison, E. *Why Growth Rates Differ: Postwar Experience in Nine Countries*. Brookings Institution, Washington, DC, 1967.

Dernburg, T. *Macroeconomics* (7th ed.), McGraw-Hill, New York, 1985.

Dornbusch, R. "Macroeconomic prospects and policies for the European Community," in O. Blanchard, R. Dornbusch, and R. Layard (eds.), *Restoring Europe's Prosperity*, MIT Press, Cambridge, MA, 1986.
Dornbusch, R. and Fischer, S. *Macroeconomics*, McGraw-Hill, New York, 1981.
Dreze, J. and Modigliani, F. "The trade-off between real wages and employment in an open economy (Belgium)," *European Economic Review*, 15 (1), 1981, 1–40.
Dreze, J. and Wyplosz, C. "Autonomy through cooperation," *European Economic Review*, 32 (2–3), 1988, 353–62.
Eckstein, O. and Brinner, R. *The inflation process in the United States: a study prepared for the Joint Economic Committee, US Congress*, U.S. Government Printing Office, Washington, DC, February 1972.
Economic Report of the President, U.S. Government Printing Office, Washington, DC, 1992.
Economic Report of the President, U.S. Government Printing Office, Washington, DC, 1993.
Esping-Andersen, E. and Korpi, W. "Social policy as class politics in post-war capitalism: Scandinavia, Austria and Germany," in J. Goldthorpe (ed.), *Order and Conflict in Contemporary Capitalism*, Clarendon Press, Oxford, 1984.
Fellner, W. "The valid core of the rationality hypothesis in the theory of expectations," *Journal of Money, Credit and Banking*, 12, November 1980, 763–87.
Fischer, S. "Monetary policy and performance in the U.S., Japan and Europe, 1973–86," *NBER Working Paper Series*, No. 2475, December 1987.
Flanagan, R., Soskice, D., and Ulman, L. *Unionism, Economic Stabilization and Incomes Policies: European Experience*, Brookings Institution, Washington, DC, 1983.
Flora, P. *State, Economy and Society in Western Europe, 1915–1975*, Vol. 1, Campus Verlag, Frankfurt, 1987.
Freeman, R. and Medoff, J. *What Do Unions Do?* Basic Books, New York, 1984.
Freeman, R. and Weitzman, M. "Bonuses and employment in Japan," *NBER Working Papers Series*, No. 1878, April 1986.
Friedman, M. "The role of monetary policy," *American Economic Review*, 58, March 1968, 1–17.
Goldthorpe, J. "The current inflation: towards a sociological account," in F. Hirsch and J. Goldthorpe (eds.), *The Political Economy of Inflation*, Harvard University Press, Cambridge, MA, 1978.
Goodwin, R. "The nonlinear accelerator and the persistence of business cycles,"*Econometrica*, Vol. 19 1951, 1–17.
Goodwin, R. "Rational politicians and rational bureaucrats in Washington and Whitehall," *Public Administration*, 60, Spring 1982, 23–41.
Gordon, R.J. "The demand for and supply of inflation," *Journal of Law and Economics*, December 1975. Vol. 18 (3), 807–836
Gordon, R.J. "Wage–price controls and the shifting Phillips curve," *Brookings Papers on Economic Activity*, No. 2, 1972.
Gramlich, E. "U.S. budget deficits: Views, Burdens and New Development," in J. Rock (ed.), *Debt and the Twin Deficits Debate*, Mayfield Publishing Co., Mountain View, CA, 1991.

272 Bibliography

Gregory, R. "Wage policy and unemployment in Australia," *Economica* (Supplement), 53, 1986, S53–S74.

Gross, R. and Keating, M. "An empirical analysis of exports and domestic markets," *Economic Outlook Occasional Studies*, OECD, Paris, December 1980.

Grubb, D. *The OECD Data Set*, Working Paper No. 615, Centre for Labour Economics, London School of Economics, March 1984.

Grubb, D. "Topics in the OECD Phillips curve," *Economic Journal*, 96, March 1986, 55–79.

Grubb, D., Jackman, R. and Layard, R. "Causes of the current stagflation," *Review of Economic Studies*, 49, 1982, 707–30.

Hall, P. *Governing the Economy: The Politics of State Intervention in Britain and France*, Oxford University Press, New York, 1986.

Hamermesh, D. "Wage bargains, threshold effects and the Phillips curve," *Quarterly Journal of Economics*, 84, August 1970, 501–17.

Hargreaves Heap, S. "Choosing the wrong natural rate: accelerating or decelerating employment and growth," *Economic Journal*, 90, 1980, 611–20.

Hayek, F. *Unemployment and the Unions* (2nd ed.), Institute of Economic Affairs, London, 1984.

Helliwell, J. "Comparative macroeconomics of stagflation," *Journal of Economic Literature*, 26, March 1988, 1–28.

Hibbs, D. "On the political economy of long-run trends in strike activity," *British Journal of Political Economy*, 8, 1978, 153–76.

Hibbs, D. *The Political Economy of Industrial Democracies*, Harvard University Press, Cambridge, MA, 1987.

Hibbs, D. "Political parties and macroeconomic policy," *American Political Science Review*, 71, December 1977, 1467–87.

Hicks, J. *The Crisis in Keynesian Economics*, Basic Books, New York, 1974.

ILO. *Yearbook of Labour Statistics*, various issues.

IMF (International Monetary Fund). *Direction of Trade Statistics*, IMF, Washington, DC, 1981.

Jackman, R. "Wage formation in the Nordic countries viewed from an international perspective," *Seminar Paper No. 4151*, Institute for International Economic Studies, University of Stockholm, August 1988.

Johnson, G. and Layard, P. "The natural rate of unemployment: explanation and policy," *Discussion Paper No. 206*. Centre for Labour Economics, London School of Economics, October 1984.

Kalecki, M. "Political aspects of full employment," *Selected Essays on the Dynamics of the Capitalist Economy 1933–1970*, Cambridge University Press, Cambridge, 1977.

Kastli, R. "The new economic environment in the 1970s: market and policy response in Switzerland," in M. de Cecco (ed.), *International Economic Adjustment: Small Countries and the European Monetary System*, St. Martin's Press, New York, 1982.

Katz, L. "Efficiency wages theories: a partial evaluation," *NBER Working Paper Series*, No. 1906, April 1986.

Katzenstein, P. "Capitalism in one country?: Switzerland in the international economy," *International Organization*, 34, Autumn 1980, 507–40.

Katzenstein, P. *Corporatism and Change: Austria, Switzerland and the Politics of Industry,* Cornell University Press, Ithaca, NY, 1984.
King, A. "Overload: problems of governing in the 1970s," *Political Studies,* 23, June–September 1974, 284–96.
Kirby, M. "A variable expectations coefficient model of the Australian Phillips curve," *Australian Economic Papers,* 20, December 1981, 351–58.
Korliras, P. "Disequilibrium theories and their policy implications: towards a synthetic disequilibrium approach," *Kyklos,* 33 (3), 1980, 449–74.
Korpi, W. *The Democratic Class Struggle,* Routledge and Kegan Paul, London, 1983.
Korpi, W. "Political and economic explanations for unemployment: a cross-national and long-term analysis," *British Journal of Political Science,* July, 1991.
Korpi, W. and Shalev, M. "Strikes, power and politics in the Western nations, 1900–1976," in M. Zeitlin (ed.), *Political Power and Social Theory,* Vol. 1, JAI Press, Greenwich, CT, 1980.
Langlois, R. "The new institutional economics: an introductory essay," in R. Langlois (ed.), *Economics as a Process,* Cambridge University Press, Cambridge, 1986.
Layard, P. and Nickell, S. "The causes of British unemployment," *National Institute Economic Review,* 111, February 1985, 62–85.
Layard, R., et al. *Unemployment: Macroeconomic Performance and the Labour Market,* Oxford University Press, Oxford, 1991.
Leijonhufvud, A. *On Keynesian Economics and the Economics of Keynes,* Oxford University Press, New York, 1968.
Lewis, W. *Growth and Fluctuations: 1870–1913,* George Allen & Unwin, London, 1978.
Lindbeck, A. and Snower, D. "Explanations of unemployment," *Oxford Review of Economic Policy,* No. 2, 1985.
Lindbeck, A. and Snower, D. "Union activity, unemployment persistence and wage–employment ratchets," *European Economic Review,* 31 (1–2), February–March 1987, 157–67.
Lindbeck, A. and Snower, D. "Wage setting, unemployment, and insider–outsider relations," *American Economic Review, Papers and Proceedings,* 76, May 1986, 235–9.
McCallum, J. "Inflation and social consensus in the seventies," *Economic Journal,* 93, December 1983, 784–805.
McCallum, J. "Unemployment in the OECD countries in the 1980s," *Economic Journal,* 96, December 1986, 942–60.
Mackie, T. and Rose, R. *The International Almanac of Electoral History,* Macmillan, London, 1991.
Maddison, A. *Economic Growth in the West,* Twentieth Century Fund, New York, 1964.
Maddison, A. *Phases of Capitalist Development,* Oxford University Press, Oxford, 1982.
Maizels, A. *Growth and Trade,* Cambridge University Press, Cambridge, 1970.
Malinvaud, E. *Mass Unemployment,* Blackwell, Oxford, 1984.
Malinvaud, E. "Wages and unemployment," *Economic Journal,* 92, March 1982, 1–12.

Modigliani, F., Monti, M., Dreze, J., Giersch, H. and Layard, R. "Reducing unemployment in Europe: the role of capital formation," in R. Layard and L. Calmfors (eds), *The Fight Against Unemployment*, MIT Press, Cambridge, MA, 1987.
National Institute Economic Review, July 1961.
Newell, A. and Symons, J. "Corporatism, laissez-faire and the rise in unemployment," *European Economic Review*, 31 (3), 1987, 567–601.
OECD, *Economic Outlook*, OECD, Paris, December 1983, June 1987, December 1988, and June 1992.
OECD, *Employment Outlook*, OECD, Paris, September 1987, July 1992.
OECD, *Historical Statistics, 1960–1983*, OECD, Paris, 1985.
OECD, *Historical Statistics, 1960–1986*, OECD, Paris, 1988.
OECD, *Historical Statistics, 1960–1990*, OECD, Paris, 1992.
OECD, *Labour Force Statistics, 1960–1971*, OECD, Paris, 1973.
OECD, *Labour Force Statistics, 1970–1981*, OECD, Paris, 1983.
OECD, *Public Expenditures, 1960–1990*, OECD, Paris, 1985.
OECD, *Public Expenditure Trends*, OECD, Paris, 1985.
OECD, *Social Expenditures, 1960–1990*, OECD, Paris, 1985.
OECD, *Towards Full Employment and Price Stability*, OECD, Paris, 1978.
Okun, A. *Prices and Quantities: A Macroeconomic Analysis*, Brookings Institute, Washington, DC, 1981.
Olson, M. "The political economy and growth rates," in D. Mueller (ed.), *The Political Economy of Growth*, Yale University Press, New Haven, CT, 1983.
Olson, M. *The Rise and Decline of Nations*, Yale University Press, New Haven, CT, 1982.
Olson, M. "Why nations rise and fall," *Challenge*, 27, March–April 1984, 15–23.
Paldam, M. "Industrial conflict and the Phillips curve—an international perspective," *Memo 80–4/5*, Institute of Economics, Aarhus University, 1980, 1–37.
Paldam, M. and Rasmusen, L. "Data for industrial conflicts in 17 OECD countries, 1948–77," *Memo 80–4/5*, Institute of Economics, Aarhus University, 1980.
Pempel, T. and Tsunekawa, K. "Corporatism without labour? The Japanese anomaly," in P. Schmitter and G. Lehmbruch (eds.), *Trends Towards Corporatist Intermediation*, Sage Publications, Beverly Hills, CA, 1979.
Perry, G. "Determinants of wage inflation around the world," *Brookings Papers on Economic Activity*, No. 2, 1975.
Phelps Brown, E. *A Century of Pay*, Macmillan, London, 1968.
Phelps, E. (ed.). *Microfoundations of Employment and Inflation Theory*, Norton, New York, 1970.
Pissarides, C. "Unemployment and macroeconomics: an inaugural address," *Centre for Labour Economics Discussion Paper*, No. 3–4, London School of Economics, March 1988.
Popper, K. *Objective Knowledge: An Evolutionary Approach*, Oxford University Press, Oxford, 1972.
Ray, G. "Labour costs and international competitiveness," *National Institute Economic Review*, 61, August 1972, 53–58.
Rock, J. (ed.). *Debt and the Twin Deficits Debate*, Mayfield Publishing Co., Mountain View, CA, 1991.

Rothschild, K. " 'Left' and 'right' in Federal Europe," *Kyklos,* 39 (3), 1986, 359–76.
Rubin, L. "The state and local government sector: long-term trends and recent fiscal pressures," *Federal Reserve Bulletin,* December 1992. Vol. 78, No. 12, 892–901.
Sargent, J. "Deregulation, debt, and downturn in the UK economy," *National Institute Economic Review,* August 1992. No. 137, 75–98.
Scharpf, F. "Economic and institutional constraints of full-employment strategies: Sweden, Austria and West Germany," *IIM/IMP Discussion Paper 83–20,* Wissenschaftszentrum, Berlin, 1983.
Scharpf, F. "The political economy of inflation and unemployment in Western Europe: an outline," *IIM/IMP Discussion Paper 81–2,* Wissenschaftszentrum, Berlin, 1981.
Schmidt, M. "The politics of unemployment: rates of unemployment and labour market policy," *West European Politics,* 7, July 1984, 5–24.
Schott, K. *Policy, Power and Order: The Persistence of Economic Problems in Capitalist States,* Yale University Press, New Haven, CT, 1984.
Schumpeter, J. *Capitalism, Socialism and Democracy,* Harper, New York, 1942.
Scitovsky, T. "Market power and inflation," *Economica,* 45, August 1978, 221–34.
Solow, R. "Unemployment: getting the questions right," *Economica* (Supplement), 53, 1986, S23–S34.
Soskice, D. "Strike waves and wage explosions, 1968–1970: an economic interpretation," in C. Crouch and A. Pizzarno (eds.), *The Resurgence of Class Conflict in Western Europe since 1969,* vol. 2, Holmes and Meir, New York, 1978.
Stewart, M. *Controlling the Economic Future,* Wheatsheaf, Brighton, 1983.
Summers, L. "Comments," *European Economic Review,* 31 (3), April 1987, 606–14.
Summers, L. "Why is the unemployment rate so very high near full employment?" *Brookings Papers on Economic Activity,* No. 2, 1986.
Tarantelli, E. "The regulation of inflation and unemployment," *Industrial Relations,* 25, Winter 1986, 1–15.
Thalberg, B. "Stabilization policy and the nonlinear theory of the trade cycle," *Swedish Journal of Economics,* Vol. 3, 1971, 294–310.
Thirlwall, A. and Hussain, M. "The balance of payments constraint, capital flows and growth rate differences between developing countries," *Oxford Economic Papers,* 34, November 1982, 498–510.
Tufte, E. *Political Control of the Economy,* Princeton University Press, Princeton, NJ, 1978.
U.S. Department of Commerce. *Economic Bulletin Board,* Office of Business Analysis, November 1992.
U. S. Department of Commerce. *Statistical Abstract of the United States,* various issues.
U. S. Department of Commerce. *Survey of Current Business,* September 1992 and January 1993.
Wachter, M. and Williamson, O. "Obligational markets and the mechanics of inflation," *Bell Journal of Economics,* 9, Autumn 1978, 549–71.
Wallich, H. and Weintraub, S. "A tax-based incomes policy," *Journal of Economic Issues,* 5, June 1971, 1–19.

Weitzman, M. "Increasing returns and the foundations of unemployment theory," *Economic Journal,* 92, December 1982, 787–804.

Woolley, J. "Monetary policy instrumentation and the relationship of central banks and governments," *Annals of the American Academy,* 434, November 1977, 151–73.

Yellen, J. "Symposium on the budget deficit," *Journal of Economic Perspectives.* Vol. 3, No. 2, Spring 1989, 17–22.

You, J. "Is taxed-based incomes policy an answer?" *Canadian Public Policy,* 8, Winter 1982, 95–101.

Zanowitz, V. "Unfilled orders, price changes and business fluctuations," *The Review of Economics and Statistics*, November 1962. Vol. XLIV, No. 4, 367–394.

Index

AD (aggregate demand) policies
  choice of, 15–25
  Clinton plan, 250, 251–52, 253
  constraints on use of, 84–86, 198, 202, 208–9, 247
  as determinant of performance, 60
  full employment and, 3, 55
  hysteresis and, 169–71
  inflation relationship, 5, 18–19, 45, 93, 133, 135, 236, 267
  as instrument of stabilization, 4
  macroequilibrium and, xxiii, xxiv
  OECD countries and stimulation of, 6–7
  Phillips curve and, 94n.6
  political-economic power link and, 69, 74, 75
  political intervention in form of discretionary, 15–16
  restimulation, 201
  shift in views on role of, 44
  strategy for determining basic causes of differences in, 18–19
  unemployment relationship, 45, 79–80, 82
  See also Restrictive AD policies; Stimulative AD policies
African Americans, unemployment rate, 255
Aggregate demand policies. *See* AD (aggregate demand) policies
Aggregate equilibrium, xii
Aiken, George, ix
Alpha strand, VPC, 50–54, 63, 153
Australia
  exchange rate, 191n.19
  inflation, 38, 130
  misery index, 130
  strike volume, 112
  unemployment, 11, 40, 130, 131
Austria
  corporatism, 100, 110
  exchange rate increase, 144
  inflation, 38, 130
  misery index, 119, 130, 136
  recovery program, xviii
  strikes, 112, 144

Austria *(continued)*
  unemployment, 11, 40, 88, 89, 90, 123, 130, 131, 136, 142–43
  wage indexation, 145

Backward-induction approach, to model design, xi
Balance of payments
  constraints, 209, 246, 247
  deterioration, 41
  difficulties and stimulative AD policies, 6
  disequilibrium with full employment, 83, 85, 86
  OECD countries, 124
  problems, 190, 191–92, 194
  shift, 186
Balance of trade. *See* Balance of payments
Bank
  mortgage loans, 220, 228
  See also Central bank
Belgium
  corporatism, 110n.2
  inflation, 38, 130
  misery index, 130
  social democratic corporatism, 100
  strike volume, 112
  unemployment, 11, 40, 88, 89, 123, 130, 131
Beta strand, VPC, 54–57, 63
Blacks, unemployment rate, 255
Booms, economic, 216–29
  recessionary, 203
  relationship between slumps and, 221–22
Bourgeois democratic corporatism, 101–3, 142
Breakdown, economic, 129–34
  in early 1970s, 29–32
  explaining, 181–96
  political economy view of, 23
  stagnation vs., 13
  studying, 263–64
  unemployment since, 40, 41, 135–51
  use of term, xxi
Bretton Woods
  agreement breakdown, 125
  exchange rate collapse, 182

Budget
  interaction of economy and, 242–44
  See also Deficit
Business cycles, causal relationship between phases of, 221–22
Business investment expenditures, 221, 223, 225
  decline in, 218
  See also Capital flight
Business. *See* Corporatism

Canada
  balance of payments, 41
  belief in free market, 260–61
  household sector indebtedness, 228*n.12*
  inflation, 38, 130
  macroperformance, 122
  misery index, 130, 136
  pain-for-gain policies, xviii
  pluralist economy, 101, 198
  recovery program, 231
  regression analysis, 178–80
  strike volume, 112
  unemployment, 11, 27, 28, 40, 88, 89, 90, 107, 130, 131, 136, 141, 203, 234, 235, 242
Capital flight, 193–94
  SDC economies, 145
Capital goods industry, ceiling, 219–20, 221, 222
Capitalist economies
  and adoption of AD policies, 20
  automatic full employment tendencies of, 45
  democracies as cause of inflation, 1–2
  evolutionary nature of twentieth-century, 26–43
  industrial relations in, 34–35
  inherently unstable system of, 232
  lack of self-regulating mechanisms, xvii, 6, 15, 44, 239
  North American/United Kingdom belief in, 260–61
  and rise of welfare states, 28–31
  rising power of labor and, 31–35
  sociological appraisal of, 231, 232
  structural changes and evolution of, 42
  success or failure of, 1–5
  See also Corporatism; Flexprice markets
Cartels. *See* Decartelization program
Central bank, 143
  as political and economic constraint, 84
Clinton administration
  and macro policy intervention, xvi

Clinton administration *(continued)*
  optimism on economic revitalization, 4
  recovery program, 4, 237, 249–53, 255
Collective bargaining, 205
  pluralist economies, 207
  unrestricted, 244
Competition
  impact of technology on, 260*n.8*
  resulting from macroeconomic restraint, xii
Consumer expenditures. *See* Household-related expenditures
Consumer investment
  growth of, 217
  leveling off of, 218
Corporatism, 97–100, 114, 199
  alternative forms of, 103–6
  bourgeois democratic, 101–3, 142
  Crouch's index, 109–11
  indices of, 98
  neocorporatism index, 119–20
  policy-making, 97–98
  social democratic, 99–100
Cost-push inflation, xvi-xvii, 90, 182, 184, 205
Credibility hypothesis, 206, 232
Credit
  suppliers, 220, 228
  See also Mortgages
Crouch, C., corporatism index, 98*n.8*, 99*n.11*, 109–11, 114
Crowding out, 240, 241
  as full-employment phenomenon, 239

Debt. *See* Credit; Deficit; Indebtedness
Decartelization program, 257–59, 260
Defense expenditures, 217, 223
Deficit, 228, 229, 230
  borrowing to cover, 190–91
  recession-caused, 240
  reduction, 242, 254, 255
  spending, 21, 213
  unacceptable growth of national, 245
  under full-employment conditions, 228, 240–41
  See also National debt
Demand-pull inflation, xvi-xvii
Democracy
  economic theory of, 70–71
  inflation and, 1–2
  See also Bourgeois democratic corporatism; Capitalist economies; Social democratic corporatism

Denmark
  inflation, 38, 130
  misery index, 130
  social democratic corporatism, 100
  strike volume, 112
  unemployment, 40, 123, 130, 131, 189
Depression (economic). *See* Great
  Depression; Recession
Diminishing marginal product of labor law,
  46
Discomfort index. *See* Misery index
Disintermediation process, 220–21, 222
Distribution of conflict, determination of,
  35–36
Duesenberry, James, x
Dummy variables, econometric theory and
  use of, 121

Eckstein-Brinner model of inflation,
  158–62, 173–80
Economic breakdown. *See* Breakdown,
  economic
Economic theory of democracy, 70–71
Employment. *See* Full employment; Labor;
  Unemployment
England. *See* United Kingdom
Equilibrium
  economic choice of alternate, xiii
  macroeconomic employment concept,
    xxiii, 67
  multiple and macro foundations of
    microeconomics, x-xiii
  rate of unemployment. *See* NAIRU
  variable-coefficient Phillips curve
    analysis of multiple, 161–62, 172
  See also Natural rate hypothesis
Equipment-deficient unemployment,
  58n.15
Eurosclerosis hypothesis, 3, 5, 7, 135, 136,
  192n.21, 257
Exchange rate
  AD policies and protection of, 193
  Australia, 191n.19
  and collapse of Bretton Woods regime,
    182
  and correction of balance-of-payments
    problems, 191, 194, 201
  depreciation, 144, 200
  flexible policy model, 146–51
Expectations-augmented Phillips curve,
  45–46, 48, 55n.11
Exports
  rapid expansion of, 124–25
  See also Balance of payments

FE. *See* Full employment
Federal Reserve System, independence of,
  255
Finland
  inflation, 38, 39, 130
  misery index, 130
  social democratic corporatism, 100
  strike volume, 112
  unemployment, 11, 40, 130, 131
Fixed investment expenditures, rate of
  growth, 225n.9
Fixprice markets, 205
  and abolition of unions, 257, 259
Flanagan, R., 188
Flexible exchange rate policy model,
  146–51
Flexprice markets, 25, 205
  decartelization and, 257–59
  full employment and, 260–62
  See also Capitalist economies
France
  balance of payments, 41
  inflation, 38, 130
  misery index, 130
  strike volume, 112
  unemployment, 11, 40, 130, 131
Free market. *See* Capitalist economies;
  Flexprice markets
Free riders, 72n.4
  inflation and, 92–93
  prisoner's dilemma and, 93
  public good and, 92
Friedman, Milton, inflation expectations
  formulation, 46
Full employment
  achieving, ix-x
  AD policies and achievement of, 3, 55
  budgetary requirements of, 243
  budget deficits and, 228, 240–41
  in corporatist economies, 198
  decartelization program and, 257–62
  demand for, 20, 26, 107
  economic structure, 106–7
  flexprice markets and, 260–62
  governmental active pursuit of, 22
  as high priority goal, 266
  inflation relationship, 22, 79, 82, 85–86,
    96–97, 125, 126, 133, 134, 267
  lack of inflationary bias, 201, 249
  OECD countries and, 87, 88n.2
  payments disequilibrium at, 83, 85, 86, 87
  pluralist economies and, 198
  political and economic side effects, 21
  and productivity growth rates, 3

Full employment *(continued)*
  rate differences with NAIRU rate, 12
  use of union power at, 90–91
  and welfare policies, 72

Game theory, 142
  See also Prisoner's dilemma
GDP (Gross Domestic Product)
  explaining behavior of, 23n.9
  growth, 27–28, 216–18, 246, 247
  OECD countries, 41, 139
  peak, 216n.1, 225, 226
  social security expenditures, 29–31
  United States, 217, 225, 226
The General Theory (Keynes), xxiv, 6, 229, 239
  discretionary AD policies, 15
  Pigou's rebuttal, 51, 67
  real wages and AD stimulation, 58
Germany
  balance of payments, 41
  corporatism, 110
  inflation, 38, 130
  misery index, 130
  second-generation incomes policy, 210
  social democratic corporatism, 100
  strike volume, 112
  unemployment, 11, 40, 130, 131, 137n.4, 186, 203
  unemployment linked with Hitler's rise, 255n.28
  union density, 32, 33
  willingness to supply full employment, 143
Governments
  unemployment choices, 16–17
  See also OECD countries; State and local governments; specific countries
Great Britain. *See* United Kingdom
Great Depression (1930s), 266, 267
  failure of constraints, 222
  Hitler's rise and, 255n.28
  OECD countries' macroeconomic performances during, 27
  recovery from, 213
Great Inflation, 182–86, 267
  causes of, 232
  stages, 183–86
  See also Hyperinflation; Real wages
Gross domestic product. *See* GDP
G7 countries, inflation and unemployment rates, 195

Hendry's specification approach, 139

Hibbs, D., strike involvement study, 34, 35
Hispanic-Americans, unemployment rate, 255
Hitler, Adolf, 255n.28
Hocking's Sp test, 139
Household-related expenditures, 219, 221, 222
  growth of indebtedness and, 227–28
Housing investment, 223–25
Hyperinflation, Germany, 255n.28
Hysteresis, 60–62, 63, 68, 265–66
  persistence of inflation and, 171–72
  policy-induced effects, 187
  restrictive AD policies inducing, 190
  and variable-coefficient Phillips curve, 167–69

Iceland, employment policies, 7n.4
Income distribution
  per capita growth, 28–29
  shift in, 253, 254
Incomes policies, 94n.6, 95, 198, 203, 245, 263
  breakdown, 154, 163–65
  first generation, 184, 188
  implementation of second-generation, 143, 210, 213, 262
  successful, 98–99
Indebtedness
  household sector, 227–28
  rising, 230
  See also Credit; Deficit
Industrial relations system
  adversarial, 18, 101, 122, 207, 209, 252–53
  characteristics of, 110, 205–6
  cooperative, 96, 106, 107
  decartelization program, 258–61
  rising power of labor and, 34–35
  strike activity, 121
  See also Unions
Inflation
  acceleration, 1–2, 132
  AD policies and, 5, 18–19, 45, 93, 133, 135, 236, 267
  bias. *See* Inflationary bias
  boom rates, 227
  constraints, 79–80, 247
  cost-push, xvi-xvii, 90, 182, 184, 205
  cross-country differences in, 118–19
  demand-pull vs. cost-push, xvi-xvii
  determinants analysis, 44–68, 146–51
  Eckstein-Brinner model of, 158–62, 173–80

Inflation *(continued)*
  expectations, 5, 45–46
  fairness and dynamics of, 155–57
  full employment relationship, 22, 79, 82, 85–86, 96–97, 125, 126, 133, 134, 267
  labor power and, 37–39, 89–91
  as main macro problem, xxiv
  mass unemployment relationship, 142n.11, 197
  modeled as a prisoner's dilemma, 91–94
  OECD countries, xviiin.3, 38, 38–41, 88–89, 90, 123, 129, 130, 136–37, 187–88, 194–96
  party control, union power, and, 89–90
  persistence of, 171–72, 181
  policy-induced unemployment and high, 152–80
  political dangers of, 255n.28
  Reagan administration's failure to curb, xv
  rising costs of, 188–90
  Scandinavian model of, 99n.10, 118, 123n.14
  stimulative AD policies and accelerated, 262
  as strike cause, 111n.5
  unemployment relationship, xxiv, 1, 18, 39–41, 48, 91, 134, 152–80, 197, 227, 252
  variable-coefficient models of, 157–66
  wage-price spiral, 155–56, 186–205
  wage-wage and wage-price mechanisms, 92–93
  See also Great Inflation; Real wages; specific countries
Inflationary bias, 7, 98, 184, 192, 195–96, 201, 204, 208
  AD restrictive policies and, 126, 141, 197, 244–45
  elimination in pluralist economies, 256
  full employment and lack of, 201, 249
  high unemployment rates and, 194, 197, 227
  need for institutions to alter, 209, 266–67
  world recovery and elimination of, 230
Institutional-analytical paradigm, xvii
Institutions
  behavior and changing, 257–63
  econometric tests of influences of, 109–26
  impact on Phillips curve, 121
  influence on economic events, 18–25, 82–86
  macroeconomic performance and, 8–9, 18, 87–108

Institutions *(continued)*
  need to alter inflationary bias, 209, 266–67
  policy-induced changes in, 22–25, 232–33
  role in determining policies, 18–19, 22
Intermediation process, 221
Investment. *See* Business investment expenditures; Capital flight; Fixed investment expenditures
Involuntary unemployment, 12, 55, 153, 242, 262
  resources and stimulative AD policies, 239
  universal nature of high, 9
  and vertical Phillips curve analysis, 55–57
Ireland
  inflation, 38, 130
  macroperformance, 122
  misery index, 130
  pluralist economy, 198
  strike volume, 112
  unemployment, 11, 40, 88, 89, 107, 122, 130, 131
IRS. *See* Industrial relations system
Italy
  balance of payments, 41
  inflation, 38, 39, 130
  macroperformance, 122
  misery index, 119, 130
  pluralist economy, 101
  strike volume, 112, 116
  unemployment, 27, 28, 40, 88, 89, 90, 107, 122, 130, 131, 141

Japan
  corporatism, 102, 104–6, 110n.2
  inflation, 38, 106, 130
  misery index, 130
  recovery program, xviii, 254
  strikes, 36, 112, 144
  unemployment, 11, 40, 88–89, 117, 130, 131, 137n.4, 142–43
J-curve effects, 191

Kalecki, M., political business cycle theory, 2–3, 20, 214
Keynes, John Maynard. *See The General Theory* Keynesian economics
Keynesian economics
  and aggregate demand policies-inflation relationship, 185n.8
  and aggregate demand policies-unemployment relationship, xxiv, 79, 263

Keynesian economics *(continued)*
  on automatic equilibrium unemployment tendencies, 51
  on government intervention in capitalist system, 44
  ideology, x, 239–42
  monetary policy ineffectiveness, 213
  on private sector lack of self-regulation, 239
  recovery policies, 6, 7
  relevancy of, 44–45
  symmetry, 5, 63, 170
  view of unemployment vs. classical unemployment, 49
Knife-edge concept, 51, 54, 62, 65, 152
Korpi, W., 138

Labor
  collective bargaining, 205, 207, 244
  diminishing marginal product law, 46
  fairness considerations, 91
  interpretation of restrictive AD policies, 207–8
  power relative to capital, 22
  power relative to inflation, 37–39, 90–91
  reduction of power of, 13
  rising political strength of, 26, 28, 31–35, 73, 76–77, 135, 192, 264, 366
  wage negotiations, 153–54
  See also Full employment; Industrial relations system; Real wages; Strike activity; Unemployment; Unions; Wages
LDCs. *See* Less-developed countries
Leftist parties
  inflation relationship, 37–38
  and strike activity, 36
  and unemployment, 88
  and union movement growth, 32–34
Less-developed countries, 201
Local governments. *See* State and local governments
Locomotive (AD restimulation), 201, 202
London School of Economics, standardized unemployment rates, 113
Long-run Phillips curve, 156–57, 160
  acceptance of theory of vertical, 133
  shifting, 162–66

Macroeconomics, 15–25
  and abstract models, x
  foundations of microeconomics, x–xiii
  goals of, x, 15
  main concern of post-war era, ix

Macroeconomics *(continued)*
  models, x–xi, 15–16
  performance and institutions, 87–108
  performances of OECD countries, 109–26
  search for micro foundation for, xi
  twentieth-century developments, 26–43
  unemployment as main problem of, xvi
  unique equilibrium employment concept, xxiii, 67
  See also Keynesian economics
Market clearing, 258, 260, 261
Marshall-Lerner conditions, 191, 192
Marxism, 69–70
Mass unemployment, 240, 262, 267
  causes for, 39, 84, 122, 181–96
  as economic and political phenomenon, 17
  as failure of institutional policy fit, 19
  goal achievement, 21–22
  inflation relationship, 142n.11, 197
  Keynesian interpretation of, 79
  model of long-run, 197–210
  and natural rate hypothesis, 50
  in Nazi Germany, 255n.28
  phase inception, 126
McCallum, J., 141
McCracken Report, xviii, 182, 183, 189, 214, 232
Mexico, 249n.19
Microeconomics, macro foundations of, x–xiii
Ministry of Trade and Industry (Japan), 105
Misery index, 90, 94, 109, 263
  cross-country differences in, 118–19
  and neocorporatism, 119
  OECD countries, 129, 130, 136–37
  strike volume correlation, 113
  See also specific countries
MITI. *See* Ministry of Trade and Industry (Japan)
Models, macroeconomics and, x–xi, 15–16
Monetarist economics, unemployment theory, 2
Monetary policy, 222–30
  ceiling, 219, 220, 221, 222
  ineffectiveness of, 213
  neutrality of, 220
  as weakened tool for AD regulation, 229
  See also Exchange rate
Money wages. *See* Wages
Mortgages, 220–21, 227
Multiple equilibria
  economic choice of alternate, xiii
  in macroeconomic employment concept, xxiii, 67

Multiple equilibria *(continued)*
  and macro foundations of
    microeconomics, x–xiii
  variable-coefficient Phillips curve
    analysis, 161–62, 172
  See also Natural rate hypothesis

NAFTA. *See* North American Free Trade
  Agreement
NAIRU (nonaccelerating inflation rate of
    unemployment), xii, 50, 79, 81,
    171–72
  AD policies' stimulative effectiveness, 5
  analysis, 152, 159
  forces behind shift of, 51–54, 64, 67
  hysteresis effects, 61–62, 63, 68
  increase since early 1970s, 10
  knife-edge properties, 51, 54, 62, 65, 152
  reliability of estimates, 65–66
  symmetry assumption, 152, 162
  unemployment rate differences and, 12,
    234–35
National debt. *See* Deficit
Natural rate hypothesis, 45–49, 67, 162
  automatic equilibrium unemployment
    tendencies, 51
  unemployment and rejection of, 50, 63
Neoclassical analysis
  as reigning paradigm, xvii
  rejection of, 25
  self-regulating tenet of, xvii–xviii
Neocorporatism index, 119–20
Neo-Keynesian asymmetry. *See*
  Post-Keynesian asymmetry
Netherlands
  corporatism, 100, 110
  inflation, 38, 130
  misery index, 130
  strike volume, 112
  unemployment, 11, 40, 130, 131
New Classical economists, xi
Newly industrializing countries
  competition from, 209
  import penetration, 197, 204
New neo-Keynesian economists, xi
New Zealand
  inflation, 38, 130
  misery index, 130
  strike volume, 112
  unemployment, 40, 130, 131
NICs. *See* Newly industrializing
  countries
Nonaccelerating inflation rate of
  unemployment. *See* NAIRU

Nonaccelerating price-level constraint,
  xii–xiii
North American Free Trade Agreement,
  249*n.19*
Norway
  corporatism, 100, 110
  exchange rate decline, 144
  inflation, 38, 130
  labor unions, 90
  misery index, 130, 136
  strikes, 112, 144
  unemployment, 11, 40, 88, 89, 123, 130,
    131, 136, 142–43
  wage indexation, 145
NRH. *See* Natural rate hypothesis

OECD countries
  AD policies, 6–7, 17, 21
  coordinated stimulation program, 231
  differences in macroeconomic
    performances, 109
  division into two groups, 129
  employment, 88–89
  full employment achievement, 86
  inflation, xviii*n.3*, 7, 38, 38–41, 88–89,
    90, 123, 130, 136–37, 187–88,
    194–96
  misery index, 129, 130, 136–37
  NAIRU calculations, 65–66
  social security expenditures, 29–31
  strike activity, 107*n.27*, 111–13, 184–85
  unemployment, xviii*n.3*, 8, 9–11, 16*n.1*,
    40–41, 90, 113, 123–25, 129, 130,
    131–32, 136–37, 140, 142, 186,
    187–88, 190, 194–96, 202, 208, 235
  votes for leftist parties, 32–34
  See also specific countries
Oil prices
  contributing to inflation, 125, 126, 186
  impact on balance of payments, 41, 126
  pressure for restrictive policies, 187, 190
Okun index, 137*n.4*
Okun's law, 60
OPEC. *See* Organization of Petroleum
  Exporting Countries
Organization for Economic Cooperation
  and Development. *See* OECD
  countries
Organization of Petroleum Exporting
  Countries
  formation, 24
  import restrictions, 202*n.5*
Organized labor. *See* Labor; Unions; Strike
  activity

Overload thesis, 1, 7

Pareto optimum, through competition of political parties, 71
Party control theory, 35–36, 122
  cross-country analysis, 75–76
  economic policy and, 76–78
  labor power and, 76–77
  of policy formation, 69, 73–74
  unemployment and, 77, 88–90
  See also Political parties
Party control variable, regression analysis, 114, 116–17, 117–18
Peak GDP, 216n.1, 225, 226
Peak organizations, 97, 110
Per capita incomes, growth of, 28–29
Phillips curve
  cross-country, 90
  differences in, 94–97
  horizontal nature of cross-country, 106–8
  shifts in, 17, 91, 147–50
  strike activity and, 184
  unemployment rates, 80–81, 82
  variable-coefficient, 153–54, 157–58
  vertical long-run, 82, 159
  See also Long-run Phillips curve; Short-run Phillips curve; Variable-coefficient Phillips curve; Vertical Phillips curve
Pigou effects, 51, 67–68, 171, 233
Pluralist economies, 100–101, 197–98
  constraints on AD policies in, 202
  elimination of inflationary bias, 230, 256
  reflationary programs, 202
  unemployment policies, 203
Political business cycle theory, 2–3, 20, 214
Political parties
  role in economic policy, 69–71, 73–74
  See also Party control theory
Popper, K., 23n.9
Post-Keynesian asymmetry, 5
Price
  mechanisms and full employment policies, 22
  setting in capitalist economies, 17–18
  stability as public good, 92
  stability sacrificed for high employment, 2
  stickiness, xi–xii
  unresponsiveness of, 205–6
  See also Inflation; Wage-price spiral
Price surprises
  and shift in short-run Phillips curve, 61
  unemployment rate fluctuation and, 47, 48, 50, 55

Prisoner's dilemma, 257
  free riders and, 93
  inflation modeled as a, 91–94
Productivity growth, 28–29, 169
  OECD countries, 124, 125
  rates, 3, 7, 40
Public choice theory, 69–72
Public goods, price and wage stability as, 92

Reagan administration
  and economic boom, 251
  failed policies of, xv
  income distribution shift during, 254
  policy acceptance, 4
  unemployment rates, 12
Real wages
  gap in, 56
  labor market determination of, 55, 58
  negotiations, 64, 153–54, 166, 189
  price inflation and rates of, 52–53, 207
  protection of, 152–53
  resistance, 192–93
  slow growth in, 266
  stickiness, 154n.3
  stimulative AD policies and, 56, 193
  unemployment rate and, 56, 59, 164–65
Recession, 225–26
  bounded by countercyclical movement, 222
  as cause of budget deficit, 240
Recessionary boom, 203
Recovery
  hierarchy of policy goals, 245–47
  obstacles to economic, 6–7
Regression analysis
  post-war unemployment, 138–41
  unemployment rates, 113–16
Restrictive AD policies
  as cause of stagnation, 7
  corporatist economies, 199
  costliness of, 204–6
  credible, 206, 207
  deficit reduction and, 242
  economic breakdown and, 126
  as first step in recovery program, 232
  impact of, 23, 166, 167–69, 170, 171
  ineffectiveness of, 182, 197, 207–8, 245, 265–66
  and inflationary bias, 244–45
  inflation reduction and, 93, 133, 135, 169, 186, 196, 236, 267
  OECD countries' utilization, 17
  oil price factor, 41
  pluralist economies, 198

Restrictive AD policies *(continued)*
  reasons for, 200
  recovery program and, 5
  and reduction in sales and profits, 106
  unemployment and, 6, 39, 40, 116
  vertical Phillips curve analysis shifts, 167–69, 189
  See also Stimulative AD policies
RHS variables, 139, 140, 145
Rothschild, K., 33

Savings and loan associations, mortgage loans, 220
Scandinavian countries
  corporatism index, 99
  See also specific countries
Scandinavian model of inflation, 99n.10, 118, 123n.14
Schumpeter, J., economic theory of democracy, 70
SDC. *See* Social democratic corporatism
Short-run Phillips curve, 46, 47, 61, 146, 156–57
Slack periods, policy-induced, 22–23
Slumps, relationship between booms and, 221–22
Social bargain, 187, 242, 252, 263, 265, 267
  acceptance of, 244–45, 247–48
  adoption of, 204, 213, 241
  corporatist policy-making and, 97–100
  kinds of, 95–96
  measures of, 109–12
  and stimulative AD policies, 241
  successful, 13, 96–97
Social democratic corporatism, 99–100
  economies, 142–45
Social expenditure. *See* Welfare state
Social security expenditures, 29–31
Sociologist, perception of capitalism, 231, 232
Spain, unemployment, 11
SPC. *See* Short-run Phillips curve
Special interest groups, power of, 72
Stagflation, 132
Stagnation, 132, 218, 228
  economic breakdown vs., 13
  restrictive AD policies as cause of, 7
  use of term, 9
State and local governments, expenditures, 222n.7, 226, 228
Stimulative AD policies
  adverse side effects, 6–7, 85, 170
  Clinton plan, 250, 251
  constraints on use of, 6, 21, 90, 246

Stimulative AD policies *(continued)*
  economic recovery and, 5, 238
  ineffectiveness of, 49–50, 55, 56–60, 63, 152
  inflation relationship, 6, 17, 18, 44–45, 125, 193, 262
  involuntary unemployment resources and, 239
  misery index and, 120
  real wages and, 56, 193
  social bargain implementation and, 241
  stage one of inflationary process and, 183
  unemployment reduction and, 17, 44, 57–60, 82, 85, 87
  unlikely use in United States, 227
  world recovery and coordinated, 200–202
  See also Restrictive AD policies
Strike activity
  bourgeois democratic corporatism and, 103
  inflation as cause of, 111n.5
  involvement, 34–35
  macroperformance and, 122
  measured by involvement, 34–35
  misery index correlation, 113
  OECD countries, 184–85
  volume, 111–13, 144
  volume variables, 120
  regression analysis, 114–16, 117
  welfare state size and, 35–37
Sustainability criterion, 243
Sweden
  corporatism, 100, 110
  exchange rate decline, 144
  inflation, 38, 130
  labor unions, 90
  misery index, 130, 136
  strikes, 112, 144
  unemployment, 11, 40, 88, 89, 123, 130, 131, 136, 142–43, 234, 235
  wage indexation, 145
Switzerland
  corporatism, 100, 102, 103–4, 105, 106, 110n.2
  inflation, 38, 130
  misery index, 118–19, 130
  party control, 117–18
  recovery program, xviii
  strikes, 36, 112, 116, 117, 118–19, 144
  unemployment, 40, 88–89, 117, 122, 130, 131, 134n.2, 137n.4, 142–43

Tarantelli, E., neocorporatism index, 119–20

Taxation, progressive system of, 253, 254
Taxed-based incomes policies, 209
Technology
 impact on competition, 260n.8
 transfers, 204
Thatcher government, 121, 194
 policy acceptance, 4
 restrictive AD policies, 198n.1
 unemployment rates, 12
 weak economic recovery of, xv
Thrift institutions, mortgage loans, 220–21
TIPs. *See* Tax-based incomes policies
Trade. *See* Balance of payments; North American Free Trade Agreement
Trade unions. *See* Unions; Strike activity

Unemployment
 AD policies and, 6, 17, 19, 39, 40, 57–60, 87, 116
 before breakdown and party control, 88–90
 causes of, 81–82
 classical vs. Keynesian, 49
 cumulative effects of high, 255
 determinants, 69–86, 138
 analysis, 44–68, 146–51
 equilibrium rate of. *See* NAIRU
 equipment-deficient, 58n.15
 exporting, 200
 growth rate comparisons and, 27–28
 impact of breakdown on, 40, 41, 135–51
 inflation relationship, xxiv, 1, 18, 39–41, 48, 91, 134, 152–80, 194, 197, 227, 252
 as major issue, xvi, 9–13
 minorities and, 255
 patterns, 131–32
 policies and government choice, 16–17
 political economics' analysis of, 79–81
 rates, ix, 113–16; *See also* specific countries
 OECD countries, xviii*n.3*, xxi, 8, 9–11, 40–41, 88–89, 90, 123–25, 129, 130, 131–32, 136–37, 140, 142, 187–88, 194–96, 202
 regression analysis for post-war, 138–41
 rise as form of malfunction, xxi
 strike volume correlation, 113
 structural explanations of high, 107*n.28*
 twentieth-century, 233–34
 unique equilibrium tendencies, xxiii
 voluntary, 48, 53–54

Unemployment *(continued)*
 See also Involuntary unemployment; Mass unemployment; specific countries
Unions
 cooperation with, 253
 density of, 32, 33
 elimination of, 256, 259, 261
 inflation relationship, 37–39, 89–90, 90–91
 Japanese, 105
 party control theory and, 88–89
 social bargain and, 95–96
 unemployment and strength of, 18, 22, 122
 See also Industrial relations system; Labor; Strike activity
Unique equilibrium employment tendencies, xxiii, 67
United Auto Workers of Canada, wage negotiations, 189
United Kingdom
 balance of payments, 41
 economic recovery, 126
 "export-led" growth, 249*n.19*
 free market belief, 260–61
 household sector indebtedness, 228*n.12*
 inflation, 38, 130, 195
 macroperformance, 122
 misery index, 130
 pluralist economy, 101, 198
 recovery program, 231
 short-term pain for long-term gain policies, xviii
 strikes, 36, 112
 unemployment, 11, 12, 40, 88, 89, 108, 130, 131–32, 141, 195, 203, 234, 235, 242
 See also Thatcher government
United States
 balance of payments, 41
 deficit borrowing, 190–91
 determining role in world economic health, 46, 214
 economic boom, 216–29
 economic recovery, 126, 230–55
 export expansion, 124
 free market belief, 260–61
 full employment support by, 143
 Gross Domestic Product, 217, 225, 226
 household sector indebtedness, 227–28
 inflation, 38, 123, 130, 194–95
 macroperformance, 122
 misery index, 118–19, 130, 136

United States *(continued)*
  party control, 117–18
  pluralist economy, 101, 198
  recessionary boom, 202–3
  short-term pain for long-term gain policies, xviii
  strike volume, 112, 117, 118–19
  technology transfers, 204
  unemployment, ix, 11, 12, 27, 28, 40, 88, 89, 90, 107, 130, 131, 136, 137n.4, 141, 186, 194–95, 203, 230, 234, 235, 242, 255
  See also Clinton administration; Reagan administration

Vacancy rates, 224, 227, 229
Variable-coefficient Phillips curve, 153–80
  hysteresis and, 167–69, 171
  restrictive AD policies and shifts in, 167–69, 189
  unemployment-inflation rate relationship, 157–58
VCPC. *See* Variable-coefficient Phillips curve
Verdoorn's law, 60, 124
Vertical long-run Phillips curve, 82, 152
Vertical Phillips curve analysis, 133
  new strands in, 49–57
  reappraisal, 44–68
Vietnam War
  growth of U.S. economy and, 218

Vietnam War *(continued)*
  increasing AD expansion and, 184
Voluntary unemployment, 48, 53–54
VPC. *See* Vertical Phillips curve analysis

Wage-price spiral, 155–56, 186, 205
Wages
  bourgeois democratic corporatism and, 103
  fairness in demands and settlements, 91, 249
  inflation and setting of, 109–10
  long-term trends in, 37–38
  negotiations in capitalist economies, 17–18
  response to price increases, 162
  stability as public good, 92
  stickiness, xi-xii
  unresponsiveness of, 205–6
  See also Real wages
Welfare state
  extension of, 22, 26, 28–31, 126, 135
  party control and, 77–78
  political-economic power linked with policies of, 69, 74, 75
  reduction of, 262
  size-strike activity relationship, 35–37
  unemployment increase and, 122
Woolley, J., 143
Workers. *See* Labor; Real wages; Strike activity; Unions; Wages
Work ethic, loss of, 255